Wadsworth College Reading Series

3rd
EDITION

Wadsworth College Reading Series

BOOK
2

Edith Alderson, Editor

WADSWORTH
CENGAGE Learning™

Australia • Brazil • Japan • Korea • Mexico • Singapore • Spain • United Kingdom • United States

WADSWORTH
CENGAGE Learning™

Wadsworth College Reading Series, Book 2, Third Edition
Edith Alderson, Editor

Publisher/Executive Editor: Lyn Uhl

Director of Developmental Studies: Annie Todd

Managing Editor, Production: Samantha Ross-Miller

Development Editor: Laurie K. Dobson

Assistant Editor: Elizabeth Rice

Editorial Assistant: Matthew Conte

Media Editor: Amy Gibbons

Marketing Manager: Sophie Teague

Marketing Assistant: Brittany Blais

Marketing Communications Manager: Courtney Morris

Design and Production Services: PreMediaGlobal

Manufacturing Planner: Betsy Donaghey

Rights Acquisition Specialist: Timothy Sisler

Cover Designer: Walter Kopec

Cover Image: Thinkstock/Getty Images

Compositor: PreMediaGlobal

Library of Congress Control Number: 2011934648

Student Edition

ISBN-13: 978-1-111-83941-3

ISBN-10: 1-111-839417

Annotated Instructor's Edition

ISBN-13: 978-1-111-84126-3

ISBN-10: 1-111-84126-8

Wadsworth
20 Channel Center Street
Boston, MA 02210
USA

Cengage Learning is a leading provider of customized learning solutions with office locations around the globe, including Singapore, the United Kingdom, Australia, Mexico, Brazil and Japan. Locate your local office at **international.cengage.com/region**

Cengage Learning products are represented in Canada by Nelson Education, Ltd.

For your course and learning solutions, visit **www.cengage.com**

Purchase any of our products at your local college store or at our preferred online store **www.cengagebrain.com**

Instructors: Please visit **login.cengage.com** and log in to access instructor-specific resources.

Printed in the United States of America
1 2 3 4 5 6 7 15 14 13 12 11

CONTENTS

PREFACE

The *Wadsworth College Reading Series,* Third Edition, is a three-level series that uses a progressive, unified approach to improving students' reading comprehension and critical thinking skills—and all at an affordable price! Praised in the second edition by users across the country, the third edition of this innovative series contains additional features and support materials that will enhance students' abilities to become effective readers.

Hallmark Features of the Text

The *Wadsworth College Reading Series,* Third Edition, includes the following features:

- **Integration of Skills and Strategies:** Along with presenting the major reading skills—identifying the main idea, supporting details, implied main idea, transitions, patterns of organization, and others—the book introduces students to a world of reading strategies that will enable them to practice good habits while reading. Strategies such as SQ3R, annotating, and note taking will help students improve their comprehension of what they read and will enable them to learn different strategies that will help them comprehend and analyze what they read.
- **Consistent Chapter Structure:** Each chapter covers skills and strategies in a consistent and clear manner.
- **Coverage of Visuals:** A different type of visual, such as diagrams, maps, and graphs, is covered at the end of each chapter. Students who do not need the instruction might skip this part of the chapter.
- **Critical Thinking:** In addition to a multitude of skills exercises designed to help students build comprehension, the text features questions at the end of the reading selections that build on important critical thinking skills. Many practice exercises, too, require the application of critical thinking.
- **Vocabulary Strategy Building:** Every chapter covers a particular vocabulary strategy and relates that strategy to reading selections from the chapters.
- **Focus on Academic Achievement:** Tips and selected readings about studying and succeeding in school are integrated throughout the text.

What's New in the Third Edition

Based on user and reviewer response, several new features have been added to the new edition of Book 2 to help students learn key concepts and strengthen their vocabulary and reading skills:

- **Reorganized Chapter Materials:** The reading strategy has been moved ahead of the reading selections. Students are encouraged to practice the chapter reading strategy on their choice of reading selections. Because there are multiple reading selections, students could possibly practice the strategy several times. The chapter review has been moved to the end of the chapter. Although most questions follow the cloze procedure format, questions in later chapters in the text require more thoroughly written answers.
- **More Longer Reading Selections:** Students and instructors now have a choice of three longer reading selections in Chapters 2 through 8. These choices allow students more practice reading longer pieces as well as a greater diversity of material to read.
- **Longer Reading Selections from Career Area Textbooks:** At least one longer reading selection in Chapters 2 through 8 has been selected from career area textbooks such as fire science, law enforcement, computer technology, and sports medicine. Many students taking developmental reading courses will pursue degrees in the career areas. These readings allow them to experience the actual textbook material from a career they may be considering. For students who are undecided in their career choice, these readings may inspire them to investigate a particular career.
- **Longer Biographical Reading Selections:** At least one longer reading selection in Chapters 2 through 8 is of biographical content. These biographies are selected to represent the great diversity that students will experience their lives. These biographies are of people they may very well read about in their career classes or in their general studies courses.
- **Updated Practice Materials:** New, updated practice materials have been largely selected from career area textbooks. Students have authentic college text materials on which to practice their reading skills. These high-interest materials have been carefully chosen to be at students' instructional reading level.
- **Streamlined Skill Explanations:** Skill explanations have been streamlined for greater ease of comprehension.
- **Chapter Tests Are Now in a Separate Document:** Chapter tests have been removed from the textbook. This allows for greater security and validity for administering chapter assessments. The Combined Skills Tests for comprehensive assessment at the end of the textbook have also been removed for

security and validity of results. All chapter tests are now available in both an Instructor's Manual and online format.

- **Web Links:** Web links have been added to allow students additional instruction and the interactive links will provide them with the opportunity for additional practice.

Chapter Organization

In addition, each chapter in each level of *The Wadsworth College Reading Series,* Third Edition, contains the following elements:

- **Goals:** A list of goals at the beginning of each chapter tells students what they will learn when they have completed the chapter.
- **Pretests:** These pretests, which appear in Chapters 2 through 8, assess the student's knowledge of the skill to be introduced. This assessment helps both instructors and students target specific areas for improvement.
- **Explanation:** Each chapter is broken up into sections, with each section devoted to explanation and practice of a particular concept. Material is divided into manageable sections of information that are followed by practice of a specific skill.
- **Exercises:** An ample number and variety of exercises is included in every chapter. Most of the exercises contain paragraphs from textbooks, magazines, newspapers, and journals so that students can read various types of selections and learn new information about a variety of different subjects. Exercises are arranged using a step-by-step progression to build concepts and skills gradually.
- **Reading Strategy:** Every chapter includes an important reading strategy that students can use to help them comprehend and remember what they've read. Students are encouraged to practice the strategy on the longer reading selections at the end of each chapter.
- **Chapter Review:** A closing exercise tests students' knowledge of the concepts presented in each chapter.
- **Longer Reading Selections:** Longer reading selections follow the explanatory material in Chapters 1 through 9 and are included to give students practice in identifying different skills in context. Readings are chosen for their high interest, diverse topics, and cultural relevance for today's students. In addition, each reading is selected with the level of student in mind as well as students' ethnic, cultural, and educational experiences. New to this edition is the "Practicing the Active Reading Strategy," which asks students to apply active reading techniques to longer selections before and after they read.

- **Questions for Discussion and Writing:** These questions ask students to think about their own experiences, as well as what they have read in the longer reading selections. The main points, topics, and theses of the longer readings are used as springboards to encourage student reflection on personal experiences and as stimuli for strengthening academic skills such as research, argument, and summary. These questions give students the opportunity to develop their writing skills by responding to a professional reading selection.

- **Vocabulary:** Vocabulary is integrated in several different ways throughout each chapter. First, definitions of words or phrases that may be new to beginning students now appear as footnotes. In addition, words that may be unfamiliar are taken from the longer reading selection that appears later in Chapters 1 through 8 and used in a vocabulary exercise that follows the selection. Students are given the opportunity to glean the meanings of certain words from context and expand their overall vocabulary. Lastly, each chapter includes instruction in a specific vocabulary strategy, such as context clues, that will help students improve their reading comprehension. The instruction is followed by one or more exercises that draw examples from readings in the text to give students practice with that particular strategy.

- **Chapter Review:** A closing exercise tests students' knowledge of the concepts presented at the end of each chapter.

Ancillaries

The *Wadsworth College Reading Series*, Third Edition, is supported by an innovative teaching and learning package.

- **Aplia**—Aplia is an online, auto-graded homework system that improves learning by increasing student effort and engagement—without requiring more work from the instructor.

- **Annotated Instructor's Edition**—The annotated Instructor's Edition includes solutions to exercises in the student edition.

- **Instructor's Manual and Test Bank**—Streamline and maximize the effectiveness of your course preparation. This time-saving resource, which includes a helpful chapter-by-chapter Q & A format, also includes a Test Bank.

- **ExamView**—Create, deliver, and customize tests and study guides (both print and online) in minutes with this easy-to-use assessment and tutorial system. ExamView offers both a Quick Test Wizard and an Online Test Wizard that guide you step by step through the process of creating tests, while its "what you see is what you get" interface allows you to see the test you are creating on the screen exactly as it will print or display online.

- ***The Wadsworth Guide to Reading Textbooks***—This guide has five full textbook chapters and an accompanying study guide section from a variety of disciplines. Following each textbook chapter are two sections of instruction and exercises for the students. The first section, "Textbook Features," explains methods for improving reading skills.

Acknowledgments

I would like to express my very deepest gratitude to my extraordinary assistants, Tanya Bahn and Michelle Lowry. Without the exceptional work of these two marvelous reading professionals, the task of revising this text would have been almost impossible.

I am greatly indebted to Laurie Dobson, my Development Editor, for her constant patience and unflagging good humor while leading me through the forest of textbook revision.

I am especially appreciative of Annie Todd, Director of Developmental Studies, for thinking that I had the knowledge and experience to bring something new and different to these books.

For their fine work on this project, I would like thank the terrific folks at Cengage Learning and PreMedia Global including: Elizabeth Rice, Assistant Editor; Matt Conte, Editorial Assistant; Beth Kluckhohn, Project Manager; Shawn De Jong, Permissions Project Manager; and Sara Golden, Photo Researcher.

I am also indebted to the wonderful students in my reading classes over the past decades for showing me what perseverance really looks like.

I would like to thank the many incredible adjunct reading instructors that I have had the great pleasure of knowing and working with over the course of my career. You all amaze me with your dedication to our students.

A huge thank you goes to Kathleen Perryman, my colleague, co-teacher, and friend, who inspired and motivated me to be a better teacher.

My gratitude also goes to my family and friends for their constant faith and support, especially my fantastic husband and sons—Daryl, David, and Michael.

I would also like to thank the following reviewers for their time and effort:

Christine Barrilleaux, Tallahassee Community College
Barbara Cox, Redlands Community College
Eric Hibbison, J. Sargeant Reynolds Community College
Miriam Kinnard, Trident Technical College
Laura Meyers, Hawkeye Community College
Darlene Pabis, Westmoreland County Community College

Hattie Pinckney, Florence-Darlington Technical College
Nancy Rice, New England Institute of Technology
Jerolynn Roberson, Miami Dade College
Deborah Spradlin, Tyler Junior College

Edy Alderson

WADSWORTH COLLEGE READING SERIES

CHAPTER 1

Dennis Drenner/Aurora/Getty Images

Improving Reading and Thinking

Goals for Chapter 1

- Explain why effective reading is critical to academic, professional, and personal success.
- Explain how reading improves thinking skills.
- Describe four techniques for improving reading skills.
- List the different goals of reading for information.
- Explain the four types of mental skills required for reading.
- Describe the organization and features of this book.
- Explain and apply the steps of active reading.
- Use general tips for reading visual aids.

Do you enjoy reading? If your answer is no, why not? Like many people, you may have several reasons for disliking the printed word. You might think reading is too passive, requiring you to sit still for too much time. You may not like it because it takes too long. You may say that most of the things you read just don't interest you or aren't relevant to your life. You may object to reading because it seems too hard—you don't like having to struggle to understand information. These are the most common reasons people give to explain their dislike of reading.

What people don't realize is that most of these reasons arise from a lack of experience and effort. When you first decided you didn't like to read, you probably began to avoid it as much as possible. This avoidance led to a lack of practice that set up a vicious cycle: lack of practice prevented skills from developing. This lack of skills meant more difficult and unrewarding experiences when you did read. As a result, you probably read less and less and failed to use opportunities to practice your reading skills. So, the cycle began again.

You can break this cycle, though, and make your reading experiences more enjoyable. The first step is realizing how much you already know about the reading process.

Reading and Academic Success

Solid reading skills will be critical to your success in college. Most college courses require a great deal of reading. Your professors will ask you to read textbooks, articles, books, stories, and handouts. You'll be responsible for remembering much of this information and revealing your knowledge of it on tests. You'll have to read the instructor's notes, and you'll have to read your own notes on lecture material to prepare for your tests. In addition, you'll be asked to conduct research that requires reading all types of sources, including websites on the Internet. Various assignments will ask you to read not only your own writing but also your classmates'.

Not only will you have to simply read and remember information, you'll be asked to evaluate it, judge it, agree or disagree with it, interpret it, compare it to something else, summarize it, and synthesize[1] it with other things you've read. All of these tasks are possible only if you can first attain a solid grasp of the ideas and information in the source.

1. **synthesize:** to put things together in new combinations

1

Exercise 1.1

In the list below, place a check mark beside every reading-related activity you've completed at least once. Then, answer the questions that follow by writing your answers on the blanks provided. Answers will vary.

_______ Read a textbook.

_______ Read a magazine or journal article assigned by a teacher.

_______ Read information on a website for a class assignment.

_______ Read a book or a novel assigned by a teacher.

_______ Researched a topic in the library by reading several sources about it.

_______ Read a memo at work.

_______ Read a letter from a friend.

_______ Read an e-mail message from a friend, teacher, or colleague.

_______ Read subtitles[1] while you watched a foreign film.

_______ Read the newspaper.

_______ Read a story to a child.

_______ Read aloud in class.

_______ Read a prepared speech to an audience.

1. If you could choose anything to read, what would it be? Why?

   Answers will vary.

2. What types of reading situations do you find the most difficult? Why?

   Answers will vary.

1. **subtitles:** translations of the dialogue

3. What do you think you need to do to become a better reader?

   Answers will vary.

4. What would you like to learn in this textbook that you think would help you become a better reader?

   Answers will vary.

Reading and Professional Success

When you enter the workforce, you might be surprised how much reading you'll need to do. Many jobs will require you to read e-mail messages, letters, memorandums, policy and procedure manuals, instructions, reports, logs and records, summaries of meetings, newsletters, and many other types of documents.

Often, a lot is at stake on your comprehension of these materials. Your personal safety may depend on your understanding of the information in manuals or other instructions. Your efficient and effective job performance may rest on your ability to comprehend written information sent to you by your supervisors and coworkers. Even your promotions and raises may depend, in part, on your ability to read and understand materials such as reports about trends, new research, or other innovations in your field.

Exercise 1.2

Read the following memo and then write your answers to the questions on the blanks provided.

To: Nursing Staff of County General Hospital

From: Barbara Benton, Head of Nursing Staff

Date: January 2, 20—

Re: Avoiding Needle Stick Injuries

To all nurses:

On behalf of the nursing staff and executive board, I'd like to thank each and every one of you for your hard work and commitment to the hospital and its patients. It has come to our attention that injuries resulting from needle sticks have risen, and we would like to give you a set of guidelines that will assist you in your patient care.

Prevention

Any sharp object that comes in contact with a patient's body fluids may carry infection. Hepatitis is a greater danger than HIV. You are likely to get an HIV infection only if the stick is very deep or if blood from the needle gets into your body.

To prevent needle stick injuries:

- Be careful when handling needles, scalpels, and any other sharp objects.
- Do not put the cap back on a used needle: do not bend or break a needle by hand, and do not take the needle off a disposable syringe.
- Put all sharp objects in a special holder that contains only sharp items.
- Always wear gloves when you touch anything that has blood or other body fluids on it.

Signs/Symptoms

If you do stick yourself, there will be only the pain and bleeding at first. Only later will you develop symptoms of infection.

Care

You'll need to be tested. You may be given shots to prevent you from getting hepatitis. If you have a positive test for HIV, the doctor may prescribe medicine to slow down the infection.

What You Should Do

- If you stick yourself with a needle used on a patient, report it immediately. Both you and the patient should be tested for hepatitis and HIV infection.
- See your doctor right away if the patient has AIDS or HIV infection or refuses to be tested.
- If you do not know which patient the needle came from, you and your doctor will need to decide what tests should be done and what treatment you should have.
- In case you've contracted hepatitis, wash your hands well before eating and after using the bathroom. Do not share food or drinks.

1

- Even if your first test shows you do not have HIV, you should get another test in six weeks and three, six, and twelve months after your needle stick injury. You should also take the steps necessary to avoid spreading HIV: Use a condom when you have sex. Do not give blood. If you are breastfeeding, use formula instead.

Call Your Doctor If . . .

- You have not been given your test results.
- You can't drink fluids or you throw up after you eat.
- Your stomach or legs become swollen, itch, or break out in a rash.
- You get a fever, a rash, or muscle pain, feel tired, or can feel lumps in your neck or under your arms within a year of the injury.
- You vomit or have diarrhea or really bad abdominal pain for more than a few days.*

1. Why is a needle stick injury potentially dangerous?

   A nurse can contract hepatitis or HIV from a needle stick.

2. What is the first thing a nurse should do if stuck with a needle?

   Report the accident immediately and get tested for hepatitis and HIV.

3. Name two things a nurse can do to prevent needle stick injuries.

   Be careful when handling needles, scalpels, and any other sharp objects. Do not put the cap back on a used needle, do not bend or break a needle by hand, and do not take the needle off a disposable syringe; put all sharp objects in a special holder that contains only sharp items; always wear gloves when touching anything that has blood or other body fluids on it. (Answers will vary.)

4. Summarize two instances in which a nurse should call his or her doctor after getting a needle stick injury.

   You have not been given your test results. You can't drink fluids or you throw up after you eat. Your stomach or legs become swollen, itch, or break out in a rash.

* From *The PDR® Family Guide Encyclopedia of Medical Care™*, copyright 1997 by The Medical Economics Company, Inc. Used by permission of Three Rivers Press, a division of Random House, Inc.

You get a fever, a rash, or muscle pain, feel tired, or can feel lumps in your neck or under your arms within a year of the injury. You vomit or have diarrhea or really bad abdominal pain for more than a few days. (Answers will vary.)

Reading and Personal Success

Many occasions exist in your personal life when you will need to read well. For example, you may want to learn more about a hobby or subject area that interests you, so you'll need to read books, articles, and website pages to increase your knowledge. You may want to find out how to improve your personal finances by learning how to save or invest your money. You may need to assemble something you purchased—such as a child's toy or a barbecue grill—by following the directions. You or one of your loved ones may become sick with a particular disease or disorder, causing you to want more information about treatment options. You may even want to read for entertainment, picking up a fashion or sports magazine or a mystery novel just for the fun of it.

You'll also need to read personal correspondence, such as letters and e-mail messages, legal documents such as contracts, and reports from your children's teachers, among other things. You'll read all of these documents more capably and confidently when you improve your reading skills.

Exercise 1.3

Read the following selection and answer the questions that follow in the blanks provided. If you need more space, use a sheet of paper or your computer. Look up any words you do not know in your dictionary.

North Dakota Wants Its Place in the Sun

North Dakota is talking about changing its name. I frankly didn't know you could do that. I thought states' names were decreed by the Bible or something. In fact, as a child I believed that when Columbus[1] arrived in North America, the states' names were actually, physically, written on the continent, in gigantic letters, the way they are on maps. I still think this would be a good idea, because if an airplane's navigational system failed, the pilot could just look out the window and see exactly where the plane was. ("OK, there's a huge "W" down there, so we're over Wyoming. Or, Wisconsin.")

1. **Columbus:** Christopher Columbus, the first historically significant European discoverer of the Caribbean and South America

1

But apparently states can change their names, and some North Dakotans want to change "North Dakota." Specifically, they don't like the word "North," which connotes a certain northness. In the words of North Dakota's former governor, Ed Schafer: "People have such an instant thing about how North Dakota is cold and snowy and flat."

We should heed the words of the former governor, and not just because the letters in "Ed Schafer" can be rearranged to spell "Shed Farce." The truth is that when we think about North Dakota, which is not often, we picture it as having the same year-round climate as Uranus.

In contrast, SOUTH Dakota is universally believed to be a tropical paradise with palm trees swaying on surf-kissed beaches. Millions of tourists, lured by the word "South," flock to South Dakota every winter, often wearing nothing but skimpy bathing suits. Within hours, most of them die and become covered with snow, not to be found until spring, when they cause a major headache for South Dakota's farmers by clogging up the cultivating machines. South Dakota put a giant fence around the whole state to keep these tourists out, and STILL they keep coming. That's how powerful a name can be.

I'll give you another example. I live in Florida, where we have BIG cockroaches.

Q. How big are they?

A. They are so big that, when they back up, they are required by federal law to emit warning beeps.

These cockroaches could harm Florida's image. But we Floridians solved that problem by giving them a new name, "palmetto bugs," which makes them sound cute and harmless. So when a guest walks into a Florida kitchen and screams at the sight of an insect the size of Charles Barkley,[1] we say: "Don't worry! It's just a palmetto bug!" And then we and our guest have a hearty laugh, because we know there's nothing to worry about, as long as we do not make any sudden moves toward the palmetto bug's sandwich.

So changing names is a sound idea, an idea based on the scientific principle that underlies the field of marketing, which is: People are stupid. Marketing experts know that if you call something by a different name, *people will believe it's a different thing*. That's how "undertakers" became "funeral directors." That's how "trailers" became "manufactured housing." That's how "We're putting you on hold for the next decade" became "Your call is important to us."

And that's why some North Dakotans want to give the state a new name, a name that will give the state a more positive, inviting, and forward-looking image. That name is: "Palmetto Bug."

No, seriously, they want to drop the "North" and call the state, simply, "Dakota." I think this change is brilliant, and could also work for other states

1. **Charles Barkley:** A former NBA player (1984–1999) who stood 6'6" and weighed 250 pounds

with image problems. New Jersey, for example, should call itself, simply, "New."

Be advised that "Dakota" is not the first shrewd marketing concept thought up by North Dakotans. Are you familiar with Grand Forks, N.D.? No? It's located just west of East Grand Forks, Minn. According to a letter I received from a Grand Forks resident who asked to remain nameless ("I have to live here," he wrote), these cities decided they needed to improve their image, and the result was—get ready—"The Grand Cities."

The Grand Cities, needless to say, have a web site (grandcities.net), where you can read sentences about The Grand Cities written in MarketingSpeak, which is sort of like English, except that it doesn't actually mean anything. Here's an actual quote: "It's the intersection of earth and sky. It's a glimpse of what lies ahead. It's hope, anticipation, and curiosity reaching out to you in mysterious ways. Timeless. Endless. Always enriching your soul. Here, where the earth meets the sky, the Grand Cities of Grand Forks, North Dakota, and East Grand Forks, Minnesota."

Doesn't that just make you want to cancel that trip to Paris or Rome and head for The Grand Cities? As a resident of Florida ("Where the earth meets the water, and forms mud") I am definitely planning to go to Dakota. I want to know what they're smoking up there.*

1. Did you enjoy reading this selection? Why or why not? ______

   Answers will vary.

   ______

2. What would be someone's primary reason for reading a selection like this one?

   Pleasure or entertainment

3. Think of some additional examples of terms that have been replaced with other words to help improve the image of the thing being named.

   Answers will vary.

   ______

4. Do you think the author makes a good argument for the statement, "So changing names is a sound idea, an idea based on the scientific principle that underlies the field of marketing, which is: People are stupid."? Why or why not?

   Answers will vary.

* From Dave Barry, "North Dakota Wants Its Place in the Sun," *Miami Herald,* August 12, 2001. © Copyright, 2001, Tribune Media Services, Inc. All Rights Reserved. Reprinted with permission.

1

Reading and Better Thinking

Not only will better reading skills help you improve your chances for academic, professional, and personal success, they will also help you improve your overall thinking skills. This is because reading requires you to follow and understand the thought processes of the writer. When you can do that effectively, you get opportunities to hone[1] a variety of mental skills:

1. You evaluate information and decide what's important.
2. You learn to see relationships among things, events, and ideas.
3. You make new connections among things, events, and ideas.
4. You practice following the logic (or seeing the lack of logic) of someone else's thoughts.
5. You add more information to your memory.

These are the very skills that will strengthen your ability to make decisions, think creatively, and think logically in every area of your life.

Exercise **1.4**

Read the following newspaper story and write on the blanks provided your answers to the questions that follow.

For Author, the (GE) Light Dawns

It was one of those days that make a struggling writer feel just great.

The intense aroma of the Seattle Mountain Colombian Decaf that filled the kitchen that morning reminded me of how pleased I had been to find such a bargain on coffee at Costco. My satisfaction increased as I switched on my Bose Wave radio to my favorite smooth jazz station and settled down with the *New York Times*, my favorite newspaper after *USA Today*.

The *Times* story that first caught my eye was about a British author who has agreed to have a jewelry store—I forget the name of it—sponsor her latest novel. For an undisclosed fee, the author, Fay Weldon, has made the jewelry store the centerpiece of her novel. It's the ultimate in "product placement."

The *Times* article was well written. But the writer's polish did not overshadow the story's content: a tale of marketing genius that gives hope to every would-be novelist in America who hasn't suffocated under the weight of publishers' rejection letters.

It opened my eyes, I can tell you.

1. **hone:** sharpen, perfect

When the kids got into an argument that morning over whether we'd go to Borders or Barnes & Noble, I flipped a coin. Borders won, but I'd have been just as happy to go to Barnes & Noble because they are both mighty fine bookstores.

We headed out into a dreary rain, and the first thing I noticed was that my Acura MDX needed gas again, but I didn't mind because it's such a joy to drive and so beautifully designed for carpooling.

Branded Bagels and Books

As usual, the kids wanted to stop at Einstein Bros. Bagels, and I was glad they did because I wanted to stop there, too. There was the usual long line, but I knew that's because it's so popular, and besides, the line moved very quickly, and the wait was worth it because the toasted sesame with lox shmear (a spread of cream cheese) was to die for.

When we got to Borders, I couldn't find the book I was looking for—*10 Steps to Salvaging a Manuscript That's Been Rejected by 20 Publishers in Only 30 Days*—but I couldn't get upset because I knew that it was in such high demand that it practically flies off the shelf.

Our next stop was at a mall called Phipps Plaza, a temple of high-end fashion and excess, and I knew that I wouldn't be disappointed there. I was astounded, in fact, by the selection at Saks, where I found an exquisite Ermenegildo Zegna cashmere sweater priced at only $800. Before I could whip out my credit card, a charming salesman sidled[1] over and whispered, "The price will be considerably lower if you come back tomorrow." I appreciate that kind of customer care.

The Devil's in the Details

When we got home, I was still thinking about how happy I was for Fay Weldon as I fired up my new Char-Broil H2O smoker, which I purchased for a very good price and assembled in only five hours. And as I laid on some succulent[2] salmon I'd bought at Publix, it finally dawned on me:

I've had so much trouble trying to write fiction. I've created some solid characters. I can write dialogue that flows like molasses in July. I've done some great sex scenes—riveting but sensitive, all entirely believable, if you ask me.

But I've neglected the kind of detail that gives stories what an editor once told me was "verisimilitude."[3] And now I understand where I went wrong.

From now on, the bed sheets won't just be bed sheets; they'll be Ralph Lauren. The bed will be from Ernest Hemingway's Kenya Collection, by

1. **sidled:** moved in a manner to avoid attracting attention
2. **succulent:** juicy and delicious
3. **verisimilitude:** appearing to be real or true

Thomasville. The before-dinner drinks will be Dry Sack, and the nightcaps will be Rémy Martin V.S.O.P.

And the love triangle that I've been fooling around with for years will be set at Home Depot: Melissa will work in Lighting, Steve in Nuts and Bolts and Cheryl at Pro Checkout.

I think I've got this thing nailed.*

1. What does Don Campbell do for a living? In your opinion, has he been successful at his profession? Why or why not? Use an example from the selection to support your answer.

   Don Campbell wants to be a published writer, but he includes several references to publishers rejecting manuscripts, so he has probably not been successful.

2. What new piece of information did you learn by reading this excerpt?

   Answers will vary.

3. How does Campbell's story actually demonstrate the very subject it's about?

   Campbell's story is about product placement, the mention of specific brands in books, TV shows, films, and other forms of media. He fills his story with mentions of many different products and retailers.

4. Why is the selection entitled "For Author, the (GE) Light Dawns"?

   This story is about the author's revelation that he should add product placements in his writing, so he even manages to mention a specific manufacturer's name (GE) in his title.

How to Improve Reading Skills

Now that you understand *why* it's so important to read well, you're probably wondering *how* you can be a better reader. The obvious answer is practice. The more you read, the more opportunities you'll have for improving your abilities. But simply reading everything in sight will not necessarily improve

* From Don Campbell, "For Author, the (GE) Light Dawns," *USA Today*, September 10, 2001, www.usatoday.com.

your skills. In general, you should commit yourself to doing four other things as well:

1. Understand the different purposes for reading.
2. Be aware of the mental skills required for reading.
3. Develop individual reading skills.
4. Learn and use different reading strategies.

Understand the Different Purposes for Reading

When you set out to read something, you should know *why* you're reading it. The two basic purposes for reading are to gain information and to be entertained. Obviously, when you read for entertainment, your primary goal is your own pleasure. When you read for information, though, you may have different goals, such as:

1. **Gaining a general understanding of the ideas or points.** For example, as you're reading this section of this textbook, you're trying to comprehend the ideas being presented.
2. **Discovering the facts or answering questions about the material.** When you read the paragraphs in the exercises of this book, for example, you read them to find answers to the questions you must answer.
3. **Memorizing the information.** You often read a textbook chapter so that you'll recall its information when you take a test.
4. **Finding information or ideas that prove a point you want to make.** When you conduct research for a paper you need to write, you read to find statements or information that back up your opinions.
5. **Making a decision based on the information.** You read business brochures, for example, to decide whether to buy a particular product or service.

When you read something, you may need to accomplish just one of the goals above or perhaps all five at the same time. In any case, getting the most of everything you read means clearly identifying your purpose before you begin.

Exercise 1.5

Read the following reading situations. Write a check mark on the blank next to all MAJOR purposes for reading that applies to that situation. You may have more than one check mark for each situation. Discuss your answers with your classmates.

1. You read the movie listings in your local paper.

_______ Gain a general understanding of the ideas or points.

___✔___ Discover the facts or answer questions.

_______ Memorize the information.

_______ Find information or ideas that prove a point you want to make.

___✔___ Make a decision based on the information.

2. You read a magazine article to find statistics you can use in a research paper you're writing.

_______ Gain a general understanding of the ideas or points.

___✔___ Discover the facts or answer questions.

_______ Memorize the information.

___✔___ Find information or ideas that prove a point you want to make.

_______ Make a decision based on the information.

3. You read the technical instructions that come with your new laptop computer.

_______ Gain a general understanding of the ideas or points.

___✔___ Discover the facts or answer questions.

_______ Memorize the information.

_______ Find information or ideas that prove a point you want to make.

_______ Make a decision based on the information.

4. You read the details of the president's new education plan, as printed in a weekly news magazine.

_______ Gain a general understanding of the ideas or points.

___✔___ Discover the facts or answer questions.

_______ Memorize the information.

_______ Find information or ideas that prove a point you want to make.

_______ Make a decision based on the information.

5. You reread a chapter about mathematical equations in preparation for a math test.

_______ Gain a general understanding of the ideas or points.

_______ Discover the facts or answer questions.

___✔___ Memorize the information.

_______ Find information or ideas that prove a point you want to make.

_______ Make a decision based on the information.

Understand the Mental Skills Required for Reading

"Reading" is actually a collection of different mental skills. They include attitude, concentration, memory, and logical thought. These skills are all interrelated and connected. Some of them depend upon others. When you become conscious that these different skills are at work, you can learn to improve them.

Attitude. A positive attitude is the first essential mental component for successful reading. Your attitude includes your feelings about reading, about *what* you read, and about your own abilities. If these feelings are negative, your reading experiences will be negative. If these feelings are positive, your experiences will be more enjoyable.

A positive attitude not only makes reading more pleasurable, it also creates the right mental environment for the acquisition of new information. As a matter of fact, all of the other mental skills required for reading are useless unless you approach each reading task in the right frame of mind. If you are quick to pronounce a particular text "boring" or "worthless," you are likely to create a mental block that will prevent you from absorbing the information. Instead, approach each new reading task with intellectual curiosity. Expect to find something of value, something you'll be able to use in your life.

Also, don't let a poor attitude about your own reading abilities get in your way. If you expect to fail, if you tell yourself you just don't get it, then you virtually guarantee your failure. If you believe you can improve, however, then you'll create the necessary mental foundation for improving your skills and becoming a good reader.

Exercise 1.6

Read the following selection with a positive attitude and answer the questions on the blanks provided.

Garlic: The Spice of Long Life

It may not do much for your breath, but perhaps no other herb can do more for your heart health than garlic. Used for centuries around the world for anything from numbing toothaches to warding off vampires, a new generation is taking to garlic with a passion. German health authorities have approved garlic as a primary defense against atherosclerosis—the buildup of fatty plaques on artery walls that can lead to heart disease—and high cholesterol levels. American consumers are now buying it in droves.

Recent research, including over 1,000 clinical trials that have been conducted on its medicinal uses, supports their enthusiasm. A study published in *Coronary Artery Disease* last fall found that of 60 mice fed high-cholesterol diets, the 30 given allicin, one of garlic's active ingredients, developed fewer fatty deposits in their arteries. A 1999 Germany study showed an 18 percent reduction in plaque buildup in the arteries of people who took 900 mg of garlic powder a day. And an Oxford University overview of 16 clinical trials involving nearly 1,000 people found that those taking 600 mg to 900 mg of dried garlic powder daily for a month or more saw a 12 percent reduction in their cholesterol levels and a 13 percent reduction in triglycerides, another type of fat found in the blood.

Garlic may have other powers, as well. A study published in *Cancer Detection and Prevention* in November found that giving garlic extract to guinea pigs with skin cancer slowed the growth of their tumors, and a study in *Microbes and Infection* last February heralded garlic as an effective treatment against certain bacteria, fungi, and viruses. Garlic is being investigated as a possible foil for infections that resist traditional antibiotics, and it's even being tested in Russia as a treatment for arthritis.

Note to garlic lovers looking for an excuse to eat more: You may have to eat a lot of raw garlic to experience its benefits, as much as five to 10 cloves a day—a prospect that may drive your friends away. Luckily, garlic supplements offer an odor-free alternative. Just remember that the herb is a blood thinner, and people taking aspirin or other anticoagulant drugs should talk to their doctors before taking the supplement.*

1. When you read the title of the selection "Garlic: The Spice of Long Life," what did you think the selection would be about? Why?

   Answers will vary, but students will probably say they thought the selection would be about garlic because it's mentioned in the title.

2. Did you assume the passage would be boring or too difficult? If so, why?

   Answers will vary.

3. As you read this passage, did you discover a fact or idea that interested you? Did you discover some information in this passage you could actually use in your life? If so, what was it?

   Answers will vary.

* From "Garlic: The Spice of Long Life," *Psychology Today*, March/April 2000, 40. Reprinted with permission from *Psychology Today Magazine*. Copyright © 2000 Sussex Publishers, Inc.

Concentration. Once your positive attitude has prepared your mind to absorb new information, you're ready to employ the second mental skill necessary for reading: concentration. **Concentration** *is the ability to focus all of your attention on one thing while ignoring all distractions.* You cannot understand or remember information unless you read with concentration.

Many people, however, find concentration difficult to achieve, especially when they read more challenging material. Too often, they succumb to distractions that pull their thoughts away from the sentences and paragraphs before them. But you can learn to concentrate better. How? By practicing effective techniques for combating the two types of distractions: external and internal.

External distractions *are the sights, sounds, and other sensations that tempt you away from your reading.* These distractions include ringing phones, people talking or walking nearby, the sound of a stereo, or a friend who stops by to chat. Though they are powerful, these external distractions are also the easier of the two types of distractions to eliminate.

To avoid having to grapple with external distractions, you merely prevent them from happening by choosing or creating the right reading environment. Try to select a location for reading—such as an individual study area in your library or a quiet room in your house—where there will be few distractions. Prior to a reading session, notify your friends and family that you'll be unavailable for conversation and socializing. If you must read in places with more activity, try wearing earplugs and/or sitting with your back to the action so you're not tempted to watch the comings and goings of others.

Internal distractions are often more challenging to overcome. *They are the thoughts, worries, plans, daydreams, and other types of mental "noise" inside your own head.* They will prevent you from concentrating on what you're reading and from absorbing the information you need to learn.

You can try to ignore these thoughts, but they will usually continue trying to intrude. So, how do you temporarily silence them so you can devote your full attention to your reading? Try the following suggestions:

1. Begin every reading task with a positive attitude. A negative attitude produces a lot of mental noise in the form of complaints about, and objections to, the task at hand. When you choose to maintain a positive attitude, you'll eliminate an entire category of noisy thoughts that interfere with your concentration.

2. Instead of fighting internal distractions, try focusing completely on them for a short period of time. For five or ten minutes, allow yourself to sit and think about your job, your finances, your car problems, your boyfriend or girlfriend, the paper you need to write, or whatever is on your mind. Better yet, write these thoughts down. Do a free-writing exercise (a quick writing of your own thoughts on paper without censoring them or worrying about grammar and spelling) to empty your mind of the

thoughts that clutter it. If you can't stop thinking about all of the other things you need to do, devote ten minutes to writing a detailed to-do list. Giving all of your attention to distracting thoughts will often clear them from your mind so you can focus on your reading.

3. Keep your purpose in mind as you read. As discussed earlier, having a clear goal when you read will help you concentrate on getting from a text what you need to know.
4. Use active reading techniques. These techniques are explained at the end of this chapter. They increase your level of interaction with the text, which will improve your concentration on the material.
5. Use visualization to increase your interest and improve your retention of the information. As you read, let the words create pictures and images in your mind. Try to "see" in your mind's eye the scenes, examples, people, and other information presented in the text.

Exercise **1.7**

On a separate sheet of paper, free-write for ten minutes about what's going on inside your mind at this moment so you can clear your mind for the reading that follows. Answers will vary.

Exercise **1.8**

Read the following passage and practice the visualization techniques you read about earlier. Answer the questions that follow on a separate sheet of paper or use your computer.

According to her own account, Mary Harris was born in Ireland in 1830 and came to the United States as a child, with her father. As a young woman, she taught school and worked as a dressmaker or seamstress, then married George Jones, an iron molder and union activist. Her expectations as a wife and mother were shattered, however, when she lost her entire family, her husband and their four children—in a yellow-fever epidemic in 1867.

On her own, she opened a dressmaking shop in Chicago. Her clients included those she called "the aristocrats of Chicago," and she witnessed "the luxury and extravagance of their lives." The contrast between the opulent expectations of her wealthy clients and tightly constrained lives of the poor left her deeply disturbed.

In 1871, her shop burned in the great fire that swept much of the city. Thereafter, she chose to give much of her time to helping workers, first through the Knights of Labor.[1] In 1882, she first took part in a strike by coal miners.

1. **The Knights of Labor:** an American labor organization started by Philadelphia tailors in 1869

Mary's, or "Mother Jones" as she came to be known, talents lay in public speaking and in organizing demonstrations to capture public attention and sympathy. In one strike in 1900, she organized miners' wives to protest against strikebreakers by pounding on pots and pans and frightening the mules that pulled the mine carts. In 1903, she took up the cause of the children who worked in textile mills. By organizing a march of mill children to the home of President Theodore Roosevelt, she captured headlines with her living, walking display of the children's deformities and injuries caused by mill work.

Mother Jones made an unusual choice in her decision to spend the last half of her life as a labor organizer and agitator.[1] But she apparently held traditional expectations about the role of women in society, arguing that their place was in the home. She seems to have seen her own work as an extension of her role as mother. Deprived of her own family, she sought to nurture and protect a much larger family of workers.*

1. Picture Mary Harris Jones, or Mother Jones, in your mind. What does she look like? What is she wearing? Answers will vary.
2. Picture the scene of Mary marching with mill children to the home of Theodore Roosevelt. What do you think this scene looked like? What do you think Roosevelt's reaction was? Answers will vary.
3. Picture the differences between "the aristocrats of Chicago" and the people that Mary chose to help—miners and child laborers, in particular. How would they be different in appearance? Answers will vary.

Memory. Memory, the ability to store and recall information, is also essential to the reading process. You use your memory constantly as you read. You must remember:

- The meanings of words.
- What you know about people, places, and things when you encounter references to them.
- All of the ideas and information presented before that point in the text.
- The text's overall main point while you read the subpoints or details.
- Your own experiences that either support or contradict the text's message.
- Other texts you've read that either agree or disagree with the new information you're reading.

1. **agitator:** one who stirs up interest in a cause

* Adapted from Berkin et al., *Making America: A History of the United States,* 2nd ed. Boston: Houghton Mifflin, 2001, 356–357. Copyright © 2001 by Houghton Mifflin Company. Reprinted with permission.

1

You can use many techniques to improve your memory. A few of the most common are:

1. **Improve your concentration.** The more intensely you focus on something, the better the chance you'll remember it.
2. **Repeat and review.** Most of the time, the more you expose yourself to new information, the more easily you'll recall it.
3. **Recite.** Saying information aloud helps strengthen your memory of it.
4. **Associate new information with what you already know.** Making connections between your present knowledge and what you need to learn helps you to store new information in your mind more effectively.

Exercise 1.9

Read the following passage through one time. Then cover it so you can't see it and test your memory of the information by writing on the blanks provided your answers to the questions that follow.

Harlem[1] became a vibrant center of black culture in the 1920s. The Mississippi-born classical composer William Grant Still moved to Harlem in 1922, pursuing his composition studies and completing his best-known work, *Afro-American Symphony* (1931). On the musical-comedy stage, the 1921 hit *Shuffle Along* launched a series of popular all-black reviews. The 1923 show *Runnin' Wild* sparked the Charleston dance craze. The Cotton Club and other Harlem cabarets[2] featured such jazz geniuses as Duke Ellington, Fletcher Henderson, and Jelly Roll Morton. Contributing too to the cultural ferment[3] were muralist Aaron Douglas, concert tenor Roland Hayes, and singer-actor Paul Robeson.*

1. During what decade did the section of New York City known as Harlem become a center of black culture? The 1920s
2. What was *Shuffle Along*? A musical comedy

1. **Harlem:** an area of New York City
2. **cabarets:** nightclubs providing entertainment
3. **ferment:** excitement; mixture

* Adapted from Boyer et al., *The Enduring Vision,* 5th ed. Boston: Houghton Mifflin, 2004, 728. Copyright © 2004 by Houghton Mifflin Company. Reprinted with permission.

3. What show sparked the Charleston dance craze? Runnin' Wild

4. Name a Harlem cabaret that was popular in the 1920s. The Cotton Club

Logical Thought. Another mental skill required for effective reading is logical thinking. Logical thought is composed of many different mental tasks, including those in the list below:

Sequencing and ordering: seeing the order of things and understanding cause/effect relationships

Matching: noticing similarities

Organizing: grouping things into categories

Analysis: understanding how to examine the different parts of something

Reasoning from the general to the particular and the particular to the general: drawing conclusions and making generalizations

Abstract thought: understanding ideas and concepts

Synthesis: putting things together in new combinations

If you want to improve your ability to think logically, try one or more of the following suggestions:

1. **Practice active reading.** Using outlining, in particular, forces you to work harder to detect relationships in information. Outlining and other active reading techniques are explained at the end of this chapter.
2. **Play with games and puzzles.** Card games, computer games, and board games like chess, checkers, and backgammon will give you opportunities to sharpen your analytical skills.
3. **Solve problems.** Work math problems. Read mysteries (or watch them on television) and try to figure out who committed the crime before the detective does. Try to think of ways to solve everyday problems both big and small. For example, come up with a solution for America's overflowing landfills. Or figure out how to alter backpacks so they don't strain your back.
4. **Practice your argument and debating skills.** Discuss controversial issues with people who hold the opposing viewpoint.
5. **Write more.** Writing requires a great deal of logical thought, so write letters to your newspaper editor or congressional representatives about issues that are important to you.

1

Exercise 1.10

Read the following article from National Public Radio. Then answer the questions that follow.

Want to Make $1,000 More a Year? Try Kindergarten

A great kindergarten experience isn't just enriching to kids mentally—it's enriching to their wallets, too. That's according to a new Harvard study that found attending a top-notch kindergarten increases a person's earnings decades later by an average of $1,000 a year. Experts used to think the effect of early childhood education wore off as students got older, but these researchers, led by Harvard economist Raj Chetty, discovered that the "kindergarten effect" resurfaces in adulthood. "Your kindergarten teacher sort of gets you off on the right track," Chetty says. "Teachers use basic skills that you might use later in life, like how to study hard, how to focus, patience, manners, things like that, in addition to better academic skills. And all these things have a long-term payoff."

Chetty used data from the Tennessee STAR, or Student/Teacher Achievement Ratio, project. It tracked 12,000 students with similar backgrounds in Tennessee who were assigned to random kindergarten classes in the 1980s. The project tracked these children into adulthood. "What we find is that the type of kindergarten class that we're assigned to has very large effects on long-term outcomes and being in a better class," Chetty says. "For instance a smaller class or having a more experienced teacher makes you do better in the long run."

The study found that moving an average student from an average-quality class to an excellent-quality class not only can increase earnings but also can affect the likelihood of being a single parent, going to college and saving for retirement. But Chetty says it's not just about kindergarten. "The study's really about early childhood education," he said. "It's not that kindergarten is some kind of fatalistic thing that determines everything. But on the other hand, it makes sense to invest resources in trying to get your child into the best classroom, because it seems to matter on average."*

1. What is the "kindergarten effect"? The positive long-term effects of a quality early childhood/kindergarten education on one's life.

2. What kind of skills do children learn in kindergarten that will help them later in life?
Study hard, focus, patience, manners, and academic skills.

* Source: http://www.npr.org/templates/story/story.php?storyId=129187436 August 14, 2010

3. Identify two characteristics of a quality kindergarten. Small class sizes and more experienced teachers.

4. Describe your kindergarten experience. Answers will vary.

5. Do you think that parents should investigate their child's kindergarten class? Why or why not?

   Answers will vary.

Develop Individual Reading Skills

Another way to improve your reading comprehension is to develop the isolated skills you must use to read well. For example, you can learn techniques for recognizing the main idea of a paragraph or for detecting patterns used to organize information. The rest of this book is designed to help you develop and practice these skills.

Exercise 1.11

Check off in the list below the skills you believe are your weaknesses. Next to each item that you check, write the number of the chapter in this book that focuses on helping you strengthen that skill.

_______ Recognizing the overall point (the main idea) of a reading selection Chapter 2

_______ Understanding how details support the main idea of a reading selection Chapter 3

_______ Figuring out how a reading selection is organized Chapter 6

_______ Understanding visuals—maps, charts, graphs—in reading selections Chapter 1–8

_______ Reading critically, or figuring out if a reading selection is accurate or trustworthy Chapter 8

_______ Figuring out implied main ideas, points that are not stated directly in a reading selection Chapter 4

1

_______ Recognizing transitions, words that link sentences and paragraphs together Chapter 5

_______ "Reading between the lines" (making inferences) by drawing conclusions from the information in a reading selection Chapter 7

Learn and Use Different Reading Strategies

Reading strategies are techniques you use when you read. Some of them—such as active reading—are designed to improve your comprehension and retention of information. Others—such as skimming and scanning—provide you with tools you can use to find what you need in certain circumstances.

This book explains a different reading strategy in each chapter. Make sure you understand each of them so you can begin using them to read better right away.

How This Book Will Help You Improve Your Reading

Goals of This Book

The Wadsworth College Reading Series is one of three books in a series designed to help you improve your reading skills. This text—the second in the sequence—focuses on the basic skills necessary to master effective reading. Each chapter concentrates on one essential skill you can use immediately to strengthen your reading comprehension.

This book, along with the other two in the series, is based on the belief that you can indeed become a better reader. Even if you have struggled in the past, you can learn and practice the skills you need to get more out of anything you read.

Organization and Features

The textbook includes eight chapters, one for each essential reading skill. Each of the eight chapters includes several helpful features.

Test Yourself. At the beginning of each chapter, a test will help you identify what you already know about the skill covered in that chapter. It will also help you pinpoint specific areas you need to target for improvement.

Exercises. Throughout each chapter, you'll have numerous opportunities to check your understanding with practice activities. As you complete each exercise and receive feedback on your answers, you will progress toward better reading comprehension.

Interesting Readings. The readings within practices, along with the longer reading selections in each chapter, are drawn from a variety of interesting sources. These readings have been carefully chosen as enjoyable and useful. They have also been selected to clearly demonstrate a particular skill or concept. Furthermore, they'll give you practice reading different kinds of sources, including textbooks, magazine articles, newspaper articles, and essays.

The longer reading selections in each chapter are followed by questions designed to check your comprehension and increase your vocabulary. They also include discussion questions that will encourage you to sharpen your thinking skills and find ways to apply the information to your own life.

Vocabulary. Each chapter presents a different vocabulary strategy. In this section, you will learn techniques for discovering the meanings of unfamiliar words. You will also learn about different types of specialized vocabulary in order to improve your overall reading comprehension. A practice activity draws from the readings in the chapter to give you an opportunity to check your understanding.

Reading Strategy. Each chapter concludes with the explanation of a different reading strategy. Strategies are techniques you can use to get more out of what you read. Using these techniques, you can begin to improve your reading comprehension right away.

Visual Feature Boxes. Each of these boxes reviews a particular type of visual aid you are likely to encounter as you read. You will learn techniques for reading and interpreting these visual aids.

Chapter Review. Filling in the blanks in a brief summary of the major points and concepts in the chapter will help you reinforce them in your mind.

Exercise 1.12

Preview this textbook. Write on the blanks provided your answers to the following questions about its features and organization.

1. How many chapters does this book contain? Eight

2. In what chapter is the topic of "Main Ideas" covered? Chapter 2

3. In what chapter will you learn the different patterns of organization that writers use? Chapter 6

4. In what chapters will you find visual material—that is, charts, graphs, maps, and photos—and find out how to read them? Chapter 1–8

5. In what chapter will you review how to use the dictionary? Chapter 1

6. Look at Chapter 7 and define the term *inference*. An inference is a conclusion you draw that's based upon the stated information.

7. In which chapter will you learn how to summarize? Chapter 5

8. In which chapter will you learn how to spot a contrast context clue? Chapter 7

Reading Strategy: Active Reading

Many people don't get everything they can out of reading simply because they are *passive* readers. Passive readers are people who try to read by just running their eyes over the words in a passage. They expect their brains to magically absorb the information after just one quick reading. If they don't understand the reading, they blame the author and pronounce the work "dull" or "too difficult." These readers don't write anything down. If they come to a word they don't know, they just skip it and keep reading. If they get bored, they let their attention wander. They "read" long sections and then realize they have no memory or understanding of the information or ideas.

To read more effectively, you must become an *active* reader. Active readers know they have to do more than just sit with a book in front of them. They know that they have to participate in reading by interacting with the text and by thinking as they read. Active readers read with a pen or pencil in their hand, marking key words or ideas or jotting down notes in the margins. They reread the text if necessary, and they consciously try to connect the text's information to their own experiences and beliefs.

Active reading is essential to understanding and remembering ideas and information, especially those in difficult reading selections. It includes any or all of the following tasks:

- Identifying and writing down the point and purpose of the reading
- Underlining, highlighting, or circling important words or phrases
- Determining the meanings of unfamiliar words

- Outlining a passage in order to understand the relationships in the information
- Writing down questions when you're confused
- Completing activities—such as reading comprehension questions—that follow a chapter or passage
- Jotting down notes in the margins
- Thinking about how you can use the information or how the information reinforces or contradicts your ideas or experiences
- Predicting possible test questions on the material
- Rereading and reviewing
- Studying visual aids such as graphs, charts, and diagrams until you understand them

Remember, the purpose of all these activities is to comprehend and retain more of what you read. So, for challenging reading, such as textbook chapters or journal articles, active reading is a must. Also, you should perform these tasks for any reading that you're expected to remember for a test.

Even if you won't have to demonstrate your mastery of a reading selection, however, you should still get in the habit of reading actively when you read for information. Even if you're just reading for your own pleasure, you'll remember more by using active reading techniques.

To read actively, follow these steps:

1. When you sit down to read a book, get pens, pencils, and/or highlighter markers ready.
2. As you read each paragraph, mark points or terms that seem important. You may choose to underline them, highlight them, or insert boxes or circles. Be sure to mark any words or key information phrases that are in bold or italic print because the author wished to call attention to them. Consider jotting down an outline or notes in the margins as you read. If you're reading a textbook, write in the margins the questions you want to remember to ask your instructor.
3. As you read, continually ask yourself these questions: How can this information help me? How can I use this information? What will my instructor probably want me to remember? How does this reading support or contradict my own ideas, beliefs, and experiences?

4. After you have read the entire selection, complete any activities that follow it.

Follow steps 1, 2, and 3 described above to actively read the Reading Selection for this chapter "Ten Terrific Self-Motivating Tips."

WEB LINK **http://www.npr.org/templates/story/story.php?storyId=130728588&ft=1&f=100**

This link provides some new insights into active studying.

Reading Selection

Practicing the Active Reading Strategy

■ Before and While You Read

You can use active reading strategies before, while, and after you read a selection. The following are some suggestions for active reading strategies that you can perform before you read and while you read.

1. Skim the selection for any unfamiliar words. Circle or highlight any words you do not know.
2. As you read, underline, highlight, or circle important words or phrases.
3. Write down any questions about the selection if you are confused by the information presented.
4. Jot notes in the margin to help you understand the material.

WEBSITE READING
Ten Terrific Self-Motivating Tips

by Mike Moore

How motivated are you to do well in college? Who is responsible for your motivation? The following reading selection will give you some tips to help you understand how to motivate yourself so that your college experience is successful.

1 No one can motivate anyone to do anything. All a person can do for another is provide them with incentives to motivate themselves. Here are ten very effective strategies to help you get up and get moving toward actualizing your enormous, untapped potential.

2 ■ Be willing to leave your comfort zone. The greatest barrier to achieving your potential is your comfort zone. Great things happen when you make friends with your discomfort zone.

3 ■ Don't be afraid to make mistakes. Wisdom helps us avoid making mistakes and comes from making a million of them.

4 ■ Don't indulge in self-limiting thinking. Think empowering, expansive thoughts.

5 ■ Choose to be happy. Happy people are easily motivated. Happiness is your birthright so don't settle for anything else.

6 ■ Spend at least one hour a day in self-development. Read good books or listen to inspiring tapes. Driving to and from work provides an excellent opportunity to listen to self-improvement tapes.

7 ■ Train yourself to finish what you start. So many of us become scattered as we try to accomplish a task. Finish one task before you begin another.

8 ■ Live fully in the present moment. When you live in the past or the future you aren't able to make things happen in the present.

9 ■ Commit yourself to joy. C. S. Lewis[1] once said, "Joy is the serious business of heaven."

10 ■ Never quit when you experience a setback or frustration. Success could be just around the corner.

11 ■ Dare to dream big dreams. If there is anything to the law of expectation, then we are moving in the direction of our dreams, goals, and expectations.

12 The real tragedy in life is not in how much we suffer, but rather in how much we miss, so don't miss a thing.

13 Charles Dubois once said, "We must be prepared, at any moment, to sacrifice who we are for who we are capable of becoming."*

■ Vocabulary

Read the following questions about some of the vocabulary words that appear in the previous selection. Circle the letter of the correct answer.

1. In paragraph 1, what is the meaning of the word *incentives*?
   - a. motives
   - b. ideas
   - c. thoughts
   - d. words

2. In paragraph 1, what is the meaning of the word *actualizing*?
   - a. beginning
   - b. opening
   - c. completing
   - d. deciding

1. **C. S. Lewis:** British author

* Mike Moore is an international speaker/writer on the role of appreciation, praise, and humor in performance motivation and human potential. You can check out his books, tapes, and manuals at www.motivationalplus.com. From http://www.topachievement.com/mikemoore.html.

1

3. In paragraph 4, what does *empowering* mean?

a. disarming
b. lame
c. wacky
d. making strong; authorizing

4. In paragraph 4, what does *expansive* mean?

a. narrow
b. broad
c. different
d. similar

Practicing the Active Reading Strategy

After You Read

Now that you have read the selection, answer the following questions using the active reading strategies that are discussed on pages 26–27.

1. Identify and write down the point and purpose of this reading selection.
2. Are there any other vocabulary words that are unfamiliar to you? If so, write a list of them. When you have finished writing your list, look up each word in a dictionary and write the definition that best describes the word as it is used in the selection.
3. Predict any possible questions that may be used on a test about the content of this selection.

Questions for Discussion and Writing

Answer the following questions based on your reading of the selection. Write your answers on the blanks provided.

1. What new information, if any, did you learn from this selection?

Answers will vary.

2. Was there any information in this selection that you already knew? If so, what was it? Answers will vary.

3. Is there any information in this selection that you can use to help you achieve your academic goals? What information or suggestions included in the selection can you incorporate into your daily life? How?

Answers will vary.

Vocabulary Strategy: Using the Dictionary

To increase your vocabulary and to ensure your comprehension of what you read, you'll want to use a dictionary. The best hard-copy dictionaries for college level reading are those that include the word *college* or *collegiate* in their title and are not older than five years. For example, *The American Heritage College Dictionary* is a good reference to have on your desk at home. You may also want to get in the habit of carrying a paperback dictionary with you to class.

However, today's students often prefer to use online dictionaries. These dictionaries allow you to simply search for a word. Online dictionaries frequently have audio so you can hear the pronunciation of a word. Whereas some dictionary sites seem to be cluttered, others are easier to use. Because not all of the dictionary sites have the same information, you may want to bookmark several good sites for easy reference. Some good dictionary sites are **www.dictionary.com, www.yourdictionary.com, www.wordnik.com, and visuwords.com**.

Most dictionaries, hard copy or online, contain the following information:

- The spelling and pronunciation of the word, including its syllables and capital letters
- The word's part of speech (noun, verb, adjective, etc.)
- Words made from the main word, including plurals and verb forms
- The different meanings of the word, including special uses
- Synonyms (words that mean the same thing) for the word
- The history of the word
- Labels that identify the word's subject area or level of usage (for example, *slang* or *informal*)

The entry for a word may also contain a sentence that demonstrates the correct usage of the word. In addition, an entry may include *antonyms*, or words with the opposite meaning.

To use the dictionary effectively, you must understand how to locate a word and how to read the entry for that word once you find it.

Guide Words

All hard-copy dictionaries list words in alphabetical order, which helps you find a word quickly. Another feature that helps you locate a particular word is the two **guide words** at the top of the page. The first guide word identifies the first word listed on that page. The second guide word tells you the last word on the page. Refer to Figure 1.1 to see an example of a dictionary page with guide words. If you want to find the word *coddle*, for example, you'd know to look for it on the page labeled with the guide words *cocktail table* and *coeno-*, because the first three letters of *cod*, come between *coc* and *coe*.

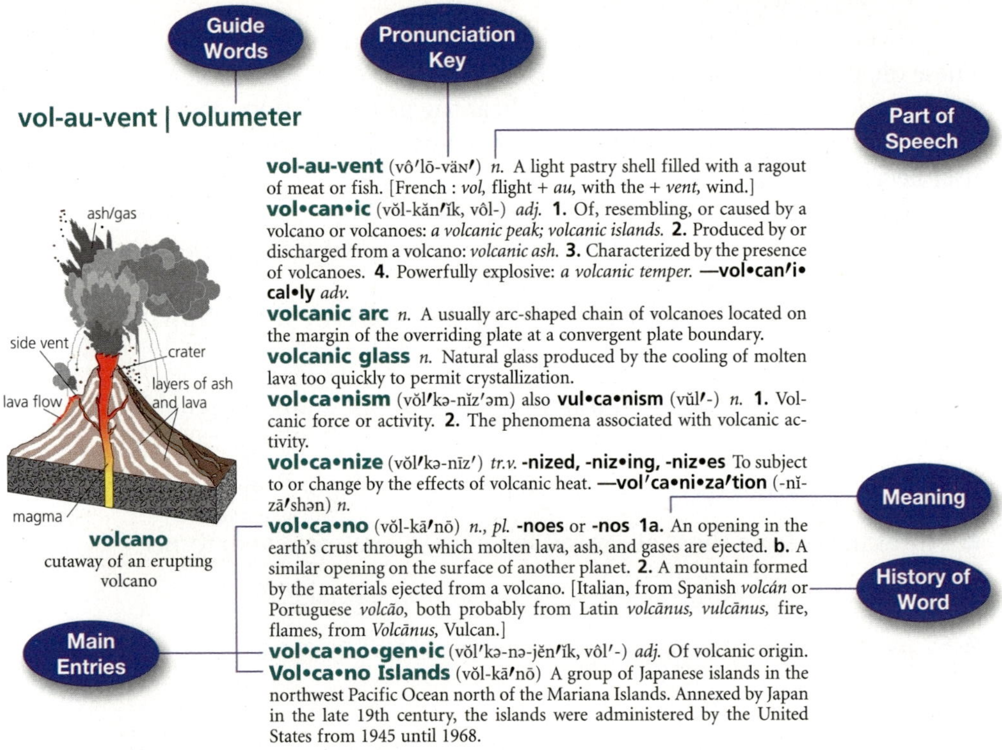

vol-au-vent | volumeter

vol-au-vent (vô′lō-väɴ′) *n.* A light pastry shell filled with a ragout of meat or fish. [French : *vol*, flight + *au*, with the + *vent*, wind.]

vol•can•ic (vŏl-kăn′ĭk, vôl-) *adj.* **1.** Of, resembling, or caused by a volcano or volcanoes: *a volcanic peak; volcanic islands.* **2.** Produced by or discharged from a volcano: *volcanic ash.* **3.** Characterized by the presence of volcanoes. **4.** Powerfully explosive: *a volcanic temper.* **—vol•can′i•cal•ly** *adv.*

volcanic arc *n.* A usually arc-shaped chain of volcanoes located on the margin of the overriding plate at a convergent plate boundary.

volcanic glass *n.* Natural glass produced by the cooling of molten lava too quickly to permit crystallization.

vol•ca•nism (vŏl′kə-nĭz′əm) also **vul•ca•nism** (vŭl′-) *n.* **1.** Volcanic force or activity. **2.** The phenomena associated with volcanic activity.

vol•ca•nize (vŏl′kə-nīz′) *tr.v.* **-nized, -niz•ing, -niz•es** To subject to or change by the effects of volcanic heat. **—vol′ca•ni•za′tion** (-nĭ-zā′shən) *n.*

vol•ca•no (vŏl-kā′nō) *n., pl.* **-noes** or **-nos 1a.** An opening in the earth's crust through which molten lava, ash, and gases are ejected. **b.** A similar opening on the surface of another planet. **2.** A mountain formed by the materials ejected from a volcano. [Italian, from Spanish *volcán* or Portuguese *volcão*, both probably from Latin *volcānus, vulcānus*, fire, flames, from *Volcānus*, Vulcan.]

vol•ca•no•gen•ic (vŏl′kə-nə-jĕn′ĭk, vôl′-) *adj.* Of volcanic origin.

Vol•ca•no Islands (vŏl-kā′nō) A group of Japanese islands in the northwest Pacific Ocean north of the Mariana Islands. Annexed by Japan in the late 19th century, the islands were administered by the United States from 1945 until 1968.

Figure 1.1 Dictionary Page

Understanding a Dictionary Entry

Every hard-copy dictionary includes a guide at the front of the book that explains how to read the entries. This guide explains the abbreviations, symbols, and organization of different meanings, so you may need to consult it to know how to decipher the information. Various dictionaries differ in these details. However, they all usually contain certain types of standard information:

The main entry. Each word in a dictionary appears in bold print with dots dividing its syllables. This word is correctly spelled, of course, and any alternative spellings for the word follow.

Pronunciation key. Usually in parentheses following the main entry, the word's pronunciation is represented with symbols, letters, and other marks. The guide at the front of the dictionary or at the bottom of the page will provide a list of the corresponding sounds for each letter or symbol. The accent mark shows you what syllable to stress when you say the word.

The part of speech. The next part of the entry is an abbreviation that identifies the word's part of speech. *N.* means noun, *v.* means verb, *adj.* stands for adjective, and so on. Refer to the list of abbreviations in the guide at the front of the dictionary to find out what other abbreviations mean.

The meanings of the word. The different meanings of a word are divided first according to their part of speech. All of the meanings related to a particular part of speech are grouped together. For example, the word *project* can function as both a noun and a verb. All of its noun meanings appear first, followed by all of its verb meanings. Dictionaries order each set of meanings in different ways, usually from most common to least common or from oldest to newest. Different senses, or shades of meaning, are numbered. Following the list of meanings, the dictionary may provide synonyms and/or antonyms for the word.

The history of the word. Some dictionaries provide information about the origin of a word. This history, or *etymology*, usually includes the word's language of origin, along with its various evolutions.

Vocabulary Exercise 1

A. To complete the exercise that follows, choose two dictionaries—one hard-copy dictionary and one online dictionary. Write down your choices here: Answers will vary.

Hard copy: ____________________

Online: ____________________

1

Answer each of the following questions twice—once for each dictionary. If the dictionary does not contain the information, write "No answer."

A. Write your answers to the following questions on the blanks provided.

1. What is the plural of *yourself*? Yourselves
2. How many different parts of speech can the word *left* be? Four (noun, verb, adjective, adverb)
3. What is a synonym for the word *yield*? Bow, defer, submit, succumb (Answers will vary.)
4. Which language does the word *ketchup* come from? Malay and/or Cantonese
5. How many different pronunciations does your dictionary provide for the word *often*? Four (Answers may vary.)
6. Does the noun *bough* rhyme with *rough* or *so* or *vow*? Vow
7. How many syllables does the word *liege* contain? One

B. Use the same two dictionaries that you chose for Exercise 1 to complete the following exercise. Look up each word twice—once in each dictionary.

On the blanks following each sentence, write the correct meaning for the italicized word. Answers will vary.

1. The camel is a common form of transportation in the *desert*.

   Definition: A dry, often sandy region of little rainfall, extreme temperatures, and sparse vegetation

   Definition: ____________________

2. A good soldier will never *desert* his post.

   Definition: Abandon

   Definition: ____________________

3. He keeps a *ferret* as a pet.

   Definition: Weasel-like mammal

   Definition: ____________________

1

4. The detective will *ferret* out those responsible for this crime.

Definition: To uncover and bring to light by searching

Definition: ______

5. The valedictorian decided to *major* in economics.

Definition: Pursue academic studies

Definition: ______

6. Before retiring, he attained the rank of *major* in the U.S. Army.

Definition: Military rank above captain and below lieutenant colonel

Definition: ______

C. List the differences that you found between your hard-copy dictionary and the online dictionary. Which dictionary would you prefer to use? Why?

Answers will vary.

Vocabulary Exercise 2

Use either an online or hard copy dictionary to look up the boldfaced, italicized words in the following passage. Write the meanings of the words in the blanks provided. Keep in mind the context of the passage when selecting the correct meaning of a word.

Over the centuries, as formal governments were established, early, ***primitive*** forms of a formal criminal justice system evolved in England. In 1285 C.E., the ***Statute*** of Winchester was ***enacted*** in England and established a ***rudimentary*** criminal justice system in which most of the responsibility for law enforcement remained with the people themselves. The statute formally established (1) the watch and ***ward***, (2) the ***hue*** and cry, (3) the ***parish constable***, and (4) the requirement that all males keep weapons in their homes for use in maintaining the public peace.*

primitive primary or basic

statute a law enacted by a legislature

* Dempsey, John, and Linda S. Forst. *An Introduction to Policing,* 5th ed. Clifton Park: Delmar, 2010. Print. Ch. 1, p. 5.

1

enacted to make into law

rudimentary primary or basic

ward a means of protection or defense

hue a loud outcry formerly used in the pursuit of one who is suspected of a crime

parish a subdivision of a county often coinciding with an original ecclesiastical parish and constituting the unit of local government

constable (British) a police officer

Reading Visuals

Visual aids, which are also known as **graphics**, *are types of illustrations that represent data or information in a visual form.* Visual aids include tables, charts, different types of graphs, diagrams, or maps. You will often encounter all of these kinds of visuals when you read, especially when the purpose of a reading selection is to inform or explain. Publications such as textbooks, magazines, journals, and instruction manuals will often include visuals to aid, or help, the reader in understanding the information. Many job-related documents will also contain visual aids.

Texts include visual aids for many reasons. For one thing, they can summarize a lot of information or complex information in a relatively small space. Think about a flow chart, for instance. A flow chart provides a visual summary of the steps in a process. It allows you to see a condensed version of even a complicated procedure.

Another reason for visual aids is their ability to clarify and reinforce textual explanations. In most publications, visual aids do not substitute for written presentation of information. Instead, they provide another way of "seeing" what the words are saying. A diagram in an instruction manual is one example. When you are assembling something like a barbecue grill or a child's swing set, it's helpful to check your understanding of the directions by looking at a diagram that labels the parts and shows how they fit together. You use both the written explanation and the visual aid to figure out what you need to do.

Visual aids also allow readers to quickly see the important data or facts. For instance, a graph reveals, at a glance, trends over time. An organizational chart allows readers to quickly grasp the chain of command within a company.

Finally, visual aids provide a way for readers to find a particular detail quickly and easily. A table, for example, that organizes facts into columns and rows allows a reader to easily locate one specific piece of information he or she needs.

General Tips for Reading Visual Aids

The following tips will help you improve your comprehension of reading selections that include visuals:

- **Don't skip a visual aid.** Passive readers ignore visual aids because they don't want to take the time to read them. Skipping visual aids, however, robs you of chances to improve and/or reinforce your understanding of the information in the text. When authors invest the time and effort necessary to create a visual, they do so because they believe a visual representation is particularly important. Therefore, get in the habit of reading over each visual as well as the text.
- **Look at a visual aid when the text directs you to do so.** As you read, you'll come across references to visual aids. Resist the urge to "save them for later." Instead, when a sentence mentions a visual, as in "See Figure 2," or "Table 1 presents the results . . ." and tells you where to find it (below, to the left, on page 163, etc.), find the visual and read it before going any further. Remember, most visuals reinforce information in a text. The writer's explanation will often state the conclusion you should draw from the visual, and the visual provides more insight into the textual explanation. So, you'll get more out of both of them when you read a passage and its corresponding visual together.
- **Follow a three-step procedure for interpreting the information in a visual aid:**
  1. First, read the title, the caption, and the source line. The title and caption or brief descriptions will usually identify the visual aid's subject and main point. They will help you understand what you're seeing. The source line, which identifies where the information comes from, will help you decide whether the information is accurate and trustworthy.
  2. Next, study the information represented in the visual and try to state the relationships you see in your own words. For example, you might say, "This graph shows that sales of sport utility vehicles have been growing since 1985," or "This table shows that teachers in the Midwest earn higher salaries than teachers in the rest of the country."
  3. Finally, check your understanding of the relationship against its corresponding explanation in the text. Locate where the visual is mentioned, and verify that the conclusion you drew is accurate.

1

Each of the next seven chapters will cover one of the most common types of visual aids and provide you with more specific tips for improving your understanding of each kind. To see what you already know about visual aids, complete the questions that follow the two visuals.

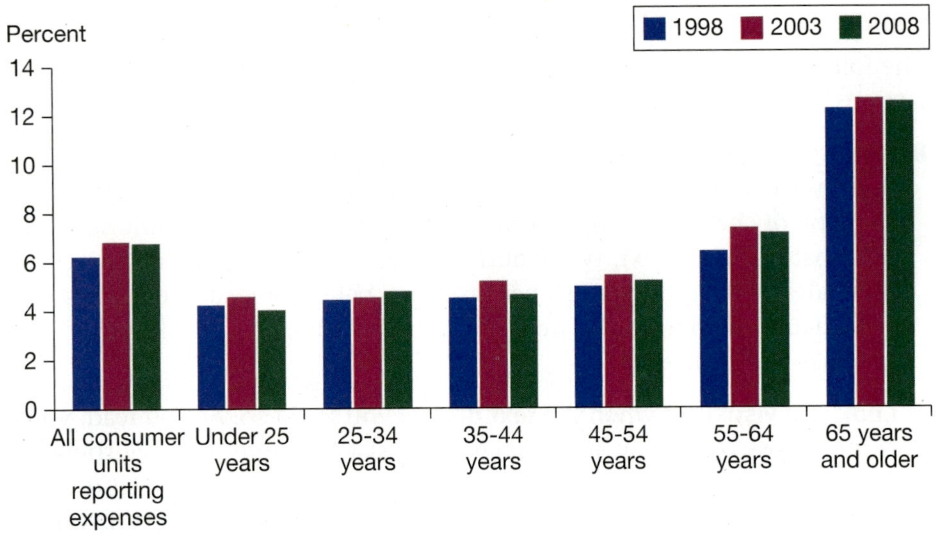

Figure 1.2 Average health care spending shares of total annual expenditures by age of reference person, Consumer Expenditure Interview Survey, 1998, 2003, 2008

Source: http://www.bls.gov/opub/focus/volume1_number8/cex_1_8.htm 10/16/2010 Web.

1. What does this visual describe? It describes the average amount of annual income that is spent on health care by age group.
2. Which group consistently spends the most on health care? 65 and older
3. For which group have expenditures risen every reporting period? 25-34 years old
4. Which group consistently spends the least on health care? under 25
5. What is the overall percentage of change between 1998 and 2008 for all groups reporting expenses? almost 7%

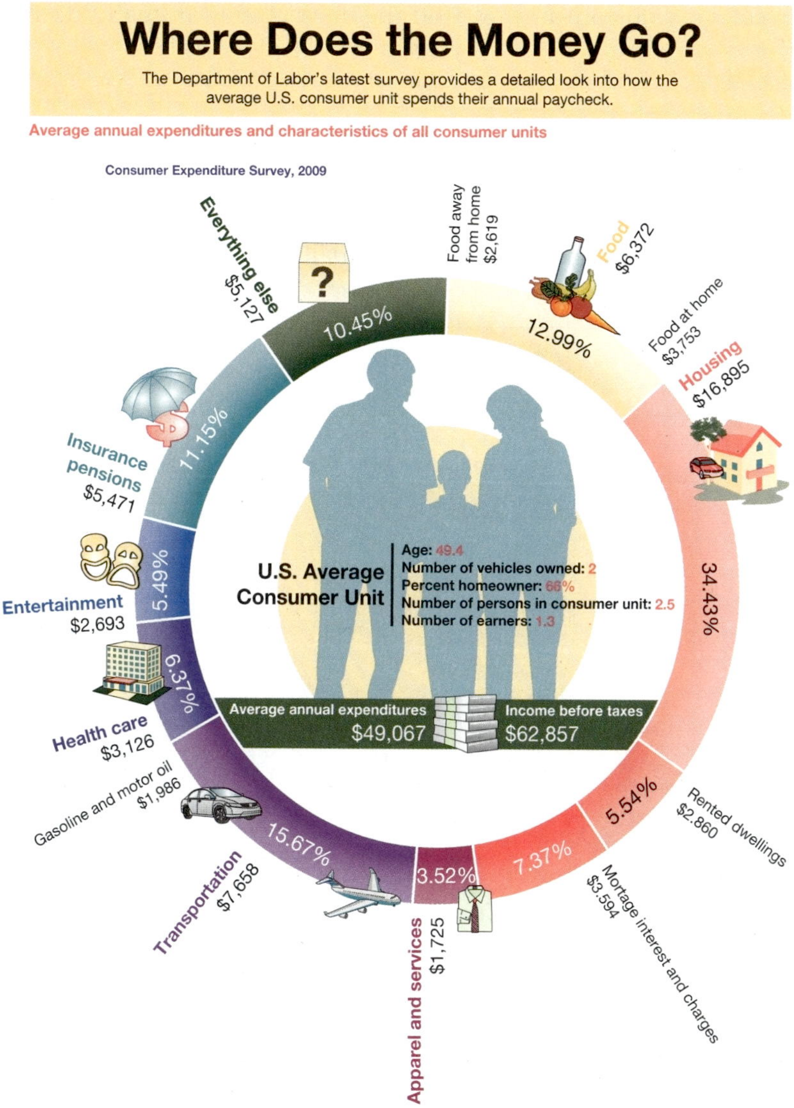

Figure 1.3

Source: http://www.visualeconomics.com/how-the-average-us-consumer-spends-their-paycheck/10/16/2010 Web.

1. What does this visual represent?

   How average consumers spend their paychecks

2. On average, do consumers spend more on healthcare or entertainment?

   Health care

3. In which category do consumers spend the most money annually? Least?

Housing; Apparel and services

4. What percentage of the annual income is spent on food?

12.99%

5. How much money do consumers spend annually on transportation?

$7,658

Chapter 1 Review

Fill in the blanks in the following statements.

1. Good reading skills are important to __academic__, personal, and __professional__ success.
2. Reading helps strengthen __thinking__ skills.
3. The two basic purposes for reading are to gain __information__ and to be entertained.
4. When you read for information, you may have one or more of the following goals: gain a general __understanding__ of the ideas or points; discover __facts__ or answer questions; memorize the information; find information or ideas that prove a __point__ you want to make; make a __decision__ based on the information.
5. Reading is actually a collection of mental skills that include __attitude__, concentration, __memory__, and __logical__ thought.
6. A positive __attitude__ makes reading more pleasurable and more productive.
7. __Concentration__ is the ability to focus all of your attention on one thing while ignoring distractions.
8. The two types of distractions are __external__ and __internal__.
9. __Memory__ is the ability to store and recall information.
10. Logical thought includes mental tasks such as sequencing and ordering, __matching__, __organizing__, analysis, __reasoning__ from the general to the particular and the particular to the general, __abstract__ thought, and synthesis.
11. Reading __strategies__ are techniques you can use to get more out of what you read.
12. __(Answers should come from the bulleted list in the Reading Strategy box.)__, ________, and ________ are three activities that active readers engage in while reading difficult text.
13. Online dictionaries do not need to use __guide__ words that are found at the top of the page in hard-copy dictionaries
14. Students who need pronunciation of a difficult word should use a(n) __online__ dictionary.
15. When reading a visual, students should read the __title__, __caption__, and the __source line__ before trying to interpret information represented in the visual.

Smith Collection/Stone/Getty Images

CHAPTER 2

Main Ideas

Goals for Chapter 2

- Define the terms *general* and *specific.*
- Order groups of sentences from most general to most specific.
- Identify the topic of a paragraph.
- Determine the main idea of a paragraph.
- Recognize the topic sentence of a paragraph.
- Recognize topic sentences in different locations in a paragraph.
- Describe the characteristics of an effective reading environment.
- Read and understand information in a table.

2

To read successfully, you must learn to determine the main idea of a paragraph or longer selection. *The* **main idea** *is the overall point the author is trying to make.* The rest of the paragraph or longer selection consists of information or examples that help the reader understand the main point.

What process do you go through to help you figure out the main idea of a selection? Take this pretest to find out how much you already know about identifying and understanding main ideas.

Pretest

Before beginning the work in this chapter, think about what you already know about the main idea and how to find it. What is the main idea of each of the following passages? Write your answers on the blanks provided.

1. One way in which almost anyone can improve his or her memory is to employ *mnemonics* (pronounced "ni-'mä-niks"). **Mnemonics** are strategies for putting information in an organized context to remember it more easily. To remember the names of the Great Lakes, for example, you could use the acronym HOMES (for Huron, Ontario, Michigan, Erie, and Superior). Verbal organization is the basis for many mnemonics. You can link items by weaving them into a story, a sentence, or a rhyme. To help customers remember where they have parked their cars, some large garages have replaced section designations such as "A1" or "G8" with the names of colors, months, or animals. Customers can then tie the location of their cars to information already in long-term memory—for example, "I parked in the month of my mother's birthday."*

   Main Idea: Mnemonics are a memory aid that many people use.

2. Verbs work in two ways within a sentence. Some verbs show the action, physical or mental, of the subject of the sentence. These verbs are called *action verbs*. Other verbs link the subject with other words in the sentence. These verbs are called *linking verbs*.†

   Main Idea: Verbs work in two ways within a sentence.

3. Memory plays a critical role in your life. Without it, you wouldn't know how to shut off your alarm, take a shower, get dressed, recognize objects, or communicate. You would be unaware of your own likes and dislikes.

* From Bernstein and Nash, *Essentials of Psychology*, 2nd ed. Boston: Houghton Mifflin, 2002, 205. Copyright © 2002 by Houghton Mifflin Company. Reprinted with permission.

† From Arlov, *Wordsmith*. Upper Saddle River: Prentice Hall, 2000, 217.

You would have no idea of who you are. The impressive capacity of human memory depends on the operation of a complex mental system.*

Main Idea: Memory plays a critical role in your life.

4. No one family structure typifies[1] contemporary American society. The 1950s model of a two-parent family with two children and a nonworking mother no longer applies. For example, only 69 percent of children younger than 18 years old lived with two parents in 2000, compared with 85 percent in 1970. Today, 26 percent of American children live with only one parent. High rates of divorce and single-parent births have contributed to this trend. Projections are that about 50 percent of current marriages will end in divorce (compared with about 15 percent in 1960), and about 32 percent of all births are to single women. Moreover, about 5 percent of children live with their grandparents, and a growing number live with gay or lesbian parents. Finally, more than 70 percent of married women with children younger than 18 years old work outside the home, compared with about 45 percent in 1975.†

Main Idea: No one family structure typifies contemporary American society.

5. Cabbage doesn't deserve its stinky reputation. Eat just one cup of cooked cabbage and you'll get double the recommended daily dose of vitamin C. And, according to the American Cancer Society, cabbage may protect against esophagus, stomach, and colon cancers. Then, of course, there's the fiber issue. Cabbage has plenty of it to help lower cholesterol, prevent constipation, and reduce hemorrhoids.‡

Main Idea: Cabbage is good for you and doesn't deserve its stinky reputation.

General and Specific

Before you practice finding main ideas, it's helpful to learn to distinguish the difference between the terms *general* and *specific*. You must apply these concepts to figure out the relationships of sentences within a paragraph. Understanding these relationships is the first step in improving your comprehension of the author's meaning.

The word **general** *means "broad" and "not limited."* When we say a word or idea is general, we mean that it includes or refers to many different things

1. **typifies:** serves as a typical example

* Bernstein, Douglas. *Essentials of Psychology*, 5th ed. Belmont: Wadsworth, 2011, Print. Ch. 6, p. 210.

† Adapted from Bukatko and Daehler, *Child Development*, 5th ed. Boston: Houghton Mifflin, 2004, 498. Copyright © 2004 by Houghton Mifflin Company. Reprinted with permission.

‡ Adapted from Bev Bennett, "Of Cabbage and Things," *Better Homes and Gardens*, October 2001, 226.

in a large category. For example, *musical instruments* is a general term that includes many different types of things, including trumpets, saxophones, and clarinets. *Relatives* is another general word that refers to a large group of items, including mothers, fathers, aunts, uncles, and cousins.

The word **specific** *means "definite" or "particular."* Specific things or ideas are limited or narrowed in scope, and they refer to one certain something within a larger group. In the previous paragraph, for instance, *trumpets, saxophones,* and *clarinets* are all certain types of musical instruments, so we say they are more specific. *Whales, dolphins,* and *seals* are all specific sea mammals. *Math, English,* and *science* are three specific subjects we study in school.

The terms **general** *and* **specific** *are relative. In other words, they depend upon or are connected to the other things with which they are being compared.* For example, you would say that *school subject* is a general term and that *science* is one specific subject. However, *science* becomes the more general term when you think of specific kinds of science, such as biology, chemistry, and physics. Words and concepts, therefore, can change from being general or specific depending on their relationships to other words and concepts. Look at this list:

food

desserts

candy

chocolate candy bar

Hershey's chocolate bar with almonds

The words in this list are arranged from most general to most specific. In other words, each item in the list is more specific than the previous one. The last item, Hershey's chocolate bar with almonds, names a specific brand of candy, so it is the most specific of all.

To read well, you will need to be able to recognize the most general idea within a passage. Let's practice that skill by looking at groups of related items in different ways. Can you select the most general word in the list?

fork   knife   utensil   spoon

Three of the words in the group are specific, and one of the words is the most general. If you chose *utensil* as most general, you are correct. The other three items are specific kinds of utensils.

Now examine this list and decide how the items are related. Come up with a word that includes all three items in the list.

basketball   hockey   soccer

Did you say *sports?* The three items above are all specific types of sports.

Finally, see if you can think of three specific examples of shoes. Some possible answers include sandals, athletic shoes, boots, and slippers.

Now that you've reviewed how words can be general and specific, you'll be able to see how the sentences that express ideas are also general and specific in relation to each other. *Paragraphs are composed of both general and specific sentences. A general sentence states the broadest idea in the paragraph. Specific sentences in a paragraph offer explanations or details that help readers understand and accept the idea in the general sentence.* Specific sentences are essential to helping readers correctly determine the meaning of the general statement.

We saw earlier how the terms *general* and *specific* are relative when applied to words. Sentences within a paragraph, too, are relatively general and specific. For example, read the following three statements:

I am afraid of several things.

For example, I fear creepy, crawly creatures.

I am terrified of spiders most of all.

The first sentence states the most general idea; then, the second sentence clarifies a specific type of thing—creepy, crawly things—that the writer fears. The third sentence is even more specific because it identifies the particular kind of creepy, crawly creatures the writer fears most. So, in this group of sentences, each statement is more specific than the previous one.

Exercise 2.1

On the blanks provided, number these sentences from most general (1) to most specific (3).

1. __2__ I like to watch reality television shows in which contestants compete to win prizes.

   __1__ I love to watch television.

   __3__ My favorite reality show is on the Food Network.

2. __2__ Homemade soups are a great meal for a big family because they are filling and nutritious.

   __1__ Cooking at home and avoiding eating out can stretch your monthly food budget.

   __3__ You can make chicken soup by adding a few vegetables and some noodles to your leftover chicken bones and meat.

2

3. __1__ Jiang Li is very organized and uses time efficiently.

__2__ Jiang Li keeps all of her appointments logged into her daytime planner.

__3__ Jiang Li checks her planner daily to see how many appointments she has and when they are.

4. __2__ Give the older child lots of verbal reassurance, but also use concrete actions.

__3__ One strategy is to give the child an important role by including him or her in daily activities with the new infant.

__1__ After the new baby arrives home, parents can do a number of things to help an older child adjust.*

5. __1__ After the September 11, 2001, terrorist attacks, the rescue effort at the World Trade Center site was overwhelming in its scope.

__2__ Many brave men and women volunteered to help find survivors.

__3__ Firefighters, in particular, spent many hours at the site looking for survivors of the disaster.

Because paragraphs are combinations of sentences that all work together to develop a main idea, sorting out the general and specific relationships among related sentences is the first step toward understanding what you read. Look at the four sentences below and try to identify the one that is the most general.

Parents provide their children with laptops, pagers, and cell phones.

Many parents today spoil their children.

Parents buy their kids cars when the kids turn sixteen.

Parents pay huge sums for their children to go to expensive camps and on international vacations.

Did you choose the second sentence as most general? The other three sentences offer specific facts—specific things parents buy their kids—that help explain the idea of "spoil their children."

Now read these three specific sentences:

Water helps the body break down and absorb nutrients from foods.

Water cushions tissues, lubricates joints, and transports waste products to the kidneys for elimination.

Water helps the bowels function and prevents constipation.†

---

* Adapted from Seifert et al., *Lifespan Development*, 2nd ed. Boston: Houghton Mifflin, 2000, 103.

† Adapted from Tedd Mitchell, M.D., "Maximize Your Liquid Assets," *USA Weekend*, August 17–19, 2001, 4.

How would you state the general idea these three sentences explain or support? All three are examples of the ways the body uses water, so the sentence, "Water is necessary to the normal functioning of the human body" would be an accurate statement of the general idea they develop.

Finally, read this general sentence:

Survivor is the best show on television.

What three specific sentences could you write to explain this sentence? Some possibilities include:

The team competitions are exciting to watch.

The interpersonal relationships are interesting.

It's fun to root for one contestant you want to win.

Exercise **2.2**

The following groups of sentences include one general sentence and three specific sentences. Label each sentence with either a G for *general* or an S for *specific.*

1. __G__ Many varieties of cupcake flavors and toppings exist.

   __S__ Carrot cake and red velvet cupcakes are usually topped with cream cheese frosting.

   __S__ Key lime cupcakes are often topped with thick meringue.

   __S__ Rich buttercream frosting is frequently used as a topping for traditional chocolate and vanilla cupcakes.

2. __S__ College freshmen take introductory writing classes to help them prepare to write essays for more advanced courses.

   __S__ College freshmen often take introductory biology courses.

   __S__ College freshmen usually take a course to introduce them to psychology.

   __G__ College freshmen take many different kinds of classes to broaden their general knowledge.

3. __S__ Most girls enjoy one-on-one play, whereas some boys like to play in large groups.

   __S__ Many boys prefer to play with trucks and trains, whereas most girls like dolls and puzzles.

___G___ Boys and girls are very different when it comes to play.

___S___ Boys, in general, like to run around and play sports, whereas many girls like to pretend and use their imaginations.

4. ___S___ Chantal is always on time and doesn't mind staying overtime if I come home late from work.

___G___ Chantal is a wonderful babysitter for my children.

___S___ Chantal enforces the rules of the house while not appearing too strict.

___S___ Chantal makes nutritious meals (which are delicious, too) for the kids.

5. ___G___ The flu can be a very serious illness.

___S___ The flu can last up to two weeks in your system, making you tired and listless.

___S___ People who get the flu often report fevers in excess of 102 degrees.

___S___ The flu is sometimes accompanied by bad coughing, aches, and the chills.

Exercise 2.3

Read the three specific sentences given. Then, in the list that follows them, circle the letter of the general sentence best supported by those three specific sentences.

1. The white jacket is an assurance to the client that the kitchen is clean. The double- breasted design allows the chef to present a clean appearance by switching sides. The double layer provides protection from hot elements and spills.*

   General Sentences:

   a. A chef's jacket serves several purposes.

   b. A dirty chef's jacket is a sign of disrespect.

   c. All chefs wear similar jackets.

2. About 50 percent of law school graduates are women, but they represent less than 17 percent of partners in the major law firms.

---

* The Chefs of the Cordon Bleu. *Le Cordon Bleu Cuisine Foundations*, 1st ed. Clifton Park: Delmar, 2011. Print. Ch. 2, p. 30.

Women have comprised more than 30 percent of MBA graduates for more than 20 years, but women make up only 2.7 percent of the top earners in *Fortune* 500 companies.

Women make up just 1 percent of *Forbes* 500 companies' CEO positions.*

General Sentences:

a. Women in corporate America are not interested in the highest positions.

b. Men are better leaders than women.

c. In the corporate world, few women are achieving top positions.

3. Some people use a system called *mnemonics* to aid their memory.

Many people take a popular over-the-counter herbal supplement called gingko biloba, which is said to help improve long-term and short-term memory.

Studies show that a good percentage of people use visualization to remember places, names, and dates.

General Sentences:

a. Many people have good memories.

b. People use a variety of techniques to aid their memories.

c. Not too many drugs are available to aid memory.

4. The Red Worm computer virus was very dangerous and had the potential to wipe out the hard drives of hundreds of thousands of computers.

The Nimda virus infected both e-mail and Internet sites.

The e-mail entitled "A Virtual Card for You" had the capacity to completely disable a computer if the user opened the attachment to the message.

General Sentences:

a. Not too many e-mail viruses are circulating.

b. Computer viruses are often found in e-mail message attachments.

c. Computer viruses are potentially dangerous and hazardous to hard drives and computers.

5. The cost of a college education, already an expensive proposition, is expected to rise by about 50 percent in the next 20 years.

The cost of tuition and fees keeps going up every year.

* Adapted from Irma D. Herrera, "'The Apprentice' Exposes Reality of Glass Ceiling," *USA Today*, April 5, 2004, 13A

Housing on college campuses is still the cheapest housing available but can cost more than $10,000 a semester, depending on where a student attends school.

General Sentences:

a. Many colleges have on-campus housing.

(b.) Going to college can be a very expensive undertaking.

c. A college education is a necessity in today's job market.

2

Exercise 2.4

Read the general sentence given and then circle the letters of the three sentences from the list that best explain or support that statement.

1. **General Sentence:** Trees improve both our environment and our quality of life.*

Specific Sentences:

(a.) Trees help conserve energy; adding 100 million mature trees in U.S. cities would save $2 billion per year in energy costs.

(b.) Trees produce the oxygen that we breathe and remove air pollution by lowering air temperature and removing particulates from the atmosphere.

c. Two of the fastest-growing trees are willow trees and poplar trees.

(d.) Trees that form a windbreak can lower a homeowner's heating bills 10 to 20 percent, and shade trees planted on a home's east and west sides can cut cooling costs 15 to 35 percent.

e. Trees can live hundreds of years.

f. Arbor Day, which was established in the 1880s, is now celebrated in all 50 states on the last Friday in April.

2. **General Sentence:** Many experts say that good note taking is the key to doing well on tests.

Specific Sentences:

a. I didn't take notes in college.

(b.) Writing down key information from lectures can help students retain information when it is time to take a test.

c. Note taking involves highlighting key information while reading textbooks.

(d.) Note taking is especially helpful for students who are "visual learners" because those students can "see" what happens in a lecture and remember it better.

* From "Trees Make a World of Difference," National Arbor Day Foundation, www.arborday.org.

e. My professor writes notes on the blackboard during class.

(f.) Writing notes in the margins of textbooks, which is called *annotating*, will help students recall the information during the test.

3. **General Sentence:** Many community college graduates report that their first two years of college gave them an enriching and rewarding academic experience.*

Specific Sentences:

a. Many students enjoy going to community colleges because they are close to home.

b. Community colleges are cheaper than four-year schools.

(c.) Smaller classes at community colleges are beneficial to students and can help them learn more in preparation for work at four-year schools.

(d.) In general, professors at community colleges take pride in their teaching and provide a rich educational experience for students.

e. There are many community colleges nationwide.

(f.) Many students report that the courses they took at community colleges were as rigorous as those found at four-year schools.

4. **General Sentence:** In medieval times, children graduated to adult status early in life.†

Specific Sentences:

(a.) Teenagers assumed adult roles in medieval times.

b. During medieval times, infants tended to be regarded rather like talented pets.

(c.) At around seven or eight, children took on major, adult-like tasks for the community during medieval times.

(d.) Children who would be in second or third grade today would be caring for younger siblings during medieval times.

e. Children in medieval times earned respect for what they did.

f. Children were still innocent a few hundred years ago.

5. **General Sentence:** Overweight people are turning to new diets and procedures to help them lose large quantities of weight in a shorter period of time.

Specific Sentences:

(a.) Gastric bypass surgery is becoming increasingly popular for people who need to lose more than 100 pounds in less than a year's time.

* Adapted from Ulrich Boser, "Ease the Leap from a Two-Year School," USNews.com, October 3, 2001.

† Adapted from Seifert and Hoffnung, *Child and Adolescent Development*, 5th ed. Boston: Houghton Mifflin, 2000, 11. Copyright © 2000 by Houghton Mifflin. Reprinted with permission.

2

b. Walking is proven to help people lose weight slower, thereby keeping it from coming back.

c. Low-carb diets, in which people consume large quantities of protein and vegetables, are proven to help people lose weight quickly.

d. The "belly band" is a procedure that overweight people can turn to if they don't want the risks of gastric bypass surgery.

e. Weight Watchers incorporates a "point" system to help people slowly lose weight.

f. If you are more than 10 pounds overweight for your height, you may want to consider going on a diet.

Determining the Topic

Now that you've reviewed the distinction between general and specific, let's look at the most general aspect of a paragraph: its topic. To understand what you read, you must be able to identify the topic, or subject, of a reading selection. *The* **topic** *is the person, place, thing, event, or idea that the passage is about, and it is usually expressed in just a word or brief phrase.* For example, read the following paragraph:

> Today, a new generation of Tony Hawk wannabes is fueling and financing a blockbuster skateboarding industry. The *Wall Street Journal* reported that participation in skateboarding has jumped 118 percent in the past eight years. Skateboard sales have tripled to $72 million since 1995. Summer camps are starting to cater to kids who like this new action sport. *The X Games*, which feature skateboarding competitions, is a hit show on ESPN. Once-disapproving parents are financing and encouraging their kids' newest obsession.*

The topic of this paragraph is skateboarding. Every sentence in the paragraph refers to or mentions skateboarding.

To find the topic of a selection, look for the person, place, thing, event, or idea that is repeated.

Exercise 2.5

Read each paragraph and write the correct topic on the blank provided.

1. There is a relationship between birth weight and intelligence, according to a recent study. It's long been known that children with abnormally low birth weights tend to score lower than normal-birth-weight children on IQ tests

* Adapted from Tim Wendel, "Going to Xtremes," *USA Weekend*, August 17–19, 2001, 7.

given at school age. But a new study of about 3,500 seven-year-olds links size to intelligence even among kids born at normal birth weight. Columbia University and New York Academy of Medicine researchers found that for every 2.2 pounds of additional weight, boys scored 4.6 IQ points higher, and girls scored 2.8 points higher. This was true even after other factors such as the mother's age, education, and economic status were considered.*

Topic: Birth weight and intelligence

2

2. Every EMS system, regardless of its size, is vulnerable to a disaster. EMS systems that are equipped to respond to disaster situations aided by well-developed disaster plans and well-trained staff who have practiced the procedures outlined in those plans have been far more successful in responding to disasters than those systems that have not prepared. Understanding disasters, planning for them, and training and drilling in advance ultimately save lives, limit disabilities, and hasten recovery of the victims of tragedies. Every community has the responsibility to actively participate in disaster planning and preparation. Every effort needs to be made to ensure that EMS plans are linked to those of fire, rescue, and law enforcement services. Disasters are everybody's business. This is especially so for EMS and other emergency services agencies.†

Topic: The vulnerability of EMS systems

3. Numerous bookstore chains have sprung up throughout the country in recent years, among them Borders, Super Crown, and Barnes and Noble. These businesses are designed to appeal particularly to young adults. Most offer comfortable chairs in which to sit, relax, and read. Some of these stores have a café area where specialty coffees, teas, muffins, and other delectables[1] are available. The evening hours are often filled with concerts, poetry readings, or other special events. Bookstores don't just sell books anymore; they sell a lifestyle. They do this because the competition is intense and economic issues pressing.‡

Topic: Bookstores

1. **delectables:** delights; things that are pleasing to the taste

* Adapted from Stephen P. Williams, "Health Notes," *Newsweek,* September 10, 2001, 71. Copyright © 2001 Newsweek, Inc. All rights reserved. Reprinted by permission.

† Walz, Bruce, Kurt Krumperman, and Jason J. Zigmont. *Foundations of EMS Systems,* 2nd ed. Clifton Park: Delmar, 2011. Print. Ch. 12, p. 216.

‡ From Leslie, *Mass Communication Ethics,* 2nd ed. Boston: Houghton Mifflin, 2004, 216. Copyright © 2004 by Houghton Mifflin Company. Reprinted with permission.

4. Cookies come in an infinite variety of shapes, sizes, flavors, and textures. Characteristics that are desirable in some are not desirable in others. For example, we want some cookies to be crisp and others to be soft. We want some to hold their shape and others to spread during baking. In order to produce the characteristics we want and to correct faults, it is useful to know what causes these characteristics.*

   Topic: Variety of cookies

5. In one small study, researchers found that people suffer motor skill deficits[1] that last more than an hour after waking. But according to Mark Rosekind, PhD, president of Alertness Solutions, a company that offers stay-awake strategies to businesses, you can substantially decrease that downtime by drinking coffee. "The amount of caffeine in a strong cup of coffee can boost both physical performance and mental alertness by up to 30 percent within 15 to 30 minutes," he says. "If you're sluggish for an hour, getting that caffeine within the first five minutes of getting out of bed may gain you a half hour's head start on your morning."†

   Topic: Coffee's effect on alertness

When you are deciding on the topic of a paragraph or passage, make sure your choice is not too *broad* or too *narrow*. A topic that is too **broad** *suggests much more than the paragraph actually offers*. A topic that is too **narrow** *does not include everything the paragraph covers*. For example, look at the following paragraph:

> The results of hypnosis can be fascinating. People told that their eyes cannot open may struggle fruitlessly to open them. They may appear deaf or blind or insensitive to pain. They may forget their own names. Some appear to remember forgotten things. Others show age regression,[2] apparently recalling or re-enacting childhood. Hypnotic effects can last for hours or days through posthypnotic suggestions—instructions about behavior to take place after hypnosis has ended (such as smiling whenever someone says "Oregon"). Some subjects show posthypnotic amnesia, an inability to recall what happened while they were hypnotized, even after being told what happened.‡

1. **deficits:** inadequacies or insufficiencies
2. **regression:** going or moving backward

* Gisslen, Wayne. *Professional Cooking, College Version,* 7th ed. Hoboken: John Wiley & Sons, 2011. Print. Ch. 33, p. 992.

† From Melissa Gotthardt, "Waking Up Is Hard to Do," *O Magazine*, September 2001, 84.

‡ Adapted from Bernstein et al., *Psychology,* 4th ed. Boston: Houghton Mifflin, 1997, 177. Copyright © 1997 by Houghton Mifflin Company. Reprinted with permission.

Which of the topics below is the correct one?

_______ hypnosis

_______ age regression

_______ effects of hypnosis

The first choice, *hypnosis*, is too broad. This paragraph focuses only on the *results* of hypnosis. The second choice, *age regression*, is too narrow because this paragraph discusses other effects besides that one. Therefore, *effects of hypnosis* is the correct topic. This paragraph describes several different results of being hypnotized.

Exercise 2.6

Following each paragraph are three topics. On each blank, label the topic B if it is too broad, N if it's too narrow, and T if it's the correct topic of the paragraph.

1. A tornado is a rapidly rotating column of air that blows around a small area of intense low pressure with a circulation that reaches the ground. A tornado's circulation is present on the ground either as a funnel-shaped cloud or as a swirling cloud of dust and debris. Sometimes called twisters or cyclones, tornadoes can assume a variety of shapes and forms that range from twisting rope-like funnels, to cylindrical-shaped funnels, to massive black wedge-shaped funnels, to funnels that resemble an elephant's trunk hanging from a large cumulonimbus cloud.*

   Tornadoes __B__

   Definition of a tornado __T__

   Tornado circulation __N__

2. One of the largest unions not associated directly with the AFL-CIO is the Teamsters Union. The Teamsters Union was originally part of the AFL-CIO, but in 1957 it was expelled for corrupt and illegal practices. The union started out as an organization of professional drivers, but it has recently begun to recruit employees in a wide variety of jobs. Current membership is about 1.3 million workers.†

* Ahrens, C. Donald, and Perry Samson. *Extreme Weather and Climate*. Belmont: Brooks/Cole, 2011. Print. Ch. 12, p. 334.

† From Pride et al., *Business,* 6th ed. Boston: Houghton Mifflin, 1999, 280.

Unions B

Current Teamsters membership N

The Teamsters T

3. A universal symbol for hospitality is the pineapple. While the exact origin of this symbol is unknown, many believe the idea was borrowed from the people—most likely inhabitants of Brazil—who first domesticated the pineapple. These people placed pineapples outside their homes to signify that visitors were welcome. European explorers introduced the fruit to Europe and the American colonies in the seventeenth century. As the exotic fruit was rarer and more costly than caviar, it symbolized the very best in hospitality. It was used to welcome and honor royal and wealthy guests.*

The pineapple as a symbol of hospitality T

Brazilian origin of the pineapple N

Fruits of the New World B

4. Today computer-aided dispatch (CAD) allows almost immediate communication between the police dispatcher and police units in the field. Numerous CAD system software packages are available for purchase by police departments. With typical CAD systems, after a 911 operator takes a call from a citizen, the operator codes the information into the computer, and the information immediately flashes on the dispatcher's screen. The CAD system prioritizes the calls on the dispatcher's screen, putting more serious calls (such as crimes in progress and heart attacks) above less serious calls (such as past crimes and nonemergency requests for assistance). The system verifies the caller's address and telephone number, as well as determining the most direct route to the location. The system also searches a database for dangers near the location to which the officers are responding, calls to the same location within the last 24 hours, and any previous history of calls to that location.†

Priority 911 calls B

Functions of CAD systems for policing T

CAD systems prioritizing N

* Chon, Kaye (Kye-Sung) and Thomas A. Maier. *Welcome to Hospitality: An Introduction,* 3rd ed. Clifton Park: Delmar, 2010. Print. Ch. 1, p. 3.

† Dempsey, John S. and Linda S. Forst. *An Introduction to Policing,* 5th ed. Clifton Park: Delmar, 2010. Print. Ch. 14, p. 462.

5. Cats have many natural instincts that they inherited from wild cats. Cats have developed hunting skills, marking behaviors, purring traits, and social skills from their ancestors. The domestication of the cat has added in the companionship factor. Similar to the dog, cats have three distinct behaviors. Each of these behaviors is displayed in the cat's body language, and most cats will display their behaviors relatively quickly. There is the happy cat, the angry cat, and the fearful cat.*

   Body language of cats ___T___

   Cats of the world ___B___

   Behaviors of domesticated cats ___Y___

Determining the Main Idea

Once you've found the topic of a paragraph, you can determine its *main idea*, the general point the writer expressed about the topic. *The* **main idea** *is what the writer wants to prove or explain.* It's the point he or she wants you to know or believe when you finish reading the paragraph. Therefore, being able to discern main ideas is a fundamental skill for successful reading.

To find the main idea, ask yourself what the writer is saying *about* the topic. For example, read this paragraph:

> The most famous recording of an alleged[1] Bigfoot is the short 16 mm film taken in 1967 by Roger Patterson and Bob Gimlin. Shot in Bluff Creek, California, it shows a Bigfoot striding through a clearing. But the film is suspect for a number of reasons. First, Patterson told people he was going out with the express purpose of capturing a Bigfoot on camera. In the intervening thirty-five years (and despite dramatic advances in technology and wide distribution of handheld camcorders), thousands of people have gone in search of Bigfoot and come back empty-handed (or with little but fuzzy photos). Second, a known Bigfoot track hoaxer[2] claimed to have told Patterson exactly where to go to see the Bigfoot on that day. Third, Patterson made quite a profit from the film, including publicity for a book he had written on the subject and an organization he had started. Furthermore, John Napier, an anatomist and anthropologist who served as

1. **alleged:** supposed
2. **hoaxer:** deceptive person or trickster

* Vanhorn, Beth, and Robert W. Clark. *Veterinary Assisting: Fundamentals and Applications*. Clifton Park: Delmar, 2011. Print. Ch. 9, p. 126.

the Smithsonian Institution's director of primate[1] biology, found many problems with the film, including that the walk and size is consistent with a man's; the center of gravity seen in the subject is essentially that of a human; and the step length is inconsistent with the tracks allegedly taken from the site.*

2

The paragraph's topic is the film of Bigfoot shot by Roger Patterson and Bob Gimlin. This film is mentioned in almost all of the paragraph's sentences. But what is the author's point about this topic? In the third sentence, he states that the film is suspect for several reasons. Then, all of the other sentences in the paragraph offer details to explain that idea.

Exercise 2.7

Read each paragraph and then answer the questions that follow by circling the letter of the correct topic and main idea.

1. Communication scholar James McCroskey, who has studied communication apprehension (CA) for more than 20 years, defines it as "an individual's level of fear or anxiety associated with either real or anticipated communication with another person or persons." As this definition suggests, communication apprehension is not limited to public speaking situations. We may feel worried about almost any kind of communication encounter. If, for example, you are preparing to have a conversation with a romantic partner who, you think, is about to suggest ending the relationship, if your professor has called you into her office to discuss your poor attendance record, or if a police officer has motioned you to pull off the road for a "conversation," you know what communication apprehension is all about.†

   Circle the letter of the correct topic.

   a. James McCroskey

   b. communication apprehension

   c. communication encounters

   Circle the letter of the main idea.

   a. Communication apprehension can occur in different kinds of communication situations.

1. **primate:** mammals characterized by developed hands and feet, shortened snouts, and large brains

* From Bernstein and Nash, *Essentials of Psychology*, 2nd ed. Boston: Houghton Mifflin, 2002, 350. Copyright © 2002 by Houghton Mifflin Company. Reprinted with permission.

† From Andrews et al., *Public Speaking*. Boston: Houghton Mifflin, 1999, 42.

b. James McCroskey is the leading expert on communication apprehension.

c. Communication encounters cause apprehension.

2. Cardiovascular disease (CVD), the underlying cause of heart attack and stroke, remains America's No. 1 medical problem. Despite widespread public awareness of risk factors such as high cholesterol, smoking, inactivity, and obesity, CVD continues to exact a devastating toll on society. As the leading cause of death in the United States, it kills more than 2,600 people a day and has an annual mortality rate greater than the next six causes of death combined. The estimated number of people in the country living with cardiovascular disease is staggering—12.4 million have coronary heart disease, 4.5 million have had a stroke, and 4.7 million have congestive heart failure. An additional 50 million have high blood pressure. The total cost to the economy of all that illness is estimated by the American Heart Association at more than $298 billion a year in medical expenses and lost productivity. The total cost in pain and suffering to individuals and families is beyond imagining.*

Circle the letter of the correct topic.

a. cardiovascular disease

b. the American Heart Association

c. the cost of CVD

Circle the letter of the main idea.

a. The American Heart Association is a great organization.

b. Cardiovascular disease affects more people than any other disease in the United States.

c. Cardiovascular disease costs Americans billions of dollars each year.

3. Is there anything a couple can do to keep the honeymoon alive? Researcher Arthur Aron and his colleagues say that after the exhilaration of a new relationship wears off, partners can combat boredom by engaging together in new and arousing activities. In a controlled experiment, they brought randomly selected couples into a laboratory, spread gymnasium mats across the floor, tied the partners' hands together at the wrist, and had them crawl on their hands and knees, over a barrier, from one end of the room to the other—all the while carrying a pillow between their bodies. Other couples were given the more mundane[1] task of rolling a ball across the mat, one partner at a time. A third group received no assignment.

1. **mundane:** ordinary

* From David Noonan, "The Heart of the Matter," *Newsweek Special Issue*, September 2001, 75. © 2001 Newsweek, Inc. All rights reserved. Reprinted by permission.

2

Afterward all participants were surveyed about their relationships. As Aron predicted, the couples who had struggled and laughed their way through the novel and arousing activity reported more satisfaction with the quality of their relationships than did those in the mundane and no-task groups. Maybe, just maybe, a steady and changing diet of exciting new experiences can help keep the flames of love burning.*

Circle the letter of the correct topic.

a. relationships

(b.) keeping love alive

c. experiments with couples

Circle the letter of the main idea.

a. The exhilaration of a new relationship wears off eventually.

(b.) One way to keep love alive is to engage as a couple in exciting new experiences.

c. Experiments with couples show that only about a third will actually stay together.

4. The scope of global marketing includes many industries and many business activities. Boeing, the world's largest commercial airline manufacturer, engages in global marketing when it sells its aircraft to airlines across the world. Likewise, Ford Motor Company, which operates automobile manufacturing plants in many countries, engages in global marketing, even though a major part of Ford's output is sold in the country where it is manufactured. Large retail chains, such as Wal-Mart, search for new products abroad to sell in the United States. As major global buyers, they too participate in global marketing.†

Circle the letter of the correct topic.

a. Ford Motor company's global market

b. marketing in a diverse society

(c.) the scope of global marketing

Circle the letter of the main idea.

a. Ford Motor company operates manufacturing plants in many countries.

(b.) The scope of global marketing includes many industries and many business activities.

c. Companies find global marketing challenging in a diverse society.

---

* Adapted from Brehm et al., *Social Psychology,* 5th ed. Boston: Houghton Mifflin, 2002, 337. Copyright © 2002 by Houghton Mifflin Company. Reprinted with permission.

† Gillespie, Kate, and H. David Hennessey. *Global Marketing,* 3rd ed. Mason: South-Western Cengage Learning, 2011. Print. Ch. 1 p. 4.

5. Population is still growing rapidly in many poor countries, but this is not the case in the world's industrialized nations. In 2000, women in developed countries had only 1.6 children on average; only in the United States did women have, almost exactly, the 2.1 children necessary to maintain a stable population. In European countries where women have been steadily having fewer babies since the 1950s, national fertility rates ranged from 1.2 to 1.8 children per woman. Italy, once renowned for big Catholic families, had achieved the world's lowest birthrate—a mere 1.2 babies per woman. Spain, Germany, and Russia were only slightly higher, while France, Poland, and Britain were clustered around 1.6 children per woman.*

   Circle the letter of the correct topic.

   a. population growth

   b. population in industrialized nations

   c. population growth in Europe

   Circle the letter of the main idea.

   a. In Europe, people have fewer children.

   b. The population is not growing as much in industrialized nations as it is in poor countries.

   c. Italians used to be known for their big families.

The Topic Sentence

The **topic sentence** *is the single statement that presents the main point or idea of the paragraph.* Topic sentences have two parts: they state the topic and they state what the author has to say about that topic. Writers do not have to include such a sentence. Chapter 4 of this book will discuss in more detail paragraphs that lack a topic sentence. However, writers often include a topic sentence to help readers see the main idea quickly and easily.

To find the topic sentence, look for the most general statement in the paragraph and then make sure the other sentences all offer information or details. See if you can locate the topic sentence in the following paragraph:

> If you want to keep your long-term memory intact, you should avoid certain foods and eat more of others. The artificial sweetener called aspartame is one food to cut back. Studies have shown that drinking more than one or two diet drinks' worth of aspartame per day has been shown to decrease long-term memory. Also, you should limit tofu. Ingredients in this soy product have been shown to cause memory loss, so you should limit servings to one a week. Foods that

* Excerpted from McKay et al., *A History of Western Society,* 7th ed. Boston: Houghton Mifflin, 2003, 1052. Copyright © 2003 by Houghton Mifflin Company. Reprinted with permission.

boost memory are those that are rich in B vitamins. These include bananas, peas, orange juice, and seafood, all of which contain B vitamins that are essential to good brain health and memory.*

If you chose the first sentence, you're right. That statement expresses the paragraph's main idea, and the rest of the paragraph explains that idea.

2

Exercise 2.8

Read the following selection about factors that influence food selection. For each of the paragraphs, write the correct topic on the blank provided. Write on the second blank provided the number of the topic sentence, which expresses the main idea.

Criteria Influencing Food Selection

A. (1) Culture influences food habits by dictating what is or is not acceptable to eat. (2) Foods relished in one part of the world may be spurned in another. (3) Grubs, which are a good protein source, are acceptable to the Aborigines of Australia. (4) Whale blubber is used in many ways in the arctic region, where the extremely cold weather makes a high-fat diet essential. (5) Dog is considered a delicacy in some Asian countries. (6) Escargots (snails) are a favorite in France. (7) Sashimi (raw fish) is a Japanese tradition fairly well accepted in the United States. (8) Locusts, a source of protein, are considered choice items in the Middle East. (9) Octopus, once thought unusual, now appears on many American menus.

Topic: Cultural influences on food habits

Topic Sentence: 1

B. (1) An increasingly diverse population in the United States, accompanied by people traveling more and communicating over longer distances, has contributed to a more worldwide community, and a food industry that continues to "go global." (2) Within the boundaries of the United States alone, many foods once considered ethnic are now commonplace: pizza, tacos, beef teriyaki, pastas, and gyros. (3) More recently arrived ethnic foods, such as Thai, Indian, Moroccan, and Vietnamese, are constantly added to the mix to meet the escalating demands for meals providing more variety, stronger flavors, novel visual appeal, and less fat.

Topic: Effects of a diverse population on food choices

Topic Sentence: 1

* Adapted from Dana Lichterman, "8 Surprising Ways to Give Your Memory a Makeover!" *Woman's World*, September 18, 2001, 35.

C. (1) Birthplace influences the foods that a person is exposed to, and helps to shape the dietary patterns that are often followed for life. (2) Salsa varies in flavor, texture, and color depending on whether the person preparing in was born in Mexico, Guatemala, Puerto Rico, or Peru. (3) Curry blends differ drastically depending on where the creator of the recipe was born. (4) In Mexican cuisine, the same dish may taste differently in various states according to the birthplace of the cook.

Topic: Influence of birthplace on food preparation

Topic Sentence: 1

D. (1) Not so long ago, geography and climate were the main determinants of what foods were available. (2) People ate food grown close to where they lived and were very rarely presented with the possibility of eating any exotic food. (3) For example, guava fruit grown in tropical regions was not even a consideration in an area such as Greenland. (4) Now the wide distribution of formerly "local" food throughout the world provides many people with an incredible variety of food choices.

Topic: Changes in availability of food choices

Topic Sentence: 4

E. (1) Culture not only influences what types of foods are chosen, but also the way they are consumed and the behavior surrounding their consumption. (2) In some parts of India, for example, only the right hand is used for eating and manipulating utensils; the left hand is reserved for restroom duties. (3) Foods may be served on banana leaves or wrapped in cornhusks. (4) It may be eaten with chopsticks, as is the custom throughout Asia, or with spoons, forks, and knives as in Europe and the Americas. (5) It is considered impolite in China not to provide your guest with a bountiful meal, so an unusually large number of food courses is served when guests are present.*

Topic: Cultural influences on food consumption

Topic Sentence: 1

Locations of Topic Sentences

Main ideas are often stated in the first sentence of the paragraph. However, they can appear in other places in a paragraph, too. Writers sometimes place the topic sentence in the middle of a paragraph or even at the end.

* Brown, Amy. *Understanding Food: Principles and Preparation,* 4th ed. Belmont: Wadsworth, 2011. Print. Ch. 1, pgs. 10–11.

Topic Sentence as First Sentence

It's very common for writers to announce the main idea in the first sentence of the paragraph. Then, the remainder of the paragraph explains why the reader should accept that point. In the following paragraph, for example, the topic sentence, which is highlighted in boldface type, is at the beginning.

> **When horse people discuss what sets Arabian horses apart, "endurance" is a word that comes up frequently.** For all their refined elegance, these are horses that can and will summon up almost unimaginable reserves of stamina and courage to help—or just to please—a trusted human friend. Arabians, and the half-Arabian, half-thoroughbred horses called *Anglo-Arabians*, dominate the long-distance sport of endurance riding in which champions regularly speed through rugged one-hundred-mile courses in under ten hours, stepping across the finish line with enough verve[1] to suggest that they'd just as soon trot twenty miles more.*

Topic Sentence as Second or Third Sentence

Sometimes, though, a writer needs to present a sentence or two of introductory information before stating the main point. Or the paragraph may begin with a question. This means the topic sentence might occur in the second or third sentence of the paragraph. Take a look at this example:

> Who smokes more? **If you have followed the trends in prevalence of smoking in North America, you know there is good news and bad news.** The numbers of smokers substantially decreased between 1993 and 2006 for all age groups, except those between age 18 and 24. Between 2003 and 2005, the percentage of high school students who reported smoking cigarettes in the past month remained stable at 22 percent to 23 percent, which is a drop from 36 percent in 1997. The reduction of smoking or the cessation of tobacco use among college students is a critical public health priority. Within the last 10 years, college student smoking prevalence has dropped from nearly 30 percent to slightly less than 20 percent.†

The main idea is "there is good news and bad news" concerning the trends in prevalence in smoking in North America. When authors begin a paragraph with a question, then the main idea is often stated in the second sentence. The remaining sentences discuss the rates for high school and college-age smokers.

1. **verve:** energy and enthusiasm

---

* Adapted from Jennifer Lee Carrell, "They Drink the Wind," *Smithsonian,* September 2001, 49.

† Gurung, Regan A. R. *Health Psychology: A Cultural Approach.* 2nd ed. Belmont: Wadsworth, 2010. Print. Ch. 7, p. 233

2

Topic Sentence in the Middle

A topic sentence can also appear somewhere in the middle of the paragraph. For example, read the following paragraph:

> Last year, the valedictorian at Brea Olinda High School in Southern California was caught electronically altering a course grade. His punishment: being banned from the graduation ceremony. Cheat on the SAT and your score will be cancelled; but you can take a retest. **It's often true that getting caught cheating does not result in harsh penalties.** It doesn't have terrible consequences for being accepted to college either. Says Don Firke, academic dean at Choate Rosemary Hall, a boarding school in Wallingford, Connecticut, "If a college really wants a kid, they're going to find a way to take him." Once on campus, a cheater is apt to find similarly lax[1] discipline. With the exception of a handful of schools like the University of Virginia, which have one-strike-and-you're-out honor-code policies, the vast majority simply dole out zeros for an assignment or course in which a student has been found cheating.*

The previous paragraph began with two of four examples that explain the main idea in the fourth sentence. After the main idea was stated, the paragraph offered two more examples.

Topic Sentence as Last Sentence

A writer might choose to save the topic sentence for the end of the paragraph, offering it as the last sentence. This next paragraph is an example of one that builds up to the main point:

> Senior citizens, a growing percentage of the U.S. population, also have recreational needs. For example, exercise has been found to reduce osteoporosis (a breakdown of calcium in the bones), especially for women in their post- menopausal years. Senior citizens need activities matched with their capabilities. On the other end of the spectrum, children have many needs for physical activity that remain unfulfilled. Daily physical education from kindergarten through the twelfth grade would greatly enhance children's movement skills and fitness capacities, if all school students were provided this instruction. Non-school sport programs can also provide opportunities for physical activity and play. **Increased fun-filled opportunities for physical**

1. **lax:** not strict

* Adapted from Carolyn Kleiner and Mary Lord, "The Cheating Game," *U.S. News and World Report*, November 22, 1999, 66.

activities will contribute to the development of a healthy lifestyle for everyone.*

In the previous paragraph, the writer offered all of his explanation first. Then, he summarized the point in a topic sentence at the paragraph's end.

Topic Sentence as First and Last Sentence

Finally, the topic sentence might occur twice: once at the beginning of the paragraph and then again, in different words, at the end. Writers often restate the topic sentence to emphasize or reinforce the main idea for the reader. Here is an example:

> **Hunting and gathering in the ocean does more than kill fish; it changes ecosystems.**[1] Each species in an ecosystem is linked to many others, as a predator, a scavenger, or a source of food or shelter. Remove some peripheral[2] species from the web and the system as a whole may continue to function just fine, so long as all the roles are still filled. But knock out a keystone[3] species and the system must find a new equilibrium, or balance. Other human impacts such as agricultural runoff and seafloor dredging may provide the final knockout blow to ecosystems, but in every case scholars analyzed, excessive fishing set the process in motion. **According to author Jeremy Jackson, we're causing fundamental shifts in ecosystems, and some of those shifts may be irreversible.**†

This paragraph identified the main point in the first sentence, offered explanation, and then made the same point again in the final sentence.

Steps for Locating the Topic Sentence

To find the topic sentence, regardless of location, look for the most general statement in the paragraph and then verify that the rest of the sentences in the paragraph offer information, details, or explanation for that general idea. Here's a specific step-by-step procedure you can follow when you're trying to determine the main idea and topic sentence in a paragraph:

Step 1: Read over the entire paragraph to get an idea of the subject matter included.

1. **ecosystems:** ecological communities
2. **peripheral:** minor or less important
3. **keystone:** important, crucial, necessary

* Lumpkin, Angela. *Introduction to Physical Education, Exercise Science, and Sport Studies,* 8th ed. New York: McGraw-Hill, 2011. Print. Ch. 1, p. 7.

† Adapted from Thomas Hayden, "Deep Trouble," *U.S. News and World Report*, September 10, 2001, 69.

Step 2: Read the first sentence to see if it gives a general picture of the entire paragraph. If it doesn't, it may provide some general background or contrasting information. Or, the first sentence may pose a question that the next few sentences go on to answer.

Step 3: If the first sentence does not state the main idea, read the last sentence to see if it gives a general picture of the entire paragraph. Turn the last sentence into a question, and then see if the other sentences in the paragraph answer that question. If they do, that last sentence may be the topic sentence.

Step 4: If either the first or the last sentence gives that general overview of the paragraph—the main idea—you have found your topic sentence.

Step 5: If neither the first nor last sentence is identified as the topic sentence, then the reader must evaluate each sentence in the middle of the paragraph to see if one of the sentences states the general idea or the main idea information. Test each possibility by turning it into a question and then determining if the other sentences in the paragraph answer that question.

Step 6: Once the topic sentence is located, then the reader must look for the general phrase located in the topic sentence that states the overall main idea.

Exercise **2.9**

Following each paragraph, write on the blank provided the number of the sentence that is the topic sentence.

A. (1) We crave high-fat foods because they're satisfying on many different levels. (2) "When we eat a fatty food, we get a drowsy, sensuous feeling," says Howard Moskowitz, PhD, a psychologist and president of Moskowitz Jacobs, Inc., a consumer research company. (3) Fat-free foods might make us feel virtuous, and they may temporarily dull a craving, but they don't make us feel deeply content in the same way fatty foods do. (4) Not to mention the fact that high-fat foods are pleasurable. (5) When you bite into a piece of dense cake or take a spoonful of rich ice cream, the creamy, rich texture that comes from fat is what feels good in your mouth. (6) Fat also makes food tender—the flaky crust, the moist muffin and the velvety frosting all owe their appeal to fat.*

Topic Sentence: __1__

B. (1) As a first precaution, take a close look at the water in a pool before you jump in. (2) Its color and texture are good indicators of its

* Adapted from Dayna Winter, "Don't Blame Your Sweet Tooth," *Family Circle*, April 24, 2001, 66.

cleanliness. (3) It should be clear enough for you to see through at least ten feet of water and distinguish objects such as a metal grating on the bottom of the pool. (4) Foamy or bubbling water along the pool's edge is a sign of potential trouble; it typically represents excessive organic matter, such as pollen or bacteria.*

Topic Sentence: 2

C. (1) What do your mother, your best friend, and your religion have in common? (2) They each constitute a way that you learn about acceptable behaviors. (3) Take parents, for example. (4) Whether we do something because they told us to (e.g., "Eat your greens!") or exactly because they told us not to (e.g., "Don't smoke!"), they have a strong influence on us. (5) If our friends exercise, we will be more likely to exercise. (6) Similarly, religions have different prescriptions for what individuals should and should not do. (7) Muslims should not eat pork or drink alcohol. (8) Hindus are prohibited from eating beef. (9) Even where we live can determine our habits and can help predict the diseases we may die from as studied in detail by the area of health geography. (10) Parents, peers, religion, and geography are a few of the key determinants of our behaviors and are examples of what makes up our culture.†

Topic Sentence: 10

D. (1) Everybody uses words to persuade people of something without actually making a clear argument for it. (2) This is called using loaded language. (3) For example: a newspaper writer who likes a politician calls him "Senator Smith"; if he doesn't like the politician, he refers to him as "right-wing [or left-wing] senators such as Smith." (4) If a writer likes an idea proposed by a person, he calls that person "respected"; if he doesn't like the idea, he calls the person "controversial." (5) If a writer favors abortion, she calls somebody who agrees with her "pro-choice" ("choice" is valued by most people); if she opposes abortion, she calls those who agree with her "pro-life" ("life," like "choice," is a good thing). (6) Recognizing loaded language in a newspaper article can give you important clues about the writer's point of view.‡

Topic Sentence: 6

E. (1) Daniel Goleman, author of *Social Intelligence,* says humans are "wired to connect." (2) And communication—verbal and nonverbal—is

* Adapted from Ian K. Smith, M.D., "A Quick Dip in a Dirty Pool," *Time Online*, July 18, 2001, www.time.com.

† Gurung, Regan A. R. *Health Psychology: A Cultural Approach,* 2nd ed. Belmont: Wadsworth, 2010. Print. Ch. 1, p. 9.

‡ Adapted from Shipman et al., *An Introduction to Physical Science*, 9th ed. Boston: Houghton Mifflin, 2000, 466. Copyright © 2000 by Houghton Mifflin Company. Reprinted with permission.

the primary way that we connect with others. (3) Marriage counselors have long emphasized the importance of communication for healthy, enduring relationships. (4) They point out that the failure of some marriages is not caused primarily by troubles and problems or even by conflict because all marriages encounter challenges and conflict. (5) A major distinction between relationships that endure and those that collapse is effective communication. (6) In fact, results of a national poll taken in 1999 showed that a majority of Americans perceive communication problems as the number one reason marriages fail—far surpassing other reasons such as sexual difficulties, money problems, and interference from family members.*

Topic Sentence: 5

2

Topic Sentences That Cover More Than One Paragraph

Sometimes a topic sentence might cover more than one paragraph. This usually occurs when the author needs to give a lot of information to explain that topic sentence. In that case, the author might choose to divide the explanation or information into two paragraphs to make it easier to read. For example, read the following paragraphs:

> **The delegates in Philadelphia, and later the critics of the new Constitution during the debate over its ratification,[1] worried about aspects of the presidency that were quite different from those that concern us today.** From 1787 to 1789 some Americans suspected that the president, by being able to command the state militia, would use the militia to overpower state governments. Others were worried that if the president were allowed to share treaty-making power with the Senate, he would be "directed by minions[2] and favorites" and become a "tool of the Senate."
>
> But the most frequent concern was over the possibility of presidential reelection. Americans in the late eighteenth century were suspicious of human nature and experienced in the arts of mischievous government. Therefore, they believed that a president, once elected, would arrange to stay in office in perpetuity[3] by resorting to bribery, intrigue, and force.†

1. **ratification:** official approval
2. **minions:** followers
3. **in perpetuity:** forever

* Wood, Julia T. *Communication in Our Lives,* 6th ed. Boston: Wadsworth, 2012. Print. Ch. 1, p. 5.

† Adapted from Wilson and DiIulio, *American Government,* 8th ed. Boston: Houghton Mifflin, 2001, 257. Copyright © 2001 by Houghton Mifflin Company. Reprinted with permission.

In this passage, the topic sentence is highlighted in boldface type. After stating the topic sentence, the author presents several concerns of early Americans to explain the main idea. Both paragraphs work together to support that one point.

2

Exercise 2.10

Identify the topic sentence of each of the following passages and write its number on the blank provided.

A. (1) Intraspecies[1] communication helps animals find food. (2) Biologist Charles Brown discovered that some birds actually establish "information centers" where they can learn where to go for food. (3) Observing cliff swallows on the plains of Nebraska for several years, he noted that the birds, on returning to their nests from a food hunt, would "rock back and forth" if their hunts were successful. (4) When they left their nests to search for more food, they were followed by their neighbors only if their body language indicated success.

(5) This bird dance, however, hardly compares to the well-documented dance of the honey bee. (6) When scouts locate a source of food, they return to their hive and inform others of its whereabouts. (7) Their scent declares what they've found; their dance gives directions and more. (8) If the food is nearby, they perform a "round dance"—they run around in circles—which simply announces the find. (9) When the location is far away, they perform a "waggle dance." (10) The waggle dance is extraordinary in its detail. (11) The movements tell the other bees how far away the food is, its precise location, and even how much there is.*

Topic sentence: ___1___

B. (1) Doppler radars are being installed at major airports to prevent plane crashes and near crashes that have been attributed to dangerous downward wind bursts known as *wind shear*. (2) These wind bursts generally result from high-speed downdrafts in the turbulence of thunderstorms but can occur in clear air when rain evaporates high above the ground. (3) The downdraft spreads out when it hits the ground and forms an inward circular pattern. (4) A plane entering the pattern experiences an unexpected upward headwind that lifts the plane. (5) The pilot often cuts speed and lowers the plane's nose to compensate.

1. **intraspecies:** within a species

* Excerpted from Remland, *Nonverbal Communication in Everyday Life*. Boston: Houghton Mifflin, 2000, 62. Copyright © 2000 by Houghton Mifflin Company. Reprinted with permission.

(6) Further into the circular pattern, the wind quickly turns downward, and an airplane can suddenly lose altitude and possibly crash if near the ground when landing. (7) Doppler radar can detect the wind speed and the direction of raindrops in clouds, as well as the motions of dust and other objects floating in the air, so it can provide an early warning of wind shear conditions.*

Topic sentence: 1

C. (1) Not all fire departments have fire prevention bureaus. (2) In some jurisdictions, traditional fire prevention bureau functions simply are not performed or are performed by another agency or agencies. (3) In the aftermath of a fire that killed 25 employees of the Imperial Foods chicken processing plant in Hamlet, North Carolina, the fire chief stated that the entire incident centered around the lack of enforcement of existing codes. (4) The fire department was not adequately staffed to perform inspections.

(5) In some areas, certain traditional fire prevention functions have been shifted to other agencies, usually in the name of streamlining government. (6) Some jurisdictions have located all inspection functions within one agency. (7) The assumption that all types of inspections are basically the same and effectively performed by any person with the title "inspector" can have serious consequences if adequate training and supervision are not provided.†

Topic sentence: 2

D. (1) Every Saturday, from March through May, managers, bankers, and lawyers from Seattle to Atlanta shed their ties and put on their cleats to compete in one of the roughest games—rugby. (2) The Harp USA Rugby Super League attracts mostly white-collar workers who say this sport helps them cope with the stress of office life. (3) As one player explained, "After a hard day's work, rugby is a great release." (4) Terry Bradshaw, former NFL football player, says exercise tends to have a cleansing effect: "If I am stressed out, I go and run three miles, or play an hour and a half of tennis. (5) When I come back, I feel so good—I am ready to tackle the world."

(6) Exercise can act as a buffer against stress, so stressful events have less of a negative impact on your health. (7) Regular aerobic exercise—walking, swimming, low-impact aerobics, tennis, or jogging, for example—can increase your stress capacity. (8) Exercise does not have

* Adapted from Shipman et al., *An Introduction to Physical Science*, 9th ed. Boston: Houghton Mifflin, 2000, 516.

† Diamantes, David. *Principles of Fire Prevention,* 2nd ed. Clifton Park: Delmar, 2011. Print. Ch. 2, p. 24.

to be strenuous to be helpful. (9) Even gentle exercise like yoga or tai chi can help you manage your daily stress load.*

Topic sentence: 6

E. (1) The Hawaiian Islands in the Pacific Ocean are a popular tourist site; indeed, tourism accounts for 70 percent of Hawaii's economy. (2) In 2005, over 7.5 million visitors traveled to Hawaii. (3) The state average is close to 185,000 visitors on average per day. (4) The average length of stay is 9.1 days, with each visitor spending roughly $174 per day, totaling 11.9 billion dollars annually. (5) Not all visitors arrive by air; in 2005, cruise ship arrivals averaged close to 321,000 visitors.

(6) Being a desirable destination, however, isn't enough to create a successful tourism trade. (7) A means to get to the destination must also exist. (8) Because there is no land passage between Hawaii and the mainland, tourists must travel by air or sea. (9) The more people who are attracted to Hawaii's shores, the more travel tickets are sold by the airlines and cruise ships to transport them there. (10) If Hawaii had nothing to offer the traveler, the airlines and cruise ships would have less trade. (11) The converse is also true: If there were no convenient or comfortable means of transportation, fewer people would visit Hawaii, and the state's tourism trade would decline. (12) The success of each component contributes to the overall success of Hawaii's tourism industry, and vice versa. (13) This interdependence of the many products and services making up the network is an important aspect of hospitality, travel, and tourism.†

Topic sentence: 12 and 13

Reading Strategy:
Creating an Effective Reading Environment

If you're like most students, you probably read both at home and outside your home: perhaps somewhere on your college campus and maybe even at work during your breaks. Your reading environment can greatly affect your comprehension. So, give some thought to how you can create or select the right reading environments. The right environment allows you to stay alert and to focus all of your concentration on the text, especially when it's a challenging one.

* Adapted from Reece and Brandt, *Effective Human Relations in Organizations*, 7th ed. Boston: Houghton Mifflin, 1999, 373.

† Chon, Kaye (Kye-Sung) and Thomas A. Maier. *Welcome to Hospitality: An Introduction*, 3rd ed. Clifton Park: Delmar, 2010. Print. Ch. 2, p. 40, 41, 42.

When you're at home, you can usually create effective conditions for reading. You might want to designate a particular place—a desk or table, for example—where you always read. Make sure the place you choose is well lit, and sit in a chair that requires you to sit upright. Reading in a chair that's too soft and comfortable tends to make you sleepy! Keep your active reading tools (pens, highlighter markers, notebook, or paper) and a dictionary close at hand.

Before you sit down for a reading session, try to minimize all potential external distractions. Turn off your phone, the television, and the radio. Notify your family members or roommates that you'll be unavailable for a while. If necessary, put a "do not disturb" sign on your door! With fewer interruptions and distractions, you will have an easier time keeping your attention on the task at hand.

Overcoming internal distractions, which are the thoughts, worries, plans, daydreams, and other types of mental "noise" inside your own head, is often even more challenging for readers. However, it's important to develop strategies for dealing with them, too. If you don't, they will inhibit you from concentrating on what you are reading. Internal distractions will also prevent you from absorbing the information you need to learn. You can try to ignore these thoughts, but they will usually continue trying to intrude. So, how do you temporarily silence them so you can devote your full attention to your reading? Instead of fighting them, try focusing completely on these thoughts for a short period of time. For 5 or 10 minutes, allow yourself to sit and think about your job, your finances, your car problems, your boyfriend or girlfriend, the paper you need to write, or whatever is on your mind. Better yet, write these thoughts down. To empty your mind onto a piece of paper, try a free-writing exercise, which involves quickly writing your thoughts on paper without censoring them or worrying about grammar and spelling. If you can't stop thinking about all of the other things you need to do, devote 10 minutes to writing a detailed "to-do" list. Giving all of your attention to distracting thoughts will often clear your mind so you can focus on your reading.

If you're reading somewhere other than at home (on your college campus, for instance), it will be more difficult to achieve ideal reading conditions. However, you can still search for places that have the right characteristics. First of all, find a location—such as the library—that is well lit and quiet. Try to sit at an individual study carrel or cubicle so you can block out external distractions. If no carrels are available, choose a table that's out of the flow of traffic, and sit with your back to others so you're not tempted to watch their comings and goings. If you must read in a more distracting place like your college cafeteria or a bench on the grounds, you might want to get in the habit of carrying a pair of earplugs in your book bag so you can reduce external noise. Finally, don't forget to keep your active reading tools and dictionary with you so you'll have them on hand no matter where you end up reading.

Write your answers to the following questions on the blanks provided:

1. Where were you when you read this information about creating an effective reading environment? Describe your surroundings.

   Answers will vary.

2. Is this the place where you do most of your reading? If not, where do you usually read?

   Answers will vary.

3. What external distractions pulled your attention from the book as you read?

   Answers will vary.

4. Could you have done anything to prevent these external distractions from happening?

   Answers will vary.

5. Did you battle any internal distractions as you read? Briefly describe the thoughts that intruded upon your concentration.

   Answers will vary.

6. Based on the information in this section, where could you create the most ideal environment for reading? What objects and/or procedures will you need to create that environment?

   Answers will vary.

WEB LINK

http://www.ucc.vt.edu/stdysk/studydis.html

This website will help you evaluate three different places where you might want to study. After you take the quick survey, this site will choose which study environment is the most beneficial to you.

2

Reading Selections

Practicing the Active Reading Strategy

Before and While You Read

You can use active reading strategies before, while, and after you read a selection. The following are some suggestions for active reading strategies that you can employ before you read and as you are reading.

1. Skim the selection for any unfamiliar words. Circle or highlight any words you do not know.
2. As you read, underline, highlight, or circle important words or phrases.
3. Write down any questions about the selection if you are confused by the information presented.
4. Jot notes in the margin to help you understand the material.

BIOGRAPHY:

Auguste Escoffier: A Master French Chef

Auguste Escoffier, who as a young boy yearned to be a sculptor, became one of the world's most famous chefs. He elevated the prestige of French cooking and restored dignity to the title of chef.

1 In 1860, Escoffier got his first taste of the restaurant business when, at the age of twelve, he worked as a cook in his uncle's restaurant, Le Restaurant Français, in Nice, France. At that time, in contrast to just a generation or so earlier, restaurant cooks were not held in high regard. Though pushed into the restaurant business by his father and grandfather, Escoffier decided that if his destiny in life was to be a cook, he would make it his mission to restore honor to the title.

2 Early—and briefly—in his career, Escoffier emulated the eighteenth century's most illustrious chef, Marie- Antoine Carême. Soon thereafter, he took on the task of modernizing and simplifying Carême's style of cuisine. Carême had been a master chef, but his elaborate style created problems for guests: hot food was rarely hot, and his towering creations were nearly impossible for most guests to eat comfortably. Escoffier soon changed all that. Reflecting both the talent he had for cooking and the gift he had for organization, he

felt that cuisine could be artistically inspired yet scientifically executed. He created simple yet elegant dishes and served them with exquisite timing to maintain proper food temperature.

3 It was after 1883, when Escoffier met César Ritz (of Ritz Hotel fame), that his talent for organizing led him to develop the kitchen brigade, a system of organizing the restaurant kitchen that some restaurants still follow today. As a duo, Escoffier and Ritz worked beautifully. For example, faced with an English-speaking clientele in Monte Carlo (where Escoffier frequently worked in the summers in the 1890s, and where his wife and three children lived), Escoffier and Ritz developed a new menu concept, prix fixe, for parties of four or more. With prix fixe, a waiter simply informed the chef of the host's name and the number of guests in the party. Escoffier then chose a selection of menu items that he felt complemented the party's tastes. The menu was noted in a special record book so that returning guests could be treated to a new selection of entrees, unless favorites were requested. This system was successful not only in Monte Carlo, but in England as well. Today, most fine dining restaurants still offer a classic prix fixe option, often referred to as the table d'hôte menu.

4 As chef at the Savoy Hotel and then the Carlton (both in London), Escoffier created many new dishes. Among the most famous was Peach Melba, named in honor of the Australian opera star Nellie Melba, who stayed at the Savoy. Among the most interesting was Chicken Jeanette, a stuffed chicken breast served atop a carved ice ship, to commemorate the ship Jeanette, which had an unfortunate and fateful run-in with an iceberg.*

■ Vocabulary

Read the following questions about some of the vocabulary words that appear in the previous selection. Before you look up the word, try to use the context of the passage to figure out the meaning. Then, circle the letter of the correct answer for each question.

1. In paragraph 2, what does *emulated* mean?

   a. imitated
   c. disliked
   b. ignored
   d. worked for

2. *Illustrious* in paragraph 2 means ______________.

   a. creative
   c. hard working
   b. highest paid
   d. famous

* Kaye (Kye-Sung) Chon and Thomas A. Maier. *Welcome to Hospitality . . . an Introduction.* 3rd ed. Clifton Park: Delmar, 2010. Print. pg. 238

3. What is *cuisine*? (paragraph 2)
   a. the origin of a food
   b. a style of preparing food
   c. the creator of a dish
   d. a restaurant in Paris

4. What is the meaning of *executed* as it is used in paragraph 2?
   a. hung by the state
   b. legally signed
   c. carried out
   d. murdered

5. *Complemented* (paragraph 3) means ______________.
   a. to praise
   b. make a change
   c. tempted
   d. to make complete or perfect

Reading Skills

Respond to each of the following questions by circling the letter of the correct answer or by writing your answer on the blank provided.

1. What is the topic sentence in paragraph 1?
   a. The first sentence
   b. The second sentence
   c. The third sentence
   d. There is no topic sentence in this paragraph.

2. What is the topic of paragraph 2?
   a. emulating a famous chef
   b. keeping food hot
   c. using science for cooking
   d. modernizing and simplifying French cuisine

3. What is the topic sentence of paragraph 2?
   a. Early—and briefly—in his career, Escoffier emulated the eighteenth century's most illustrious chef, Marie- Antoine Carême.
   b. Soon thereafter, he took on the task of modernizing and simplifying Carême's style of cuisine.
   c. Escoffier soon changed all that.
   d. He created simple yet elegant dishes and served them with exquisite timing to maintain proper food temperature.

4. What is the topic of paragraph 3?
   a. creative partnership of Ritz and Escoffier
   b. creation of the kitchen brigade
   c. creation of the prix fixe menu
   d. impact of Escoffier on today's restaurants

5. Which sentence is the topic sentence of paragraph 4?
   a. The first sentence
   b. the second sentence
   c. the third sentence
   d. There is no topic sentence in this paragraph.

Practicing the Active Reading Strategy

■ After You Read

Now that you have read the selection, answer the following questions, using the active reading strategies that you learned in Chapter 1.

1. Identify and write down the point and purpose of this reading selection.
2. Did you circle or highlight any words unfamiliar to you? Can you figure out the meaning from the context of the passage? If not, then look up each word in a dictionary and find the definition that best describes the word as it is used in the selection. You may want to write the definition in the margin next to the word in the passage for future reference.
3. Predict any possible questions that may be used on a test about the content of this selection.

■ Questions for Discussion and Writing

Respond to each of the following questions based on your reading of the selection.

1. Identify two of the important changes Escoffier made to the restaurant system.

   Students should choose from the following: Escoffier created simple, elegant dishes that could be served at the proper temperature. He developed the kitchen brigade system for organizing the kitchen. Along with Ritz, he created the prix fixe menu

2. Would you like to have a chef select your menu for you? Why or why not?

Answers will vary.

3. Describe the most elegant restaurant meal you have ever had.

Answers will vary.

Practicing the Active Reading Strategy

Before and While You Read

You can use active reading strategies before, while, and after you read a selection. The following are some suggestions for active reading strategies that you can employ before you read and as you are reading.

1. Skim the selection for any unfamiliar words. Circle or highlight any words you do not know.
2. As you read, underline, highlight, or circle important words or phrases.
3. Write down any questions about the selection if you are confused by the information presented.
4. Jot notes in the margin to help you understand the material.

TEXTBOOK READING – HOSPITALITY

An Age-Old Industry

Historians have traced the development of the hospitality industry through thousands of years and many cultures. Viewing the industry through the lens of history is helpful because it reveals the strong relationship between the shape of hospitality and the needs and expectations of different societies. This passage describes the type of inns and hotels earlier travelers encountered on their travels.

1 Historians speculate that the first overnight lodging structures were erected along Middle Eastern trade and caravan routes around four thousand years ago. These structures, the *caravanserai,* were at eight-mile intervals and operated much like the present-day Middle Eastern *kahns* in that they provided shelter (for both humans and beasts) but nothing else. Provisions—food, water, and bedding—were supplied by the traveler. Early accounts of these establishments reveal physical conditions that would be considered harsh by today's standards. However, the spirit of hospitality was strong, perhaps especially so in the Middle East. A traditional Middle Eastern saying illustrates devotion to hospitality: "I am never a slave—except to my guest."

2 In many countries, the quality of hospitality services varied according to the fees paid and the location of an establishment. Some early accounts tell of vermin-infested inns and poor-quality food, but not all were bad. For example, *lesches,* social gathering places in ancient Greece, had a reputation for good food. Guests could choose from a variety of delicacies, including goat's milk cheese, barley bread, peas, fish, figs, olives, lamb, and honey. Guests also had their choice of *lesches* to frequent—Athens alone had 360!

3 Fine service could also be found in ancient Rome, circa A.D. 43. There were hotels on all main roads and in the cities, the better ones having a restaurant, a lavatory, bedrooms with keys or bolts...and also a yard and stabling. An inn at Pompeii had six bedrooms round two sides of an inner courtyard, with a kitchen on the third side. Its large bar and restaurant were a little ways away, on the main street.

4 Roman society had a singular influence on the hospitality industry. Many of Rome's citizens were wealthy enough to travel for pleasure, and well-built Roman roads gave them easy access to most of the known world. As soldiers conquered new areas, Roman citizens could visit exotic places in comfort. Communication between guest and host presented no problems, as Latin had become a universal language. (In fact, much hospitality terminology springs from Latin: *hospe* means host or guest; *hospitium* means a guest chamber, inn, or quarters. Other related words with this root include *hospice, hostel, hospital,* and *hotel.*)

5 With the fall of the Roman Empire, travel declined and inns became almost nonexistent. From the fourth through the eleventh centuries, the Roman Catholic Church kept the hospitality industry alive by encouraging religious pilgrimages between monasteries and cathedrals throughout Europe. Roads were built and maintained by clergy from the local monasteries. Hostels built on church grounds offered places to eat and sleep. Churches did not charge for these accommodations, although travelers were expected to make a contribution to the Church. When

travel and trade gradually increased in Europe, the monasteries remained a major hospitality provider for both the business and recreational traveler.

6 Besides priests and missionaries, other travelers, including traders, merchants, diplomats, and military personnel, traveled the expanding Mediterranean and European roadways. Not all these wayfarers were taken care of by the Church; independent innkeepers also welcomed travelers on their journeys. When a group of Italian innkeepers incorporated in the year 1282, hospitality evolved from an act of charity to a full-fledged business.*

Vocabulary

Read the following questions about some of the vocabulary words that appear in the previous selection. Before you look up the word, try to use the context of the passage to figure out the meaning. Then, circle the letter of the correct answer for each question.

1. When historians *speculate* about the beginnings of travel lodging, what are they doing? (paragraph 1)
   a. imagining
   b. doing research
   c. questioning
   d. traveling
2. In paragraph 2, the author writes about vermin-infested inns. What are *vermin?*
   a. criminals
   b. loud people
   c. harmful insects or animals
   d. drunks
3. What is a *singular* influence? (paragraph 4)
   a. unusual
   b. poor
   c. frequent
   d. expensive
4. Religious people made *pilgrimages*. What were they doing? (paragraph 5)
   a. traveling by donkey
   b. traveling to a holy place
   c. traveling in a group
   d. traveling to see family
5. A *hostel* is a type of ________. (paragraph 5)
   a. restaurant
   b. shop
   c. inn
   d. recreation center

* Chon, Kaye (Kye-Sung), and Thomas A. Maier. Welcome to Hospitality: An Introduction, 3rd ed. Clifton Park: Delmar, 2010. Print. Ch. 1, pp. 6–9.

2

■ Reading Skills

Respond to each of the following questions by circling the letter of the correct answer.

1. The topic of paragraph 1 is
   a. the spirit of hospitality
   b. early provisions
   c. the first overnight lodging structures
   d. Middle Eastern hospitality
2. The topic sentence of paragraph 2 is
   a. Sentence 1
   b. Sentence 2
   c. Sentence 3
   d. Sentence 4
3. The main idea of paragraph 4 is
   a. Latin became a universal language.
   b. Wealthy Romans traveled to exotic places.
   c. Wealthy Romans had an important effect on the hospitality industry.
   d. Roman roads allowed citizens to travel widely.
4. The topic sentence for paragraph 5 is
   a. Sentence 2
   b. Sentence 4
   c. Sentence 5
   d. Sentence 6
5. The main idea of paragraph 6 is
   a. Hospitality evolved into a business when Italian innkeepers incorporated in 1282.
   b. The Church refused to take in certain travelers.
   c. Travel became more widespread.
   d. Different kinds of people began to travel.

Practicing the Active Reading Strategy

■ After You Read

Now that you have read the selection, answer the following questions, using the active reading strategies that you learned in Chapter 1.

1. Identify and write down the point and purpose of this reading selection.

2. Did you circle or highlight any words that are unfamiliar to you? Can you figure out the meaning from the context of the passage? If not, then look up each word in a dictionary and find the definition that best describes the word as it is used in the selection. You may want to write the definition in the margin next to the word in the passage for future reference.
3. Predict any possible questions that may be used on a test about the content of this selection.

Questions for Discussion and Writing

Respond to each of the following questions based on your reading of the selection.

1. Identify two reasons that early people needed to travel.

   Pleasure and religious pilgrimages

2. Why did the Roman Catholic Church play such an important role in keeping the hospitality industry alive?

   The monasteries built and maintained roads and hostels.

3. What are some of the hardships that early travelers encountered?

   In some cases the traveler had to supply all of the provisions. In other cases the food might be poor and the sleeping conditions filthy.

Practicing the Active Reading Strategy

Before and While You Read

You can use active reading strategies before, while, and after you read a selection. The following are some suggestions for active reading strategies that you can perform before you read and while you read.

1. Skim the selection for any unfamiliar words. Circle or highlight any words you do not know.
2. As you read, underline, highlight, or circle important words or phrases.
3. Write down any questions about the selection if you are confused by the information presented.
4. Jot notes in the margin to help you understand the material.

TEXTBOOK READING – COLLEGE SUCCESS

Coping with Procrastination

2

What do you put off doing? Why? What are the results of your procrastination? Most people procrastinate about things they dislike doing. Unfortunately, those things still need to be done! This selection discusses some of the effects of procrastination and offers some suggestions to dealing with it.

1 Any discussion of time management would not be complete without an examination of the most well-intentioned person's worst enemy—procrastination. The dictionary (*Webster's New Collegiate*) defines *procrastination as* "the act of putting off intentionally and habitually the doing of something that should be done." Interestingly, most procrastinators do not feel that they are acting intentionally. On the contrary, they feel that they fully *intend* to do whatever it is, but they simply cannot, will not, or—bottom line—they *do not* do it. Procrastinators usually have good reasons for their procrastination (some would call them excuses): "didn't have time," "didn't feel well," "couldn't figure out what to do," "couldn't find what I needed," "the weather was too bad"—the list is never-ending.

2 Even procrastinators themselves know that the surface reasons for their procrastination are, for the most part, not valid. When procrastination becomes extreme, it is a self-destructive course, and, yet, people feel that they are powerless to stop it. This perception can become reality if the underlying cause is not uncovered. Experts have identified some of the serious underlying causes of procrastination. Think about them the next time you find yourself struck by this problem.

3 Often procrastination stems from a real or imagined fear or worry that is focused not so much on the thing you are avoiding but its potential consequences. For instance, your procrastination over preparing for an oral presentation could be based on your fear that no matter how well prepared you are, you will be overcome by nerves and forget whatever you are prepared to say. Every time you think about working on the speech, you become so worried about doing "a bad job" that you have to put the whole thing out of your mind to calm down. You decide that you will feel calmer about it tomorrow and will be in a much better frame of mind to tackle it. Tomorrow the scenario gets repeated. The best way to relieve your anxiety would be to dig in and prepare so well that you can't possibly do poorly.

4 Being a perfectionist is one of the main traits that spawns fear and anxiety. Whose expectations are we afraid of not meeting? Often it is our own harsh judgment of ourselves that creates the problem. We set standards that are too high and then judge ourselves too critically. When you picture

yourself speaking before a group, are you thinking about how nervous the other students will be as well, or are you comparing your speaking abilities to the anchorperson on the six o'clock news? A more calming thought is to recall how athletes measure improvements in their performances by tracking and trying to improve on their own "personal best." Champions have to work on beating themselves in order to become capable of competing against their opponents. Concentrating on improving your own past performance, and thinking of specific ways to do so, relieves performance anxiety.

5 On the surface this would seem to be the reason for all procrastination, and the obvious answer is for the procrastinator to find a way to "get motivated." There are situations where lack of motivation is an indicator that you have taken a wrong turn. When you seriously do not want to do the things you need to do, you may need to reevaluate your situation. Did you decide to get a degree in Information Systems because everyone says that's where the high paying jobs are going to be, when you really want to be a social worker or a travel agent? If so, when you find yourself shooting hoops or watching television when you should be putting in time at the computer lab, it may be time to reexamine your decision. Setting out to accomplish something difficult when your heart isn't in it is often the root cause of self-destructive behavior.

6 Often procrastination is due to an inability to concentrate or a feeling of being overwhelmed and indecisive. Although everyone experiences these feelings during a particular stressful day or week, a continuation of these feelings could indicate that you are in a state of burnout. Burnout is a serious problem that occurs when you have overextended yourself for too long a period of time. It is especially likely to occur if you are pushing yourself both physically and mentally. By failing to pace yourself, you will "hit the wall," like the long-distance runner who runs too fast at the beginning of the race. Overworking yourself for too long without mental and physical relaxation is a sure way to run out of steam. Learning to balance your time and set realistic expectations for yourself will prevent burnout.

7 Sometimes you put off doing something because you literally don't know how to do it. This may be hard to admit to yourself, so you may make other excuses. When you can't get started on something, consider the possibility that you need help. For example, if you get approval from your favorite instructor for a term paper topic that requires collecting data and creating graphics, you can be stymied if you don't have the necessary skills and tools to do the work and do it well. Does the collection and analysis of the data require the use of a software program that you don't have and cannot afford to buy? Sometimes it is difficult to ask for help and sometimes it is even hard to recognize that you need help. When you feel stymied, ask

yourself, "Do I need help?" Do you need information but haven't a clue as to where to go to get it? Have you committed to doing something that is really beyond your level of skills? Being able to own up to personal limitations and seek out support and resources where needed is a skill used every day by highly successful people.*

WEB LINK

http://www.studygs.net/attmot3.htm

This link gives you some further suggestion in dealing with procrastination. Don't put off looking at it!!

■ Vocabulary

Read the following questions about some of the vocabulary words that appear in the previous selection. Circle the letter of the correct response.

1. This selection is about procrastination. What does *procrastination* mean?
   - a. speediness
   - b. immediacy
   - c. putting off or delaying
   - d. carrying out
2. In paragraph 2, the authors write, "Even procrastinators themselves know that the surface reasons for their procrastination are, for the most part, not valid." What does *valid* mean?
   - a. logical
   - b. sound
   - c. defined
   - d. unbalanced
3. What is an *underlying cause* (paragraph 2)?
   - a. complicated
   - b. fundamental
   - c. conflicting
   - d. disturbing
4. In paragraph 4, the authors write that "[b]eing a perfectionist is one of the main traits that spawns fear and anxiety." What does *spawn* mean?
   - a. consume
   - b. bring forth
   - c. destroy
   - d. disturb
5. What does *stymied* mean? Reread paragraph 7, "… you can be stymied if you don't have the necessary skills and tools to do the work and do it well."
   - a. puzzled
   - b. misunderstood
   - c. styled
   - d. comprehensive

* From Rebecca Moore, Barbara A. Baker, and Arnold H. Packer, "Coping with Procrastination," *College Success*. Upper Saddle River: Prentice Hall, 1997. Used by permission of the authors.

Reading Skills

Answer the following questions by circling the letter of the correct answer.

1. What is the topic of paragraph 3?
   a. procrastination
   b. oral presentations
   c. the fear of public speaking
   d. worry as a source of procrastination

2. What is the topic sentence of paragraph 3?
   a. "Often procrastination stems from a real or imagined fear or worry that is focused not so much on the thing you are avoiding but its potential consequences."
   b. "For instance, your procrastination over preparing for an oral presentation could be based on your fear that no matter how well prepared you are, you will be overcome by nerves and forget whatever you are prepared to say."
   c. "Every time you think about working on the speech, you become so worried about doing 'a bad job' that you have to put the whole thing out of your mind to calm down."
   d. "Tomorrow the scenario gets repeated."

3. What is the topic of paragraph 5?
   a. procrastination
   b. lack of motivation as a cause of procrastination
   c. making decisions
   d. choosing a career

4. In paragraph 5, the topic sentence is
   a. Sentence 1
   b. Sentence 2
   c. Sentence 6
   d. Sentences 2 and 6

5. What is the main idea of paragraph 4?
   a. Harsh self-judgment can lead to procrastination.
   b. Performance anxiety is a paralyzing condition.
   c. Champion athletes should focus on achieving their own "personal best."
   d. Perfectionism is the result of an individual's upbringing and temperament.

2

Practicing the Active Reading Strategy

■ After You Read

Now that you have read the selection, answer the following questions, using the active reading strategies that are discussed in Chapter 1.

1. Identify and write down the point and purpose of this reading selection.
2. Did you circle or highlight any words that are unfamiliar to you? Can you figure out the meaning from the context of the passage? If not, then look up each word in a dictionary and find the definition that best describes the word as it is used in the selection. You may want to write the definition in the margin next to the word in the passage for future reference.
3. Predict any possible test questions that may be used on a test about the content of this selection.

■ Questions for Discussion and Writing

Answer the following questions based on your reading of the selection. Write your answers on the blanks provided.

1. Would you describe yourself as a procrastinator? Why or why not?

   Answers will vary.

2. What skills, if any, did you learn from this article that will help you avoid procrastinating?

   Answers will vary.

3. Have you ever experienced burnout, as described in paragraph 6?

   Answers will vary.

Vocabulary Strategy: Synonyms

Synonyms *are words that have the same, or similar, meanings*. Synonyms serve four purposes in texts. First of all, they add variety to a reading selection. Instead of writing the same word over and over, authors will use different words with the same meanings to keep sentences lively and interesting. For example, in the specific sentences about computer viruses, the author describes those viruses as being able to *wipe out, infect, or disable* a hard drive. Second, authors use synonyms to express their thoughts as precisely as possible. For example, the paragraph about skateboarding says "skateboard sales have tripled to $72 million." The author could have used the word *risen* or *increased*, but he used the more specific *tripled*, which expresses exactly how much they increased.

A third use of synonyms is to connect ideas and sentences and to reinforce ideas. Do you remember the paragraph about improving long-term memory? Notice how the boldface, italicized words are synonyms that help keep the paragraph focused on the main idea:

> If you want to keep your long-term memory intact, you should ***avoid*** certain foods and eat more of others. The artificial sweetener called aspartame is one food to ***cut back***. Studies have shown that drinking more than one or two diet drinks' worth of aspartame per day has been shown to decrease long-term memory. Also, you should ***limit*** tofu. Ingredients in this soy product have been shown to cause memory loss, so you should ***limit*** servings to one a week. Foods that boost memory are those that are rich in B vitamins. These include bananas, peas, orange juice, and seafood, all of which contain B vitamins that are essential to good brain health and memory.

Finally, texts include synonyms to help readers figure out what other words mean. For example, in the sentence below, the author provides a synonym to help the reader understand what the word *equilibrium* means:

> But knock out a keystone species and the system must find a new equilibrium, or ***balance***.
>
> *Balance* is another way to say *equilibrium*; it's a synonym used to define a word.

Vocabulary Exercise 1

On the blank following each paragraph, write in the synonyms the paragraph includes for the boldfaced, italicized word or phrase.

1. Communication scholar James McCroskey, who has studied communication ***apprehension*** (CA) for more than 20 years, defines it as "an individual's level of fear or anxiety associated with either real or anticipated communication with another person or persons." As this definition suggests, communication apprehension is not limited to public speaking situations. We may feel worried about almost any kind of communication encounter.

   Three synonyms for italicized word: fear, anxiety, worry

2. There is a relationship between birth weight and intelligence, according to a recent study. It's long been known that ***children*** with abnormally low birth weights tend to score lower than normal-birth-weight children on IQ tests given at school age. But a new study of about 3,500 seven-year-olds links size to intelligence even among kids born at normal birth weight.*

Two synonyms for italicized word: 7-year-olds, kids

3. On September 19, 1991, a German couple chanced upon one of the most remarkable archaeological discoveries of the century, a 5,300-year-old mummy that came to be known as the *Iceman*. They were hiking in the Italian Alps. At 10,530 feet above sea level, they thought they had left civilization and its problems behind until they stumbled on an unexpected sight: the ***body of a dead man*** lying in the melting ice. Nor was that their only surprise. At first they thought the corpse was the victim of a recent accident.

Two synonyms for italicized phrase: mummy, corpse

4. Numerous ***bookstore chains*** have sprung up throughout the country in recent years, among them Borders, Super Crown, and Barnes and Noble. These businesses are designed to appeal particularly to young adults. Most offer comfortable chairs in which to sit, relax, and read. Some of these stores have a café area where specialty coffees, teas, muffins, and other delectables[1] are available. The evening hours are often filled with concerts, poetry readings, or other special events. Bookstores don't just sell books anymore; they sell a lifestyle.†

Three synonyms for italicized phrase: businesses, stores, bookstores

Vocabulary Exercise 2

Circle the eight synonyms used for the word *crying* in the following passage.

The saying goes: "Never let them see you sweat." But in today's macho workplace, we don't mind sweat. It's tears we can't handle. Work is the vessel into which we pour so much of ourselves—hope and disappointment, elation and rage, satisfaction and frustration. Yet any damp display of these emotions is seen as a weakness. "Do anything you can," Marjorie Brody, a career consultant, said, "to keep from crying at work. . . ."

1. **delectables:** delights; things that are pleasing to the taste

* Adapted from Williams, "Health Notes," *Newsweek*, September 10, 2001, 71.

† From Leslie, *Mass Communication Ethics*, © 2004, Houghton Mifflin, 216.

Weeping can paralyze a workplace. Cass Burton-Ward, who now works at the Stevens Institute of Technology in Hoboken, N.J., remembers an employee from a previous job who could be found sobbing after the slightest criticism. She was also reduced to whimpering by minor problems. "If someone inadvertently[1] left company letterhead in the laser printer, making her have to reprint her two- or three-page document," Burton-Ward said, "she would sometimes launch into a wailing tantrum. . . ." You just can't have that person bawling at the photocopy machine. It took the intervention of a psychologist to get this employee's emotions under control, Burton-Ward says. . . .

Brody, whose book is titled *Help! Was That a Career Limiting Move?* (Career Skills Press, 2001), warns that this is not an ideal world. "I hate to sound unsympathetic," she says of blubbering on the job, "but it might be better to stay away from the workplace for a while if you can't control your emotions."*

2

Reading Visuals: Tables

A **table** *is a visual aid that organizes information or data in rows and columns*. A table might list types, categories, figures, statistics, steps in a process, or other kinds of information. Its purpose is to summarize many related details in a concise format so that readers can read them easily and find specific facts quickly.

Tables contain the following parts:

- **Title.** The title states the visual aid's subject.
- **Column headings.** These labels identify the type of information you'll find in the vertical lists.
- **Row headings.** These labels identify the type of information you'll find in each horizontal list.
- **Source line.** The source line identifies who collected or compiled the information in the table.

1. **inadvertently:** accidentally, unintentionally

* Adapted from Lisa Belkin, Life's Work; Crying Shame? Tears in the Office, *New York Times*, September 26, 2001. Copyright © 2001 by the New York Times Company. Reprinted by permission

2

These parts are labeled in Table 2.1 below.

Title

Table 2.1 The Thirteen Most Intense Hurricanes (at Landfall) to Strike the United States from 1900 through 2007

Column headings

Row headings

Rank	Hurricane (Made Landfall)	Year	Central Pressure (Millibars/Inches)	Category	Death Toll
1	Florida (Keys)	1935	892/26.35	5	408
2	Camille (Mississippi)	1969	909/26.85	5	256
3	Andrew (South Florida)	1992	922/27.23	5	53
4	Katrina (Louisiana)	2005	920/27.17	3*	>1500
5	Florida (Keys)/South Texas	1919	927/27.37	4	>600†
6	Florida (Lake Okeechobee)	1928	929/27.43	4	>2000
7	Donna (Long Island, New York)	1960	930/27.46	4	50
8	Texas (Galveston)	1900	931/27.49	4	>8000
9	Louisiana (Grand Isle)	1909	931/27.49	4	350
10	Louisiana (New Orleans)	1915	931/27.49	4	275
11	Carla (South Texas)	1961	931/27.49	4	46
12	Hugo (South Carolina)	1989	934/27.58	4	49
13	Florida (Miami)	1926	935/27.61	4	243

Source line

*Although the central pressure in Katrina's eye was quite low, Katrina's maximum sustained winds of 110 knots at landfall made it a Category 3 storm.

†More than 500 of this total were lost at sea on ships. (The > symbol means "greater than.")

Source: Ahrens, Donald C., and Perry Samson. *Extreme Weather and Climate*. Belmont: Brooks/Cole, 2011. Print. Ch. 13, p. 382.

To understand the information in a table, first read the title, which will identify the kind of information the table includes. Next, familiarize yourself with the column and row headings. They will identify the kind of details included. Then, form an understanding of the relationships first by moving your eyes down each column to see how details compare, and then across each row to see how those details are related. Finally, try to state in your own words the overall point revealed by the table's lists.

In Table 2.1, the title states that this visual aid will focus on the thirteen most intense hurricanes (at landfall) to strike the United States from 1900 through 2007. The first column lists the rank of these intense hurricanes. Then, the next columns give specific information about each of these hurricanes. You can see which states have suffered the most intense hurricanes, compare death tolls, and look for relationships between category and central pressure. Look at the years in which the hurricanes occurred. You could create a timeline showing the decades with the worst hurricanes.

Now, study Table 2.2 on page 95 and then answer the questions that follow.

Table 2.2 **Trends in Number of Fires and the Number of Injuries and Fatalities from Fires**

Year	Fires	Deaths	Injuries	Direct Dollar Loss in Millions
1999	1,823,000	3,570	21,875	$10,024
2000	1,708,000	4,045	22,350	$11,207
2001[1]	1,734,500	3,745	20,300	$10,583
2001[2]	—	2,451	800	$33,440
2002	1,687,500	3,380	18,425	$10,337
2003	1,584,500	3,925	18,125	$12,307
2004	1,550,500	3,900	17,875	$9,794[3]
2005	1,602,000	3,675	17,925	$10,672
2006	1,642,500	3,245	16,400	$11,307
2007	1,557,500	3,430	17,675	$14,639
2008	1,451,500	3,320	16,705	$15,478

[1] Excludes the events of September 11, 2001.

[2] These estimates reflect the number of deaths, injuries, and dollar loss directly related to the events of September 11, 2001.

[3] The decrease in direct dollar loss in 2004 reflects the Southern California wildfires with an estimated loss of $2,040,000,000 that occurred in 2003. The dollar loss estimate for 2007 includes the California Fire Storm with an estimated property loss of $1,800,000,000. For 2008, the direct dollar loss includes the California Wildfires at an estimated loss of $1,400,000,000.

Source: Diamantes, David. *Principles of Fire Prevention,* 2nd ed. Clifton Park: Delmar, 2011. Print. Ch. 1, p. 3. U.S. Fire Administration

1. What does the chart represent? The downward trend in the number of fires, and number of injuries and fatalities from fire.

2. In what year did the most number of fires occur? How many were there?
1999; 1,823,000

3. How many deaths occurred from fires in 2008?
3,320

4. In what year were there 17,875 injuries from fires?
2004

5. How much money was lost due to fires in 2000?
$11,207

6. Why are there two listings in the chart for 2001? (Hint: see footnotes below chart)
One listing is exclusively for the events of September 11, 2001. The other listing is for all other events that year.

2

Chapter 2 Review

Try to answer the following questions without looking back in your text.

1. Paragraphs are composed of general and specific statements.
2. The most general sentence in the paragraph expresses its main idea the idea or point the writer wants you to know or to believe.
3. The sentence that states the writer's main idea is called the topic sentence.
4. The topic sentence has two parts: the topic, or subject, of the paragraph and what the writer wants to say about that subject.
5. The topic sentence can occur anywhere in the paragraph.
6. A topic sentence can cover more than one paragraph.
7. What are the four purposes that synonyms serve in a text?
   a. Add variety
   b. To express thoughts as precisely as possible
   c. To connect ideas and sentences and to reinforce ideas
   d. To help readers figure out what other words mean
8. What are two strategies for overcoming internal distractions?
   a. "Empty" your mind by focusing for a few minutes on your distractions
   b. Write down your distracting thoughts
9. How is information in a table organized? In rows and columns
10. The purpose of a table is Summarizing related details in a concise format.

Roberto Westbrook/Blend Images/Corbis

CHAPTER 3

Supporting Details, Mapping, and Outlining

Goals for Chapter 3

- Define the terms *major details* and *minor details.*
- Recognize major and minor details in paragraphs.
- Use mapping to show major and minor details in a paragraph.
- Use outlining to show major and minor details in a paragraph.
- Describe the principles of effective time management.
- Read and understand information in an organizational chart.

In the previous chapter, you practiced finding the main idea of a paragraph. The main idea is the general point the writer wants you to know or to believe when you've finished reading the paragraph. Often, though, readers cannot understand or accept this point as true unless they get more information. The *supporting details* in a paragraph provide this information.

Before continuing, take the following pretest to find out what you already know about supporting details.

3

Pretest

Identify each paragraph's main idea and write it on the blank. Then, choose one sentence that offers a *major* supporting detail and write the number of that sentence on the blank labeled "Major Supporting Detail."

1. (1) Many colleges offer students an opportunity to practice altruism in service learning experiences, which combine community service with classroom instruction and personal reflection. (2) In a recent survey of students at 504 colleges and universities, an average of one in three reported doing some form of community service. (3) More than half of the schools surveyed noted an increase in student involvement in community service. (4) Various studies have shown that students find service learning personally and professionally enriching and are more likely to continue volunteer work after college.*

   Main Idea: Many colleges offer students an opportunity to practice altruism in service learning experiences, which combine community service with classroom instruction and personal reflection.

   Major Supporting Detail: Sentence 2, 3, or 4. (Answers will vary.)

2. (1) You can do several things to help your child avoid being bitten by insects. (2) The best protection against insect bites is to apply an EPA[1]-approved insect repellent to a child's skin and clothing as directed. (3) However, insect repellents should be used sparingly on infants and young children. (4) Another prevention technique involves avoiding areas where insects nest or congregate,[2] such as garbage cans, stagnant[3] pools

1. **EPA:** Environmental Protection Agency
2. **congregate:** gather together
3. **stagnant:** not moving

* Hales, Diane. *An Invitation to Wellness: Making Healthy Choices*. Belmont: Thomson Higher Education, 2007. Print. Ch. 7, p. 140.

of water, and orchards and gardens where flowers bloom. (5) In addition, when you know your child will be exposed to insects, dress him in long pants and a lightweight long-sleeved shirt; avoid dressing your child in clothing with bright colors or flowery prints as they are known to attract insects.*

Main Idea: You can do several things to help your child avoid being bitten by insects.

Major Supporting Detail: Sentence 2, 4, or 5 (Answers will vary.)

3. (1) Laboratory studies show that certain ways of administering punishment to children are more effective than others. (2) One important factor is making sure the punishment closely follows the child's transgression[1] so that the child makes the connection between her wrongdoing and the consequences. (3) Another powerful factor is providing an explanation for why the behavior is not desirable. (4) The effectiveness of punishment also depends on the consistency with which it is applied. (5) If parents, for example, prohibit a behavior on one occasion and permit it on another, then children tend to become particularly disobedient and aggressive.†

Main Idea: Laboratory studies show that certain ways of administering punishment to children are more effective than others.

Major Supporting Detail: Sentence 2, 3, or 4. (Answers will vary.)

4. (1) Many parents overindulge kids for different reasons. (2) Guilt often has a lot to do with it. (3) Mothers and fathers of all income levels, caught up in a whirl of a busy world, often try to substitute presents for presence. (4) For example, a divorced dad may arrive bearing a Santa's load of presents. (5) As a working mom, I wouldn't dream of returning from a business trip without gifts for my 14-year-old daughter. (6) Also, parents may overindulge because giving in—whether to a toddler's pleas to stay up late yet again or a grade-schooler's demands for a hot new video game—is often easier than trying to just say no. (7) Furthermore, some parents, remembering their own less bountiful childhoods, just don't want to deny their beloved offspring anything—from computers to riding lessons to pricey designer clothes.‡

1. **transgression:** violation of a law, rule, or duty

* Adapted from Kirsten Matthew, "Safety in Sun, Sand, and Summer Pursuits!" *Westchester Parent,* June 2001, 25.

† Adapted from Bukatko and Daehler, *Child Development,* 5th ed. Boston: Houghton Mifflin, 2004, 504. Copyright © 2004 by Houghton Mifflin Company. Reprinted with permission.

‡ Adapted from Dianne Hales, "Spoiled Rotten?" *Ladies' Home Journal,* May 2000, 114–16.

3

Main Idea: Many parents overindulge kids for different reasons.

Major Supporting Detail: Sentence 2, 3, 6, or 7. (Answers will vary.)

5. (1) Coping with stress takes two general forms: problem-focused coping and emotion-focused coping. (2) Problem-focused coping is a coping style that involves behaviors or actions targeted toward solving or handling the stress-inducing problem itself. (3) One example might be compromising with a coworker with whom one is experiencing conflict. (4) Emotion-focused coping, on the other hand, involves cognitive or thought-related strategies that minimize the emotional effects of stress-inducing events. (5) Examples of emotion-focused coping include rationalizing[1] or intellectualizing,[2] looking for the "silver lining," and making the best of a bad situation.*

Main Idea: The two general forms of coping with stress are problem-focused coping and emotion-focused coping.

Major Supporting Detail: Sentence 2 or 4. (Answers will vary.)

Major and Minor Details—Supporting Details

Supporting details *are the specific facts, statistics, examples, steps, anecdotes, reasons, descriptions, definitions, and so on that explain or prove the general main idea stated in the topic sentence*. They support, or provide a solid foundation for, this main idea.

Supporting details should answer some or all of the questions raised by the topic sentence. For example, read the following statement: **Children are especially vulnerable to dog bites.** This topic sentence immediately raises the question *"why?"* in the reader's mind. To answer the question, the paragraph must go on to offer the reasons and other explanations that prove this point.

As you read this next paragraph, notice how the supporting details clarify the main idea, which is underlined, and explain why it's true:

> Today's American society believes a number of myths that perpetuate absentee fathers. One misconception is that raising children

1. **rationalizing:** devising self-satisfying but incorrect reasons for one's behavior
2. **intellectualizing:** avoiding psychological insight into an emotional problem through intellectual (rational) analysis

* Adapted from Paul E. Levy, *Industrial/Organizational Psychology.* Boston: Houghton Mifflin, 2003, 319. Copyright © 2003 by Houghton Mifflin Company. Reprinted with permission.

is women's work. Many people believe that it's not masculine to care for kids. Another misconception is that small children do not really need a father's influence. Many dads believe they can cultivate a relationship with their kids when they're older, but by then, the kids will resent their father's lack of involvement. A similar myth says that girls don't need fathers. Research shows, though, that girls with active dads are more successful and well adjusted. A final misconception is fathers can make up for being gone with short periods of "quality time." This is a myth, though, because kids need dads who help them cope with life on a daily basis, not just take them to an amusement park every now and then.*

The topic sentence of this paragraph raises the question *What are these myths?* Then, the paragraph goes on to answer that question by describing four common misconceptions about absentee fathers. The reader cannot understand the topic sentence without reading the details in the rest of the paragraph. It is important to learn to recognize supporting details because they determine your level of understanding and interpretation.

There are two kinds of supporting details: major details and minor details. **Major details** *are the main points that explain or support the idea in the topic sentence.* They offer *essential* reasons or other information that the reader must have in order to understand the main idea.

Minor details *offer more explanation of the major details.* Minor details are not usually critical to the reader's comprehension of the main idea, although they do offer more specific information that helps clarify the points in the paragraph.

To see the difference between major and minor details, read the following paragraph:

Many people hold a superstitious fear of certain numbers. One especially ominous[1] number is 13. Some people, for example, do not like being on the thirteenth floor of a building, and some are apprehensive about Friday the thirteenth. Another troubling number is 666. Because the Bible associates 666 with Satan, for instance, residents of Colorado and New Mexico have tried to change the name of U.S. Highway 666 to something else.†

The topic sentence of this paragraph, which is underlined, raises the question *What are these certain numbers people fear?* The second and fourth sentences of the paragraph are major details that answer that question. They tell the

1. **ominous:** menacing, threatening

* Adapted from Ron Klinger, "What Can Be Done About Absentee Fathers?" *USA Today*, July 1998, 30.
† Adapted from Gerald F. Kreyche, "Playing the Numbers Game," *USA Today*, July 1998, 98.

reader that the numbers 13 and 666 are the ones that trouble people. The other sentences in the paragraph offer minor details that give examples of ways people demonstrate their fear of these two numbers. Therefore, they offer nonessential information that helps further explain the main idea.

Do you remember the explanation of general and specific sentences in Chapter 2? You learned that the topic sentence is the most general statement in a paragraph, whereas the other sentences offer more specific information. Well, these other sentences (the supporting details) are also related to each other in general and specific ways. It might be helpful to visualize these relationships in a diagram form:

Many people hold a superstitious fear of certain numbers.

One especially ominous number is 13.	Another troubling number is 666.
Some people, for example, do not like being on the thirteenth floor of a building, and some are apprehensive about Friday the thirteenth.	Because the Bible associates 666 with Satan, for instance, residents of Colorado and New Mexico have tried to change the name of U.S. Highway 666 to something else.

This diagram offers a useful visual image of the general and specific relationships among sentences in paragraphs. The major details—represented in the blocks beneath the topic sentence—provide the solid foundation of support for the main idea. You could not remove any of these blocks without significantly weakening the base on which the main idea rests. The minor details in the next row of blocks make the structure even sturdier. Though the main idea would still be supported by the major details even if the minor details were removed, the minor details make the whole base even stronger.

To better understand what you read, you may want to try to visualize the sentences in a diagram like the previous one. Sorting out these relationships is critical not only to comprehending a paragraph but also to deciding whether you can agree with the author's ideas.

Exercise 3.1

Read the following paragraphs, and then label each of the sentences in the list as MI for main idea, MAJOR for major detail, or MINOR for minor detail.

1. **(1)** People seek out frightening situations like scary movies and haunted houses for different reasons. **(2)** One reason is curiosity and a desire to learn to control their emotional reactions. **(3)** When you move through a Halloween haunted house, for example, you know the threat isn't real,

so you can practice feeling and managing your fear. (4) A second reason people seek out scary situations is to experience the opposite reaction that follows an experience of intense emotion. (5) After seeing a scary movie, many people feel more calm and peaceful.*

MI Sentence 1

MINOR Sentence 3

MAJOR Sentence 4

2. (1) Weathering plays a vital role in our daily lives, with both positive and negative outcomes. (2) It frees life-sustaining minerals and elements from solid rock, allowing them to become incorporated into our soils and eventually into our foods. (3) Indeed, we would have very little food without weathering, as this process produces the very soil in which much of our food is grown. (4) But weathering can also wreak havoc[1] on the structures we build. (5) Countless monuments, from the pyramids of Egypt to ordinary tombstones, have suffered drastic deterioration from freezing water, hot sunshine, and other climatic forces.†

MI Sentence 1

MAJOR Sentence 4

MINOR Sentence 5

3. (1) If you want your kids to learn to like Brussels sprouts and other vegetables, you can use three strategies. (2) First, don't promise them a cupcake if they eat their Brussels sprouts. (3) This sends the message that vegetables are work and sugar is fun. (4) Second, you can actually mix the two. (5) One doctor recommends mixing a tablespoon of sugar in half a cup of water and pouring it over broccoli or another vegetable to sweeten it slightly without altering its taste. (6) Third, serve the Brussels sprouts at least 10 times. (7) Food preferences are learned; after people eat a repellent[2] food 10 times, the taste receptors in their brains actually change, and they will learn to like the food.

MI Sentence 1

MAJOR Sentence 2

MAJOR Sentence 6

1. **wreak havoc:** cause destruction
2. **repellent:** distasteful, disgusting

* Adapted from "Everybody Loves a Halloween Scare," *USA Today,* September 1998, 8.

† From Chernicoff and Fox, *Essentials of Geology,* 2nd ed. Boston: Houghton Mifflin, 2000, 85.

3

4. (1) Weather and climate play a major role in our lives. (2) Weather, for example, often dictates the type of clothing we wear, whereas climate influences the type of clothing we buy. (3) Climate determines when to plant crops as well as what type of crops can be planted. (4) Weather determines if these same crops will grow to maturity. (5) Although weather and climate affect our lives in many ways, perhaps their most immediate effect is on our comfort. (6) In order to survive the cold of winter and heat of summer, we build homes, heat them, air condition them, insulate them—only to find that when we leave our shelter, we are at the mercy of the weather elements.*

MI Sentence 1

MAJOR Sentence 2

MAJOR Sentence 4

MAJOR Sentence 5

5. (1) Scientists still have not determined what lack of sleep has to do with putting on weight. (2) Some cite inflammation reactions. (3) The less you sleep, the stronger the trigger for inflammation. (4) Others contend that those who sleep less have other unhealthy lifestyle habits, which may be partly responsible for their weight gain. (5) Yet other experts focus on the activation of the hormones *leptin* and *ghrelin* in response to lack of sleep. (6) These hormones can affect appetite and, as a result, increase the amount of food you consume.†

MAJOR Sentence 2

MAJOR Sentence 3

MAJOR Sentence 4

Exercise 3.2

Read each paragraph and write an abbreviated form of each sentence in the boxes to indicate their general and specific relationships.

1. Studies show that America's children do not get enough physical activity, but we can change that. One way to improve kids' fitness level is to require daily physical education in schools. Studies show that children

* Ahrens, C., Donald and Perry Samson. *Extreme Weather and Climate*. Belmont: Brooks/Cole, 2011. Print. Ch. 1, p. 25.

† http://www.parade.com/health/your-healthy-home/articles/the-healing-power-of-sleep.html. Web. 9/29/2010. Here's the additional info: Dr. Ranit Mishori, The Healing Power of Sleep.

who participate in daily PE classes have better cardiovascular endurance than kids who participate in weekly PE classes. A second way to improve fitness levels is to offer active after-school programs. Kids who engage in games such as tag, scavenger hunts, and obstacle courses get more exercise in target heart rate zones, which improves their overall health.*

Studies show that America's ...

One way to improve ...	A second way to improve fitness levels ...
Studies show that children ...	Kids who engage in games ...

2. The need for reforesting is fairly clear. The old trees are dying, victims of age and drought[1] conditions in recent years. More than 70 of the oldest trees that surround George Washington's home in Mount Vernon have died over the past century, and only 13 of the trees planted under Washington's direction are left. Also, deer keep eating new trees as soon as they break through the ground. According to Dean Norton, who supervises planting at Mount Vernon, these animals are preventing anything new from growing.†

The need for reforesting ...

The old trees are dying ...	Also, deer keep eating new trees ...
More than seventy of the oldest trees ...	According to Dean Norton ...

1. **drought:** long period of low rainfall

* Adapted from Arlene Ignico, "Children's Sedentary Lifestyle: A Forerunner of Unhealthy Adulthood," *USA Today,* May 1998, 59.

† Adapted from Dan Vergano, "Mount Vernon Clones History," *USA Today,* June 20, 2001, 7D.

3. If you set out to write an ideal story for a baseball player, you couldn't do better than Cal Ripken, Jr.'s. The son of a father-teacher hones his craft in the family business, gets drafted by the hometown team—the one he has loved as far back as memory goes—and stays for two storybook seasons. Then, he wins one World Series, two Most Valuable Player awards, and the admiration of millions. And, he breaks Lou Gehrig's consecutive-game streak of 2,632 games played.*

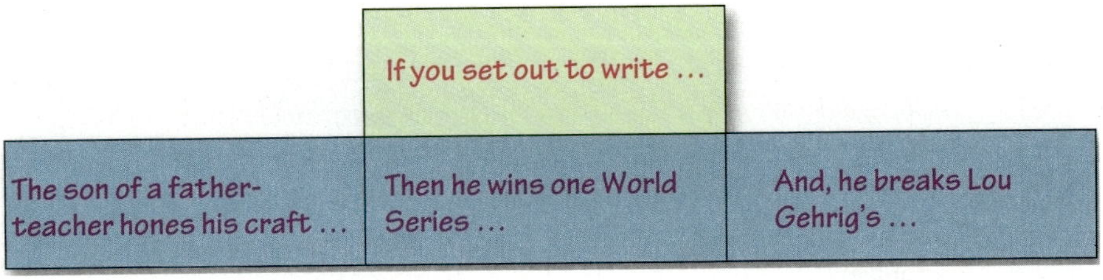

3

4. Although our culture associates napping with laziness, brief naps can be good for you. A 10- to 15-minute nap every day makes you more productive during the day. As one devoted napper says, "Fatigue and safety are the antithesis[1] of each other and when you're fatigued, you're not working at your best, and you're probably grumpy; that makes a bad work environment." Researchers also find that napping cuts down on stress on the job. For example, people who nap during the workday report feeling more relaxed while they work, call in sick less than their non-napping counterparts,[2] and enjoy their workday more.†

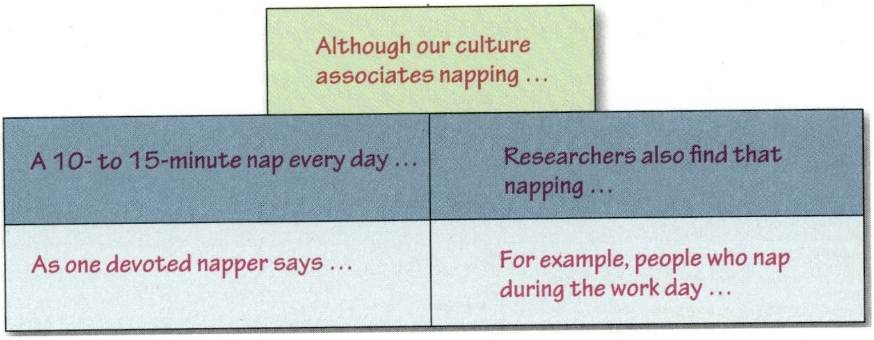

1. **antithesis:** exact opposite
2. **counterparts:** those with the same function and characteristics

* Adapted from Erik Brady, "Ironman Age Ending," *USA Today,* June 20, 2001, 1C.

† Adapted from Michael Precker, "Bosses Awaken to the Benefits of Naptime," *The Journal News,* June 25, 2001, 1D.

5. If you commute to college, it may be less convenient for you to become involved in activities and events than it would be if you lived on or near campus, but there are ways for you to take a more active part in campus life. For one thing, many clubs and organizations on your campus would be happy to have you as a member. If you join one of these groups, you will meet people who share your interests, and you may learn even more about an activity you already enjoy. You could also drop by your student government office and introduce yourself. Someone there can tell you about the many activities and upcoming events in which you can take part. Forming a study group that meets on campus or scheduling some on-campus study time is another way to remain on campus and stay involved.*

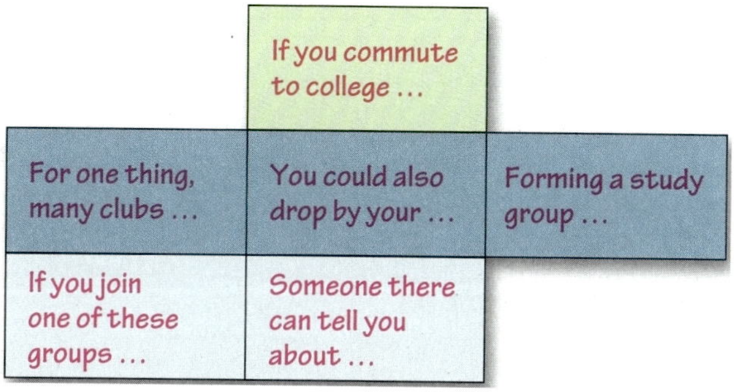

Mapping and Outlining

Earlier in this chapter, you saw how to visualize the relationships between sentences in a paragraph by inserting each one into a block. The main idea went into the block at the top, the major supporting details went into the row of blocks just beneath the main idea, and the minor details, if any, were in the third row.

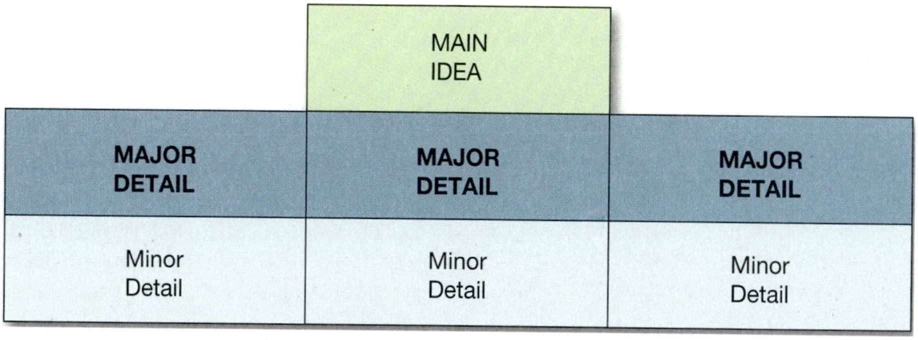

* Adapted from Kanar, *The Confident Student,* 5th ed. Boston: Houghton Mifflin, 2004, 24. Copyright © 2004 by Houghton Mifflin. Reprinted with permission.

This diagram is a form of **mapping**, *a technique that involves using lines, boxes, circles, or other shapes to show how sentences in a paragraph are related.*

In mapping, you lay out a visual to help you see the main idea, major supporting details, and minor supporting details. Here are some other ways to visualize these relationships:

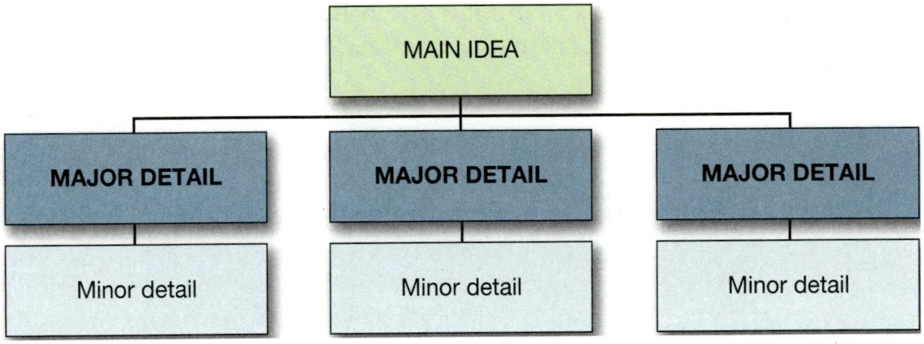

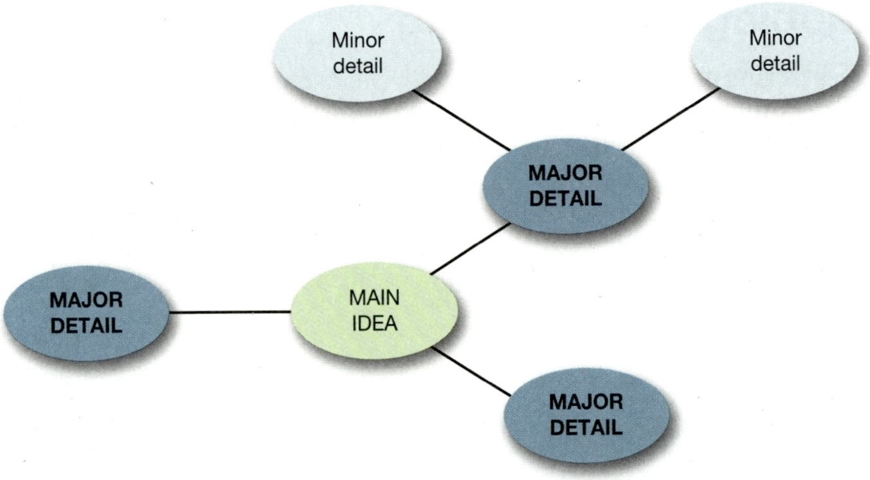

For example, using the diagram above, you might map the paragraph about absentee fathers on pages 100–101 as shown here.

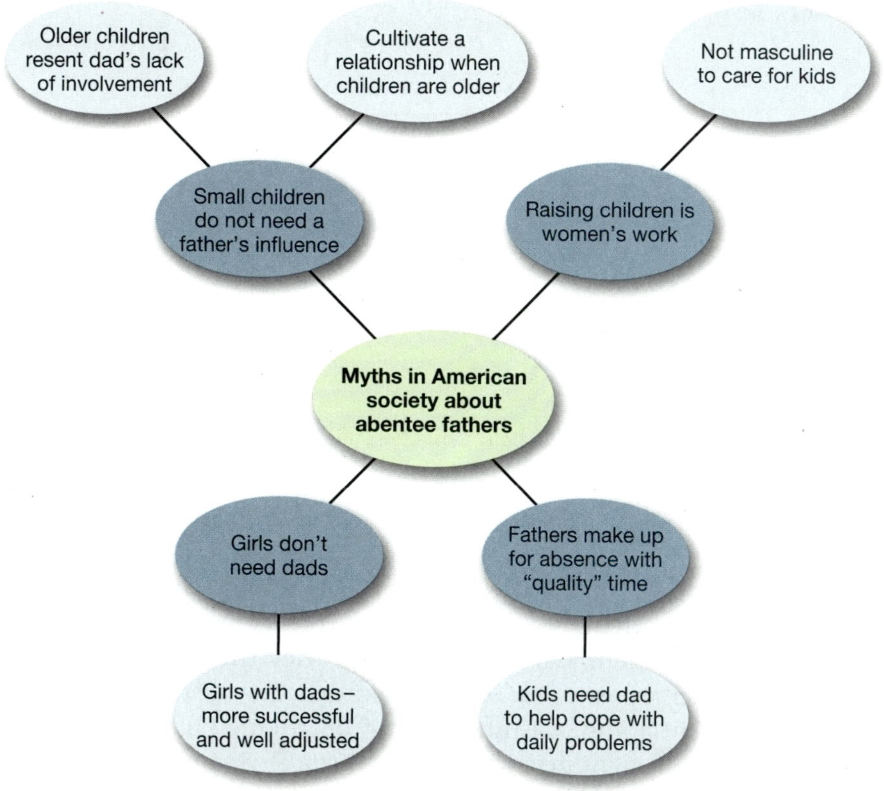

3

Exercise 3.3

Read each paragraph and fill in the map that follows with an abbreviated form of each sentence.

1. When family members talk to one another, there are often two meanings to what they say. The *message* is the meaning of the words and sentences spoken, what anyone with a dictionary and a grammar book could figure out. For example, a husband might ask his wife, "What's in this turkey stuffing?" The *metamessage* (the prefix *meta*- means, among other things, going beyond or higher) is meaning that is not stated: it's the way something is said, who is saying it, or the fact that it is said at all. The wife, for instance, may interpret her husband's question as critical if he has expressed disapproval of her cooking in the past.*

* From Deborah Tannen, "What's That Supposed to Mean?" *Reader's Digest*, July 2001, 103.

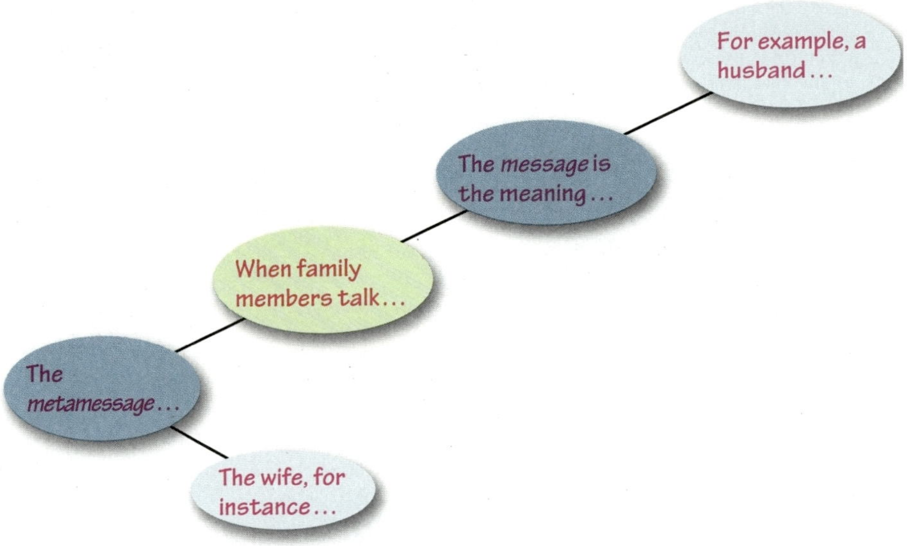

2. People cope with the distressing state of loneliness in different ways. When college students were asked about the behavioral strategies they use to combat loneliness, 93 percent said they tried extra hard to succeed at another aspect of life. Others said that they distracted themselves by running, shopping, washing the car, or staying busy at other activities. Still others sought new ways to meet people. Some talked to a friend, relative, or therapist about the problem. Though fewer in number, some are so desperate that they use alcohol or drugs to wash away feelings of loneliness.*

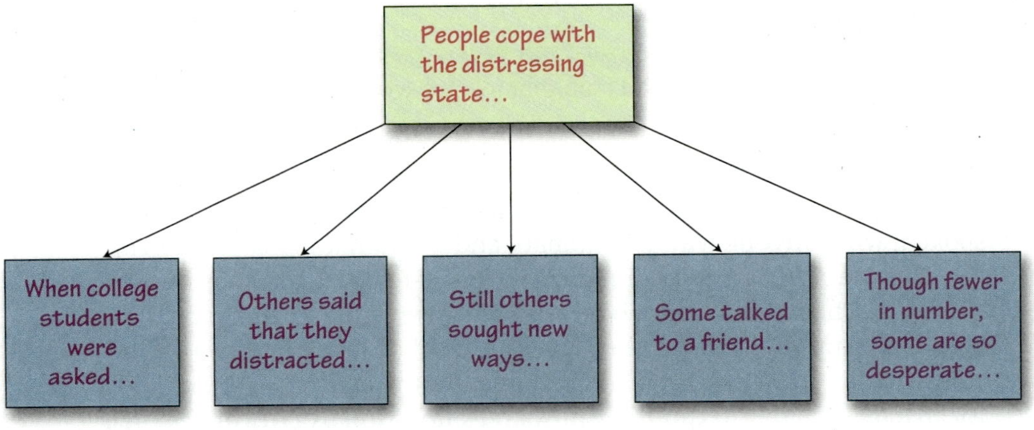

* Adapted from Brehm et al., *Social Psychology*, 5th ed. Boston: Houghton Mifflin, 2002, 305. Copyright © 2002 by Houghton Mifflin Company. Reprinted with permission.

3. Questions offer a variety of benefits. Questions open up inquiries that otherwise might never take place, waking people up and leading them to examine an issue that otherwise might go unexamined. For instance, if you want to take better notes, you can write, "What's missing for me in taking notes?" or "How can I gain more skill in taking notes?" Besides being helpful to you, questions can help you develop your relationship with a teacher. Teachers love questions because they reveal interest and curiosity. Questions are also great ways to improve relationships with friends and coworkers. When you ask a question, you bring a huge gift to people—an invitation for them to speak their brilliance and an offer to listen to their answers.*

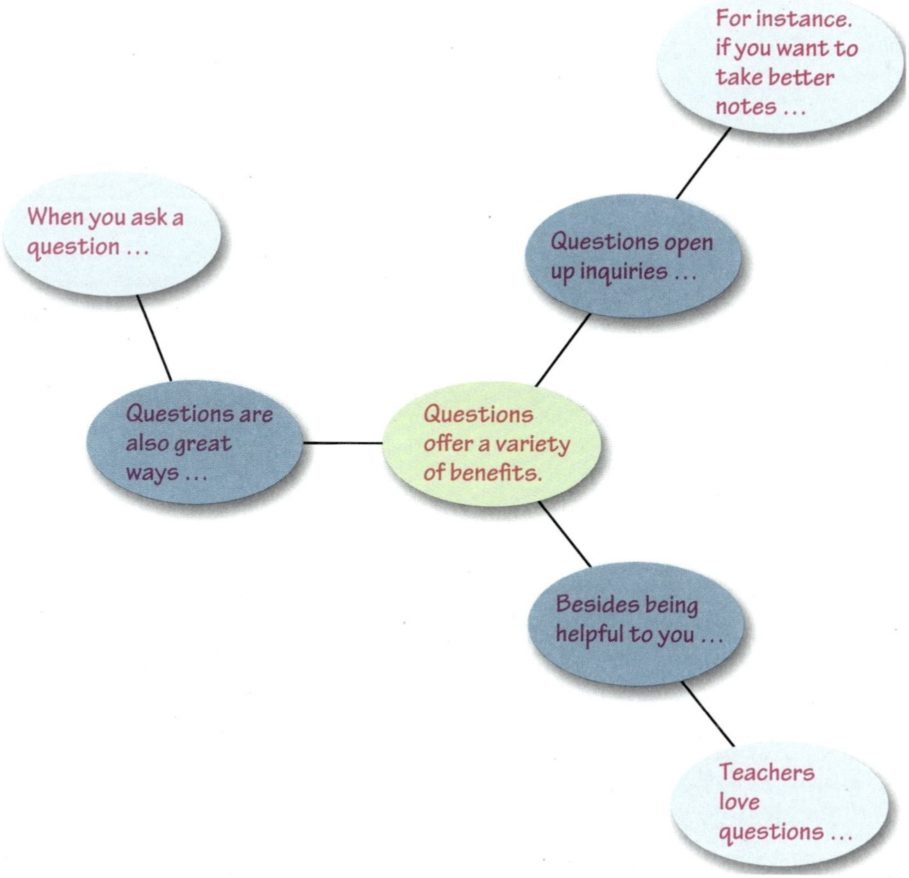

* Adapted from Dave Ellis, *Becoming a Master Student*, 9th ed. Boston: Houghton Mifflin, 2000, 230.

3

4. The best way to help kids get into a good saving habit is to create a scenario in which it becomes stupid not to save. You can do this by creating a "mini-matched savings plan," in which a parent agrees to match dollar for dollar the child's savings, with the stipulation[1] that the money cannot be withdrawn until some point in the future without a substantial penalty. Even though they don't get to spend the money right away, kids love the idea because they are getting the immediate gratification[2] of more money now. Another plan would be to open up a passbook savings account where a child opens a savings account and is given a passbook that records each deposit and withdrawal you or your child makes to the account. This is a good way for children to see money grow in their account or, conversely, disappear if they take money out to buy a treat or a special thing they might want.*

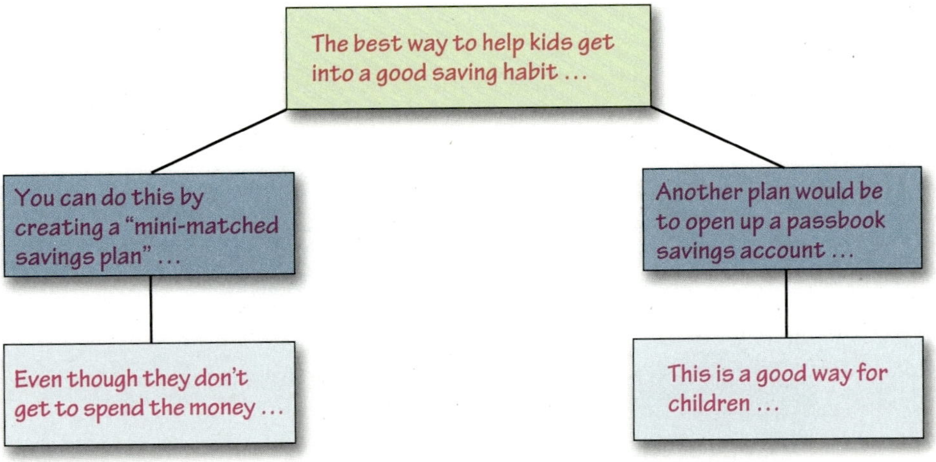

5. If you can learn to predict change where your job or your corporation is concerned, you'll be in a much stronger position when it hits. To stay current, join professional organizations, read business journals, and attend every convention or conference you can. Within your company, it's never been more important to make friends, and not just with the high and mighty. Assistants often know things other people would like to know

1. **stipulation:** condition, requirement
2. **gratification:** satisfaction of a desire

* Adapted from Cynthia Davies, "Raising Money-Savvy Kids," *Westchester Family*, July 2001, 35. Used by permission of the author.

and can tip you off on new software programs or even new personnel. Also, start reading job postings to get a sense of the skills your front office considers most desirable these days. Check out key websites, too. Look at your employer's site to see what kinds of new directions and strategies are being announced, and also examine the websites posted by your company's competition.*

Another good way to identify the main idea and supporting details is to create an outline. *An* **outline** *is a list of these details labeled with a system of numbers and letters that show their relationships to one another.* Outlines often use the Roman numeral system, which effectively identifies the main idea and different topics or details. Outlines can be in sentence form or in topic form.

* Adapted from Anne Field, "How to Handle Change at the Office," *Good Housekeeping*, May 2000, 94.

The latter is useful for creating a brief summary that allows you, at a glance, to see the general and specific relationships.

I. Main Idea

   A. Major detail
      1. Minor detail
      2. Minor detail

   B. Major detail
      1. Minor detail
      2. Minor detail

For example, you could outline the paragraph about absentee fathers on pages 100–101, as follows:

I. Myths in American society about absentee fathers

   A. Raising children is women's work
      1. Not masculine to care for kids

   B. Small children do not need a father's influence
      1. Cultivate a relationship when children are older
      2. Older children resent dad's lack of involvement

   C. Girls don't need dads
      1. Girls with active dads—more successful and well adjusted

   D. Fathers make up for absence with "quality time"
      1. Kids need dad to cope with daily problems

To create an outline, line up the major details along one margin and label them with capital letters. Beneath each major detail, indent minor details with numbers: 1, 2, 3, and so forth.

Exercise 3.4

Complete the outline that follows each paragraph.

1. For more than 50 years, Congress has been periodically holding hearings on television violence and its possible effects on children. During that time, Congress passed no legislation regulating content, but it did pressure the television networks to adopt some changes. In 1975, the TV industry tried a self- regulatory policy called the "family hour" where programmers pushed violence and other material regarded as being harmful to children later into the evening, leaving the first hour of primetime solely for content appropriate for so-called *family viewing*. However, several stations filed suit, citing infringement of free speech, and won their suit in court.

Then the omnibus[1] Telecommunication Act of 1996 included an amendment mandating that all TV receivers sold in the United States after 1999 should have a V-chip, which is a screening device that allows TV owners to program their sets to avoid programs with certain ratings for violence, sex, and language.*

I. Congressional hearings on the effects of television violence on children

A. Pressure networks to adopt changes

B. Adoption of the "family hour"

C. Lawsuit over freedom of speech

D. Telecommunications Act of 1996 mandating V-chips in all televisions

2. Wikipedia's greatest challenge early on was generating interest among the general public to volunteer to create articles for the encyclopedia without being paid. It met this challenge and by 2008 had generated close to 2.3 million articles and was growing by about 600,000 articles each year in the English edition. Now its challenge is to check the article writing and editing for accuracy. Also, there is a continuing challenge to ensure that people with certain political or religious orientations do not distort entries for their own purposes. For example, in 2006, Wikipedians noticed that unmet campaign promises of Congress people were being deleted from articles on those Congress people. It was discovered that these deletions were coming from web addresses of congressional aides for those Congress people. Also, it was found that the Justice Department was removing references to certain groups they felt were involved in terrorist activities. And they noticed that supporters of the Church of Scientology were entering a pro-Scientology viewpoint while critics were editing that out in favor of a critical viewpoint. In all of these (and many more instances), Wikipedia had to lock out those people from the editing function.†

I. Wikipedia's challenges

A. Creating public interest to create articles without payment

B. Checking the article writing and editing for accuracy

C. Ensuring that people with certain political or religious orientations do not distort entries for their own purposes

1. **omnibus:** including or covering many things

* Potter, W. James. *Media Literacy,* 5th ed. Thousand Oaks: SAGE Publications, Inc., 2011. Print. Ch. 5, p. 65.

† Potter, W. James. *Media Literacy,* 5th ed. Thousand Oaks: SAGE Publications, Inc., 2011. Print. Ch. 13, p. 214.

1. Unmet campaign promises of Congress people were being deleted from articles on those Congress people.

2. The Justice Department was removing references to certain groups they felt were involved in terrorist activities.

3. Supporters of the Church of Scientology were entering a pro-Scientology viewpoint while critics were editing that out in favor of a critical viewpoint.

3. Small physical and behavioral differences between the sexes appear early on and tend to increase over the years. For example, girls suffer less often than boys from speech, learning, and behavior disorders; mental retardation; emotional problems; and sleep disorders. They tend to speak and write earlier and to be better at grammar and spelling. They nurture others more than boys do and show more emotional empathy. Their play tends to be more orderly. At the same time, boys tend to be more skilled than girls at manipulating objects, constructing three-dimensional forms, and mentally manipulating complex figures and pictures. They are more physically active and aggressive and more inclined to hit obstacles or people. They play in larger groups and spaces and enjoy noisier, more strenuous physical games.*

I. Physical and behavioral differences between the sexes

A. Girls

1. Suffer less than boys from speech, learning, and behavior disorders; mental retardation; emotional problems; and sleep disorders

2. Tend to speak and write earlier and be better at grammar and spelling

3. Nurture others more than boys do and show more empathy

4. More orderly play

B. Boys

1. More skilled than girls at manipulating objects, constructing three-dimensional forms, and mentally manipulating complex figures and pictures

* Adapted from Bernstein and Nash, *Essentials of Psychology*, 2nd ed. Boston: Houghton Mifflin, 2002, 327–28. Copyright © 2002 by Houghton Mifflin Company. Reprinted with permission.

2. More physically active and aggressive and more inclined to hit obstacles or people

3. Play in larger groups and spaces and enjoy noisier, more strenuous physical games

4. Bed-and-breakfasts are flourishing for several reasons. Business travelers are growing weary of the complexity of check-ins and check-outs at some commercial hotels. Also, many leisure-time travelers are looking for lodging on a scale somewhere between that of a large, formal hotel and the private home of a friend or family member. Bed-and-breakfasts offer a friendly, homelike atmosphere. Many guests say that arriving at a B & B at the end of the day is like returning home after a hard day's work. Community breakfasts with hosts and other guests seem to enhance that feeling, as do shared bath-rooms (although these are rapidly disappearing). Each B & B is as distinctive as its owner. People might be attracted to a carefully preserved antebellum home in the deep South, a restored Victorian home in the Northeast, or an old seaside cottage restored to perfection.*

I. Reasons for the success of bed-and-breakfasts

A. Complex check-in and -out for business travelers at commercial hotels

B. Between large hotel and private home in size for leisure travelers

C. Offer friendly homelike atmosphere

1. Like returning home after a hard day's work

2. Community breakfasts

3. Shared baths

D. Distinctive as their owners

1. Antebellum home in the deep South

2. Restored Victorian home in the Northeast

3. Restored seaside cottage

5. There are three types of marriages. The first type has been characterized as an *equal-partner relationship*. In this kind of marriage, everything (who works, who cooks, who pays the bills) is open to negotiation. Instead of a preset assignment of roles and responsibilities, both partners expect change as they and their relationship grow and develop. A second type

* Chon, Kay (Kye-Sung) and Thomas A. Maier, *Welcome to Hospitality: An Introduction,* 3rd ed. Clifton Park: Delmar. 2010. Print. Ch. 10, p. 341.

3

of marriage is the *conventional relationship*, in which the man is the head of the household and the sole economic provider and the woman is the mother and the homemaker, responsible for all domestic tasks. A third type of relationship, the *junior-partner relationship*, has elements of both equal partnerships and conventional relationships. The junior partner, typically the wife, brings in some of the income and takes on some decision-making responsibilities. The senior partner, usually the husband, often *helps* the wife at home, but he does not share family responsibilities such as cooking and child care.*

I. Three types of marriages
   A. Equal-partner relationship
      1. Everything is open to negotiation
      2. No preset roles and responsibilities
   B. Conventional marriage
      1. Man is head of household and sole economic provider
      2. Woman is mother and homemaker
   C. Junior-partner relationship
      1. Junior partner brings in some of income and takes on some decision making
      2. Senior partner often helps at home but doesn't share family responsibilities

Reading Strategy: Reading and Time Management

How often should you read? How long should you try to read in one sitting? How many times should you read a chapter? Is it better to read the whole chapter at once or just a section at a time?

No right or wrong answers exist to these questions. The most effective length, amount, and frequency of reading time will differ from student to student and from class to class. You will have to experiment to discover what works best for you, and you will probably need to make adjustments for each different course you take.

* Adapted from Seifert et al., *Lifespan Development*, 2nd ed. Boston: Houghton Mifflin, 2000, 480–81. Copyright © 2000 by Houghton Mifflin Company. Reprinted with permission.

However, be aware of the following general principles of effective time management:

- Schedule time to read. Don't just try to fit reading in whenever you can; actually make an appointment to read by blocking out regular times on your calendar. Try to schedule time for multiple readings of the same chapter.
- The best time to read is the time of day or night when you are most mentally alert. If you're a night owl, read at night. If you're a morning person, try to fit in your reading time at the beginning of your day.
- Take frequent breaks during reading sessions. Regularly stand up and stretch, walk around, and rest your eyes for a few minutes.
- Keep up with the reading assignments in a course by following the schedule provided by your instructor. Following the schedule will give you the basic understanding of the material you'll need in order to get the most out of class lectures, discussions, and activities.
- Repeated exposure to information helps increase your retention of the material. If you hurriedly read large chunks of information all at once just before a test, you probably won't remember much of it. If you digest information slowly and regularly over a longer period of time, you'll remember more.

Answer the following questions on a separate sheet of paper, or use your computer.

1. Describe the typical length, amount, and frequency of reading time that seems to work best for you.
   Answers will vary.
2. Describe a time when you took a class that required you to alter significantly the length, amount, and/or frequency of your reading.
   Answers will vary.
3. At what time of day are you most mentally alert? Is that the time of day when you usually read?
   Answers will vary.
4. Which of the guidelines listed above do you already practice?
   Answers will vary.

5. Which of the guidelines above do you think you should implement in order to get more out of your reading?
Answers will vary.

Use the following interactive websites to help you determine what is most important for you to do every day and to help you schedule your time so you can accomplish everything you would need to do.

WEB LINK

http://www.studygs.net/stressb.htm
http://www.studygs.net/schedule/index.htm
http://www.studygs.net/schedule/weekly.html

Reading Selections

Practicing the Active Reading Strategy

Before and While You Read

You can use active reading strategies before, while, and after you read a selection. The following are some suggestions for active reading strategies that you can employ before you read and as you are reading.

1. Skim the selection for any unfamiliar words. Circle or highlight any words you do not know.
2. As you read, underline, highlight, or circle important words or phrases.
3. Write down any questions about the selection if you are confused by the information presented.
4. Jot notes in the margin to help you understand the material.

BIOGRAPHY: The Navajo Code Talkers

It is a great American story that is still largely unknown—the story of a group of young Navajo men who answered the call of duty, who performed a service no one else could, and in the process became great warriors and patriots. Their unbreakable code saved thousands of lives and helped end WWII.

1 During the early months of WWII, Japanese intelligence experts broke every code the U.S. forces devised. They were able to anticipate American actions at an alarming rate. With plenty of fluent English speakers at their disposal, they sabotaged messages and issued false commands to ambush Allied troops. To combat this, increasingly complex codes were initiated. At Guadalcanal, military leaders finally complained that sending and receiving these codes required hours of encryption[1] and decryption[2]—up to two and a half hours for a single message. They rightly argued the military needed a better way to communicate.

2 When Phillip Johnston, a civilian living in California learned of the crisis, he had the answer. As the son of a Protestant missionary, Johnston had grown up on the Navajo reservation and was 1 of less than 30 outsiders fluent in their difficult language. He realized that since it had no alphabet and was almost impossible to master without early exposure, the Navajo language had great commanders, he was given permission to begin a Navajo Code Talker test program.

3 Their elite unit was formed in early 1942 when the first 29 Navajo Code Talkers were recruited by Johnston. Although the code was modified and expanded throughout the war, this first group was the one to conceive it. Accordingly, they are often referred to reverently as the "original 29." Many of these enlistees were just boys; most had never been away from home before. Often lacking birth certificates, it was impossible to verify ages. After the war it was discovered that recruits as young as 15 and as old as 35 had enlisted. Age notwithstanding, they easily bore the rigors of basic training, thanks to their upbringing in the southwestern desert.

4 The code they created at Camp Pendleton was as ingenious as it was effective. It originated as approximately 200 terms—growing to over 600 by war's end—and could communicate in 20 seconds what took coding machines of the time 30 minutes to do. It consisted of native terms that were associated with the respective military terms they resembled. For example, the Navajo word for turtle meant "tank," and a dive-bomber was a "chicken hawk." To supplement those terms, words could be spelled out using Navajo terms assigned to individual letters of the alphabet—the selection of the Navajo term being based on the first letter of the Navajo word's English meaning. For instance, "Wo-La-Chee" means "ant," and would represent the letter A. In this way the Navajo Code Talkers could quickly and concisely communicate with each other in a manner even uninitiated Navajos could not understand.

5 Once trained, the Navajo Code Talkers were sent to Marine divisions in the Pacific theater of WWII. Despite some initial skepticism by commanding officers, they quickly gained a distinguished reputation for their remarkable

1. **encryption:** process of changing information into code
2. **decryption:** process of changing code to plain text

abilities. In the field, they were not allowed to write any part of the code down as a reference. They became living codes, and even under harried battle conditions, had to rapidly recall every word with utmost precision or risk hundreds or thousands of lives. In the battle for Iwo Jima, in the first 48 hours alone, they coded over 800 transmissions with perfect accuracy. Their heroism is widely acknowledged as the lynchpin of victory in the pivotal conflict.

6 After the war, the Navajo Code Talkers returned home as heroes but without a heroes' welcome. Their code had been so successful, it was considered a military secret too important to divulge. They remained silent heroes until more than two decades later. Even after declassification of the code in 1968, it took many years before any official recognition was given. In 2001, nearly 60 years after they created their legendary code, the Navajo Code Talkers finally received well-deserved Congressional Medals of Honor.

7 Now, in their 80s and 90s, only a few of these silent heroes remain. Many of their stories have yet to be documented for posterity. At the Navajo Code Talker Association, work is being done to create a lasting record of the Navajo Code Talker legacy.*

■ Vocabulary

Read the following questions about some of the vocabulary words that appear in the previous selection. Before you look up the word, try to use the context of the passage to figure out the meaning. Then circle the letter of the correct answer for each question.

1. In paragraph 1 ". . . they [the Japanese] *sabotaged* messages." What were the Japanese doing?

   a. writing
   b. destroying
   c. ignoring
   d. sending

2. In paragraph 3, what does *conceive* mean?

   a. create
   b. understand
   c. teach
   d. remember

3. The code is described in paragraph 4 as *ingenious*. What does that mean?

   a. difficult
   b. long
   c. clever
   d. easy

4. What does *harried* mean, as used in paragraph 5?

   a. noisy
   b. rushed
   c. confusing
   d. frightening

*Source: http://navajocodetalkers.org/code_talker_story/. Web. 10/23/2010

5. What is a *lynchpin*? (paragraph 5)

   a. most important element   c. of no importance
   b. a supporting role   d. forgotten about

Reading Skills

Respond to each of the following questions by circling the letter of the correct answer or by writing your answer on the blank provided.

1. What is the topic of paragraph 1? Difficulty of creating an unbreakable code
2. Write the topic sentence for paragraph 4. The code they created at Camp Pendleton was as ingenious as it was effective.
3. Two minor detail sentences are in paragraph 4. Which sentences are they?

   a. 1 and 7   c. 2 and 5
   b. 4 and 6   d. 3 and 7
4. In paragraph 5, major details are contained in which of the following sentences?

   a. 3 and 4   c. 4 and 6
   b. 1 and 2   d. 2 and 6
5. What is the main idea of paragraph 6? After the war, the Navajo Code Talkers returned home as heroes but without a heroes' welcome.

3

Practicing the Active Reading Strategy

After You Read

Now that you have read the selection, answer the following questions, using the active reading strategies that you learned in Chapter 1.

1. Identify and write down the point and purpose of this reading selection.
2. Did you circle or highlight any words that are unfamiliar to you? Can you figure out the meaning from the context of the passage? If not, then look up each word in a dictionary and find the definition that best describes the word as it is used in the selection. You may want to write the definition in the margin next to the word in the passage for future reference.
3. Predict any possible questions that may be used on a test about the content of this selection.

■ Questions for Discussion and Writing

Respond to each of the following questions based on your reading of the selection.

1. Explain how the Navajo language played an important role in the battle for the Pacific in World War II.

   It consisted of native terms that were associated with the respective military they resembled. To supplement those terms, words could be spelled out using Navajo terms assigned to individual letters of the alphabet—the selection of the Navajo term being based on the first letter of the Navajo word's English meaning.

2. How did the Navajo men earn respect from commanding officers?

   They quickly gained a distinguished reputation for their remarkable abilities. They became living codes, and even under harried battle conditions, had to rapidly recall every word with utmost precision or risk hundreds or thousands of lives.

3. Why did honoring these heroes take so long? Their code had been so successful, it was considered a military secret too important to divulge.

Practicing the Active Reading Strategy

■ Before and While You Read

You can use active reading strategies before, while, and after you read a selection. The following are some suggestions for active reading strategies that you can perform before you read and while you read.

1. Skim the selection for any unfamiliar words. Circle or highlight any words you do not know.
2. As you read, underline, highlight, or circle important words or phrases.
3. Write down any questions about the selection if you are confused by the information presented.
4. Jot notes in the margin to help you understand the material.

TEXTBOOK READING: PSYCHOLOGY

Physical Attractiveness

What do you look for in a friend or romantic partner? Intelligence? Kindness? A sense of humor? How important, really, is a person's looks?

1 As children, we were told that "beauty is only skin deep" and that we should not "judge a book by its cover." Yet as adults, we react more favorably to others who are physically attractive than to those who are not. According to studies that inspired Nancy Etcoff's 1999 book *Survival of the Prettiest*, beauty is a major force in the affairs of our social world.

2 The bias for beauty is everywhere. In one study, fifth-grade teachers were given background information about a boy or girl, accompanied by a photograph. All teachers received identical information; however, those who saw an attractive child saw that child as being smarter and more likely to do well in school. In a second study, male and female experimenters approached students on a college campus and tried to get them to sign a petition. The more attractive the experimenters were, the more signatures they were able to get. In a third study, Texas judges set lower bail and gave lower fines to suspects who were rated as attractive rather than unattractive on the basis of photographs. In a fourth study conducted in the United States and Canada, economists discovered that physically attractive men and women earn more money than others whose only difference was being less attractive in their appearance.

3 It all seems so shallow, so superficial. But before we go on to accept the notion that people prefer others who are physically attractive, let's stop for a moment and consider a basic question. What constitutes physical beauty? Is it an objective and measurable human characteristic like height, weight, or hair color? Or is beauty a subjective quality, existing in the eye of the beholder? There are advocates on both sides.

4 Some researchers believe that certain faces are naturally more attractive than others. There are three sources of evidence for this conclusion. First, when people are asked to rate faces on a 10-point scale, there is typically a high level of agreement—among children and adults, men and women, and people from the same or different cultures. For example, Michael Cunningham and others asked Asian and Latino students, along with black and white American students, to rate the appearance of women from all these groups. Overall, the ratings were highly consistent. Investigators concluded that people everywhere share an image of what is beautiful. People also tend to agree about what makes for an attractive body. For example, men tend to be drawn to the "hourglass" figure seen in women of average weight whose waists are narrower than their hips.

3

3

This shape is thought to be associated with reproductive fertility. In contrast, women like men with waist and hips that form a tapering V-shape. If marriage statistics are any indication, women also prefer height. Comparisons made in Europe indicate that married men are a full inch taller, on average, than unmarried men.

5 Second, some researchers have identified physical features of the human face that are linked to judgments of attractiveness. For example, women who are seen as attractive tend to have large eyes, prominent cheekbones, a small nose, and a wide smile. Men are seen as attractive if they have a broad jaw. Even more interesting, perhaps, are studies showing that people like faces in which the eyes, nose, lips, and other features are not too different from the average. Judith Langlois and Lori Roggman showed college students both actual yearbook photos and computerized photos blending the "averaged" features from 4, 8, 16, or 32 of the photos. Time and again, they found that the students preferred the blended photographs to the individual faces. They also found that the more faces used to form the blend, the more highly it was rated. Other studies have since confirmed this result.

6 It seems odd that "average" faces are judged attractive when, after all, the faces we find the most beautiful are anything but average. What accounts for these findings? Langlois and others believe that people like average faces because they seem more familiar to us. Consistent with this idea, research shows that people are also attracted to average dogs, birds, and wristwatches. Other studies indicate that the computerized averaging technique produces faces that are also equal on both sides. It may be the balance that we find attractive. Why do people prefer faces in which the paired features on the right and left sides mirror each other? Some psychologists speculate that balance is naturally associated with health, fitness, and fertility. These qualities are highly desirable in a mate.

7 A third source of evidence for the view is that beauty is an objective quality. Babies, who are too young to have learned the culture's standards of beauty, show a preference for faces considered attractive by adults. Picture the scene in an infant laboratory. A baby, lying on its back in a crib, is shown a series of faces previously rated by college students. The first face appears and a clock starts ticking as the baby stares at it. As soon as the baby looks away, the clock stops and the next face is presented. The result: Young infants spend more time looking at attractive faces than at unattractive ones. It doesn't matter if the faces are young or old, male or female, or black or white. Other studies similarly reveal that infants look longer at faces that are "average" in their features. "These kids don't read *Vogue* or watch TV," notes Langlois, "yet they make the same judgments as adults."

8 In contrast to this objective perspective, other researchers argue that physical attractiveness is subjective. They point for evidence to the influences of culture, time, and the circumstances of our perception. One source of support for this view is that people

from different cultures increase their beauty in very different ways. They use face painting, makeup, plastic surgery, scarring, tattoos, hairstyling, the molding of bones, the filing of teeth, braces, and the piercing of ears and other body parts. All contribute to the "enigma of beauty." What people find attractive in one part of the world is often seen as disgusting in another part of the world.

9 Ideals also vary when it comes to bodies. Judith Anderson and others looked at preferences on female body size in 54 cultures. In places where food is often in short supply, heavy women are judged more attractive than slender women. In one study, for example, Douglas Yu and Glenn Shepard found that Matsigenka men living in the Andes Mountains of southeastern Peru see female forms with "tubular"[1] shapes (rather than hourglass shapes) as healthier, more attractive, and more desirable in a mate. Differences in preference have also been found among racial groups within a given culture. Michelle Hebl and Todd Heatherton asked black and white female college students from the United States to rate thin, average, and overweight women from a set of magazine photographs. The result: The white students saw the heavy women as the least attractive. The black students, however, did not agree. Why the difference? White Americans are, on average, thinner than black Americans. Therefore, one possible explanation is that they simply prefer a body type that is more typical of their group. Another possibility is that white Americans identify more with the "mainstream" weight-obsessed culture as portrayed in TV shows, magazine ads, and other media.

10 Standards of beauty also change over time, from one generation to the next. Brett Silverstein and others examined the measurements of female models appearing in women's magazines from 1901 to 1981. They found that "curviness" (as measured by the bust-to-waist ratio) varied over time, with a boyish, slender look becoming particularly desirable in recent years. Apparently, the ideal body for women has changed a great deal from the larger proportions preferred in the past to the slender, athletic form popular now. Ideas about facial attractiveness are also subject to change over time. Would the face that launched a thousand ships toward the Trojan War[2] get more than a passing glance today?

11 Still other evidence for the subjective nature of beauty comes from research laboratories. Time and again, social psychologists have found that our judgments of someone's beauty can be inflated or deflated[3] by various

1. **tubular:** shaped like a tube
2. **the face that launched . . . Trojan War:** a reference to Helen, the beautiful woman said to have caused the Trojan War in ancient Greece
3. **deflated:** reduced in size

3

3

circumstances. Research shows, for example, that people often see others as more physically attractive after they have grown to like them. In fact, the more in love people are with their partners, the less attracted they are to others of the opposite sex. On the other hand, men who viewed gorgeous nude models in *Playboy* and *Penthouse* magazines later gave lower attractiveness ratings to average-looking women, including their own wives. These lower ratings were the unfortunate results of a contrast effect. Even our self-evaluations change in this way. Research shows that people feel less attractive after viewing supermodel-like members of the same sex than after viewing less attractive persons. And they aren't happy about it. Douglas Kenrick and others found that exposure to highly attractive members of the opposite sex put people into a good mood. Exposure to attractive members of the same sex, though, had the opposite effect.*

■ Vocabulary

Read the following questions about some of the vocabulary words that appear in the previous selection. Circle the letter of the correct response.

1. What does the word *superficial* mean, as used in paragraph 3?
   - a. not pleasant
   - b. not deep
   - c. not understanding
   - d. not true
2. As used in paragraph 3, what does the word *subjective* mean? "Or is beauty a *subjective* quality, existing in the eye of the beholder?"
   - a. personal
   - b. subject to discussion
   - c. popular
   - d. close-minded
3. In paragraph 4, what does *tapering* mean?
   - a. pleasing
   - b. wide
   - c. upside down
   - d. gradually narrowing
4. In paragraph 5, what does *prominent* mean?
   - a. pink
   - b. low and long
   - c. sunken
   - d. immediately noticeable

* Adapted from Brehm et al., *Social Psychology*, 5th ed. Boston: Houghton Mifflin, 2002, 307–11. Copyright © 2002 by Houghton Mifflin Company. Reprinted with permission.

5. What is an *enigma* as used in paragraph 8: "All contribute to the '*enigma* of beauty'"?

   a. solution
   b. clue
   c. mystery
   d. story

Reading Skills

Answer the following questions by circling the letter of the correct answer.

1. What is the topic of paragraph 2?

   a. intelligence
   b. the bias for beauty
   c. fifth-grade teachers
   d. attractive college students

2. Which of the following sentences from paragraph 9 states the main idea of that paragraph?

   a. "Ideals also vary when it comes to bodies."
   b. "In places where food is often in short supply, heavy women are judged more attractive than slender women."
   c. "Therefore, one possible explanation is that [black Americans] simply prefer a body type that is more typical of their group."
   d. "Another possibility is that white Americans identify more with the 'mainstream' weight-obsessed culture as portrayed in TV shows, magazine ads, and other media."

3. Which of the following sentences from paragraph 2 does NOT state a major supporting detail?

   a. "In one study, fifth-grade teachers were given background information about a boy or girl, accompanied by a photograph."
   b. "All teachers received identical information; however, those who saw an attractive child saw that child as being smarter and more likely to do well in school."
   c. "In a second study, male and female experimenters approached students on a college campus and tried to get them to sign a petition."
   d. "In a fourth study conducted in the United States and Canada, economists discovered that physically attractive men and women earn more money than others whose only difference was being less attractive in their appearance."

4. Which of the following sentences from paragraph 9 states a minor supporting detail?

   a. "Ideals also vary when it comes to bodies."

   b. "In places where food is often in short supply, heavy women are judged more attractive than slender women."

   c. "In one study, for example, Douglas Yu and Glenn Shepard found that Matsigenka men living in the Andes Mountains of southeastern Peru see female forms with 'tubular' shapes (rather than hourglass shapes) as healthier, more attractive, and more desirable in a mate."

   d. "Differences in preference have also been found among racial groups within a given culture."

5. Which of the following sentences from paragraph 11 includes a transition that indicates a minor supporting detail?

   a. "Time and again, social psychologists have found that our judgments of someone's beauty can be inflated or deflated by various circumstances."

   b. "Research shows, for example, that people often see others as more physically attractive after they have grown to like them."

   c. "Research shows that people feel less attractive after viewing supermodel-like members of the same sex than after viewing less attractive persons."

   d. "Douglas Kenrick and others found that exposure to highly attractive members of the opposite sex put people into a good mood."

Practicing the Active Reading Strategy

■ After You Read

Now that you have read the selection, answer the following questions using the active reading strategies that are discussed in Chapter 1.

1. Identify and write down the point and purpose of this reading selection.
2. Did you circle or highlight any words that are unfamiliar to you? Can you figure out the meaning from the context of the passage? If not, then look up each word in a dictionary and find the definition that best describes the word as it is used in the selection. You may want to write the definition in the margin next to the word in the passage for future reference.
3. Predict any possible questions that may be used on a test about the content of this selection.

Questions for Discussion and Writing

Answer the following questions based on your reading of the selection. Write your answers on the blanks provided.

1. Respond to the two questions posed in the first paragraph: "What do you look for in a friend or romantic partner? How important, really, is a person's looks?"

   Answers will vary.

2. What do you think makes someone physically beautiful?

   Answers will vary.

3. Are standards of beauty different for different cultures? Give an example.

   Answers will vary.

Practicing the Active Reading Strategy

Before and While You Read

You can use active reading strategies before, while, and after you read a selection. The following are some suggestions for active reading strategies that you can perform before you read and while you read.

1. Skim the selection for any unfamiliar words. Circle or highlight any words you do not know.
2. As you read, underline, highlight, or circle important words or phrases.
3. Write down any questions about the selection if you are confused by the information presented.
4. Jot notes in the margin to help you understand the material.

TEXTBOOK READING: COLLEGE SUCCESS

Time Management for College Students

How well do you plan your time? College students lead very busy lives and must accomplish many tasks. Successful college students understand the importance of planning their time in order to complete the many things they must do.

1 You've got an exam on Friday and a paper due on Monday. You know you've got to get to work. Just then the phone rings. A group of friends from your dorm is going out for a snack. You know you shouldn't join them, but you've got to eat anyway, so you go along. When you return home you need a little time to unwind. You turn on the television. Two hours later you're relaxed, but you're also tired. You decide to call it a night. There's always tomorrow!

2 If this scenario sounds familiar, it should. It happens to all of us now and then. As a college student, however, it's very important to learn to manage your time effectively. The first step in managing your time effectively is to know where you're going. It helps to set goals for yourself. Although we may have vague notions of what we want from life, like being happy, or being a credit to society, or being financially secure, these generalized plans should be made concrete. Goals must be real. They must be examined closely. You should consider three different types of goals: long-range goals, medium-range goals, and short-range goals.

3 Long-range goals are usually personal wishes. They have to do with your career aims, your educational plans, and your social desires. Think about where you would like to be 5 or 10 years from now. The education you are now receiving in college should be a stepping-stone to help you achieve your long-range goals. Besides achieving the benefit of learning, a college education pays off in dollars. College graduates earn about $700,000 more during their lifetimes than their counterparts who have no degrees. Depending on your career plans, the grades you earn in your courses will help determine whether or not you will be able to fulfill your long-range goals. To achieve long-range goals, they need to be broken into smaller parts and examined closely.

4 Medium-range goals, sometimes called *mid-term goals*, can be accomplished in one to five years. They help you achieve your long-range goals. They can be set two or three times a year. For example, if you plan to enter medical school after graduation, you will need a considerable number of As in your courses. A medium-range goal would be to get four or five As in your courses for four years. Another medium-range goal might be to join a club or improve your skills in your favorite sport. Let's say that your grades last semester weren't the best. A medium-range goal for you might then be to improve your grades. If you're saving money to buy a car,

then watching your budget more carefully might be a reasonable goal to set.

5 Short-range goals, also called *short-term goals*, can be accomplished in a year or less. These goals involve taking care of your daily tasks and keeping up with your assignments. Reading a chapter in a book, completing an assignment, or writing a paper are examples of short-term goals.

6 Your college years are likely to be among the most demanding and enjoyable years of your life. During this time there are activities that will compete for your attention. Studying, developing relationships, and handling your financial affairs are among the most important challenges that will require your energy, creativity, and brain power. Learning to deal successfully with the different facets of your life can be accomplished by developing good coping skills. These are skills that will remain with you throughout your life and can be applied to just about any situation you'll encounter.*

Vocabulary

Read the following questions about some of the vocabulary words that appear in the previous selection. Before you look up the word, try to use the context of the passage to figure out the meaning. Then circle the letter of the correct answer.

1. In paragraph 2, what does the word *scenario* mean?
   - a. sequence of events
   - b. a floor plan
   - c. a map
   - d. an area
2. What does the word *considerable* mean in paragraph 4?
   - a. not too many
   - b. substantial
   - c. worrisome
   - d. positive
3. What are *vague notions* (paragraph 2)?
   - a. faulty conclusions
   - b. unrealistic dreams
   - c. crazy schemes
   - d. unclear ideas

Reading Skills

Respond to each of the following questions by circling the letter of the correct answer.

1. The topic sentence for paragraph 2 is
   - a. Sentence 3
   - b. Sentence 7
   - b. Sentence 5
   - d. Sentence 9

* From Sherman and Sherman, *Essential Concepts of Chemistry*. Boston: Houghton Mifflin, 1999. Copyright © 1999 by Houghton Mifflin Company. Reprinted with permission.

2. The topic of paragraph 3 is

   a. personal goals
   b. importance of grades
   (c.) long-range goals
   d. cost of college

3. In paragraph 4, sentence number 4 is a

   a. Major detail
   (b.) Minor detail

4. For paragraph 5, match the sentence to the kind of information it represents.

   a. Sentence 1 __2__
   b. Sentence 2 __3__
   c. Sentence 3 __1__

   1. Minor detail
   2. Topic sentence
   3. Major detail

3

Practicing the Active Reading Strategy

■ After You Read

Now that you have read the selection, answer the following questions using the active reading strategies that are discussed in Chapter 1.

1. Identify and write down the point and purpose of this reading selection.
2. Besides the vocabulary words included in the previous exercise, are there any other vocabulary words that are unfamiliar to you? If so, write a list of them. When you have finished writing your list, look up each word in a dictionary and write the definition that best describes the word as it is used in the selection.
3. Predict any possible questions that may be used on a test about the content of this selection.

■ Questions for Discussion and Writing

Answer the following questions based on your reading of the selection. Write your answers on the blanks provided.

1. Explain the differences between long-range, medium-range, and short-range goals.

   Long range goals are personal wishes about where you want to be in five to ten years. Medium range goals help to achieve long term goals and can be accomplished in one to five years. Short term goals can be accomplished in a year or less and include the daily work to achieve long term and medium range goals.

2. Identify two benefits to managing time well. Learning to manage time well will help you to achieve your goals. Also, developing good coping skills can help throughout life and be applied to many different situations.

Answers will vary.

3. What changes can you make in the way you manage your time?

Answers will vary.

4. Write down a long-range goal, a medium-range goal, and a short-range goal and summarize the steps you will have to take to achieve each goal.

Answers will vary.

Vocabulary Strategy: Context and Meaning

When you encounter an unfamiliar word as you read and go to the dictionary to look it up, you'll often find several different meanings and variations for that word. How do you know which definition is the right one? You have to look at the **context**—*the words, phrases, and sentences surrounding that word*—to determine which meaning applies.

To figure out the right definition, you may need to first determine the word's part of speech in the sentence. Many words can function as different parts of speech (for example, the word *left* can be a noun, a verb, an adjective, or an adverb), so you'll have to figure out how the word is being used before you can decide which definition applies. For example, the word *park* is both a noun that means "a recreation area" and a verb that means "to stop a moving vehicle." Is it the noun or the verb that is being used in the following sentence?

> This is a myth, though, because kids need dads who help them cope with life on a daily basis, not just take them to an amusement *park* every now and then.

You know the word refers to a recreation area because of the other words (in particular, the adjective *amusement*) around it.

Vocabulary Exercise 1

The following sentences all come from paragraphs throughout Chapters 2 and 3. Look up the italicized words in a dictionary and write down the definition that best describes how each word is being used.

1. His growth was arrested by periods of illness, *grave* hunger, or metal poisoning. Serious, significant
2. Kids who *engage* in games such as tag, scavenger hunts, and obstacle courses get more exercise in target heart rate zones, which improves their overall health. To involve oneself or participate
3. Although our *culture* associates napping with laziness, brief naps can be good for you. The totality of socially transmitted behavior patterns, arts, beliefs, institution, and so forth
4. Also, parents may overindulge because giving in—whether to a toddler's pleas to stay up late yet again or a grade-schooler's demands for a *hot* new video game—is often easier than trying to just say no. Popular
5. Countless monuments, from the pyramids of Egypt to ordinary tombstones, have suffered drastic deterioration from freezing water, *hot* sunshine, and other climatic forces. Warm in temperature
6. A code of ethics . . . outlines *uniform* policies, standards, and punishments for violations. Unvarying; consistent
7. Another newly synthesized compound exhibits an unusual *property* and will vastly contribute to the reduction of pollution. A characteristic trait
8. Questions open up inquiries that otherwise might never take place, waking people up and leading them to examine an *issue* that otherwise might go unexamined. A point or matter of concern
9. To stay *current*, join professional organizations, read business journals, and attend every convention or conference you can. Belonging to the present time
10. They [boys] are more physically active and aggressive and more *inclined* to hit obstacles or people. Likely; disposed

3

Vocabulary Exercise 2

Carefully consider the context and part of speech for each of the boldfaced, italicized words in the passage that follows. Before looking up each word in a dictionary try to write a definition for each word. Although some of the words are familiar, they may be used in less familiar ways.

We all live in two ***worlds***: the real world and the media world. Attaining higher levels of media literacy does not mean avoiding the media world. Instead, it means being able to tell the two worlds apart as the two ***merge*** together under pressures from newer message formats and newer technologies that seem to make the boundary lines between the two worlds very fuzzy.

Most of us feel that the real world is too limited; that is, we cannot get all the experiences and information we want in the real world. To get those experiences and information, we ***journey*** into the media world. For example, you might feel that your life is too boring and you want to ***experience*** some exciting romance. You could read a novel, go to a movie, or watch a television program to get this kind of experience. Or you might be curious about what happened in your city today, so you watch the evening news, where reporters take you to all the places of the day's actions—crime scenes, fire locations, courthouses, sporting arenas. Although these are all real-world locations, you are not visiting them in the real world. Instead, you enter the media world to visit them.

We are continually entering the media world to get experiences and information we cannot get very well in our real lives. We ***enter*** the media world to expand our real-world experience and to help us understand the real world better. But those experiences we have in the media world are different than if we had experienced them directly in the real world. We often forget this as we bring media-world experiences back into our real world. As we constantly cross the ***border*** between the real world and the media world, the border sometimes gets blurred, and over time we tend to forget which memories are from experiences in the real world and which were originally experienced in the media world.

This blurring of the line and the ***interlacing*** of memories makes it important that we spend some mental energy considering the ***nature*** of reality and how the reality of the two worlds is different.*

3

* Potter, W. James. *Media Literacy,* 5th ed. Thousand Oaks: SAGE Publications, Inc. 2011. Print. Ch. 9, p. 126.

1. world human society
2. merge join or come together
3. journey travel
4. experience to participate in
5. enter become a participant
6. border a boundary
7. interlacing intersperse
8. nature characteristics and qualities of a thing

3

Reading Visuals: Organizational Charts

An **organizational chart** *is one that shows the chain of command in a company or organization.* It uses rectangles and lines to show the managerial relationships between the individuals within a group. Its purpose is to represent the lines of authority and responsibility in the organization.

An organization chart contains the following parts:

- **Title.** The title usually identifies the organization.
- **Boxes.** Each box, or rectangle, represents one entity within the organization. That entity might be an individual or a group of individuals, such as a department. Each box will be labeled with a name, a job title, or a department name. These boxes are arranged in a hierarchy, or ranking. The person or group with the most authority and responsibility is at the top of the chart. Each subsequent row of boxes represents the next layer of authority, a group of people or groups who are equal in rank and who all report to the individual(s) in the layer above.
- **Lines.** The lines connect boxes to show managerial relationships. They indicate who reports to whom. The source line, if applicable, identifies who collected or compiled the information in the chart.

These parts are labeled in the organizational chart that follows.

To understand an organizational chart, begin at the top. Read the label in the box at the top, and then follow the lines to see which individuals and groups are related to each other.

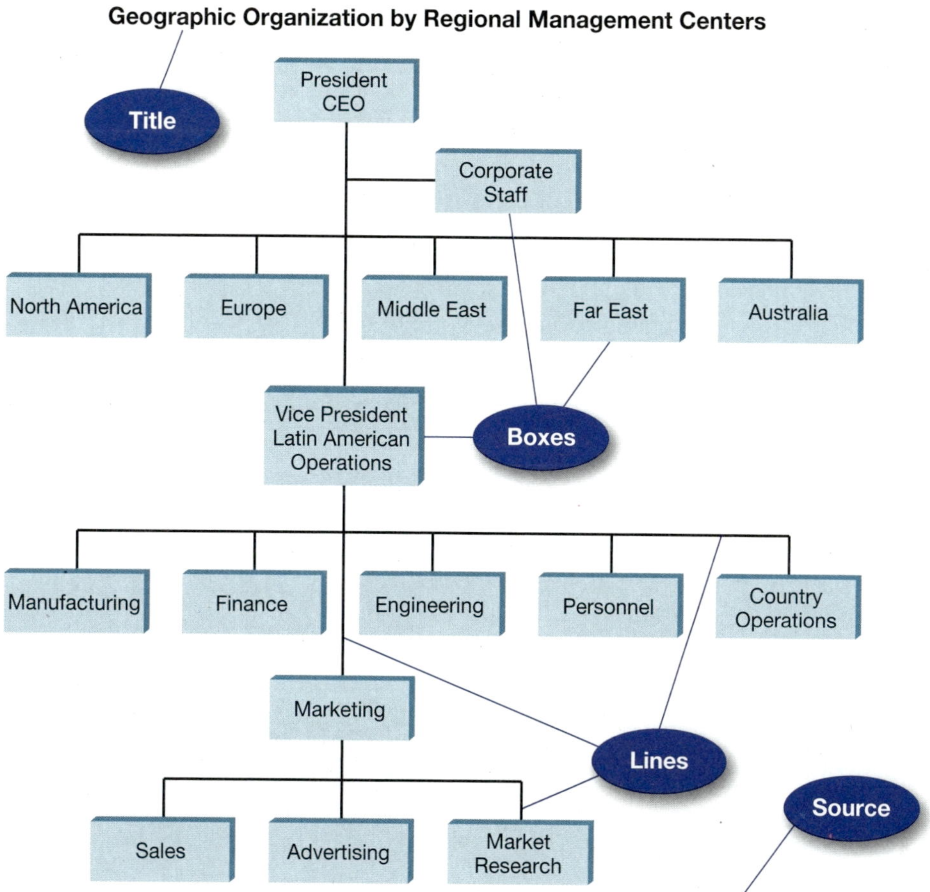

Gillespie, Kate, and David Hennessey. *Global Maketing,* 3rd ed. Mason: South-Western Cengage Learning, 2011. Print. Ch. 16, p. 473.

This organization chart shows a company structure for an international organization that places the president, or CEO, at the top of the hierarchy. That individual has the most authority and responsibility. He is supported by the corporate staff. Each region reports directly to the president. In this chart only one region is expanded—the Latin American operations. Under the vice president are the various departments that report directly to him. The only department that is expanded is marketing to show who reports to the director of marketing. All other regions would have a similar structure.

3

Typical Hotel Organization Chart

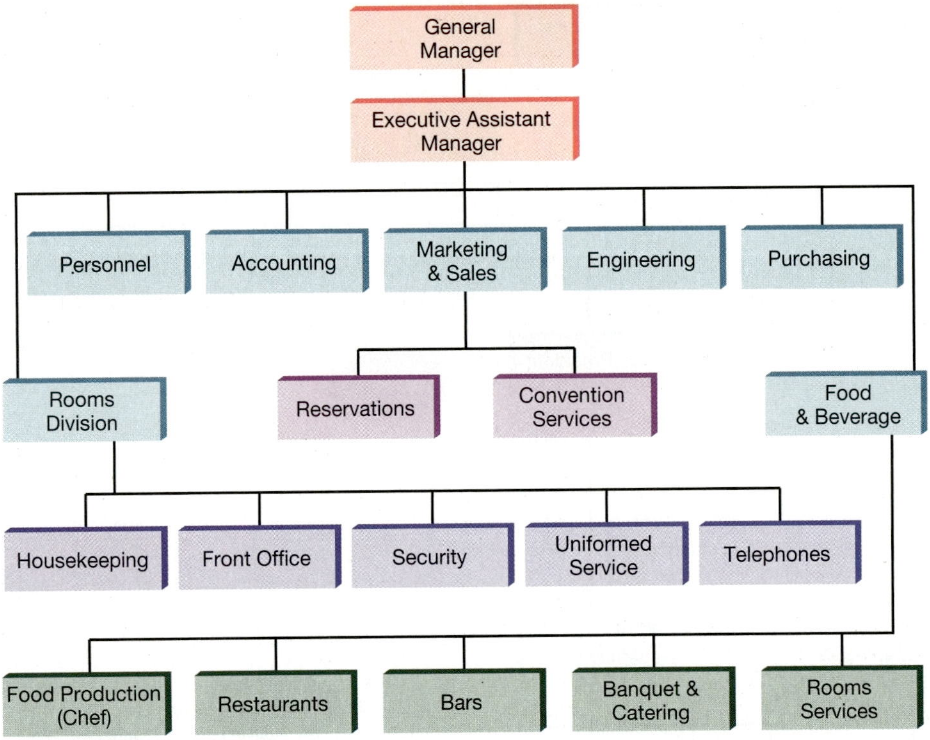

O'Fallon, Michael J., and Denney G. Rutherford. *Hotel Management and Operations,* 5th ed. Hoboken: John Wiley & Sons, Inc., 2011. Print. Ch. 2, p. 70.

Now, study the organizational chart above and then answer the questions that follow.

1. What is the title of the person with the most responsibility in this organization? General Manager
2. Who reports directly to the General Manager? Executive Assistant Manager
3. How many departments report directly to the Executive Assistant Manager? List two of these departments. 7; answers will vary
4. List the two groups that report directly to Marketing and Sales Department. Reservations and Convention Services
5. What department does housekeeping report to? Rooms Division
6. Which groups (there are 5) report to the Food and Beverage Department? Food production, restaurants, bars, banquet/catering, and room service

Chapter 3 Review

Fill in the blanks in the following statements.

1. Supporting details are the specific facts, statistics, examples, steps, anecdotes, reasons, descriptions, definitions, and so on that explain or prove the general main idea stated in the topic sentence.

2. There are two kinds of supporting details: major details and minor details. The major details are the main points that explain or support the idea in the topic sentence. Minor details offer more explanation of the major details.

3. Mapping is a technique that involves using lines, boxes, circles, or other shapes to show how sentences in a paragraph are related.

4. An outline is a list of supporting details labeled with a system of numbers and letters that show their relationships to one another.

5. Identify three of the principles of effective time management for reading.

   Answers may vary, but should be based on the Reading Strategy.

6. What is *context* as it applies to unfamiliar words? The words, phrases, and sentences surrounding the unfamiliar word

7. What do organizational charts show? The chain of command in a company or organization

James Lauritz/moodboard/Corbis

CHAPTER 4

Implied Main Ideas

Goals for Chapter 4

- Define the term *implied main idea.*
- Form generalizations based on specific details.
- State the implied main idea of a paragraph.
- Apply the steps of the SQ3R Strategy to reading selections.
- Read and understand information in a flow chart.

When you read Chapter 2 of this book, you learned that many paragraphs include a topic sentence that clearly states the main idea. Other paragraphs, however, do not contain a topic sentence. Does that mean they don't have a main point? No, it means that readers must do a little more work to figure out what that point—which is called an *implied main idea*—is. To see how much you already know about drawing conclusions about a main idea, take the following pretest.

Pretest

The following paragraphs do not include a stated main idea. Read each paragraph and see if you can determine its main point. Circle the letter of the sentence that best states the main idea.

4

1. In Charlotte, North Carolina, parents or other volunteers who accompany field trips, tutor, or serve as reading buddies or assistant athletic coaches, and may be alone with a child, must go through personal interviews, training sessions, and criminal background checks. They must also provide three personal references. Those who mentor children or chaperone overnight trips must be fingerprinted, and those who drive children around must have their driving histories, insurance, and licenses checked. Boys and Girls Clubs, scout groups, the Catholic Church, and even some Red Cross chapters now run criminal background checks on at least some volunteers.*

   a. A large percentage of volunteers have criminal records.

   b. Many organizations require background checks of volunteers who will be working with children.

   c. Everyone who works with children should be fingerprinted.

   d. The Catholic Church now runs criminal background checks on potential volunteers.

2. In an early laboratory study, researchers observed that Arabs sat closer together than Americans did, and that Arabs and Middle Easterners touched more than Americans, Britons, and Australians. Another early study found that Latin American individuals adopted closer distances in their conversations than did Americans. In two field studies, communication researcher Robert Shuter photographed couples in Italy, Germany, the United States, Costa Rica, Panama, and Colombia. Among his findings

* Adapted from Tamar Lewin, "Want to Volunteer in Schools? Be Ready for a Security Check," *New York Times*, March 11, 2004, www.nytimes.com.

were the observations that Italians and Germans stood closer to each other than Americans did, Italian men touched more than German or American men did, and Costa Ricans used closer distances and more touch than Panamanians or Colombians. In a study of cultural differences in Europe, my colleagues and I found that southern Europeans were more inclined to use touch than northern Europeans. Brief observations of nearly 1,000 couples at numerous train stations in 15 countries revealed differences in the percentages of couples in which one person touched the other. For example, among countries with at least 50 observed couples, the highest incidence of touch occurred for those in Greece (32 percent), Spain (30 percent), Italy (24 percent), and Hungary (23 percent). The lowest was found in the Netherlands (4 percent), Austria (9 percent), England (11 percent), Belgium (12 percent), and Germany (16 percent).*

a. Europeans touch more than Americans.

b. American couples exhibit more loving behaviors than Europeans or Latin Americans.

c. Cultures differ in the distance of their communication style.

d. Many studies report differences between men and women in their preferred communication styles.

3. The intelligent doctor listens carefully to patients' complaints before diagnosing the cause of their illnesses. Investment counselors listen to clients' accounts of how they currently manage their financial portfolios before suggesting any changes. The *good* car salesperson listens to customers' comments on what they are looking for in a vehicle before showing them around the lot. Assembly-line workers and construction workers have to listen to and master safety regulations if the company or crew is to remain accident free. The wise manager listens to subordinates'[1] concerns and ideas before moving forward with some bold, potentially costly venture.†

a. Listening is very important no matter what you do for a living.

b. Many managers of white-collar workers are good listeners.

c. Many managers of blue-collar workers have poor listening skills.

d. Subordinates use a variety of techniques to get their managers to listen to them.

1. **subordinates:** people of lower rank or status

* Excerpted from Remland, *Nonverbal Communication in Everyday Life*. Boston: Houghton Mifflin, 2000, 160–61.

† From Andrews et al., *Public Speaking*. Boston: Houghton Mifflin, 1999, 20.

4. Informational ads rely primarily on a recitation[1] of facts about a product to convince target consumers that it is for them. An example is an advertisement in *Stereo Review* that carefully details the specifications[2] of speakers. Hard-sell ads are messages that combine information about the product with intense attempts to get the consumer to purchase it as soon as possible. One example is a TV commercial in which a car salesman speaks a mile a minute about the glories of his dealership, shouts about a two-day-only sale this weekend, and recites the address of the dealership four times before the spot ends. Soft-sell ads aim mostly to create good feelings about the product or service by associating it with music, people, or events that creators feel would appeal to the target audience. An example of this is TV commercials for a wide variety of products, including soft drinks, beer, and athletic footwear. Think of a jingle, or catchy tune, and it probably comes from a soft-sell ad.*

   a. Car salesmen use informational ads to get sales.

   b. There are many types of TV commercials.

   c. Many different types of advertisements help sell products.

   d. Print advertisements can be very helpful in selling a product.

5. Whether you're frying an onion or baking a batch of cookies, try using olive or canola oil instead of butter. The types of fat in these oils can improve the levels of cholesterol and other lipids in your blood and combat the narrowing of arteries that often occurs with age. Also, instead of relying on red meat for protein, try fish, poultry, or legumes. And when you're feeling like you need to eat meat, select lean meats such as pork tenderloin or extra-lean ground beef. They pack less artery-clogging saturated fat than pork loin or low-grade hamburger. To cut out some white flour from your diet, switch from flour tortillas to whole-grain (corn or wheat) tortillas, and snack on whole-grain crackers.†

   a. It is easy to fry an onion.

   b. You can make healthy changes to your diet in several different ways.

   c. You should use canola oil in cooking.

   d. There are different types of fat in oil.

1. **recitation:** act of delivering information orally
2. **specifications:** details, particulars

* Adapted from Turow, *Media Today.* Boston: Houghton Mifflin, 1999, 34.

† Adapted from Harvard Medical School, "Eating Healthfully, and Enjoying Every Bite," *Newsweek Special Issue*, September 2001, 46.

Understanding Implied Main Ideas

Every paragraph contains a main idea. Sometimes that main idea is stated outright in a topic sentence. Sometimes, though, the main idea is implied. *An* **implied main idea** *is one that is suggested but not said.* To determine the implied main idea, you examine the details presented and draw from them a conclusion about the overall point.

If you think about it, you figure out implied main ideas quite often in your daily life. For example, look at the following conversation:

Wife: What is your new boss like?

Husband: Well, she welcomed me and personally introduced me to each of her staff members. She listened carefully to the ideas everyone shared during a staff meeting. She complimented several people for their work on a particular project, and she thanked everyone for their effort.

The husband answered his wife's question with a series of specific details. What conclusion can you draw from them? Every one of the boss's actions indicates that she is pleased with her employees, so it's safe to conclude that she values her staff and their work.

Here's another example:

You're in the mall parking lot. You see a Rolls Royce pull up and stop. Out of the car steps a woman wearing a fur coat and diamonds.

What conclusion do you make? Most people would say the woman is probably very wealthy.

You notice details, add them together, and draw conclusions all the time. In Chapter 3 of this book, you practiced recognizing supporting details, the information that proves or explains a main idea. A paragraph with an implied main idea contains *only* supporting details. These details are the clues that you put together to figure out the author's point.

To improve your ability to draw these conclusions while you read, it's helpful to remember what you learned about the terms *general* and *specific* in Chapter 2. Figuring out an implied main idea requires you to form a generalization based on a series of specific items or ideas. Look at the following group of words:

Band-Aid	Ace Bandage
antibacterial ointment	gauze

What generalization can you make about this list of items? They're all things you use to treat injuries, so the general phrase that describes them is *items found in a first-aid kit.*

Now, examine another list:

cracker	waffle
slice of bread	washrag

4

This group is a little trickier. When you read the first three items, you may have thought they were *things to eat*. But, the last item isn't in that category. When you add up all the details and look for the similarities, you realize that these are all *things that are square*.

As you will remember from Chapter 2, a group of specific sentences can also support a general idea. For example, read the sentences below:

Paul runs five miles on Mondays, Wednesdays, and Fridays.

Paul lifts weights on Tuesdays and Thursdays.

Paul either swims laps or rides his bicycle on Saturdays.

What general statement would include all three of those specific sentences? One possibility is *Paul exercises regularly*.

4

Exercise **4.1**

On the blank following each group of sentences, write a general sentence that includes all of the specific details given.

1. Pumpkins are used for pie making.
   In Japan, pumpkins are used in tempura[1] dishes.
   My mother makes a delicious pumpkin soup.

   General sentence: Pumpkins are an ingredient of several types of dishes.

2. Soy milk is low in sodium (salt).
   Soy milk is cholesterol free.
   Soy milk doesn't have lactose (milk sugar), which many people of Asian, Native American, and African descent can't easily digest.*

   General sentence: Soy milk is a healthy beverage.

3. Chicago's winters are usually cold, snowy, and windy.
   Summers in Chicago are often quite warm and can be very humid.
   Typically, spring and fall are relatively short, mild seasons in Chicago.

   General sentence: Chicago enjoys a variety of weather conditions throughout the year.

1. **tempura:** food dipped in batter and deep-fried

* From Jane Kirby, "Don't Have a Cow," *Real Simple*, October 2001, 52.

4. Infant massage stimulates the nerves, increases blood flow, and strengthens the immune system.

   Infant massage can relieve a host of childhood complaints from colic[1] to constipation.[2]

   Massaging an infant's chest can ease congestion.*

   General sentence: Massage is beneficial to infants.

5. One factor affecting taste is the temperature of a food or beverage.

   There is considerable genetic information among individuals' sensitivity to basic tastes.

   Other factors influencing taste include the color of the food; time of day it is eaten; and the age, gender, and degree of hunger of the taster.†

   General sentence: A number of factors can influence taste.

Determining Implied Main Ideas

To figure out the implied main idea in a paragraph, you can often use a methodical, step-by-step approach. Basically, this procedure involves looking for clues in the supporting details, adding them together, and drawing a logical conclusion based on the evidence. These next sections will explain and give you practice with each of the three steps in this process:

Step 1: Find the subject of each sentence.

Step 2: Determine a general topic based on the specific details.

Step 3: State an implied main idea that includes both the topic and what the author is saying about that topic.

As you become a more proficient reader, you will be able to complete all of these steps in your head most of the time.

Step 1: Find the Subject of Each Sentence

The first step in discovering an implied main idea is to closely examine the supporting details. The major and minor details in a paragraph will provide you with the

1. **colic:** Severe abdominal pain
2. **constipation:** difficult or infrequent purging of the bowels

* From Sheila Kotay Globus, "Touch Me, I'm Yours," *Westchester Family,* September 2001, 42.

† Brown, Amy. *Understanding Food: Principles and Preparation,* 4th ed. Belmont: Wadsworth, 2011. Print. Ch. 1, p. 4.

clues you need to draw a conclusion about the author's point. For example, read the following paragraph:

(1) When the United States celebrated 2000 as the start of a new millennium, the Buddhist calendar marked that year as 2543. (2) According to the Muslim calendar, which began in the Christian A.D. 610 and counts only 354 days in one year, the year was 1420. (3) China's calendar began in the corresponding Christian year of 2637 B.C., so in 2000, the Chinese year was 4697. (4) Year One of the Hebrew calendar was 3761 B.C., and Hebrew years include only 354 days, so those of Jewish faith marked the year 2000 as the year 5760. (5) The Hindu calendar noted the same year as 1921.*

Here are the subjects in each of the sentences:

Sentence 1: the Buddhist year

Sentence 2: the Muslim year

Sentence 3: the Chinese year

Sentence 4: the Hebrew year

Sentence 5: the Hindu year

Exercise 4.2

On the blanks following each paragraph, write the subject of each sentence.

1. (1) Computer-based fingerprint identification systems can track criminals across multiple jurisdictions.[1] (2) Computer mapping of crime "hot spots" and trends, pioneered by New York City's COMPSTAT, facilitates police planning and response by linking crime statistics to Geographic Information Systems. (3) Video cameras and acoustic[2] sensors can detect crime activity and even identify a weapon type by the sound of the discharge. (4) And DNA tests can positively match criminals to crimes committed.†

   Sentence 1 subject: computer-based fingerprint identification systems

   Sentence 2 subject: computer mapping

   Sentence 3 subject: video cameras and acoustic sensors

   Sentence 4 subject: DNA tests

1. **jurisdictions:** law enforcement territories
2. **acoustic:** related to sound or the sense of hearing

* Adapted from David Ewing Duncan, "The Year 2000 Is . . .," *Life Year in Pictures*, 16–20.

† Excerpted from Bowman and Kearney, *State and Local Government*, 5th ed. Boston: Houghton Mifflin, 2002, 453.

2. (1) Classical, or traditional, yoga—in which physical postures are used—is the type of yoga with which people are most familiar. (2) Gentle yoga is a less physical type of yoga and is often used as a warm-up to more rigorous types of yoga. (3) Restorative yoga incorporates physical postures like classical yoga, but its postures are more restful and rejuvenating.[1] (4) Meditative yoga emphasizes a gentle approach in which the yoga practitioner focuses on going within and focusing. (5) Ashtanga yoga is often known as "power" yoga because it emphasizes strength and agility.

Sentence 1 subject: classical or traditional yoga

Sentence 2 subject: gentle yoga

Sentence 3 subject: restorative yoga

Sentence 4 subject: meditative yoga

Sentence 5 subject: Ashtanga yoga

3. (1) Former Pittsburgh Steelers quarterback Terry Bradshaw has attention deficit hyperactivity disorder (ADHD). (2) Accomplished actress Mariette Hartley says that both she and her daughter have ADHD. (3) Successful political guru[2] James Carville says that, according to his mother, when he was a child he could never sit still. (4) Celebrated painter Salvador Dali's impulsiveness may have arisen from ADHD. (5) Albert Einstein was four years old before he could speak, which has been attributed by some to inattentiveness. (6) And inventor Thomas Edison was described as "addled"[3] by his teachers.*

Sentence 1 subject: Terry Bradshaw

Sentence 2 subject: Mariette Hartley

Sentence 3 subject: James Carville

Sentence 4 subject: Salvador Dali

Sentence 5 subject: Albert Einstein

Sentence 6 subject: Thomas Edison

1. **rejuvenating:** stimulating, invigorating
2. **guru:** a recognized leader in a field
3. **addled:** confused

* Adapted from Marianne Szegedy-Maszak, "Dazed, Famous," *U.S. News and World Report*, April 26, 2004, 56.

4. **(1)** *The Fantastiks* was the longest-running off-Broadway show in New York before it closed in 2001. **(2)** *Cats* was the longest-running Broadway show and enjoyed a run of many years before it closed. **(3)** *A Chorus Line*, which enjoyed record-breaking ticket sales in the 1970s and 1980s, also ran for a very long time, and was released as a movie in the 1980s. **(4)** The Broadway production of *Beauty and the Beast* is so beloved by children that it will probably stay a stage production for many years to come.

Sentence 1 subject: The Fantastiks

Sentence 2 subject: Cats

Sentence 3 subject: A Chorus Line

Sentence 4 subject: Beauty and the Beast

5. **(1)** According to studies, people who are more forgiving report experiencing less stress and less hostility, which is a risk factor for heart disease. **(2)** People who imagine forgiving their offenders note immediate improvement in their cardiovascular, muscular, and nervous systems. **(3)** Even people who have experienced devastating losses report feeling better psychologically and emotionally when they forgive. **(4)** On the other hand, people who fail to forgive have higher incidences of illnesses such as cardiovascular disease and cancers. **(5)** People who imagine not forgiving someone who has wronged them show negative changes in blood pressure, muscle tension, and immune response.*

Sentence 1 subject: people who are more forgiving

Sentence 2 subject: people who imagine forgiving their offenders

Sentence 3 subject: people who have experienced devastating losses

Sentence 4 subject: people who fail to forgive

Sentence 5 subject: people who imagine not forgiving their offenders

Step 2: Determine a General Topic Based on the Specific Details

Once you've discovered the supporting details' subjects, you can make a generalization about the general topic. You must make this generalization before you can complete the final step. In using logic to perceive an overall category for the details, you are figuring out the overall topic of the paragraph. You'll need to be able to include this topic in your statement of the main idea.

* Adapted from Fred Luskin, *Forgive for Good*. San Francisco: Harper, 2002.

Exercise 4.3

Read each of the following paragraphs and fill in the blanks after each one.

1. (1) The name *Arkansas* comes from the Sioux word *quapaw,* which means "downstream people." (2) The word *Illinois* comes from the Algonquin word *illini,* "warrior men." (3) *Kentucky* comes from the Iroquois word *ken-ta-ke,* which means "meadow" or "plains." (4) The name *Michigan* comes from the Chippewa *mica gama,* meaning "grand waters." (5) *Oklahoma* is named after the Choctaw term for "red people," *okla humma.**

   Sentence 1 subject: the name Arkansas

   Sentence 2 subject: the word Illinois

   Sentence 3 subject: Kentucky

   Sentence 4 subject: the name Michigan

   Sentence 5 subject: Oklahoma

   General topic of paragraph: origin of the names of some states

2. (1) In today's busy world, do you have an understudy if something unexpected comes up? (2) First, organize a handful of friends, neighbors, or relatives and deputize1 one another; you look out for them, and they look out for you. (3) Second, pass out blank copies of the plan—a list with important names, numbers, and other contacts—to the people who've agreed to participate. (4) Third, share whatever medical information you feel comfortable sharing with the people you trust most. (5) The information you provide can help you feel more comfortable whether you are home or away from home.†

   Sentence 2 subject: organize and deputize friends, neighbors, or relatives

   Sentence 3 subject: pass out copies of plan

   Sentence 4 subject: share medical information

   General topic of paragraph: steps in creating understudies

3. (1) Judge Larry Standley of Harris County, Texas, required a man who slapped his wife to sign up for a yoga class as part of his punishment.

1. **deputize:** appoint a person to act for someone

* Adapted from "The Origins of State Names," latin.about.com/library/friendly/nblstatenames.htm.

† Adapted from "Just in Case," no author credited, *Real Simple*, October 2001, 88.

4

(2) Municipal Judge Frances Gallegos in Santa Fe often sentences people convicted of domestic violence or fighting to a twice-a-week, New Age[1] anger-management class, where offenders experience tai chi,[2] meditation, acupuncture, and Eastern philosophy as means of controlling rage. (3) Municipal Judge David Hostetler of Coshocton, Ohio, ordered a man who had run away from police after a traffic accident to jog for an hour every other day around the block where the jail is located. (4) Hostetler also received worldwide attention in 2001 when he ordered two men to dress in women's clothing and walk down Main Street as a sentence for throwing beer bottles at a car and taunting a woman. (5) Judge Mike Erwin of Baton Rouge ordered a young man who hit an elderly man in an argument to listen to a John Prine song, "Hello in There," about lonely senior citizens and write an essay about it.*

Sentence 1 subject: Judge Larry Standley

Sentence 2 subject: Judge Frances Gallegos

Sentence 3 subject: Judge David Hostetler

Sentence 4 subject: Judge David Hostetler

Sentence 5 subject: Judge Mike Erwin

General topic of paragraph: judges who have imposed unusual sentences

4. (1) When people don't listen well on the job, they may miss information that can affect their professional effectiveness and advancement. (2) In a survey, 1,000 human resource professionals ranked listening as the number one quality of effective managers. (3) Skill in listening is also linked to resolving workplace conflicts. (4) Doctors who don't listen fully to patients may misdiagnose or mistreat medical problems. (5) Ineffective listening in the classroom diminishes learning and performance on tests. (6) In personal relationships, poor listening can hinder understanding of others, and listening ineffectively to public communication leaves us uninformed about civic issues.†

Sentence 1 subject: effects of not listening well on the job

Sentence 2 subject: number one quality of effective managers

Sentence 3 subject: linked to resolving workplace conflicts

1. **New Age:** relating to spiritual and consciousness-raising movements of the 1980s
2. **tai chi:** a Chinese system of physical exercises for self-defense and meditation

* Adapted from Donna Leinwand, "Judges Write Creative Sentences," *USA Today*, February 24, 2004, 3A.

† Wood, Julia T. *Communication in Our Lives*, 6th ed. Boston: Wadsworth, 2012. Print. Ch. 4, pp. 74–75.

Sentence 4 subject: negative effects of doctors who don't listen

Sentence 5 subject: negative effects of poor listening in the classroom

Sentence 6 subject: negative effects of poor listening in personal lives

General topic of paragraph: negative effects of poor listening

5. (1) Tornadoes have accomplished some astonishing feats, such as lifting a railroad coach with its 117 passengers and dumping it in a ditch 80 feet away. (2) Showers of toads and frogs have poured out of a cloud after tornadic winds sucked them up from a nearby pond. (3) Other oddities include chickens losing all of their feathers, pieces of straw being driven into metal pipes, and frozen hot dogs being driven into concrete walls. (4) Miraculous events have occurred, too. (5) In one instance, a schoolhouse was demolished and the 85 students inside were carried over 100 yards without one of them being killed.*

Sentence 1 subject: lifting a railroad coach

Sentence 2 subject: showers of toads and frogs

Sentence 3 subject: other oddities

Sentence 5 subject: students surviving a schoolhouse being lifted and carried away

General topic of paragraph: Tornadic winds have produced some very strange occurrences and sometimes miracles, too.

As you complete this step, remember what you learned in Chapter 2 about topics that are too broad or too narrow. Make sure the topic you choose is neither.

Exercise 4.4

After each paragraph, label each topic N if it's too narrow, B if it's too broad, and T if it's the correct topic.

1. Presidential candidates, mindful of Florida's 25 electoral votes,† regularly make pilgrimages[1] to South Florida to denounce Cuba's communist[2] policies, a popular position among Cuban American voters there. In Texas, local

1. **pilgrimages:** long journeys
2. **communist:** related to an economic system in which the government (rather than individuals) controls all goods and property and is supposed to distribute them equally to all citizens

* Ahrens, C. Donald and Perry Samson. *Extreme Weather and Climate,* 1st ed. Belmont: Brooks/Cole, 2011. Print. Ch. 12, p. 339.

† Florida now has 27 electoral votes.

4

groups called Communities Organized for Public Service (COPS) bring politicians to Hispanic neighborhoods so that poor citizens can meet their representatives and voice their concerns. They also organize voter registration drives that boost Hispanic participation. Similarly, the Southwest Voter Registration Project (SWVRP) has led more than a thousand voter registration drives in such states as California, Texas, and New Mexico. Groups like Latino Vote USA have targeted Hispanics in recent elections, to encourage them to register to vote and to turn out on Election Day. Such movements have increased Hispanic voter registration by more than 50 percent.*

__B__ a. Hispanics

__T__ b. Hispanics and voting

__N__ c. Hispanics in South Florida

4

2. Is it better for the child's development if parents are strict in their demands and discipline, or will the child have better psychological adjustment if parents are more permissive and less authoritarian[1] in their behavior? It is known that the effects of both permissiveness and strictness are negative if the family environment tends to be cold and hostile. A hostile and permissive environment is likely to produce an aggressive and delinquent[2] child, whereas a hostile-suppressive or restrictive family environment fosters children who are anxious and inhibited. However, several early studies revealed that children raised in warm and reasonably permissive, democratic families that allowed the child freedom of choice tended to be friendly, assertive, and creative, whereas children raised in warm but strict and controlling homes tended to be conforming, low in curiosity, and well behaved.†

__B__ a. discipline

__T__ b. effects of parental demands and discipline

__N__ c. parents who are strict disciplinarians

1. **authoritarian:** favoring absolute obedience and restriction of personal freedom
2. **delinquent:** failing to do what law or duty requires

---

* Adapted from Barbour and Wright, *Keeping the Republic: Power and Citizenship in American Politics*. Boston: Houghton Mifflin, 2001, 136. Copyright © 2001 by Houghton Mifflin Company. Used with permission.

† Adapted from Feshbach et al., *Personality*, 4th ed. Boston: Houghton Mifflin, 1996, 352. Copyright © 1996 by Houghton Mifflin Company. Reprinted with permission.

3. The primary benefit of exercise is to the cardiovascular system. Regular aerobic exercise counteracts the age-related decreases in cardiovascular[1] functioning. People who exercise maintain higher levels of cardiac functioning and blood flow than those who do not. The heart can more efficiently supply blood to the other tissues of the body, and the respiratory, muscular, and nervous systems all benefit as well. The benefits do not stop there, however; exercise improves endurance, helps to optimize[2] body weight, builds or maintains muscle tone and strength, and increases flexibility. It reduces or controls hypertension (abnormally high blood pressure) and improves cholesterol levels. Exercise also seems to improve mood and self-esteem and reduce stress. People who exercise tend to engage in fewer health-compromising behaviors, including smoking, alcohol consumption, and poor diet. Weight gain is one of the key age-related changes that people try to counteract with exercise.*

T a. benefits of exercise

B b. exercise

N c. cardiovascular benefits of exercise

4. In the early volunteer days, firefighters needed only a place to store their fire pumps. A small shed was perfectly suitable, and stables for the horses were added later. The advent of the professional full-time firefighter created a need for sleeping quarters and for personal space where each individual could store equipment and fire apparatus. To meet this need, many communities built a firehouse to serve the needs of firefighters serving 24-hour shifts. A firehouse usually consists of a kitchen, a bedroom, and an apparatus bay where fire equipment is stored. As technology and engineering design improve, so does the state of the firehouse.†

N a. need for sleeping space for firefighters

B b. firehouses

T c. changing design of firehouses

4

1. **cardiovascular:** relating to the heart and blood vessels
2. **optimize:** to make perfect or most effective

* Adapted from Seifert et al., *Lifespan Development*, 2nd ed. Boston: Houghton Mifflin, 2000, 424–25. Copyright © 2000 by Houghton Mifflin Company. Reprinted with permission.

† Loyd, Jason B. *Fundamentals of Fire and Emergency Services*. Upper Saddle River: Pearson Education, Inc., 2010. Print. Ch. 1, p. 11.

5. An excellent example of a proactive[1] stance to social responsibility is the Ronald McDonald House program undertaken by McDonald's Corp. These houses, located close to major medical centers, can be used by families for minimal cost while their sick children are receiving medical treatment nearby. Sears offers fellowships that support promising young performers while they develop their talents. Target has stopped selling guns in its stores. Some national toy retailers, such as KayBee and Toys "R" Us, have voluntarily stopped selling realistic toy guns.*

N a. Ronald McDonald House

B b. American corporations

T c. corporations that take a proactive stance to social responsibility

4

Step 3: State an Implied Main Idea

If you have successfully completed steps 1 and 2, you have systematically gone through each thinking stage necessary to state the paragraph's main idea. It is in this last step that you put together all of the clues you examined to come up with a statement of the main idea in your own words. This requires you not only to recognize the subjects in the supporting details but also *to draw a general conclusion based on what is being said about each of these subjects*.

Remember what you learned about main ideas and topic sentences in Chapter 2. *The main idea has two parts: the topic and the point the author wants to make about that topic.* The implied main idea is no different. It, too, should include both of those parts. Your statement will begin with the general topic you discovered in step 2 of this process. Then, it will go on to express the conclusion you drew from adding together the specific supporting details.

For example, look again at the paragraph about years on page 150. What is being said about each culture's year? Each sentence points out another culture's equivalent to the year 2000:

2543 (Buddhist) 5760 (Hebrew)
1420 (Muslim) 1921 (Hindu)
4697 (Chinese)

What generalization can you make about the items in this list? Obviously, there is a wide variety of opinion about what year it is.

1. **proactive:** acting in advance to deal with an expected problem

* Adapted from Griffin, *Management,* 7th ed. Boston: Houghton Mifflin, 2002, 118.

To form a statement of the main idea, begin with the topic you determined in step 2: years according to various cultures' calendars. Then, add the generalization above to state the main idea: **The year varies widely according to the calendars of various cultures, which did not celebrate the year 2000 with the United States.** This is the overall point suggested by the paragraph's specific supporting details.

As a final illustration, let's go through all three steps for another paragraph:

> (1) Emory University historian Michael Bellesiles, author of the critically acclaimed but controversial book *Arming America: The Origins of a National Gun Culture,* said some of his crucial research notes had been destroyed in a flood in his office. (2) He said he had relied on microfilm records in the federal archive in East Point, Georgia, but it has no such records. (3) He said he had examined probate[1] records in 30 places around the country, such as the San Francisco Superior Court, but those records were destroyed in the 1906 earthquake. (4) Well, then, he said he had seen them in the Contra Costa County Historical Society, but the society has no such records, and no record of Bellesiles's visiting the society. (5) Then he said he did the research somewhere else, but is not sure where. (6) Researchers have found that he consistently misrepresents extant[2] records in Providence, Rhode Island, and Vermont. (7) When he tried to buttress[3] his case by posting evidence on his website, critics found grave errors there, too, and he blamed the errors on a hacker[4] breaking into his files.*

4

Step 1: *Sentence 1:* Bellesiles's explanation of his research notes
Sentence 2: No such records exist
Sentence 3: Records were destroyed
Sentence 4: No record of visit
Sentence 5: Not sure where research was done
Sentence 6: Misrepresents existing records
Sentence 7: Errors on website, blames hackers

1. **probate:** related to legal proceedings about wills
2. **extant:** still in existence
3. **buttress:** support, prop up
4. **hacker:** a computer expert who illegally enters an electronic system

* Adapted from George F. Will, "Gunning for a Bad Book," *Newsweek,* May 20, 2002, 76. © George F. Will. Originally appeared in *Newsweek*. Reprinted by permission.

Step 2: **Paragraph's Topic:** Bellesiles's questionable research

Step 3: **Implied Main Idea:** The many excuses and untruths Bellesiles offers about his research indicate that his book is not based on reliable facts.

As you can see, determining implied main ideas is not only a necessary reading skill, it also helps you sharpen your thinking skills. You must analyze and apply logic as you complete each step of this process to draw a final conclusion. This kind of practice will lead to better thinking in general.

Exercise 4.5

Complete the blanks that follow each of the paragraphs below.

4

1. (1) Most commonly, the veterinary health care team including veterinarians, veterinary technicians, and veterinary assistants will dress in professional scrub uniforms, including tops and pants. (2) It is also common for these veterinary members to wear lab coats. (3) Scrub uniforms and lab coats are worn to prevent dress clothing from becoming contaminated, soiled, or torn. (4) These items are easily washed and replaced when necessary. (5) Some facilities have a set dress code or color for all staff members. (6) The kennel staff and receptionists may have a similar dress code or may be asked to wear special hospital shirts, such as polo shirts, and dress pants such as khakis. (7) All employees should wear fully enclosed shoes that are nonslip, preferably sneaker-type shoes. (8) This is for safety as well as for ease of cleaning and controlling the spread of contaminants. (9) When working in a veterinary facility, hazards such as animal bites, needles, and glass can cause a foot injury. (10) In large-animal facilities, employees may wear heavier boot-type footwear for protection.*

Sentence 2 subject: wear lab coats

Sentence 3 subject: prevent dress clothing from becoming contaminated, soiled, or torn

Sentence 4 subject: clothing easily washed and replaced

Sentence 5 subject: dress codes and colors

Sentence 6 subject: dress code for staff and receptionists

Sentence 7 subject: proper footwear

Sentence 8 subject: purpose of proper footwear

Sentence 9 subject: causes of foot injuries

* Vanhorn, Beth, and Robert W. Clark, *Veterinary Assisting: Fundamentals and Applications*. Clifton Park: Delmar, 2011. Print. Ch. 5, p. 51.

Sentence 10 subject: proper footwear in large-animal facilities

General topic of paragraph: proper clothing for employees in veterinary facilities

Implied main idea: Veterinary facilities need to require specific clothing and footwear for employees.

2. (1) For the past few weeks, the Reverend Martha Sterne has noticed that people she has never seen before have come into her church, St. Andrew's Episcopal, in Maryville, Tennessee, knelt down, bowed their heads, and prayed. (2) James Mulholland has observed more people attending services at the Irvington Friends Meeting House in Indianapolis where he's the pastor. (3) And Rabbi Chaim Stern says some members who only came occasionally to services at Temple Israel of Greater Miami are now coming more often.*

Sentence 1 subject: Reverend Martha Sterne

Sentence 2 subject: Pastor James Mulholland

Sentence 3 subject: Rabbi Chaim Stern

General topic of paragraph: recent observations by religious leaders

Implied main idea: Religious leaders have observed that more people are attending religious services recently.

3. (1) Weather often dictates the type of clothing we wear, whereas climate influences the type of clothing we buy. (2) Climate determines when to plant crops as well as what type of crops can be planted. (3) Weather determines if these same crops will grow to maturity. (4) Although weather and climate affect our lives in many ways, perhaps their most immediate effect is on our comfort. (5) In order to survive the cold of winter and heat of summer, we build homes, heat them, air condition them, insulate them—only to find that when we leave our shelter, we are at the mercy of the weather elements.†

Sentence 1 subject: effect of weather and climate on clothing

Sentence 2 subject: effect of climate on crops

Sentence 3 subject: effect of weather on crops

Sentence 4 subject: effect of weather and climate on comfort

Sentence 5 subject: surviving weather in homes

4

* Adapted from Nanci Hellmich, "Prayer's Abiding Power," *USA Today*, October 2, 2001, 6D.

† Ahrens, C. Donald, and Perry Samson, *Extreme Weather and Climate*. Belmont: Brooks/Cole, 2011. Print. Ch. 1, p. 25.

General topic of paragraph: numerous effects of climate and weather

Implied main idea: Climate and weather have numerous effects on our lives.

4. (1) Psychologist Rebecca Lee surveyed nearly two hundred adults and learned that, although both sexes are likely to work out to gain a feeling of accomplishment, only women are spurred by the desire to feel better about themselves in relation to others. (2) "Women—not men—were motivated by social comparison, the desire to perform as well as or better than peers," Lee says. (3) Enjoyment and outside pressures prompted both genders to exercise, but neither was particularly enthused[1] by material rewards, such as money or prizes. (4) The surprise finding of the study, according to Lee, was that men and women who stick to an exercise program are motivated by payoffs that are internal (such as a sense of achievement) *and* external (improved appearance or opportunities to socialize)—not internal benefits alone, as psychologists previously suspected.*

Sentence 1 subject: reasons why women and men work out

Sentence 2 subject: motivation of men and women

Sentence 3 subject: why women and men exercise

Sentence 4 subject: men's and women's motivation to exercise

General topic of paragraph: men's and women's motivations to exercise

Implied main idea: There are similarities and differences in men's and women's motivations to exercise.

5. (1) Drinking more than the recommended amount of alcohol can raise a woman's risk for many types of cancer. (2) For example, a recent study of 150,000 women published in Britain's *Journal of Cancer* found that when a woman drinks more than two drinks a day, every extra drink she consumes daily on a regular basis increases her breast cancer risk by 7 percent. (3) Drinking too much alcohol may also exacerbate[1] depression. (4) Alcohol can also transform prescription or over-the-counter drugs into toxic chemicals. (5) High doses of acetaminophen (Tylenol)—2,000 milligrams a day—mixed with alcohol can cause liver damage, whereas a regular aspirin regimen mixed with alcohol can trigger stomach bleeding. (6) Alcohol can lead women to gain weight, too. (7) Not only is alcohol

1. **exacerbate:** worsen

* From Bonita L. Marks, "Sweat Inspiration," *Allure*, October 2001, 162.

highly caloric—a 12-ounce beer packs 144 calories; a seven-ounce daiquiri has about 200—but it can also lead to overeating. (8) Alcohol stimulates the appetite by increasing the production of saliva and gastric acids, and it can also lower inhibitions and a woman's diet resolve.*

Sentences 1–2 subject: alcohol's effect on cancer risk

Sentence 3 subject: alcohol's effect on depression

Sentences 4–5 subject: alcohol's effect when combined with drugs

Sentences 6–8 subject: alcohol's effect on weight gain

General topic of paragraph: effects of alcohol on women

Implied main idea: Drinking too much alcohol damages women's health.

Exercise 4.6

Read each paragraph and complete the sentence that follows to correctly state the paragraph's main idea.

1. What once required criminals to work in disguise, under the cover of darkness, or forcefully take from another can now be done from the comfort of their own homes with little threat to their own personal safety. Why engage in a risky bank robbery where the average take is less than $5,000 when you can pull off a high-tech identity theft from your living room and make an average of $10,200. High-tech crimes are generally much safer physically than committing a traditional crime against persons. Furthermore, the low cost of the Internet and its perceived level of anonymity enable it to be used by criminals of all demographics and socioeconomic statuses.†

   Computers and the World Wide Web are now being used by criminals.

2. New York City is renowned[1] for its high-end, celebrity-chef food culture. It also offers a host of budget-priced options for good food and drinks. Many of the best meal deals are found in the ethnic enclaves[2] that dot the city. In addition to good values on down-home classics, New York

1. **renowned:** famous
2. **enclaves:** areas

* Adapted from Kristyn Kusek, "Toast to Your Health," *Real Simple*, August 2003, 110. © 2003.

† Knetzger, Michael R., *Investigating High-Tech Crime*. Upper Saddle River: Pearson Education, Inc. 2008. Print. Ch. 3, p. 52.

serves up thrifty[3] East Indian curries, Moroccan couscous, Greek kebabs, West Indian callaloos, Senegalese *thiebu djen* (fish stews), Mexican chimichangas, and many more culinary[4] treats from around the globe.*

New York City offers a wide variety of food choices.

3. Scandals in basketball began to occur in the 1950s and have continued sporadically since then whenever gamblers have been able to entice athletes to affect the point spread of games. Today, the biggest gambling concern is the amount of money that is gambled illegally on collegiate sports. The commercialization of intercollegiate athletics is illustrated by athletic administrators who eagerly seek corporate dollars as they sell logos on uniforms and signage in stadiums and arenas. Will corporate sponsorship of teams be next? Despite mandatory testing, drug use and abuse by college athletes threatens to undermine equity between competitors as some athletes seem to be seeking every advantage to win. Another major issue today is the inordinate influence of television, which often determines dates for competitions, starting times, and sometimes even locations for intercollegiate competitions. Disruption to the educational pursuits of the athletes, who play games during the academic week and arrive back on campus shortly before classes begin the next day, seems irrelevant to institutions reaping the financial revenues promised by national and cable networks.†

   Several of the issues that threaten collegiate athletics today are negative.

4. In one experiment, researcher Ilene Bernstein gave a group of cancer patients Mapletoff ice cream an hour before they received nausea-provoking chemotherapy. A second group ate the same kind of ice cream on a day they did not receive chemotherapy. A third group got no ice cream. Five months later, the patients were asked to taste several ice cream flavors. Those who had never tasted Mapletoff and those who had not eaten it in association with chemotherapy chose it as their favorite. Those who had eaten Mapletoff before receiving chemotherapy found it very distasteful.‡

   A dislike of a certain taste can be learned.

4

3. **thrifty:** economical; wisely managing money
4. **culinary:** related to food

* From Jonell Nash, "A Cheap Bite of the Apple," *Essence*, October 2001, 156.

† Lumpkin, Angela, *Introduction to Physical Education, Exercise Science, and Sport Studies*, 8th ed. New York: McGraw-Hill, 2011. Print. Ch. 9, p. 278.

‡ Adapted from Bernstein et al., *Psychology*, 6th ed. Boston: Houghton Mifflin, 2003, 193. Copyright © 2003 by Houghton Mifflin Company. Reprinted with permission.

5. Peter Karafotas, 26, really likes the idea of a chocolate and strawberry wedding cake at his June 19 nuptials[1] in Washington, DC, but a new temptation has him doubting his commitment. A chocolate-raspberry combo, he declares, also seems appealing. After several one-on-one visits with florists, Chris Coffman, 24, of Menlo Park, California, has settled on white bouquets and a modern, clean look for the centerpieces at his wedding reception, also this June. "We're doing heavy, square, clear-glass vases, some with glass beads, some with candles, and some with floating flowers," he says. But when it comes to wedding involvement, Jason Fox Jackson, 27, takes the groom's cake. The Texan spent four hours sewing beads on his bride's wedding gown before they said "I do" in December. "She was doing it by hand," he says. "I wanted to help."*

Many grooms are becoming more involved in wedding planning.

Reading Strategy: SQ3R

In Chapter 1, you learned how to use active reading techniques to increase your comprehension of the material you read. One specific type of active reading strategy is called the **SQ3R method.** This abbreviation stands for

S urvey
Q uestion
R ead
R ecite
R eview

This series of five steps gives you a clear, easy-to-remember system for reading actively. Step 1 is to *survey* the text. To **survey** *means to look over the text to preview it.* Surveying gives you an overall idea of a reading selection's major topics, organizations, parts, and features. When you complete this step, you'll be able to form a mental framework that will allow you to better understand how specific paragraphs, sections, or chapters fit in. At this stage, your purpose is not to read the whole text but to get an overview of what to expect.

1. **nuptials:** wedding ceremony

* Adapted from Vicky Hallett, "Grooms for Improvement," *U.S. News and World Report,* March 22, 2004, www.usnews.com.

If you're preparing to read a longer text, such as a book, read over the title and glance through the table of contents to understand the major topics covered and how they are organized. Flip to one of the chapters and make yourself aware of its important features. A textbook, like this one, for example, may include a list of goals at the beginning of the chapter and a review summary at the end. It will probably also include headings that divide and identify sections of information. It's likely to emphasize key words or concepts with a distinctive typeface such as bold print.

Prior to reading a shorter selection—such as one particular chapter, an article, or an essay—survey it by reading any introductory material, the headings throughout, and the first sentence of each paragraph or each section. Read any review summaries or questions at the end of the chapter to get an idea of the major concepts covered in the selection. Also, glance over any illustrations and their captions.

The second step is to **formulate questions.** *Turn the title and the headings into questions;* then, when you read, you can actively look for the answers to those questions. For example, if the heading is "The Stamp Act Crisis," you could turn it into "What was The Stamp Act Crisis?" or "What caused The Stamp Act Crisis?" If the heading is "IQ Scores in the Classroom," you would create the question "What are the effects of IQ scores in the classroom?"

The next three steps are the three Rs of the SQ3R process. Step 3 is to **read.** In this step, you *read entire sentences and paragraphs in a section.* However, you read only one section at a time; for example, in a textbook, you'd read from one heading to the next and then stop. As you read, look for the answers to the questions you formed in step 2. Mark the text as you go. Highlight or underline those answers and other important information. You may want to write the answers or other details in the margins.

Step 4 is to *recite.* **Reciting** *means saying something aloud.* After you read a section of material, stop and speak the answers to the questions you created in step 2. If you can't answer a question, reread the information until you can. Move on to the next section only when you can say the answers for the section you just read.

The last step of the SQ3R method is to *review.* **Reviewing** *means "look at again."* After you've read the entire selection, go back through it and see if you can still answer all of the questions you formed in step 2. You don't have to reread unless you can't answer a particular question.

Practice the SQ3R active reading method with the any of the following reading selections.

The following links will further explain and demonstrate how to use the SQ3R system. Also included is a link to a form that can help you to organize for SQ3R.

WEB LINK

http://www.studygs.net/texred2.htm
http://ccis.edu/departments/writingcenter/studyskills/sq3r.html
http://www.bhsd228.com/reading/docs/pdf/SQ3RReadingWorksheet.pdf

Reading Selections

Practicing the Active Reading Strategy

Before and While You Read

You can use active reading strategies before, while, and after you read a selection. The following are some suggestions for active reading strategies that you can perform before you read and while you read.

1. Skim the selection for any unfamiliar words. Circle or highlight any words you do not know.
2. As you read, underline, highlight, or circle important words or phrases.
3. Write down any questions about the selection if you are confused by the information presented.
4. Jot notes in the margin to help you understand the material.

BIOGRAPHY:
Soledad O'Brien: A Life of Perpetual Motion

The racial slurs she heard as a child fueled journalist Soledad O'Brien's drive to succeed. Soledad is the fifth of six children raised in suburban Smithtown on Long Island by her father Edward, an Australian of Irish descent, and mechanical engineering professor, and her mother, Estrella, who is Afro-Cuban, and a teacher of French and English.

One day in 1977, when Soledad was only eleven years old, she went with her fourteen year old sister Estela to a local photography studio to have their pictures taken as a gift for their parents. When the young photographer politely asked the girls if they would forgive him for wondering if they were black, Estela reacted with fury. Younger Soledad was confused and puzzled, not understanding why being black could be offensive. Her reaction to this incident sent her on a lifelong quest for answers.

1 I think this was the day it began, my life of perpetual motion. There was a time when I was always walking away from comments or stares. There was the store where someone explained that I couldn't be black because black people were thieves and killers. Um, gonna put down this jacket and leave now. I didn't feel rejected; I felt annoyed and confused. I was proud of my identity. I thought I fit in comfortably in my suburban town. It was off-putting when someone came out with something nasty, something that signaled that not everyone saw me the way I saw myself. I always expected the best from folks so it came as a surprise. It would take me a moment to figure out if that's what they *really* meant to say. Then I would refuse to let it get to me. I was a middle-class girl in a middle-class Long Island suburb, but my young life became like those games of dodgeball we played in the school yard. When you move, you can't get hit. You survive to play again. By doing that you come out the winner.

2 There was the day I was walking down the hall to sixth-period science class. An older kid, eighth grade, came right up to me. "If you're a nigger why don't you have big lips?" he asked. It killed me that not only could I hear him: I actually could feel myself trying to formulate an answer, as if the question necessitated a response. There was no hostility in his voice. It was just this question he hurled at me in the rush to change class. He wasn't much bigger than me; he wasn't even scary. Just a guy with long sandy brown bangs swinging past his eyes like windshield wipers. I rushed past him, recording for some reason the colors on his short-sleeve shirt. I could pick him out of a lineup today, almost thirty-three years later. That day, I just pursed my mouth and kept moving, walking away. I wouldn't dignify him. I had to get to class.

3 I've been a journalist now for more than twenty years. I go sprinting from story to story. My life moves fast. I am a big version of the little girl in Smithtown except now I'm walking toward something rather than away from it. I force people to consider every word they've said in interviews. I dig in to the awkward question. I revel in making people rethink their words. Nothing stops me. I am not the type to dwell on bad things. I have no patience for people who do. I am the glass half full, the one who insists there must be a way to fix things. It's not that I'm propelled by unfounded optimism. I just can't suffer the small stuff or the bad stuff or the meanness we encounter in the world. I think better of life.*

Soledad O'Brien graduated, along with all of her siblings, from Harvard University. She is currently an anchor and special correspondent for CNN. You can read more about her career and many honors and awards on the following website: http://en.wikipedia.org/wiki/Soledad_O'Brien.

---

* O'Brien, Soledad with Rose Marie Arce. *The Next Big Story: My Journey Through the Land of Possibilities.* New York: New American Library, 2010. pgs. 10–11.

Vocabulary

Read the following questions about some of the vocabulary words that appear in the previous selection. Before you look up the word, try to use the context of the passage to figure out the meaning. Then circle the letter of the correct answer for each question.

1. "...*perpetual* motion" in paragraph 1 refers to ______________.
   a. slow
   b. fast
   c. continuing indefinitely
   d. difficult
2. When you *formulate* an answer, what are you doing? (paragraph 2)
   a. put into words
   b. write a mathematical formula
   c. guess
   d. frighten away
3. *Necessitated* in paragraph 2 means ______________.
   a. failed
   b. frightened
   c. deserved
   d. questioned
4. *Pursed* lips are ______________. (paragraph 2)
   a. bitten
   b. puckered
   c. tightened
   d. frowned
5. In paragraph 3, Ms. O'Brien states that she is not moved by unfounded *optimism*. What does *optimism* mean?
   a. disappointment
   b. sadness
   c. a positive outlook
   d. humor

4

■ Reading Skills

Respond to each of the following questions by circling the letter of the correct answer or by writing your answer on the blank provided.

1. The topic sentence in paragraph 1 is I think this was the day it began, my life of perpetual motion.

2. The implied main idea of paragraph 2 is ______.
   a. There will always be bullies everywhere.
   (b.) Soledad learned to ignore rude comments and keep moving.
   c. Soledad can't forget the insults of her childhood.
   d. Insults don't hurt very much when you are a child.

3. In paragraph 2 the statement "I had to get to class." is an example of a.
   a. Major detail (b.) Minor detail.

4. The implied main idea in paragraph 3 is Soledad used the insults of her youth in a positive manner for her life and career.

5. The sentence "I revel in making people rethink their words." is an example of a
   (a.) Major detail b. Minor detail

4

Practicing the Active Reading Strategy

■ After You Read

Now that you have read the selection, answer the following questions, using the active reading strategies that you learned in Chapter 1.

1. Identify and write down the point and purpose of this reading selection.
2. Did you circle or highlight any words that are unfamiliar to you? Can you figure out the meaning from the context of the passage? If not, then look up each word in a dictionary and find the definition that best describes the word as it is used in the selection. You may want to write the definition in the margin next to the word in the passage for future reference.
3. Predict any possible questions that may be used on a test about the content of this selection.

Questions for Discussion and Writing

Respond to each of the following questions based on your reading of the selection.

1. How has Soledad used her early experiences to help her in her career?
   Answers will vary.

2. Have you ever experience any kind of prejudice? Explain what happened.
   Answers will vary.

3. How can anger become something positive? Answers will vary.

4

Practicing the Active Reading Strategy

Before and While You Read

You can use active reading strategies before, while, and after you read a selection. The following are some suggestions for active reading strategies that you can employ before you read and as you are reading.

1. Skim the selection for any unfamiliar words. Circle or highlight any words you do not know.
2. As you read, underline, highlight, or circle important words or phrases.
3. Write down any questions about the selection if you are confused by the information presented.
4. Jot notes in the margin to help you understand the material.

TEXTBOOK READING: LAW ENFORCEMENT

Modern-Day Piracy

Pirates have terrorized the high seas for centuries. Although "old-fashioned" pirates make fun Halloween costumes and entertaining movies, the pirates of today are extremely dangerous and can cost shipping companies millions of dollars in lost lives and cargo.

1 Beginning in the 1990s, one of organized crime's oldest enterprises started making a major comeback. Maritime piracy reappeared as an organized criminal enterprise, particularly in shipping lanes off the coasts of Southeast Asia and Africa. Modern-day piracy is a crime of

theft on the high seas that carries the danger of significant environmental damage, because so many ships today carry environmentally hazardous cargoes. In addition, modern maritime piracy is a significant danger to navigation on the high seas because of the common practice of leaving vessels underway with no crew, thereby drastically increasing the dangers of collision and grounding.

2 Direct financial losses from maritime piracy are estimated to be about $450 million a year. Since 1994 the number of reported incidents of maritime piracy has more than doubled to an average of 200 to 300 such incidents per year. Like many crimes, however, officially reported incidents of high-seas piracy severely underestimate the total number of such incidents. Many, if not most, instances of piracy go unreported, particularly those involving coastal fishermen and recreational sailors. In 1999, 185 attacks occurred on ships at sea, at anchor, or in ports. In those attacks, 408 crew members were taken hostage as a result of ship boardings by pirates.

3 Acts of maritime piracy are most likely to occur in unpatrolled or lightly patrolled waterways. Pirates prefer coastal waterways or narrow straits through which ships must pass. These locations allow for a relatively fast, often well-concealed approach to the target vessel to avoid any warning to the crew. Piracy is a major problem along the coastlines of Indonesia, Malaysia, Thailand, and the Philippines. These nations have heavy concentrations of islands, archipelagoes, and peninsulas from which attacks on shipping can be easily staged. Numerous maritime choke points between land masses slow shipping and make for easy targets by pirates. In addition, similar conditions, along with virtually nonexistent governmental patrolling, have also made the west coast of Africa a prime site for pirate activity, particularly the coasts of Nigeria, Senegal, and Somalia. The east coast of Africa provides a different kind of target for pirates. Heavy volumes of maritime shipping into the ports of Mombasa, Kenya, and Dar es Salaam, Tanzania, make these harbors attractive locations for attacks on anchored or berthed ships. Most pirate attacks are crimes of opportunity, undertaken quickly when an appropriate and easy target is located. However, some of these attacks involve ships that are specifically targeted for the cargo they are carrying. In these cases, pirates often attack as agents for sellers who have already prearranged for black market sales of the stolen goods.

4 Criminal networks active in piracy usually operate as independent groups, but many have business ties to other organized crime groups, either as specialized agents to conduct the theft or as patrons to use the capabilities of larger organized crime groups to dispose of stolen goods. Current criminal networks involved in piracy are both more sophisticated and more violent than their earlier counterparts. The ever-increasing frequency of pirate attacks

has begun to have a chilling effect on maritime commerce, particularly in Asia. Modern-day pirates are more likely than their earlier counterparts to engage in multiship attacks and to disguise their own vessels.

5 These pirate networks use corrupt officials to obtain shipping schedules and the routes that they use to coordinate their attacks. In addition, pirates today tend to avoid attacks on large shipping companies, concentrating their efforts on small shipping lines that could own only one or two vessels. Finally, modern-day pirates are well armed and show a consistent inclination to use force when seizing the ships they have targeted. In an alarming trend, the number of crew members killed or injured in pirate attacks has increased every year since 1995.*

Vocabulary

Read the following questions about some of the vocabulary words that appear in the previous selection. Before you look up the word, try to use the context of the passage to figure out the meaning. Then circle the letter of the correct answer for each question.

1. What does *maritime* mean in paragraph 2?

   a. pertaining to the sea

   b. pertaining to land

   c. violent

   d. pertaining to the time of day

2. In paragraph 3, the author writes, "Pirates prefer coastal waterways or narrow *straits* through which ships must pass." What is a *strait*?

   a. bridge

   b. predicament

   c. narrow waterway

   d. tunnel

3. What does *vessel* mean in paragraph 3?

   a. victim

   b. ship

   c. basin

   d. attack

* Lyman, Michael D., *Organized Crime*, 5th ed. Upper Saddle River: Pearson Education, Inc., 2011. Print. Ch. 4, pp. 118, 119.

4. In paragraph 3, the author writes, "These nations have heavy concentrations of *archipelagoes*, and peninsulas from which attacks on shipping can be easily staged." What is the meaning of *archipelagoes* based on this sentence?

   a. islands

   b. mountains

   c. oceans

   d. deserts

5. What is the meaning of the word *seizing* in paragraph 5?

   a. to stop

   b. to disown

   c. to release

   d. to take by force

■ Reading Skills

Respond to each of the following questions by circling the letter of the correct answer or by writing your answer on the blank provided.

1. What is the topic of paragraph 3? where acts of maritime piracy occur

2. Which sentence in paragraph 3 is the topic sentence? sentence 1

3. What is the implied main idea of paragraph 5? Modern-day piracy is a very strategic and violent type of crime.

4. In paragraph 3, which sentence is an example of a major detail sentence?

   a. Sentence 1

   b. Sentence 3

   c. Sentence 5

   d. Sentence 2

5. In paragraph 3, which sentence is an example of a minor detail sentence?

   a. Sentence 1

   b. Sentence 5

   c. Sentence 2

   d. Sentence 4

Practicing the Active Reading Strategy

After You Read

Now that you have read the selection, answer the following questions, using the active reading strategies that you learned in Chapter 1.

1. Identify and write down the point and purpose of this reading selection.
2. Did you circle or highlight any words that are unfamiliar to you? Can you figure out the meaning from the context of the passage? If not, then look up each word in a dictionary and find the definition that best describes the word as it is used in the selection. You may want to write the definition in the margin next to the word in the passage for future reference.
3. Predict any possible questions that may be used on a test about the content of this selection.

Questions for Discussion and Writing

Respond to each of the following questions based on your reading of the selection.

1. Give a few reasons as to why modern-day pirates prefer unpatrolled or lightly patrolled waterways.

   The chance is decreased that they will get caught in an unpatrolled or lightly patrolled waterway. They prefer to attack the vessels in a concealed approach, especially when they can avoid any warning to the crew.

2. How do modern-day pirate networks operate as an "organized" crime group?

   Some modern-day pirate networks have business ties to other organized crime groups either as patrons or special agents.

3. What are modern-day pirates often looking for when they target a specific vessel?

   They are often looking for specific cargo that is prearranged for black market sale.

4. What might ships do to protect themselves from modern-day pirates?

   Answers will vary.

Practicing the Active Reading Strategy

■ Before and While You Read

You can use active reading strategies before, while, and after you read a selection. The following are some suggestions for active reading strategies that you can employ before you read and as you are reading.

1. Skim the selection for any unfamiliar words. Circle or highlight any words you do not know.
2. As you read, underline, highlight, or circle important words or phrases.
3. Write down any questions about the selection if you are confused by the information presented.
4. Jot notes in the margin to help you understand the material.

WEBSITE READING: BIOLOGY

A Whale of a Trip

By Raphael G. Satter, Associated Press

The humpback whale is one of the largest and most fascinating creatures on earth. Scientists have been tracking and studying them for years, but this very special whale took them all by surprise!

1 It wasn't love. It could have been adventure. Or maybe she just got lost. It remains a mystery why a female humpback whale swam thousands of miles from the reefs of Brazil to the African island of Madagascar, which researchers believe is the longest single trip ever undertaken by a mammal—humans excluded. While humpbacks normally migrate along a north-to-south axis to feed and mate, this one—affectionately called AHWC No. 1363—made the unusual decision to check out a new continent thousands of miles to the east.

2 Marine ecologist Peter Stevick says it probably wasn't love that motivated her—whales meet their partners at breeding sites, so it's unlikely that this one was following a potential mate. "It may be that this is an extreme example of exploration," he said. "Or it could be that the animal got very lost." Stevick laid out the details of the whale's trip on Wednesday in the Royal Society's Biology Letters, calculating that, at a minimum, the whale must have traveled about 6,200 miles to get from Brazil to Madagascar, off the coast of east Africa. "No other mammal has been seen to move between two places that are further apart," said Stevick, who works at the Maine-based College of the Atlantic. And while he said "the distance

alone would make it exceptional no matter where it had gone," there was an added element of interest.

3 Humpbacks are careful commuters, taking the same trip from cold waters where they hunt plankton, fish, and krill to warm waters where they mingle and mate "year after year after year," he said. The location of their feeding and breeding spots sometimes varies, but their transoceanic commute doesn't usually change much. Swapping a breeding ground in Brazil for one in Madagascar was previously unheard of. "That's almost 90 degrees of longitude—so a quarter of the way around the globe," Stevick said. "Not only is this an exception, but it's a really remarkable exception at that."

4 Humpback whales are powerful swimmers, and the 40-ton behemoths typically clock up 5,000 miles in their trips from the frosty waters of the North Atlantic and the Antarctic to more temperate areas around the equator. They're known for their eerie songs—composed of moans and cries—which travel huge distances underwater and whose precise function remains a mystery. They're also cherished by whale-watchers for their spectacular out-of-the-water jumps, called breaching.

5 Their numbers have recovered since they were almost hunted to extinction in the mid-20th century. But improvements have been uneven and scientists have been studying the whales and their movements to understand why. It's to that end that Stevick and other experts have been trawling the Web for photos taken by tourists and whale-watchers, hoping to help build on a worldwide catalog of humpback whales which can be used to track where they travel.

6 It was by browsing photo-sharing site Flickr that one of Stevick's colleagues found a photo of this particular humpback, taken by a Norwegian tourist from a whale-watching vessel off the coast of Madagascar in 2001. The photo had been taken with a film camera and the negative sat undeveloped in a drawer for years. Eventually, it was scanned and posted to the Web, where it was spotted and added to the catalog. Stevick's colleagues matched the Flickr photo to a picture of the whale taken two years earlier in Abrolhos, an area of small volcanic islands off the Brazilian coast.

7 So how did Stevick and his colleagues recognize the whale as the same one photographed by researchers in 1999? Carole Carlson, Stevick's colleague, said the key to identifying humpback whales is in their tails. Humpbacks have big tail fins called "flukes," which are spotted and ridged. Carlson compared them to "huge fingerprints." Stevick elaborated: "There's an enormous amount of information in those natural markings. There's the basic underlying pattern of the black and white pigment on it, numerous scars across the tail, and the edge is very jagged—each of those things provides a piece of information. The likelihood that two animals would have every single one of those things identical would be vanishingly small."

8 Simon Ingram, a professor of marine conservation at the University of Plymouth in southern England, expressed confidence the two photos showed the same whale, saying that photo identification was a "very, very powerful technique." But Ingram, who wasn't involved in the research, said he was less excited by the length of the whale's trip than its destination. "To my mind, the remarkable thing isn't the distance but the difference," he said. Whale communities were sometimes thought of as discrete communities, seldom mixing. "This shows that's not always the case," he said. As to why the whale went the way it did, Ingram said that, "the fact is, we just don't know. You can track them, but you don't know what's motivating them."*

■ Vocabulary

Read the following questions about some of the vocabulary words that appear in the previous selection. Before you look up the word, try to use the context of the passage to figure out the meaning. Then circle the letter of the correct answer for each question.

1. What does *migrate* mean in paragraph 1?

   a. stay
   b. move
   c. remain
   d. leave

2. In paragraph 4, the author writes about the "40-ton *behemoths.*" What are *behemoths*?

   a. giants
   b. fish
   c. runts
   d. ships

3. What does *temperate* mean in paragraph 4?

   a. stormy
   b. violent
   c. balmy
   d. cold

4. In paragraph 4 the author writes "They're known for their *eerie* songs." What does *eerie* mean?

   a. silly
   b. pleasant
   c. normal
   d. mysterious

* Source: http://www.usatoday.com/tech/science/2010-10-13-humpback-whale_N.htm. Web. Posted 10/13/2010.

5. In paragraph 4, the author writes "It's to that end that Stevick and other experts have been *trawling* the Web for photos taken by tourists and whale-watchers, hoping to build on a worldwide catalog of humpback whales which can be used to track where they travel." From rereading this sentence, can you determine the correct meaning of *trawling*?

   a. searching c. ignoring
   b. fishing d. traveling

Reading Skills

Respond to each of the following questions by circling the letter of the correct answer or by writing your answer on the blank provided.

1. What is the implied main idea of paragraph 4? Humpback whales are unique and amazing animals.
2. What is the topic sentence of paragraph 3? sentence 1
3. Reread paragraph 2. Is sentence 3 an example of a MAJOR or MINOR detail? MAJOR
4. What is the topic of paragraph 7?
   a. the diet of a humpback whale
   b. identifying humpback whales by their tails
   c. the migration patterns of humpback whales
   d. the near extinction of humpback whales
5. What is the topic sentence of paragraph 7?
   a. Sentence 1 c. Sentence 3
   b. Sentence 2 d. Sentence 4

4

Practicing the Active Reading Strategy

After You Read

Now that you have read the selection, answer the following questions, using the active reading strategies that you learned in Chapter 1.

1. Identify and write down the point and purpose of this reading selection.
2. Did you circle or highlight any words that are unfamiliar to you? Can you figure out the meaning from the context of the passage? If not, then look up each word in a dictionary and find the definition that best describes the word as it is used in the selection. You may want to write the definition in the margin next to the word in the passage for future reference.

3. Predict any possible questions that may be used on a test about the content of this selection.

Questions for Discussion and Writing

Respond to each of the following questions based on your reading of the selection.

1. Why is it uncommon for a humpback whale to make such a long migration?
They are careful commuters; usually their transoceanic commute doesn't vary. Also, they don't typically travel that long of a distance to eat or mate.

2. How are experts trying to track the travel of humpback whales? Experts are using photos taken by tourists who were whale-watching to create a catalog of humpback whales.

3. What led Stevick and his colleagues to believe that the humpback whale taken in each picture (one in 1999 in Brazil and one in 2001 in Madagascar) was the same whale?
By comparing the tails of the humpback whales in each picture they were able to identify that it was the same whale; the tails of a humpback whale are considered their "huge fingerprints."

4

Vocabulary Strategy: The Definition/Restatement Context Clue

When you encounter an unfamiliar word as you read, you may be able to figure out its meaning by using context clues. *The context of a word is its relationship to the other words, phrases, and sentences that surround it.* Sometimes these nearby elements offer clues you can use to get a sense of what a particular word means.

One type of context clue is **definition or restatement**. In this type of clue, either *the word's meaning is directly stated, or synonyms are used to restate it*. The following sentence, which comes from one of the paragraphs in Chapter 3, uses restatement:

> One important factor is making sure the punishment closely follows the child's ***transgression***, so that the child makes the connection between her wrongdoing and the consequences.

The word *wrongdoing* is another way to say *transgression*.

Vocabulary Exercise 1

The following sentences all come from paragraphs in this chapter. In each one, underline the definition or restatement context clue that helps you understand the meaning of the boldfaced, italicized word:

1. The neuron's ability to communicate efficiently also depends on two other features: the "excitable" surface membrane of some of its fibers, and the minute gap, called a ***synapse***, between neurons.
2. Soy milk doesn't have ***lactose*** milk sugar, which many people of Asian, Native American, and African descent can't easily digest.
3. ***Classical***, or traditional, yoga—in which physical postures are used—is the type of yoga with which people are most familiar.
4. Exercise reduces or controls ***hypertension*** abnormally high blood pressure, and improves cholesterol levels.
5. Think of a ***jingle***, or catchy tune, and it probably comes from a soft-sell ad.
6. Dr. Sears, though, advocates the "***attachment parenting***" approach in which parents hold and cuddle their babies in the "family bed" until the children fall asleep.
7. The name *Arkansas* comes from the Sioux word ***quapaw***, which means "downstream people."
8. Recycling would be essential in all aspects of the mission, but ***regenerating*** systems tend to weigh more as well.

Vocabulary Exercise 2

In the following passage, circle the six words or phrases that are defined with definition/restatement context clues.

To understand diabetes, it's important to know a bit about how our body works. Here's a little biology lesson:

As mammals, we burn glucose (a form of sugar) as our predominant fuel. We eat food, it's digested and broken down into simpler components in the intestines, then it's transported to the bloodstream. The glucose component floats around to provide the body's cells with fuel. Glucose is moved into the

4

cells by a hormone called insulin, produced in the pancreas. If the pancreas doesn't produce enough insulin or if the body's cells become resistant to insulin, the cells are starved for energy because the glucose stays in the bloodstream. This rise in blood sugar, detectable by your doctor, is diabetes.

There are two basic types of diabetes. Type 1, or juvenile diabetes, occurs when the pancreas fails to produce insulin. It's an autoimmune disease in which the immune system destroys insulin-making cells. As a result, there's zero insulin, so the cells consume other fuel, with deadly results.

Far more common is Type 2 diabetes. The number of sufferers has tripled in the past 30 years. That alarming increase has paralleled another American phenomenon—obesity, which also has tripled in the past few decades. The vast majority of people with Type 2 diabetes are overweight. Being too heavy reduces the body's sensitivity to insulin, leading to a rise in blood sugar.*

Reading Visuals: Flow Charts

A **flow chart** *is a visual aid composed of boxes, circles, or other shapes along with lines or arrows.* The purpose of a flow chart is to represent the sequence of steps or stages in a process.

The parts of a flow chart are:

- **Title.** The title identifies the process or procedure summarized in the chart.
- **Boxes or other shapes.** Each box contains one step in the process. They are arranged either top to bottom or left to right.
- **Lines or arrows.** These show the sequence of steps.
- **Source line.** The source line, if applicable, identifies who collected or compiled the information in the chart.

These parts are labeled in the flow chart on page 183:

* Adapted from Tedd Mitchell, M.D., "Get Moving on Diabetes," *USA Weekend,* November 2–4, 2001, 4. Reprinted with permission from the author.

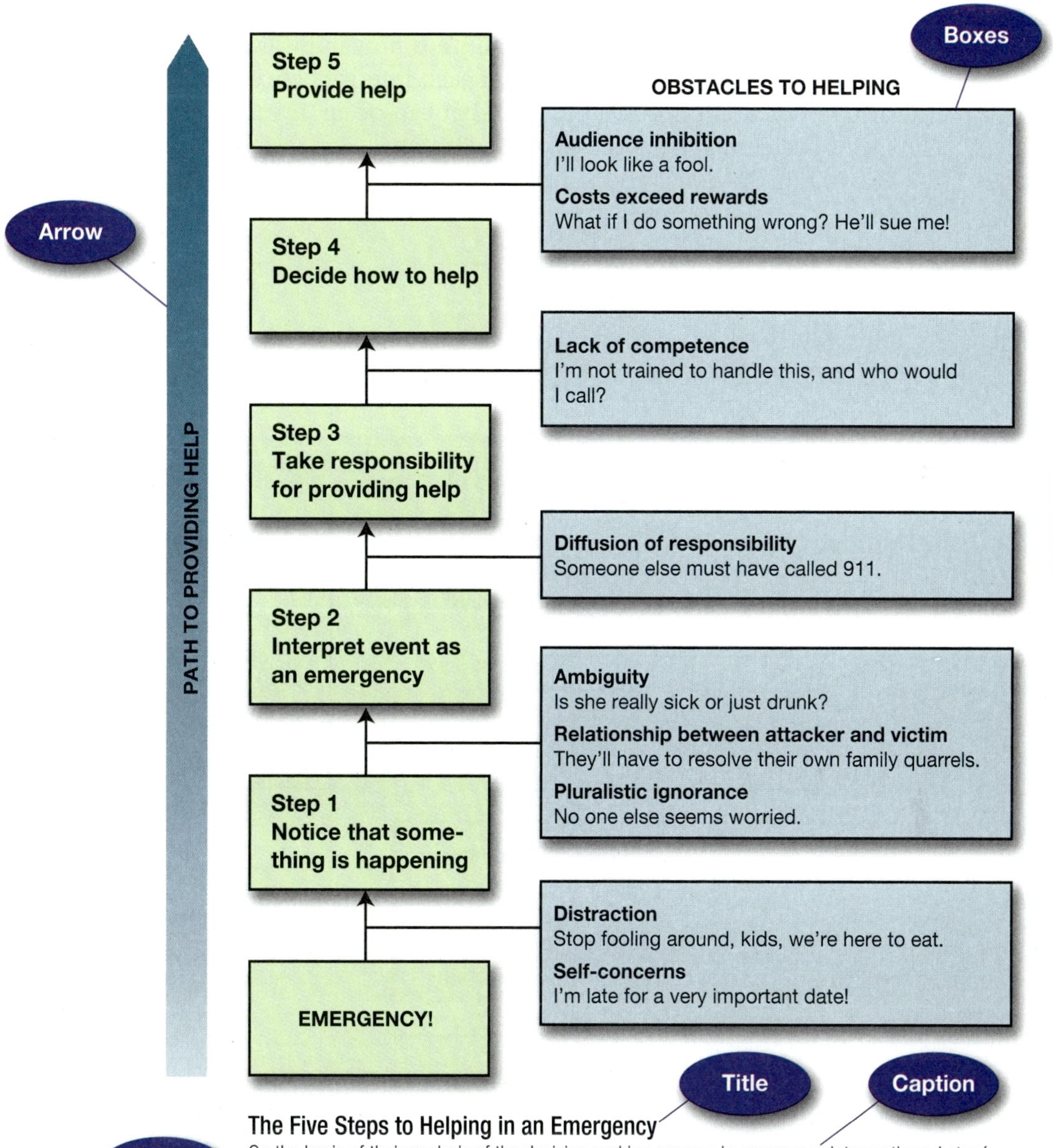

The Five Steps to Helping in an Emergency

On the basis of their analysis of the decision-making process in emergency interventions, Latané and Darley (1970) outlined five steps that lead to providing assistance. But there are obstacles that can interfere; and if a step is missed, the victim won't be helped.

Source: Excerpted from S. Brehm et al., Social Psychology, 5th ed. Boston: Houghton Mifflin, 2002, 361. Copyright © 2002 by Houghton Mifflin Company. Reprinted with permission

To interpret a flow chart, first read the chart's title so you'll know what process is being summarized. Read each step in order, following the lines and arrows to understand their sequence.

4

As the arrows in this flow chart indicate, the steps begin with the box at the bottom, the one labeled *Emergency!* The steps move upward, and each one is identified as Step 1, Step 2, and so on. At each interval between steps, a dotted-line arrow indicates a specific obstacle that can occur. If each obstacle occurs and is not overcome, the entire process will stop.

Now, study the flow chart below and then answer the questions that follow.

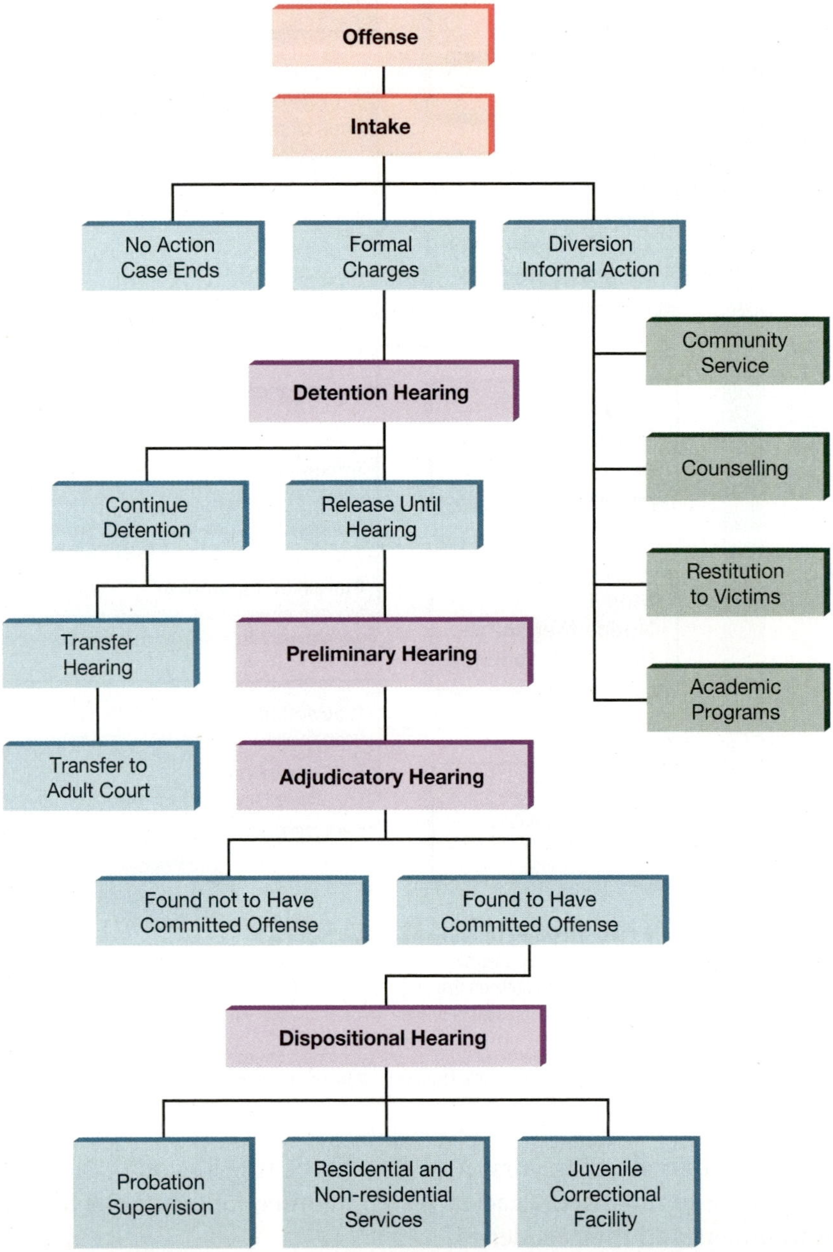

http://www.cjcj.org/files/Juvenile_Justice_Flowchart.pdf. Web. 10/27/2010

1. What is the first step in the juvenile judicial system? Offense
2. List the possible steps that follow the intake. No action, formal charges, diversion
3. If there are formal charges, how many possible hearings may there be? 4
4. According to this chart, can you send a juvenile to a correctional facility directly after a preliminary hearing? No
5. What are the possible informal actions that can occur after intake? (hint: There are four)

   community service, counseling, restitution to victim, academic program.

Chapter 4 Review

Fill in the blanks in the following statements.

1. An implied main idea is one that is suggested but not stated.

2. An implied main idea paragraph contains specific supporting details but no topic sentence.

3. To determine the implied main idea of a paragraph, you can follow four steps:

   a. Find the subject of each sentence.

   b. Determine the type of supporting details in the paragraph.

   c. Determine a general topic based on the specific details.

   d. Draw a conclusion from the supporting details and state an implied main idea in your own words.

4. An implied main idea, like one that's stated in a topic sentence, includes both the topic and what is being said about it.

5. Briefly explain each step in the SQ3R process. How can this process help you to become a better student?

   Survey – to look over or the preview the material Question – Turn the headings into questions and look for the answers as you read. Read – Read only one section at a time, marking as you go. Recite – Speak the answers to the questions you wrote using the headings. Review – After completing the reading selection, go back over the questions and see if you can still answer them.

6. What information will be given for a definition context clue? The word's meaning is directly stated, or synonyms are used to restate it.

Reza Estakhrian/Stone/Getty Images

CHAPTER 5

Transitions

Goals for Chapter 5

- Define the term *transition.*
- Recognize common transitions used to indicate a list of items.
- Recognize common transitions used to indicate sequence.
- Recognize common transitions used to indicate cause/effect.
- Recognize common transitions used to indicate comparison/contrast.
- Recognize common transitions used to indicate definition and examples.
- Recognize transitions in paragraphs organized according to more than one pattern.
- Practice the steps involved in summarizing a reading selection.
- Read and understand information in a pie chart.

In Chapters 3 and 4, you learned how to recognize supporting details within paragraphs. To help you understand how those details are related to one another, paragraphs include transitions that help you follow the author's train of thought. To discover what you already know about transitions, take the following pretest.

Pretest

Circle the transition words in the following paragraphs.

1. Throughout the first four decades of the century, the *Journal,* the *Post,* and many of the other mass-circulation magazines thrived. During the 1920s, more specialized magazines made their successful debut. One type revolved around the idea of distilling information for busy people. For example, *Reader's Digest,* a compendium[1] of "must read" articles, and *Time,* a weekly news summary, appeared in 1922 and 1923, respectively. Both had their predecessors in magazine history, and both had their imitators. The second type of magazine reflected an elite, knowing cynicism[2] and humor that seemed to be the mark of the so-called Jazz Age, the 1920s. The *New Yorker,* for instance, was the most successful of these.*

2. Problems in life such as money troubles, illness, final exams, or unhappy relationships often create upsetting thoughts and worry. Consequently, upsetting thoughts create anxiety. These thoughts become particularly difficult to dismiss when you are under stress or feel incapable of dealing effectively with the problems you are worried about. So, as the thoughts become more persistent, anxiety increases. An action such as cleaning may temporarily relieve the anxiety, but that action does nothing to eliminate the obsessive thoughts. Therefore, they become compulsive, endlessly repeated rituals that keep the person trapped in a vicious circle of anxiety. Thus, social-learning theorists see obsessive-compulsive disorder as a learned pattern sparked by distressing thoughts.†

3. You, too, can bring back a lost art of communication by learning to whistle with your fingers. First, wash your hands. Then, move your pinkies in a V shape toward your mouth. Next, place them underneath your

1. **compendium:** collection of various items
2. **cynicism:** attitude characterized by distrust of others' motives, virtue, or integrity

---

* From Turow, *Media Today*. Boston: Houghton Mifflin, 1999, 97.

† Adapted from Bernstein and Nash, *Essentials of Psychology,* 2nd ed. Boston: Houghton Mifflin, 2002, 423.

5

tongue, about an inch to an inch and a half past the tip, and lift your tongue slightly. Close your lips over your first knuckles and tighten them against your fingers and teeth. Finally, press slightly against your tongue, pursing your lips as needed, and blow.*

4. If you want to train your dog, Henry, to sit and to "shake hands," you need to shape Henry's behavior. Shaping is accomplished by reinforcing *successive approximations,* or responses that come successively closer to the desired response. For example, you might first give Henry a treat whenever he sits down. Then, you might reinforce him only when he sits and partially lifts a paw. Next, you might reinforce more complete paw lifting. Eventually, you would require Henry to perform the entire sit-lift-shake sequence before giving the treat. Shaping is an extremely powerful, widely used tool. Animal trainers have used it to teach chimpanzees to roller-skate, dolphins to jump through hoops, and pigeons to play Ping-Pong.†

5. Today's versions of the information-processing model emphasize these constant interactions among sensory, short-term, and long-term memory. For example, sensory memory can be thought of as that part of your knowledge base (or long- term memory) that is momentarily activated by information sent to the brain via the sensory nerves. And short-term memory can be thought of as that part of your knowledge base that is the focus of attention at any given moment. Like perception, memory is an active process, and what is already in long-term memory influences how new information is encoded.‡

Transitions

Transitions *are words and phrases whose function is to show the relationships between thoughts and ideas.* The word *transition* comes from the Latin word *trans,* which means "across." Transitions bridge the gaps across sentences and paragraphs and reveal how they are related.

Transitions make sentences clearer, so they help readers understand the ideas in a passage more easily. Without them, the readers have to figure out

* Adapted from Bryan Mealer, "The Lost Art of Whistling with Your Fingers," *Esquire,* February 2002, 95.

† Adapted from Bernstein et al., *Psychology,* 5th ed. Boston: Houghton Mifflin, 2000, 191.

‡ Bernstein, Douglas A. *Essentials of Psychology,* 5th ed. Belmont: Wadsworth, 2011. Print. Ch. 6, p. 214.

relationships on their own. For example, read these two sentences: **We've called ourselves African Americans, Japanese Americans, Mexican Americans, and Irish Americans. We're all just plain Americans.**

When you read these two sentences, which are not connected with a transition, you have to pause to figure out how they're related. Now look at how the addition of a transition more clearly reveals the contrast between the two thoughts. **We've called ourselves African Americans, Japanese Americans, Mexican Americans, and Irish Americans. *However,* we're all just plain Americans.**

Characteristics of Transitions

You should be aware of three characteristics of transitions:

1. Some of them are synonyms. In other words, they mean the same thing. For instance, the transitions *also, in addition,* and *too* all have the same meaning. Therefore, they are usually interchangeable with one another.
2. Some transitions can be used in more than one pattern of organization. For example, you may see the word *first* in both lists and process paragraphs.

   First, you must choose a topic for your speech. (sequence)

   The ***first*** reason to assign your child chores is to develop his or her sense of responsibility. (list)
3. Different transitions can create subtle but significant changes in the meaning of sentences. For example, reread an earlier example that includes a contrast transition: **We've called ourselves African Americans, Japanese Americans, Mexican Americans, and Irish Americans. *However,* we're all just plain Americans.**

The transition *however* suggests a contradiction or reversal of the idea in the first sentence. Notice, though, how a different transition changes the relationship between the two sentences: **We've called ourselves African Americans, Japanese Americans, Mexican Americans, and Irish Americans. *Now,* we're all just plain Americans.**

Substituting the transition *now,* which is a sequence word, suggests a change over time rather than a contradiction. Changing that one transition subtly alters the meaning of those two sentences.

As you read, then, you'll need to pay attention to transitions so you can accurately follow the train of thought within a reading selection. The remainder of this chapter explains and illustrates the different types of transition words that accompany various patterns of organization. (For more information about patterns of organization, see Chapter 6.)

Transition Words that Indicate a List

Certain transition words show readers that the sentence will *add another item* to a list. A **list** *may consist of examples, reasons, or some other kind of point.* Here are some common list transitions:

List Transitions

also	furthermore	finally
in addition	first, second, third	lastly
too	first of all	most importantly
another	and	moreover
one	for one thing	next

The following pairs of sentences illustrate the use of list transitions:

If you know how to respond productively under pressure, stress can actually increase your energy. ***Also,*** good stress can boost your confidence and help you achieve your goals.

Frequent memory lapses are one early warning sign of Alzheimer's disease. ***Another*** sign is getting lost or disoriented about the time or the place.

When asked to name the key ingredients of a successful intimate relationship, people most often mention affection. ***In addition,*** they believe emotional expressiveness is very important.

Now, read a paragraph that includes list transition words (boldface, italicized). Notice how each transition indicates the addition of another item in the list:

Three different temperature scales are commonly used in measuring heat intensity. ***One of these*** is the Fahrenheit temperature scale, which was devised by Gabriel Daniel Fahrenheit, a German scientist, in 1724. On this scale the freezing point of pure water is at 32 degrees (32°F), and the boiling point of water is at 212 degrees (212°F). Thus, 180 Fahrenheit degrees separate the freezing point and the boiling point of water. The ***second,*** the Celsius temperature scale, was devised in 1742 by Anders Celsius, a Swedish astronomer. His objective was to develop an easier-to-use temperature scale; he did so by assigning a nice, round 100 Celsius degrees between the freezing and boiling points of pure water. On the Celsius scale, the freezing point of water is at zero degrees (0°C), and the boiling point of water is at

5

100 degrees (100°C). (The Celsius scale is also sometimes referred to as the centigrade scale.) ***Third,*** the Kelvin temperature scale is an *absolute* temperature scale. That is, its zero point (0 K) is an absolute zero, the lowest possible temperature theoretically attainable. The divisions of the Kelvin scale are the same size as Celsius degrees, but they are called *kelvins* (abbreviated K) rather than degrees.*

This paragraph presents a list of three different kinds of temperature scales. The list transitions *one, second,* and *third* indicate each new kind.

Exercise 5.1

Fill in the blanks in the following sentences and paragraphs with appropriate list transitions. Choose words or phrases from the box on page 191. Try to vary your choices. Answers will vary.

5

1. The first thing you should do when you are flying in a commercial air plane is to check to see locations of the exits. Second __________, make sure you know how to access your oxygen mask should the airplane cabin have a loss in pressure.

2. By age three or so, children begin to use auxiliary verbs[1] and to ask questions using *what, where, who,* and *why.* In addition __________, they begin to put together clauses to form complex sentences.†

3. We'll need a couple of things for our trip. First __________, a canteen for fresh water would be helpful. Second __________, sunscreen always comes in handy in case it gets hot and sunny. Third __________, it is crucial that you remember to bring enough food for three days.

4. Human motivation stems from four main sources. First __________, we can be motivated by physiological factors, such as the need for food and water. Next __________, emotional factors can motivate behavior. Panic, fear, anger, love, and hatred can influence behavior ranging from selfless giving to brutal murder. Cognitive factors provide a third __________ source of motivation. Your perceptions of the world, your beliefs about what you can do, and

1. **auxiliary verbs:** verbs such as *have, can,* or *will,* which accompany the main verb

* Adapted from Sherman and Sherman, *Basic Concepts of Chemistry,* 6th ed. Boston: Houghton Mifflin, 1996, 40–41. Copyright © 1996 by Houghton Mifflin Company. Reprinted with permission.

† Adapted from Bernstein and Nash, *Essentials of Psychology,* 2nd ed. Boston: Houghton Mifflin, 2002, 234. Copyright © 2002 by Houghton Mifflin Company. Reprinted with permission.

your expectations of how others will respond generate certain behaviors. For example, even the least musical contestants who try out for *American Idol* and other talent shows seem utterly confident in their ability to sing. Finally ________, motivation can stem from social factors, including the influence of parents, teachers, siblings, friends, television, and other sociocultural forces.*

5. To conduct an effective search on the web you need to be aware of a few factors. First ________, search engines often provide a superficial[1] view of what might be available and often return an incomplete listing of their findings. Each of these engines uses different criteria for a search and will return information based on those criteria. Also ________, you can search for relevant information via links that you encounter. Links are a central component of the Web. Lastly ________, the Uniform Resource Locator[2] provides another way to investigate your topic. If you obtain the URL of a particular website that is likely to have information you can use, travel there directly by using the Open Location command and entering the URL.†

5

Transition Words that Indicate Sequence

Some transition words signal that the sentence is providing *another event, step,* or *stage within a chronological order of details*. Here is a list of common **sequence** transitions:

Sequence Transitions

first, second, third	once	last
before	today	meanwhile
now	previously	finally
then	often	over time
after	as	in the end
while	when	during, in, on, *or* by (*followed* by a date)
next	until	
soon	later	
in the beginning	eventually	

1. **superficial:** shallow; related to the surface only
2. **Uniform Resource Locator (URL):** website address

* Bernstein, Douglas A. *Essentials of Psychology,* 5th ed. Belmont: Wadsworth, 2011. Print. Ch. 8, p. 299.
† Adapted from Andrews et al., *Public Speaking.* Boston: Houghton Mifflin, 1999, 151–52.

The following pairs of sentences illustrate the use of sequence transitions:

> ***In 1941,*** the Japanese attacked America's Pearl Harbor. ***In 1942,*** 120,000 Japanese-Americans were rounded up and imprisoned in internment[1] camps.

> The massive earthquake destroyed buildings and homes. ***Then*** a giant tsunami swept over the devastated island.

> Eating breakfast foods that are high in sugar and carbohydrates, such as doughnuts, causes blood sugar to rise quickly. ***By mid-morning,*** blood sugar drops rapidly, making you feel lethargic[2] and irritable.

Now, read a paragraph that uses sequence transition words (boldfaced and italics). Notice how each transition indicates another event in the timeline:

> Following certain guidelines will ensure that your interview will be efficient and productive. ***Before*** the interview, research the topic and plan your questions. Dress nicely to show that you take the interview seriously, and to show respect for the person you are interviewing. ***On the day of the interview,*** arrive on time. ***When*** you meet your expert, engage in a little small talk before you get to your prepared questions. ***After*** the initial tension is reduced, begin by asking your first question. ***Then,*** let the expert do most of the talking ***while*** you listen and take notes. ***At the end of the interview,*** summarize what you heard so the expert can verify the accuracy of your understanding. ***Soon after the interview,*** send the expert a thank-you note as a professional courtesy.*

This paragraph offers advice about each step of the interviewing process. Each new detail is introduced with a sequence transition to help the reader easily follow the order of the steps.

Exercise 5.2

Fill in the blanks in the following sentences and paragraphs with appropriate sequence transitions. Choose words or phrases from the box on page 193. Try to vary your choices. Answers will vary.

1. **internment:** confinement
2. **lethargic:** state of sluggishness and low energy

* Adapted from Michael Osborn and Suzanne Osborn, *Public Speaking*, 4th ed. Boston: Houghton Mifflin, 1997, 164. copyright 1997 by Houghton Mifflin Company. Reprinted with permission.

1. Even though there are few charging stations available now, electric cars are starting to hit the market. Eventually________, there will be thousands of charging stations, making this purchase a sensible one for the future.

2. Right now, Deena and her family live in a small apartment in Hoboken, New Jersey. Soon________, they would like to move to a bigger place or perhaps even a house.

3. Fred put the steak on the grill to cook. Meanwhile________, Doris made a salad to serve with it.

4. Washing your own car is a satisfying endeavor.[1] Here's how to do it right. First________, park in the shade so your car won't dry too quickly and spot. Next________, soak the exterior to loosen dirt so it won't scratch the finish when you wash. Keep the car wet during the entire process. Use a soapy sponge to clean painted areas and a soft brush to clean tires and wheels. Open the doors, hood, fuel door, and trunk to clean the jambs. Spray wheel wells to remove road grime and salt. Afterwards________, dry with bath towels that have been washed without fabric softener, which can cause streaks. Let the car sit with the doors, trunk, and hood open so remaining moisture can evaporate. Finally________, apply a tire dressing to make that rubber shine. Every spring and fall, finish painted surfaces with paste wax.*

5. For a long time________, many scientists believed that the human lifespan (the maximum age to which the perfectly maintained, disease-free body could remain alive before it simply wore out and broke down) was infinitely extendible. The average lifespan early in the evolution of *Homo sapiens*[2] is thought to have been just 20 years. By________ the beginning of the twentieth century, that figure had more than doubled—to a still-brief 47 years. At the same time________, life expectancy (the number of years you can expect to live before being claimed by illness or accident) has been exploding, with people in the developed world now able to live deep into their 70s and beyond. Now________, though, scientists

5

1. **endeavor:** activity; effort toward a goal
2. ***Homo sapiens:*** the modern species of human beings

* Adapted from Barry Rice, "The Lost Art of Washing Your Own Car," *Esquire,* February 2002, 93.

understand that lifespan has remained fixed at a hard ceiling of about 125 years.*

Transition Words that Indicate Cause/Effect

Certain transition words indicate that an occurrence about to be presented in a sentence is either **a cause** (*a reason for*) or **an effect** (*a result of*) *an occurrence presented in a previous sentence*. These are the transitions that reveal cause or effect relationships between thoughts. The most common cause/effect transition words are listed below:

Cause Transitions

because of	due to
for this reason	since
led to	caused by

Effect Transitions

therefore	so	as a result
in response	hence	thus
consequently	as a consequence	

5

The following pairs of sentences illustrate the use of cause/effect transitions:

The existing financial safety net for farmers proved inadequate. ***So,*** Congress approved a new bill that provides support for grain, cotton, and soybean producers.

Carrying a grudge around saps your energy and happiness. ***For this reason,*** you should learn to forgive the mistakes or thoughtlessness of other people.

Cigarettes cost more, and American culture has shifted away from smoking. ***As a result,*** there has been a dramatic drop in the number of teenagers who pick up the habit.

* Adapted from Jeffrey Kluger, "Can We Learn to Beat the Reaper?" *Time,* http://www.time.com/time/covers/1101020121/aging.html

Next, read a paragraph that uses cause/effect transition words (boldfaced and italics). Notice how each transition indicates another effect:

> From the 1880s onward, popular newspapers increasingly nurtured people's fascination with the sensational.[1] Joseph Pulitzer, a Hungarian immigrant who bought the *New York World* in 1883, pioneered this trend by filling his newspaper with stories of disasters, crimes, and scandals. ***As a result,*** the *World's* daily circulation increased from 20,000 to 100,000, and by the late 1890s, it had reached one million. ***Consequently,*** other publishers, such as William Randolph Hearst, who started an empire of mass-circulation newspapers, adopted Pulitzer's techniques. ***Hence,*** sensationalist journalism became a nationwide phenomenon.*

This paragraph is arranged according to the chain-reaction type of cause/effect. Each transition indicates that the detail is the result of a previous occurrence.

Exercise 5.3

5

Fill in the blanks in the following sentences and paragraphs with appropriate cause/effect transitions. Choose words or phrases from the box on page 196. Try to vary your choices. Answers will vary.

1. Due to __________ added security measures at airports around the country, it is taking longer to get to your departure gates. Therefore __________, you should leave extra time to get through all of the checkpoints.

2. Ashton missed the notice from his professor that there was a test on Friday; consequently __________, he did very poorly.

3. Second-hand smoke has been proven to be as dangerous as smoke that is directly inhaled from cigarettes, so __________ do your best to stay away from smokers.

4. Because __________ of the unusual amount of rain on the East Coast this spring, the pollen count was very high.

5. "Net," abbreviated from "Internet," refers to the internetworking of computers around the world. Advances in software and hardware and a

1. **sensational:** arousing strong curiosity through exaggerated or shocking details

* Adapted from Norton et al., *A People and a Nation,* 5th ed., Vol. 2. Boston: Houghton Mifflin, 1998, 560.

common interface[1] allow people from around the globe to communicate and to exchange information almost instantaneously. As a result, the Internet has grown exponentially.[2] New sites appear every minute, adding to the millions already there. Organizations, companies, corporations, agencies, schools, colleges, universities, libraries, repositories,[3] interest groups, and politicians have scrambled to establish a presence. Therefore, on the Internet you can encounter information and opinions on any topic imaginable, and not only in text form, but also in images, sound, and video.*

6. When the United States entered World War I in 1917, a team of psychologists was asked to develop group-administered tests that could identify the mental ability of army recruits and guide their assignment to appropriate jobs. Soldiers who could speak and read English were tested on mental tasks that required verbal skills, such as defining words, whereas the rest were asked to visualize objects and perform other nonverbal tasks. Unfortunately, the verbal tests contained items that were unfamiliar to many recruits. Further, tests were often given under stressful conditions in crowded rooms where instructions were not always audible[4] or, for non-English speakers, understandable. Thus, almost half of the soldiers tested appeared to have a mental age of 13 or lower. As a result, testers were led to draw seriously incorrect conclusions about their lack of intelligence—especially in cases of those who did not speak English. Hence, later tests developed by David Wechsler were designed to correct some of the weaknesses of earlier ones.†

Transition Words that Indicate Comparison/Contrast

Paragraphs include **comparison** transitions to help readers see *similarities* between two or more things. They include **contrast** transitions to point out *differences*.

1. **interface:** point of interaction
2. **exponentially:** multiplying in large quantities
3. **repositories:** places where things are put for safekeeping
4. **audible:** able to be heard

* Adapted from Andrews et al., *Public Speaking*. Boston: Houghton Mifflin, 1999, 150–51.

† Adapted from Bernstein and Nash, *Essentials of Psychology*, 2nd ed. Boston: Houghton Mifflin, 2002, 238.

First, let's examine the *comparison* transitions, which appear in the list below:

Comparison Transitions

also	similarly	in the same way
too	in a similar manner	along the same line
likewise	just like, just as	in both cases

The following pairs of sentences illustrate the use of comparison transitions:

Religious Sunni Muslims participate in prayer services in which they bow their heads toward the holy city of Mecca and recite verses from their holy book, the Quran. ***Likewise,*** Shiite Muslims worship in the same ways.

Tobacco is a highly addictive substance that accounts for more deaths than do all other drugs, car accidents, suicides, homicides, and fires combined. ***Similarly,*** alcohol is a potentially addictive drug that can lead to major health problems.

To nineteenth-century Americans, the West represented opportunity. The machine, ***too,*** fired American optimism; between 1860 and 1930, the U.S. Patent Office registered 1.5 million new inventions.

The following paragraph uses comparison transition words (boldfaced and italics). Notice how each transition indicates another point of comparison:

Scientists are simulating a Martian lifestyle on Devon Island, a polar desert in the Canadian Arctic, because conditions there are like those on the planet Mars. The terrain of Devon Island is strikingly similar to the landscape of Mars. ***Like*** Mars, Devon Island is characterized by canyons and crevasses[1] created by, some scientists theorize, the movement of ancient glaciers. Both seem rocky and lifeless. ***As*** on Devon Island, researchers speculate, the seemingly dead rocks on Mars may contain microbial[2] life or fossils. The climate is similar, **too.** Mars is extremely cold. ***Likewise,*** Devon Island is cold, requiring scientists to wear protective suits with helmets. On Mars, scientists would conduct experiments. ***In the same way,*** researchers on Devon Island collect soil samples, study rocks, use sensors to search for water, and test a solar-powered robot that might actually be used someday on our neighboring planet.*

1. **crevasses:** deep cracks or chasms
2. **microbial:** relating to tiny life forms

* Adapted from John B. Carnett, "Mars Boot Camp," *Popular Science,* October 2001, 52–58.

5

Exercise 5.4

Fill in the blanks in the following sentences and paragraphs with appropriate comparison transitions. Choose words or phrases from the box on page 199. Try to vary your choices. Answers will vary.

1. A table of contents in a book helps you find information contained in the pages of that book. Likewise, directories on the Internet offer extensive lists of web pages, all grouped by topic.

2. Workers in many different types of professions have formed unions to ensure recognition of their profession's importance and adequate pay. Teachers are one group of professionals that formed a union. In like manner, nurses have a union to look out for them.

3. Meat is so packed with nutrients, it gave early humans a break from constant feeding, allowing them to eat at less regular intervals.[1] Similarly, lions and tigers didn't have to eat around the clock just to keep going.*

4. Islam and Christianity are similar in many ways. Islam is a monotheistic[2] religion that recognizes God (Allah) as the Creator. Christianity, too, is monotheistic. Islam holds that God is omnipotent and omniscient.[3] Likewise, Christians believe in an all-powerful God. Followers of Islam believe that God has a unique relationship with humans and makes agreements or Covenants with them. Similarly, Christians believe that humans can have meaningful relationships with God. Both religions believe that humans have an eternal soul or spirit, which continues its existence after physical death. Those who practice Islam believe that God will judge each human after the end of the world and evaluate his or her actions in compliance with a moral code. Christians also believe that God will hold humans accountable for their deeds on Earth.†

1. **intervals:** amounts of time between two events or states
2. **monotheistic:** worshipping one god
3. **omnipotent and omniscient:** all-powerful and all-knowing

* Adapted from Michael D. Lemonick, "How We Grew So Big," *Time,* June 7, 2004.

† Adapted from "Islam and Christianity: Similarities and Differences," http://forum.pressdemocrat.com/viewtopic.php?f=6&t=3233#p34841

5

5. In his studies of how infants form attachments to their caregivers, Harry Harlow isolated some newborn monkeys from all social contact. After a year of this isolation, the monkeys showed dramatic disturbances. When visited by normally active, playful monkeys, they withdrew to a corner, huddling or rocking for hours. When some of the females had babies (through artificial insemination), they tended to ignore or even physically abuse them.

In a similar manner______, humans who spend their first fewyears without a consistent caregiver exhibit many of the same problems. Like______ Harlow's deprived monkeys, abandoned children discovered at Romanian and Russian orphanages were withdrawn and engaged in constant rocking. Even after being adopted, the children were depressed, stared blankly, and demanded attention. Just as______ the deprived monkeys lashed out at their own babies, some of the children could not control their own tempers and interacted poorly with their adopted mothers. Neurologists suggest that the dramatic problems observed in both isolated monkeys and humans are the result of developmental brain dysfunction and damage brought on by a lack of touch and body movement in infancy.*

Now, let's look at the *contrast* transitions:

Contrast Transitions

however	nevertheless	unfortunately
but	on the one hand	in contrast
yet	on the other hand	conversely
although	unlike	even though
instead	rather	still
in opposition	on the contrary	nonetheless
in spite of	actually	whereas
just the opposite	despite	in reality
though	while	as opposed to

The following pairs of sentences illustrate the use of contrast transitions:

More than 8,000 fifth graders failed state reading and math tests. ***Yet,*** 75 percent of these children were promoted by principals to the sixth grade.

5

* Adapted from Bernstein et al., *Psychology*, 5th ed. Boston: Houghton Mifflin, 2000, 426.

Las Vegas, America's most colorful city, is best known for its casinos and showgirls. ***However,*** no less than five fine-art museums are determined to bring class and culture to the neon strip.

The common view is that the East has been so heavily logged that there are no old trees left. ***On the contrary,*** several forests in New York, Pennsylvania, New Hampshire, and Massachusetts contain trees as old as four or five hundred years.

Next, read a paragraph that includes contrast transition words (boldfaced and italics). Notice how each transition indicates another point of contrast.

If you want whiter teeth, should you try one of the do-it-yourself whitening kits, or should you book an appointment with your dentist? The home kits and dentist treatments differ in terms of time, cost, and results. At-home bleaching, such as Crest's Whitestrips, contains tape or trays that you wear on your teeth from 30 minutes to 3 hours at a time over several weeks. ***In contrast,*** the dentist's treatment often includes lasers that speed the process, which takes only two or three sessions in the chair. The cost of the various treatments differs widely. Crest Whitestrips cost only about $44 for a 2-week supply, ***but*** dentist treatments can cost up to one thousand. The results, too, will differ. Crest guarantees "noticeably whiter" teeth. Dentists, ***however,*** are more specific; they say they can lighten the teeth 8 to 10 shades.*

Exercise 5.5

Fill in the blanks in the following sentences and paragraphs with the appropriate contrast transition. Choose words or phrases from the box on page 201. Try to vary your choices. Answers will vary.

1. Many people feared the Second World War would be a repetition of the First. However, it was much bigger in every way.†

2. Jeff Moran and some friends from Troop 1320 dropped onto the lawn near Trading Post 13 one sweltering Tuesday morning during the Fifteenth Boy Scouts Jamboree at Fort A. P. Hill near Fredericksburg, Virginia. In spite of the heat wave, over the next 10 days they would help 32,000 other Scouts burn through 76,000 hamburgers, 479,000 eggs, and 10 tons of beef stew.‡

* Adapted from Patty Rhule, "White Might," *USA Weekend,* October 5–7, 2001, 12.

† From Bulliet et al., *The Earth and Its Peoples,* Brief Edition. Boston: Houghton Mifflin, 2000, 539. Copyright © 2000 by Houghton Mifflin Company. Reprinted with permission.

‡ Adapted from David France, "Scouts Divided," *Newsweek,* August 6, 2001, 45.

3. Although ______ we often think of a speech as "being over" when the speaker has delivered his or her conclusion, many times the conversation with the audience is just beginning.*

4. The Roman Empire was built through wars whereby emerging civilizations were conquered and put under control of Roman leaders. Unlike ______ the Greeks, who thought that other civilizations were barbaric and had nothing to offer Greek civilization, the Romans were quite willing to adopt practices of those they conquered if they appeared to be more useful than Roman practices. Whereas ______ Greek city-states created philosophy, music, art, and drama, the Romans typically adopted cultural practices of those they conquered.†

5. Females and males physically differ in a number of ways, including the makeup of their chromosomes,[1] their genitalia,[2] and levels of certain hormones. Females are physically more mature at birth, whereas ______ males show a special physical vulnerability during infancy. Compared with females, males are more likely to be miscarried, die in infancy, or develop hereditary diseases. Later in infancy and childhood, females walk, talk, and reach other developmental milestones earlier than males. Males, on the other hand ______, are more physically active and more likely to engage in vigorous rough-and-tumble play. By later childhood and adolescence, females reach puberty[3] earlier and males develop greater height, weight, and muscle mass than females.‡

Transition Words that Indicate Definition

One final set of transition words are those that signal **definitions** and **examples.** This pattern usually includes two parts—*a definition of a term and the examples that illustrate that term.* Because the definition pattern of organization often includes one or more examples, this type of transition will often

5

1. **chromosomes:** in cells, the material that carries hereditary information
2. **genitalia:** sex organs
3. **puberty:** stage at which an individual becomes capable of sexual reproduction

* From Andrews et al., *Public Speaking.* Boston: Houghton Mifflin, 1999, 287.

† Siedentop, Daryl. *Introduction to Physical Education, Fitness, and Sport,* 7th ed. New York: McGraw-Hill, 2009. Print. Ch. 2, p. 24.

‡ Adapted from Bukatko and Daehler, *Child Development,* 5th ed. Boston: Houghton Mifflin, 2004, 468. Copyright © 2004 by Houghton Mifflin Company. Reprinted with permission.

appear in definition paragraphs. However, transitions that indicate examples can appear in other types of paragraphs, too. Anytime authors want to illustrate an idea or make it clearer, they often identify the beginning of an example with one of the following transitions:

Definition Transitions	
is	defined as

Example Transitions		
for example	as an illustration	in one case
for instance	in one instance	more precisely
to illustrate	such as	specifically

5

The following pairs of sentences illustrate the use of definition/example transitions:

Special operations troops are the U.S. military's elite forces. The army's Delta Force, ***for example, is*** a clandestine[1] unit that specializes in hostage rescue and high-risk missions.

A learning disability ***is defined as*** a significant discrepancy[2] between measured intelligence and academic performance. Thomas Edison, ***for instance,*** did not have a low IQ, yet he experienced problems with reading, writing, and math in school.

A joint venture is a partnership formed to achieve a specific goal or to operate for a specific period of time. ***In one case,*** the Archer Daniels Midland Company (ADM), one of the world's leading food processors, entered into a joint venture with Gruma SA, Mexico's largest corn and flour tortilla company.

Now, read a paragraph that includes example transition words (boldfaced and italics). Notice how the transitions introduce the two examples:

A U.S. Pentagon publication ***defines*** asymmetric[3] warfare as "unanticipated or nontraditional approaches" that "exploit an adversary's

1. **clandestine:** secret or hidden
2. **discrepancy:** difference
3. **asymmetric:** unbalanced, unequal, uneven

vulnerabilities." More simply put: It is dirty fighting that gives the weak the best chance to defeat the strong. It often involves unexpected sneak attacks, which may occur in urban areas where civilians are present. ***For example,*** a 1983 guerilla[1] attack in Lebanon killed 241 American service members. ***In another instance,*** Somali militiamen downed two U.S. helicopters and killed 18 American troops in 1993.*

Exercise 5.6

Fill in the blanks in the following sentences and paragraphs with appropriate example transitions. Choose words or phrases from the box on page 204. Try to vary your choices. Answers will vary.

1. The speaker who wants to help the audience understand concepts that are complicated, abstract, or unfamiliar will give a speech of explanation. A professor's lecture, for example, is a speech aimed at explaining abstract or difficult concepts to students.†

2. *Trade paperbacks* is a term that refers to standard-size books that have flexible covers. They are designed to sell primarily in so-called mass-market outlets such as newsstands, drug stores, discount stores, and supermarkets.‡

3. There are two types of motivation: extrinsic and intrinsic. Extrinsic means from the outside. One who is extrinsically motivated is driven by some type of external reward, such as money or praise. Extrinsic motivation is based on the goals, interests, and values of others. Intrinsic motivation comes from within. It is behavior for its own sake, rather than for the rewards or outcomes the behavior might reap. Intrinsically motivated behaviors, such as personal achievement, enjoyment, self-confidence, or feeling positive emotions, require no external support or reinforcement.§

1. **guerilla:** related to a member of an irregular military unit

* Adapted from Mark Mazzetti and Richard J. Newman, "The Far Horizon," *U.S. News and World Report,* October 8, 2001, 14–15.

† Adapted from Andrews et al., *Public Speaking.* Boston: Houghton Mifflin, 1999, 300.

‡ Adapted from Turow, *Media Today.* Boston: Houghton Mifflin, 2000, 105.

§ France, Robert C. *Introduction to Sports Medicine and Athletic Training,* 2nd ed. Clifton Park: Delmar, 2011. Print. Ch. 10, p. 174.

4. Group marriage (also known as co-marriage) is a rare arrangement in which several men and women have sexual access to one another. Among Eskimos in northern Alaska, for example, sexual relations between unrelated individuals implied ties of mutual aid and support. In order to create or strengthen such ties, a man could share his wife with another man for temporary sexual relationships.*

5. Senators opposed to a bill can engage in a *filibuster,* which is an effort to tie up the floor of the Senate in debate to stop the members from voting on a bill. More precisely a filibuster is considered "hardball politics." In one case a filibuster occurred when southern senators temporarily derailed Minnesota senator Hubert Humphrey's efforts to pass the Civil Rights Act of 1964.†

Transitions in Combinations of Patterns

5

Supporting details in paragraphs can be organized according to more than one pattern. For example, a paragraph may include both *sequence* details and *effect* details. In such paragraphs, it will be particularly important for you to notice transition words and phrases, for they will provide clues about the various relationships among different kinds of details. For an example of a paragraph that includes more than one pattern and, therefore, different kinds of transitions, read the following:

> ***Ecotourism is*** relatively low-impact group travel or tour packages to destinations in nature. In other words, ecotourists travel to natural areas without disturbing the environment or contributing to the destruction of resources. ***For example,*** they might go to the South Pacific to see forests and endangered birds, or canoe down the Amazon in South America. Engaging in this type of travel has several benefits. It respects the diversity and fragility[1] of the environment of the Earth, so you won't cause more damage to natural resources or animal habitats. It ***also*** allows you to help support indigenous[2] cultures with your travel dollars. It offers you opportunities to broaden

1. **fragility:** easily damaged or destroyed
2. **indigenous:** living or growing in a certain area; native to

* Haviland, William A., et. al. *The Essence of Anthropology,* 2nd ed. Belmont: Wadsworth, 2010. Print. Ch. 12, p. 234.

† Adapted from Barbour and Wright, *Keeping the Republic.* Boston: Houghton Mifflin, 2001, 177–79.

your horizons, ***too,*** because you travel off the beaten path into excitingly different places. ***Finally,*** it will help you rediscover your passion for life, for your experience is bound to help you discover something personal and meaningful.*

This paragraph begins with a *definition* of ecotourism that includes examples. Then, it offers a *list* of reasons for becoming an ecotourist. Therefore, it includes both *example* and *list* transitions.

Exercise 5.7

Read each of the following paragraphs and circle the transition words or phrases. Then, in the list below the paragraph, place a check mark next to the two or three patterns used to organize the details.

1. Fashion occurs in almost every aspect of life. One of the many definitions of fashion is that fashion is what the majority of a group is wearing. However, apparel and accessories are not the only products subject to fashion influences. Fashion's pervasive nature becomes evident in many products areas, including food, interiors, architecture, automobiles, lifestyles, technology, and many other consumer goods. The red thread that connects these different aspects of fashion is usually a larger, more pervasive trend. For example, as the green movement gains momentum in consumer products and lifestyles, it affects what is fashionable in many consumer products, such as organic foods, sustainable environments, hybrid automobiles, postconsumer recycling, eco-friendly products, and organic apparel. Another pervasive trend might be the concept of streamlining. Apparel may reflect simple designs, interiors may feature minimalist décor, and automobiles and buildings may become sleeker and less ornate.†

   __✓__ list　　______ comparison/contrast

   ______ sequence　　__✓__ definition

   __✓__ cause/effect

2. Three styles of leadership have been identified: authoritarian, laissez-faire, and democratic. The first type, the authoritarian leader, holds all authority and responsibility, with communication usually moving from top to bottom. This leader assigns workers to specific tasks and expects orderly, precise results. The leaders at United Parcel Service, for instance,

* Adapted from www.ecotourism.org website.

† Stall-Meadows, Celia. *Fashion Now: A Global Perspective.* Upper Saddle River: Pearson Education, Inc., 2011. Print. Ch. 1, p. 5.

5

employ authoritarian leadership. At the other extreme is the laissez-faire[1] leader, who gives authority to employees. With the laissez-faire style, subordinates are allowed to work as they choose with a minimum of interference. For example, leaders at Apple Computer are known to employ a laissez-faire style. The third type, the democratic leader, holds final responsibility but also delegates authority to others, who participate in determining work assignments. An example of this leadership style is the manager who employs a communication style that is active both upward and downward. Managers for both Wal-Mart and Saturn have used democratic leadership.*

__✓__ list　　______ comparison/contrast

______ sequence　　__✓__ definition

______ cause/effect

3. The tradition of painting fire engines red dates back to at least the early 1920s. When Henry Ford made motor cars affordable for the average American family, he let it be known that his vehicles could be bought in any possible color—just as long as it was black. Pretty soon the nation's highways and byways were crowded with black vehicles, and quite logically the fire service began painting their vehicles red in an effort to stand out. Today's consumers can buy vehicles in just about any imaginable color, and so can the fire service. In addition to the traditional red fire engine, it is not uncommon to see white, yellow, blue, orange, green, or even black fire trucks. Many fire departments have, however, stuck loyally to the time-honored red engine.†

______ list　　__✓__ comparison/contrast

__✓__ sequence　　______ definition

______ cause/effect

4. A debate that began in the late 1970s suggested that the content of curriculum taught in U.S. classrooms should reflect the diverse character of the nation's population, or be *multicultural*. It should, for instance, dispense knowledge about this country's diverse cultural groups. This multicultural approach was recommended for several reasons. First, advocates argued that the curriculum should better represent the actual contributions

1. **laissez-faire:** French for "let do," or "leave alone"

* Adapted from Pride et al., *Business*, 6th ed. Boston: Houghton Mifflin, 1999, 153.

† Loyd, Jason B. *Fundamentals of Fire and Emergency Services*. Upper Saddle River: Pearson Education, Inc., 2010. Print. Ch. 1, p. 11.

made by various cultural groups to this country's society. Second, a multicultural curriculum would educate children of majority status as to the many accomplishments and contributions to U.S. society by individuals of minority status. Third, multicultural education was perceived as a school reform movement that could improve the content and process of education within schools.*

___✓___ list
______ sequence
______ cause/effect
______ comparison/contrast
___✓___ definition

5. Halloween is a plastic holiday. Unlike Christmas, Easter, and their cousins from other cultures, Halloween lacks religious foundations. Unlike Thanksgiving and the Fourth of July, it has no patriotic underpinnings.[1] It even lacks the single-minded sentimentality of the synthetic Mother's Day. Instead, Halloween has been mauled[2] and molded to fit the needs of each generation. In the 1600s, Puritans[3] intent on survival in a new world and salvation in the next ignored it. In the next two centuries, a hard-pressed immigrant population let off steam in its honor. In the 1800s and early 1900s, a Victorian society tamed it. In the twentieth century, World Wars I and II and even Vietnam undermined it. And a newly powerful postwar nation gave it a social conscience.†

______ list
___✓___ sequence
______ cause/effect
___✓___ comparison/contrast
______ definition

5

Exercise 5.8

The following groups of sentences have been scrambled. Number them in the order they should appear (1, 2, 3, etc.) so that they make sense. Use the transitions to help you figure out the right order. Then, in the list below each group, write a check mark next to the pattern or patterns used to organize the details.

1. **underpinnings:** support or foundation
2. **mauled:** injured by beating or rough handling
3. **Puritans:** group of sixteenth- and seventeenth-century English Protestants who advocated strict religious observance and morality

* Adapted from Garcia, *Student Cultural Diversity: Understanding and Meeting the Challenge,* 3rd ed. Boston: Houghton Mifflin, 2002.

† Adapted from Ellen Feldman, "Halloween," *American Heritage,* October 2001, 69. Reprinted by permission of *American Heritage.*

1. __2__ From 1942 to 1943, fighting street by street, the Soviets managed to defend their city in what was arguably the pivotal[1] military engagement of World War II.

__1__ Although the Germans reached Stalingrad by late 1942, they could not achieve a knockout.

__3__ By the end of January 1943, the Soviets had captured what remained of the German force, about 100,000 men.

__4__ The victory came at an immense price: A million Soviet soldiers and civilians died at Stalingrad, but by February 1944, Soviet troops had pushed the Germans back to the Polish border.*

Pattern(s) of organization:

_____ list

__✓__ sequence

_____ cause/effect

_____ comparison/contrast

_____ definition

5

2. __5__ Finally, if you need to evacuate the aircraft, leave your bags on the plane.

__1__ You can increase your chances of surviving an airplane crash.

__3__ Also, you should listen to the flight attendants' preflight safety briefing.

__2__ For one thing, when you fly, wear clothing of natural fabrics and don't wear high heels.

__4__ In addition, examine the emergency hatches and figure out how they operate.†

Pattern(s) of organization:

__✓__ list

_____ sequence

_____ cause/effect

_____ comparison/contrast

_____ definition

1. **pivotal:** important, crucial

* Adapted from Noble et al., *Western Civilization,* 2nd ed. Boston: Houghton Mifflin, 1999, 666. Copyright © 1999 by Houghton Mifflin Company. Reprinted with permission.

† Adapted from Sally B. Donnelly, "How to Survive a Crash," *Time,* November 13, 2000, 91.

3. __3__ This reduced activity in the locus coeruleus, in turn, tends to cause cognitive changes and a release of inhibitions.

__2__ In particular, alcohol depresses activity in a specific region of the brain called the *locus coeruleus*.

__1__ Alcohol affects specific brain regions.

__4__ As a result, some drinkers talk loudly, act silly, or tell others what they think of them.*

Pattern(s) of organization:

______ list ______ comparison/contrast

______ sequence ______ definition

__✓__ cause/effect

4. __1__ In literature, several twentieth-century novelists used the stream-of-consciousness technique, a type of narration in which the author presents a character's thoughts, feelings, and reactions with no comment or explanation.

__3__ Another example is William Faulkner's *The Sound and the Fury* (1922), in which much of the drama is seen through the eyes of a person with a learning disability.

__2__ One example is Virginia Woolf's *Jacob's Room* (1922), a novel made up of a series of internal monologues,[1] in which ideas and emotions from different periods of time bubble up randomly.

__4__ James Joyce's *Ulysses* (1922), which abandoned conventional grammar and blended foreign words, puns, bits of knowledge, and scraps of memory together in bewildering confusion, is a third—and perhaps the most famous—example.†

Pattern(s) of organization:

__✓__ list ______ comparison/contrast

______ sequence __✓__ definition

______ cause/effect

1. **monologues:** speeches made by one person

* Adapted from Bernstein and Nash, *Essentials of Psychology,* 2nd ed. Boston: Houghton Mifflin, 2002, 135.

† Adapted from McKay et al., *A History of Western Civilization,* 7th ed. Boston: Houghton Mifflin, 2003, 929–30. Copyright © 2003 by Houghton Mifflin Company. Reprinted with permission.

5

5. __3__ However, tiredness, fever, headache, and major aches and pains probably indicate the flu.

__1__ A cold and the flu are alike in some ways, but their symptoms and length differ.

__4__ These flu symptoms can continue for several weeks and lead to more serious problems, like the lung disease pneumonia.

__2__ A stuffy nose, sore throat, and sneezing are usually signs of a cold.

Pattern(s) of organization:

_____ list

_____ sequence

_____ cause/effect

__✓__ comparison/contrast

_____ definition

5

Reading Strategy: Summarizing

When you **summarize** *a reading selection, you briefly restate, in your own words, its most important ideas.* A summary usually focuses on the most general points, which include the overall main idea and some of the major supporting details. As a result, summaries are much shorter than the original material. A paragraph can usually be summarized in a sentence or two, an article can be summarized in a paragraph, and a typical textbook chapter can be summarized in a page or two.

Summarizing is an important reading skill that you will use for three specific academic purposes: studying, completing assignments and tests, and incorporating source material into research projects.

Studying. Writing summaries is an effective way to gain a better understanding of what you read. If you need to remember the information in a textbook chapter, for instance, you will know it more thoroughly after you have summarized its main ideas. Also, the act of writing down these ideas will help reinforce them in your memory.

Completing assignments and tests. Summaries are one of the most common types of college writing assignments. Professors in a variety of disciplines often ask students to summarize readings such as journal articles. Also, "summarize" is a common direction in tests that require written responses.

Incorporating source material into research projects. You will use summaries of other sources to support your ideas in research projects such as term papers.

To write a summary, follow these three steps:

1. Using active reading techniques, read and reread the original material until you understand it.
2. Identify the main idea and major supporting points. In particular, underline all of the topic sentences. You might also want to create an outline or map that diagrams the general and specific relationships among sentences (in a paragraph) or paragraphs (in an article or chapter).
3. Using your own words, write sentences that state the author's main idea along with the most important major details. This rewriting, or paraphrasing, should be accurate; it should not add anything that did not appear in the original or omit anything important from the original. It should also be objective. In other words, don't offer your own reactions or opinions; just restate the author's points without commenting on them. If you use a phrase from the original, enclose it in quotation marks to indicate that it is the author's words, not yours.

Follow the three steps described above to write a one- or two-paragraph summary for any one of readings in the Reading Selections starting on page 214. Answers will vary.

The following web links will provide you with additional information and practice with the very important skills of summarizing.

WEB LINK

http://users.drew.edu/~sjamieso/summary.html
http://www.tc.umn.edu/~jewel001/CollegeWriting/WRITEREAD/Summary/samples.htm

Reading Selections

Practicing the Active Reading Strategy

Before and While You Read

You can use active reading strategies before, while, and after you read a selection. The following are some suggestions for active reading strategies that you can perform before you read and while you read.

1. Skim the selection for any unfamiliar words. Circle or highlight any words you do not know.
2. As you read, underline, highlight, or circle important words or phrases.
3. Write down any questions about the selection if you are confused by the information presented.
4. Jot notes in the margin to help you understand the material.

BIOGRAPHY: Rosa Parks: An American Hero

Rosa Parks, a Montgomery, Alabama, seamstress, simply refused to relinquish her seat on a city bus to a white man on December 1, 1955. Her act of courage sparked the Montgomery Bus Boycott and brought the Civil Rights Movement to national attention. She has been called the mother of the Civil Rights Movement.

1 In Montgomery, Alabama, in 1955, segregation laws governed and interfered with many aspects of people's lives. Among the regulations were laws pertaining to the city bus system: African American people were required to pay their fare to the bus driver in the front, then get off, walk to the rear entrance, and board the bus from there. African American riders were only allowed to sit in the rows toward the back of the bus, and even then, if White riders ran out of seats in the rows toward the front, the bus driver would require Black passengers to vacate additional rows to accommodate them. The African American riders would then have to move farther back or stand up. Black passengers were not allowed to sit across the aisle from Whites in the same row. Sometimes bus drivers would allow Black passengers to pay their fares, and then spitefully close the doors and drive away before they made it to the back door to board. About two-thirds of Montgomery's bus riders were African American and subject to these indignities.[1]

2 Rosa Parks was born *Rosa Louise McCauley,* in Tuskegee, Alabama, on February 4, 1913. Her father was a carpenter and her mother a teacher. Her mother advised her daughter and her students to "take advantage of the opportunities, no matter how few they were." Rosa Parks attended Alabama State Teachers College, married Raymond Parks, and moved to Montgomery with her husband. The couple was active in the Montgomery chapter of the NAACP and helped work on hate crime cases against local African Americans. The cases, though numerous, did not receive much publicity from the White-controlled press.

3 Rosa Parks, 42 years old in 1955, had dealt with the discriminatory practices in the public transit system for some time. Contrary to popular legend,

1. **indignities:** offensive acts

she was not the first person to challenge the fairness of the regulations; nor did she merely refuse to vacate her seat because she was so tired she did not want to stand up, or because her feet hurt after a long day at work. She has said that on December 1, 1955, she had indeed, worked all day, but was no more tired on that day than any other. Even though she worked as a seamstress for a department store (most African Americans had extremely limited opportunities under segregation), Rosa Parks was a college-educated and politically aware woman. She, and many others, felt that the inherent[1] unfairness of segregation laws needed to be addressed in court. Eight months earlier, a fifteen year-old girl, Claudette Colvin, had experienced a similar incident on a bus and was arrested for not giving up her seat. NAACP officials met with Miss Colvin to determine whether she would stand up to media scrutiny if her case was used as a test case against the transit system's segregation policy, but they decided against it. In October of the same year, another young woman, Mary Smith, was also arrested for the same thing. NAACP leaders decided not to pursue her case either.

4 Yet the incident on December 1, involving Rosa Parks was unplanned; she later stated that she "did not get on the bus to get arrested," *but* she "got on the bus to go home." On that day, Mrs. Parks got on the bus and took the last available seat on the bus, toward the back, behind the rows where the White passengers were sitting. After two or three stops, some more White people boarded the bus, and one of them remained standing, without a seat. When the bus driver saw him standing, he ordered the four African American passengers in Mrs. Parks's row to vacate the row of seats so the White man could occupy one of the seats. The other three Black passengers stood up, but Rosa Parks did not. When the bus driver questioned her as to whether she was going to stand up, she calmly replied that she was not. The driver then told her that he would have her arrested, and she replied, "You may do that." The driver stopped the bus and called the police, and Mrs. Parks was arrested.

5 Her bail was posted that Thursday night by a lawyer who was the husband of her former employer. Word of the incident spread rapidly in the African American Community. Rosa Parks, a respected, stable member of that community, and a woman of unimpeachable character, would prove to be perfect for the test case that Black activists had been waiting for. The next night a meeting was held at the Dexter Avenue Baptist Church, where Dr. Martin Luther King was the pastor. The Women's Political Council printed 35,000 handbills urging African Americans to do whatever was necessary to avoid riding the city buses on Monday, December 5, the day of Mrs. Parks's trial. The handbills were passed out at schools, and the word spread over the weekend. Martin Luther King, Jr., said, "If we are wrong, justice is a lie. And we are determined here in Montgomery to work and fight until justice runs down like water."

6 On Monday morning, the Black citizens of Montgomery stayed off the buses in mass. People with cars used their vehicles to taxi others who worked

1. **inherent:** existing as an essential part

5

too far to walk. When Mrs. Parks arrived at the courthouse on Monday morning, a crowd was waiting in front; she was impeccably dressed in a black dress and gray coat, with white gloves and a hat. One young onlooker was heard to exclaim, "Oh, she's so sweet! They've messed with the wrong one now!"

7 Rosa Parks's trial lasted only 30 minutes, and she was found guilty and ordered to pay a fine. The case was appealed, and during the appeal, the boycott of the Montgomery public transit system continued for over a year. Dr. Martin Luther King, Jr., led the boycott and his leadership propelled him to the forefront of the Civil Rights Movement, which had finally begun to receive publicity and national attention since the arrest of Mrs. Parks. On December 21, 1956, the U.S. Supreme Court ruled that segregation on public transit was illegal.

8 Rosa Parks and her family were threatened and harassed by die-hard segregationists until they moved to Detroit, Michigan, in 1957. In 1965, she joined the staff of Rep. John Conyers, D-Michigan, and worked for him until 1988, the year she retired. After her husband Raymond passed away, Rosa Parks founded the Rosa and Raymond Parks Institute for Self Development to benefit children in the Detroit area. She was active in her church, and continued to speak out against racial injustice.[1]

9 In 1999, President Clinton, along with House and Senate leaders, awarded her a Congressional Gold Medal.

10 On October 24, 2005, at the age of 92, Rosa Parks quietly died in her apartment. She had been diagnosed the previous year with progressive dementia. Her death was marked by several memorial services, among them lying in state at the Capitol Rotunda in Washington, DC, where an estimated 50,000 people viewed her casket. Rosa was interred between her husband and mother at Detroit's Woodlawn Cemetery in the chapel's mausoleum. Shortly after her death the chapel was renamed the Rosa L. Parks Freedom Chapel.*

■ Vocabulary

Read the following questions about some of the vocabulary words that appear in the previous selection. Before you look up the word, try to use the context of the passage to figure out the meaning. Then circle the letter of the correct answer for each question.

1. **injustice:** violation of another's rights or of what is right

* Source: http://www.biography.com/articles/Rosa-Parks-9433715. Web. 10/30/2010
http://www.gibbsmagazine.com/RosaParks.htm. Web. by Susan Robinson Republished 4/18/05

5

1. What does *vacate* mean in paragraph 1?

   a. to fill
   b. to give up
   c. to occupy
   d. to share

2. In paragraph 3, the author writes about the "public *transit* system." What does *transit* refer to?

   a. transportation
   b. maintenance
   c. money
   d. food

3. What does *scrutiny* mean in paragraph 3?

   a. ignorance
   b. violence
   c. harassment
   d. examination

4. In paragraph 5, what does *unimpeachable* mean?

   a. questionable
   b. assertive
   c. pure
   d. corrupt

5. In paragraph 6, the author writes, ". . . she was *impeccably* dressed in a black dress and gray coat, with white gloves and a hat." What does *impeccable* mean?

   a. perfectly
   b. conservatively
   c. strangely
   d. flamboyantly

Reading Skills

Respond to each of the following questions by circling the letter of the correct answer or by writing your answer on the blank provided.

1. What is the main idea of paragraph 1? In Montgomery, Alabama, in 1955, segregation laws governed and interfered with many aspects of people's lives.

2. What is the topic of paragraph 3? discriminatory practices that Rosa Parks had to deal with

3. Write one example of a contrast transition from paragraph 3.

   contrary or even though

4. The transitions in paragraph 4 (on that day, after two or three stops) are examples of which type of transition?

   a. Compare/contrast
   b. Sequence
   c. Definition/example

5. Which sentence is a minor detail sentence from paragraph 1?

   a. Sentence 4
   b. Sentence 3
   c. Sentence 2
   d. Sentence 5

6. Which sentence is a major detail sentence from paragraph 1?

   a. Sentence 4
   b. Sentence 1
   c. Sentence 6
   d. Sentence 2

5

Practicing the Active Reading Strategy

After You Read

Now that you have read the selection, answer the following questions, using the active reading strategies that you learned in Chapter 1.

1. Identify and write down the point and purpose of this reading selection.
2. Did you circle or highlight any words that were unfamiliar to you? Can you figure out the meaning from the context of the passage? If not, then look up each word in a dictionary and find the definition that best describes the word as it is used in the selection. You may want to write the definition in the margin next to the word in the passage for future reference.
3. Predict any possible questions that may be used on a test about the content of this selection.

Questions for Discussion and Writing

Respond to each of the following questions based on your reading of the selection.

1. How did Rosa Parks break the law? Do you feel she was justified in doing so? Why or why not?

   She refused to give up her seat to a White passenger. Answers will vary.

2. Why did Rosa Parks refuse to give up her seat that day? She wanted to prove a point and did not feel she needed to give up her seat; not because she was tired from work.

3. What influence did Rosa Parks's actions have on the Civil Rights Movement?

Her actions led to the Montgomery public transit boycott, which was led by Dr. Martin Luther King, Jr.

Practicing the Active Reading Strategy

Before and While You Read

You can use active reading strategies before, while, and after you read a selection. The following are some suggestions for active reading strategies that you can employ before you read and as you are reading.

1. Skim the selection for any unfamiliar words. Circle or highlight any words you do not know.
2. As you read, underline, highlight, or circle important words or phrases.
3. Write down any questions about the selection if you are confused by the information presented.
4. Jot notes in the margin to help you understand the material.

5

TEXTBOOK READING: HEALTH PSYCHOLOGY

Environmental Stress

1 Working and living in a noisy environment can lead to many problems. Noise can even retard learning in children. Children living close to an airport where constant roars of jet engines interrupt their daily lives were found to have higher levels of stress and more learning difficulties than students not living close to an airport. A similar study showed that children living in noisy homes near busy roadways had greater difficulties with reading tasks than did children who lived in quiet homes. A classic series of studies on the effects of noise had students work on different tasks and then exposed them to bursts of sound. Unpredictable bursts of sound hindered their performance the most, but those students who faced consistent background sounds during early tasks performed badly on later tasks. Noise can play a large role in how stressed we feel and is often implicitly influencing our well-being.

2 Just as noise can be a problem, crowding can also be stressful. If you

grew up in a nice, quiet city or town with a population of between 30,000 and 100,000 or less, your experiences with crowding are very different from mine. I grew up in Mumbai (previously Bombay), a city with a population tilting the scales at 20,000,000 (yes, 20 million). Overcrowding can often produce negative moods for men, though not so much for women, physiological arousal (e.g., higher blood pressure), increased illness, more aggression, and a host of other stressful outcomes. Even if you do not live in a big city, you can see the effects of crowding at large gatherings. Large rock concerts, state fairs, or amusement parks during holiday weekends can become overcrowded, making people feel stressed and frustrated.

3 Environmental stressors can be divided into three main categories: back-ground stressors, natural disaster stressors, and techno-political stressors. Background stressors include crowding and noise, together with air pollution and chemical pollution. All of these can be long-term stressors and affect a large number of people. A second major category of environmental stressors is natural disaster stressors. These are short-term stressors and are often more severe than long-term stressors. For example, natural disasters such as flooding, earthquakes, and hurricanes can kill thousands of people and survivors often experience severe psychological consequences lasting a lifetime. Take Hurricane Katrina. It hit New Orleans in 2005 and damaged 80 percent of the city. Almost the entire city was evacuated, and close to 1,500 died. Not surprisingly, this major disaster had stressful effects resulting in mental illness, suicides, and post-traumatic stress disorder (PTSD), a specific form of mental illness related to the experience of severe stress, that influenced thousands. Two years after Katrina, the rate of PTSD was 10 times higher in New Orleans than in the general public.

4 The third category of stressors can be called techno-political stressors. Although these types of stressors can be unpredictable and uncontrollable like natural disasters, they are directly linked to technological or political causes. Some examples are nuclear reactor accidents (e.g., Three Mile Island in Pennsylvania and Chernobyl in Russia), chemical plant accidents (e.g., the Union Carbide accident in Bhopal, India), and dam-related flooding (e.g., Buffalo Creek in West Virginia). Political tragedies, such as wars and acts of terrorism, are also extremely stressful. In a longitudinal study of over 2,000 adults, it was found that stress responses to the 9/11 attacks predicted increased heart problems even three years after the attacks.*

* Gurung, Regan A. R. *Health Psychology: A Cultural Approach,* 2nd ed. Belmont: Wadsworth, 2010. Print. Ch. 4, pp. 134–35.

Vocabulary

Read the following questions about some of the vocabulary words that appear in the previous selection. Before you look up the word, try to use the context of the passage to figure out the meaning. Then circle the letter of the correct answer for each question or write the answer on the blank.

1. In paragraph 1, the author states ". . . sound *hindered* their performance." What does *hindered* mean?
   a. advanced
   b. improved
   c. got in the way of
   d. had no effect on
2. Paragraph 1 states ". . . *implicitly* influencing." What does *implicitly* mean?
   a. obviously
   b. unnoticed
   c. barely
   d. greatly
3. What is a *physiological* arousal, as in paragraph 2?
   a. related to biology
   b. related to psychology
   c. related to philosophy
   d. related to medicine
4. *Aggression* (paragraph 2) refers to an assault or attack.
5. What does *longitudinal* in paragraph 4 mean?
   a. over distance
   b. over a long time
   c. a short time
   d. a new map

5

Reading Skills

Respond to each of the following questions by circling the letter of the correct answer or by writing your answer on the blank provided.

1. The topic of paragraph 1 is problems caused by a noisy environment.
2. What is the comparison signal found in paragraph 1? similar
3. Identify the topic sentence in paragraph 2. Just as noise can be a problem, crowding can also be stressful.
4. Circle the transition words in paragraph 3. Check the patterns that are used in this paragraph.

   ✓ list
   ____ sequence
   ____ cause
   ____ comparison
   ____ definition
   ✓ example

5. Write the major transitions from paragraph 4. third, although, some examples, such as

Practicing the Active Reading Strategy

■ After You Read

Now that you have read the selection, answer the following questions, using the active reading strategies that you learned in Chapter 1.

1. Identify and write down the point and purpose of this reading selection.
2. Did you circle or highlight any words that are unfamiliar to you? Can you figure out the meaning from the context of the passage? If not, then look up each word in a dictionary and find the definition that best describes the word as it is used in the selection. You may want to write the definition in the margin next to the word in the passage for future reference.
3. Predict any possible questions that may be used on a test about the content of this selection.

5

■ Questions for Discussion and Writing

Respond to each of the following questions based on your reading of the selection.

1. Identify two negative effects that a noisy environment can have on students.
   Unpredictable bursts of sound hindered their performance the most, but those students who faced consistent background sounds during early tasks performed badly on later tasks.
2. Why is crowding stressful? Overcrowding can often produce negative moods for men, though not so much for women, physiological arousal (e.g., higher blood pressure), increased illness, more aggression, and a host of other stressful outcomes.
3. What environmental stressor do you experience in your daily life? What can you do to relieve those stressors?
   Answers may vary.

Practicing the Active Reading Strategy

■ Before and While You Read

You can use active reading strategies before, while, and after you read a selection. The following are some suggestions for active reading strategies that you can employ before you read and as you are reading.

1. Skim the selection for any unfamiliar words. Circle or highlight any words you do not know.
2. As you read, underline, highlight, or circle important words or phrases.
3. Write down any questions about the selection if you are confused by the information presented.
4. Jot notes in the margin to help you understand the material.

WEBSITE READING: LINGUISTICS

Signing, Singing, Speaking: How Language Evolved

by Jon Hamilton

Humans did not always speak they way they do now. Over millions of years speech and language have evolved so the people can communicate more clearly with each other. How language developed has been a fascinating subject of study for scientists for decades.

1 These words you are reading are really just a collection of arbitrary symbols. Yet, after some decoding by your brain, these symbols convey meaning. That's because humans have evolved a brain with an extraordinary knack for language. And language has given us a major advantage over other species. Yet scientists still don't know when and how we began using language. "The Earth would not be the way it is if humankind didn't have the ability to communicate, to organize itself, to pass knowledge down from generation to generation," says Jeff Elman, a professor of cognitive[1] science at the University of California, San Diego. "We'd be living in troops of very smart baboons," he says.

2 Instead, language has allowed us to cooperate in groups of millions instead of dozens, he says. It also lets us share the complex ideas produced by our brains, and it's flexible in ways you don't find in the communication systems of other species. Bees, for example, use an elaborate communication system to tell one another precisely how to get from the hive to a source of pollen, Elman says. "But that's all it does," he says. "They can't talk about politics. They can't talk about who's having an affair with what other bee—and these are things that we can do."

3 There's no single module[2] in our brain that produces language. Instead, language seems to come from lots of different circuits. And many of those

1. **cognitive:** relative to learning
2. **module:** part or unit

5

circuits also exist in other species. For example, some birds can imitate human speech. Some monkeys use specific calls to tell one another whether a predator is a leopard, a snake, or an eagle. And dogs are very good at reading our gestures and tone of voice. Take all of those bits and you get "exactly the right ingredients for making language possible," Elman says.

4 But language is a behavior, not a physical attribute. So there is no fossil record of when it first appeared, says David Armstrong, who spent decades studying the origin of language before retiring from Gallaudet University, a university for the deaf and hard of hearing in Washington, DC. "We have no way of knowing exactly when or how people began to speak, or in the case of sign language, when they began to sign or to gesture in a way that was complex enough for us to consider it to have been language," Armstrong says. Language means more than just having a label for an ax—it means being able to convey a message like, "The ax works better if you hold it this way."

5 There are several competing hypotheses[1] about how that ability emerged. Armstrong says he thinks gestures involving the hands may well have been the earliest form of complex human communication. Evidence from fossils supports that idea, Armstrong says. It shows that a modern hand capable of sign language evolved not long after our ape-like ancestors stopped walking on their knuckles a few million years ago. In contrast, the modern vocal tract[2] seems to have arrived much later, Armstrong says. And the modern version of a gene called FOXP2, which is important for speech and language, didn't appear until perhaps 100,000 years ago, he says. Early human ancestors probably used gestures to communicate, Armstrong says, because "articulate speech of the sort that we employ would have been probably difficult."

6 Also, sign language would have suited the early human lifestyle, Armstrong says. Groups of hunters could have used visual signs to communicate during a hunt without alerting their prey. It's possible that gestures eventually became associated with sounds, which got more sophisticated as the human vocal tract evolved, Armstrong says. Even now, there are close links between the brain centers involved in speech and those involved in sign language. Of course, once spoken language appeared, Armstrong says, it would have given our ancestors a huge advantage when they weren't hunting. They would have been able to communicate in the dark and while using hand tools.

7 Another idea about the origin of language is that it came from song. Ani Patel of The Neurosciences Institute in San Diego says this idea just feels right to a lot of people. "We feel music just taps into this kind

1. **hypotheses:** undeveloped explanations
2. **tract:** part of the body where speech originates

of pre-cognitive archaic part of ourselves," he says. So it seems to make sense that music came "before we had this complicated articulate language that we use to do abstract[1] thinking." Even Charles Darwin "talked about our ancestors singing love songs to each other before we could speak articulate language," Patel says. And musical ability is similar to language in that you can see aspects of it in other species. Some monkeys can recognize dissonant[2] tones, songbirds use complicated patterns of pitch and rhythm, and a few parrots can even dance to a beat.

8 And modern humans still combine music and speech in ways that seem innate,[3] Patel says. When a parent speaks to a baby, "it's this kind of lilting intonation," he says. "There is a lot of rhythm, a lot of exaggerated pitch contours, and people have speculated that this way of communicating with infants may have been one of the important roots to language in our species." Moreover, our brains process music and language in a similar fashion.

9 But just finding a connection between music and language doesn't prove that music came first, Patel says. He says it's possible that language emerged without help from either gestures or music. It might have come from a behavior you see in another smart mammal with a long life span: the killer whale. Scientists have shown that calls from whales in the same pod share a distinctive dialect, which seems to help them identify one another. Our ancestors also lived in small groups "where affiliation and identity was important," Patel says. So perhaps they began making distinctive sounds for the same reason whales did, he says, and these sounds eventually led to language.*

5

Vocabulary

Read the following questions about some of the vocabulary words that appear in the previous selection. Before you look up the word, try to use the context of the passage to figure out the meaning. Then circle the letter of the correct answer for each question or write the definition that best fit the context on the line.

1. What are *arbitrary* symbols? (paragraph 1)

   a. organized c. fixed

   b. random d. rare

1. **abstract:** existing in the mind
2. **dissonant:** lacking harmony
3. **innate:** inborn, or present at birth

* http://www.npr.org/templates/story/story.php?storyId=129155123&ps=cprs Web. 8/16/2010

2. *Convey* in paragraph 1 (and used again in paragraph 4) means to _____.

   (a.) communicate c. organize
   b. prevent d. sound out

3. To have a *knack* for language is to have an ability or talent. (paragraph 1)

4. ". . . *articulate* speech . . ." is what kind of speech? (paragraph 5)

   a. mumbled (c.) clear and effective
   b. distorted d. used in many languages

5. In paragraph 7, what is meant by *archaic?*

   a. useful c. interesting
   (b.) primitive d. unknown

Reading Skills

Respond to each of the following questions by circling the letter of the correct answer or by writing your answer on the blank provided.

5

1. Identify the kind of transition that begins paragraph 2. contrast

2. Circle the transitions in paragraph 3 and then list them here. instead, and, for example, some, and

3. Write the topic sentence for paragraph 4. But language is a behavior, not a physical attribute.

4. Identify the kind of transition that begins paragraph list

5. What patterns are used to organize paragraph 5?

   ✓ list _____ sequence
   ✓ contrast _____ cause
   _____ definition _____ example

Practicing the Active Reading Strategy

After You Read

Now that you have read the selection, answer the following questions, using the active reading strategies that you learned in Chapter 1.

1. Identify and write down the point and purpose of this reading selection.

2. Did you circle or highlight any words that are unfamiliar to you? Can you figure out the meaning from the context of the passage? If not, then look up each word in a dictionary and find the definition that best describes the word as it is used in the selection. You may want to write the definition in the margin next to the word in the passage for future reference.
3. Predict any possible questions that may be used on a test about the content of this selection.

Questions for Discussion and Writing

Respond to each of the following questions based on your reading of the selection.

1. What are the two hypotheses discussed in the article about how language evolved? Gestures involving the hands may well have been the earliest form of complex human communication. Language may have evolved from song.
2. Why would sign language have benefitted early man? Early man would have been able to communicate in the dark and while using hand tools.
3. How is language like music? Humans combine music and speech in a way that seems inborn. Also, our brains process music and language in a similar fashion.

5

Vocabulary Strategy: The Explanation Context Clue

In Chapter 4, you learned about the definition/restatement context clue. A second type of context clue is **explanation.** *In this type of clue, the words, phrases, or sentences near an unfamiliar word will explain enough about that word to allow you to figure out its meaning.* For example, read this next sentence, which comes from one of the paragraphs in this chapter:

> In 1941, the Japanese attacked America's Pearl Harbor. In 1942, 120,000 Japanese-Americans were rounded up and imprisoned in **internment** camps.

What does *internment* mean? There are a few explanation clues in this sentence. First of all, it's an adjective that describes a type of camp. Secondly, it's where people are imprisoned. Therefore, you can conclude that it must refer to a place where large numbers of people are confined or locked up.

Vocabulary Exercise 1

The following examples all come from paragraphs in this chapter and Chapter 4. In each one, use the explanation context clue to help you determine the meaning of the boldfaced word and write a definition for this word on the blank provided.

1. A learning disability is defined as a significant **discrepancy** between measured intelligence and academic performance. Thomas Edison, for instance, did not have a low IQ, yet he experienced problems with reading, writing, and math in school. difference

2. For example, *Reader's Digest,* a **compendium** of "must-read" articles, and *Time,* a weekly news summary, came out in 1922 and 1923, respectively. collection of items

3. Finally, press slightly against your tongue, **pursing** your lips as needed, and blow. puckering

4. Eating breakfast foods that are high in sugar and carbohydrates, such as doughnuts, causes blood sugar to rise quickly. By mid-morning, blood sugar drops rapidly, making you feel **lethargic** and irritable. sluggish

5. *Ecotourism* is relatively low-impact group travel or tour packages to destinations in nature. In other words, ecotourists travel to natural areas without disturbing the environment or contributing to the destruction of resources. For example, they might go to the South Pacific to see forests and endangered birds, or canoe down the Amazon in South America. Engaging in this type of travel has several benefits. It respects the diversity and fragility of the environment of the Earth, so you won't cause more damage to natural resources or animal habitats. It also allows you to help support **indigenous** cultures with your travel dollars. It offers you opportunities to broaden your horizons, too, because you travel off the beaten path into excitingly different places. living in an area or environment

6. In today's busy world, do you have an understudy if something unexpected comes up? First, organize a handful of friends, neighbors, or relatives and **deputize** one another; you look out for them, and they look out for you. appoint or empower a person to act for another

7. New York City is renowned for its high-end, celebrity-chef food culture. It also offers a host of budget-priced options for good food and drinks. Many of the best meal deals are found in the ethnic **enclaves** that dot the city. areas within a larger unit

5

8. New Orleans lies below sea level, in a bowl bordered by **levees** that fend off Lake Pontchartrain to the north and the Mississippi River to the south and west. embankments that keep bodies of water from overflowing

Vocabulary Exercise 2

Read the following textbook passage, and then use explanation context clues to write a definition of each boldfaced word on the blanks provided.

We think of the family as comprised of a married couple and their biological children. This couple is happily married; the children all feel **nurtured** and supported by their parents; and each family member's experience of the family is the same—all share the perception of the family as a safe haven providing for each member's physical and emotional needs.

This idealized image of the intact, multigenerational family household distorts the diversity and instability that has always characterized American families. The 1950s model of the white, middle-class, intact **nuclear** family, headed by a breadwinner father and supported by a homemaker mother, is only a narrow band on the broad spectrum of contemporary families. In its place, the "**postmodern** family" has emerged, characterized by a multitude of family structures—working mothers and two-earner households; divorced, single-parent, remarried, and adoptive families; and domestic partners, both gay and straight.

Consider as well the fact that a century ago, only 5 percent of married women participated in the **labor market**. In 1940, fewer than one married woman in seven worked outside the home. Since 1995, the dual-income family has become more common than the formerly more traditional one-income married household. Now over 60 percent of wives work outside the home.

Recent data suggest that since the mid-1980s the divorce rate in the United States has decreased slightly. Even so, **demographers** expect that 25 percent of contemporary marriages will dissolve by their seventh year, and approximately half will end before their twentieth year as a result of divorce. With few exceptions, divorce has been defined as an undesirable end to marriage. Many studies have been devoted to the documentation of the **deleterious** short- and long-term effects of divorce on children and adults, and divorce has been viewed as a social disorder whose frequency approaches epidemic proportions and urgently needs to be reduced. A lot is at stake; in other words, when marriages fail to function as the **pivotal** and key subsystem within the family system.

In addition, the typical image of the family distorts the wide range of **interpersonal** dynamics found within the contemporary family. Certainly, most of us would be reluctant to label U.S. families as violent. "Violence" and "family" are not words that go together. Yet, research tells a different tale. The home is the single most violent location in U.S. society. Statistics on intimate partner violence indicate that it is a widespread problem. The National Violence Against Women Survey found that of the over 16,000 men and women surveyed, nearly 25 percent of the women and 7.6 percent of the men said that they have been raped or physically **assaulted** by a spouse, partner, or date at some point in their lifetimes.*

1. nurtured to educate; bring or train up
2. nuclear relating to the core family structure of parents and children
3. postmodern of, relating to, or being a theory that involves a radical reappraisal of modern assumptions about culture, identity, history, or language
4. labor market work or career
5. demographers people who study the statistics of human populations, especially with reference to size and density, distribution, and vital statistics
6. deleterious harmful
7. pivotal vitally important
8. interpersonal between people
9. assaulted attacked

Reading Visuals: Pie Charts

In previous chapters, you've examined organizational charts and flow charts. A third kind of chart is called a **pie chart.** *This visual aid is a circle that is divided into wedges or slices, like the pieces of a pie.* The purpose of a pie chart is to show the composition of something; it indicates the amounts of each part that make up the whole. Each part is identified with a percentage or other quantity that indicates its size in relation to all of the other parts. One common use of pie charts is to represent financial information such as budgets or expenditures.

* Anderson, Stephen A. *Family Interaction: A Multigenerational Developmental Perspective*, 5th ed. Boston: Allyn & Bacon, 2011. Print. Ch. 1, pp. 4–6.

Pie charts contain the following parts:

- **Title.** The title identifies the whole entity that is being divided into parts.
- **Lines.** The lines radiate from the center of the circle, dividing the pie into pieces that represent the amount of each part. These pieces are different sizes because they are designed to be proportional to the whole.
- **Labels for names of parts.** Each piece is labeled to identify one part and its quantity in relation to the whole.
- **Source line.** The source line identifies who collected or compiled the information.

These parts are labeled in the following pie chart.

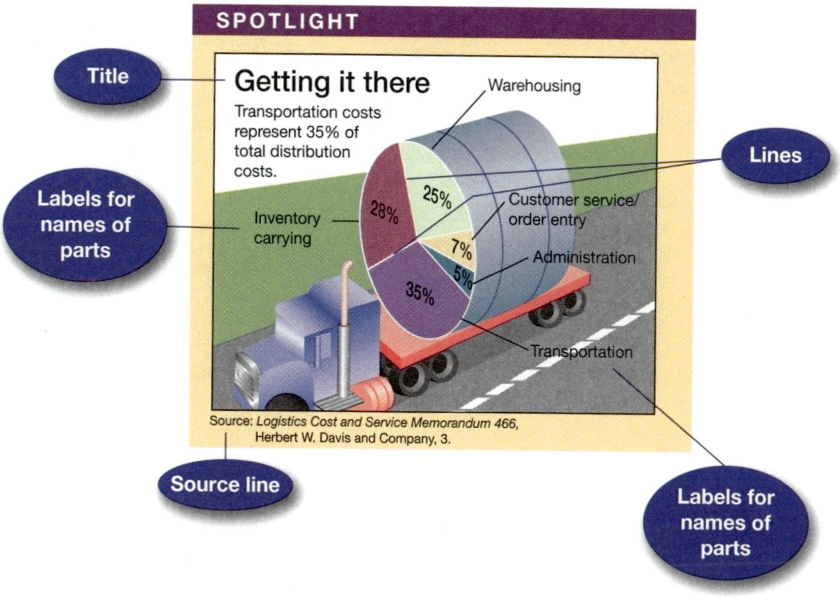

To read a pie chart, first look at its title so you'll know the whole entity that is being divided. Then, read each label and amount. Try to summarize in your own words the relationships you see and notice the biggest part, the smallest part, and parts that are about equal.

The pie chart "Getting It There" shows the amounts of five different kinds of distribution costs involved in getting products to consumers. The largest piece of the pie is transportation costs, which account for 35 percent of all costs. Inventory carrying is the next biggest cost, and administration is the smallest. The percentages all add up to 100 percent to represent the whole. The pie chart is cleverly drawn as a load carried on a truck to increase visual interest.

Now, study the pie charts "Volunteers by type of main organization" and "NYC Waste Characterization Study," and then answer the questions that follow.

Volunteers by type of main organization for which volunteer activities were performed, September 2009

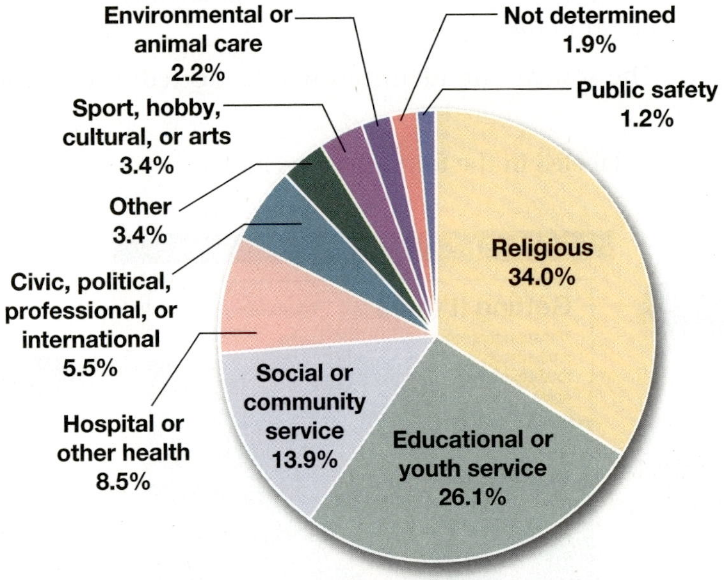

Source: http://economix.blogs.nytimes.com/2010/02/05/where-did-you-volunteer/

1. What does this pie chart represent? volunteers by type of main organization for which volunteer activities were performed
2. What is the source of this pie chart? U.S. Bureau of Labor Statistics
3. Which organization received the most volunteers? religious
4. What percentage of people responded that they volunteer in educational or youth service organizations? 26.1%
5. Which group received 8.5% of the volunteers? hospital or health organizations

5

NYC Waste Characterization Study
2004/05 Waste Composition
Annualized Results

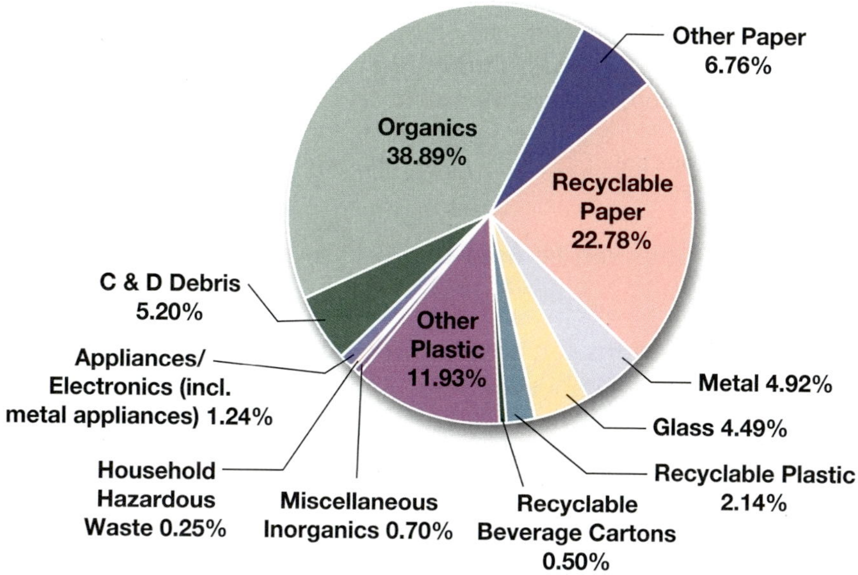

Source: http://www.nyc.gov/html/nycwasteless/html/resources/wcs.shtml.

1. What are the three largest categories of recycled material? What is the total percentage of these three categories? *organics, recyclable paper, and other plastics; 78.60%*

2. Which category has the least percentage of material recycled? *hazardous household waste*

3. What is the percentage difference between recycled glass and recycled metal? *.43%*

4. This study is a report for which city? *New York City*

5

Chapter 5 Review

Fill in the blanks in the following statements.

1. Transitions are words and phrases whose function is to show the relationships between thoughts and ideas.

2. Some transitions are synonyms; in other words, they mean the same thing.

3. Some transitions can be used in more than one pattern of organization.

4. Different transitions can create subtle but significant changes in the meaning of sentences.

5. List transitions indicate the addition of another reason, example, type, or other point.

6. Sequence transitions signal another event, step, or stage within a chronological order of details.

7. Cause/effect transitions indicate either a reason for or a result of an occurrence presented in a previous sentence.

8. Comparison transitions point out similarities, and transitions point out differences.

9. Definition transitions illustrate ideas in definition paragraphs as well as other types of paragraphs.

10. Paragraphs organized according to more than one pattern will often include different kinds of transitions.

11. Identify three occasions that you will need to use for summary writing in college. studying, completing assignments, and tests, and incorporating source material into research projects and papers

12. How do explanation context clues function? The words, phrases, or sentences near an unfamiliar word will explain enough about that word to allow you to figure out its meaning.its meaning.

Jim Craigmyle/Corbis

Patterns of Organization

CHAPTER 6

Goals for Chapter 6

- Define the term *pattern* as it relates to paragraphs.
- Name the five broad patterns for organizing supporting details in paragraphs.
- Recognize words in topic sentences that indicate certain patterns.
- Recognize supporting details within a list pattern.
- Recognize supporting details within a sequence pattern.
- Recognize supporting details within a cause/effect pattern.
- Recognize supporting details within a comparison/contrast pattern.
- Recognize supporting details within a definition pattern.
- Take notes on a reading selection.
- Read and understand information in a line graph.

Now that you've practiced examining supporting details and transitions, you're ready to look at some common patterns for arranging those details. *A* **pattern** *is a consistent form or method for arranging things.* To find out what you already know about patterns of organization in paragraphs, take the pretest below.

Pretest

Look at the following paragraphs and decide which pattern of organization arranges the details. Write a check mark next to the correct pattern in the list below each paragraph.

1. Most professional grill jockeys prefer charcoal to gas and with good reason. Charcoal generally burns hotter than gas, so you get a more truly grilled taste. Charcoal grills are more versatile than gas grills: it's easier to toss wood chips or herbs on the coals, and you get a better smoke flavor. Not to mention the fact that they give you something to do during the barbecue (in other words, they require constant attention), which will make you feel like a real pit master, not a cook whose stove happens to be outdoors. Charcoal grills cost a lot less than gas grills, and you can use them to burn both charcoal and wood. Visit a barbecue festival, like Memphis in May or the Kansas City Royal, and you won't find a gas grill around for miles.*

   ______ list ✔ comparison/contrast

   ______ sequence ______ definition

   ______ cause/effect

2. Any memory of a specific event that happened while you were present is defined as an *episodic memory*. It is a memory of an episode, or event, in your life. For example, what you had for dinner yesterday, what you did last summer, or where you were last Friday night are episodic memories.†

   ______ list ______ comparison/contract

   ______ sequence ✔ definition

   ______ cause/effect

3. You can get yourself out of bed in several unconventional ways, as suggested by readers of Oprah Winfrey's magazine, *O*. One thing you can do if you are having trouble getting out of bed is to get a dog. As long as it

* Adapted from Steven Raichlen, "Cooking Outside: What Are Your Options?" *Consumers' Research*, August 2001, 29.

† Adapted from Bernstein and Nash, *Essentials of Psychology*, 2nd ed. Boston: Houghton Mifflin, 2002, 181. Copyright © 2002 by Houghton Mifflin Company. Reprinted with permission.

6

has to go out, you have to get up. Another thing you can do is place a huge bird feeder outside the bedroom window so the neighborhood robins serve as your alarm clock. You can also do yoga. It is the most relaxing way to bring your energy level up. One reader suggested having children and remarked that it is less relaxing than yoga but equally effective!*

__✔__ list
______ comparison/contrast
______ sequence
______ definition
______ cause/effect

4. Eating a low-fat diet has several healthy effects, particularly for patients with a history of heart disease or high cholesterol. You can lower your blood fats and maintain a healthy heart. Many patients have also reported lower cholesterol and a higher energy level than before. Studies have also shown that people who eat low fat or a diet rich in vegetables and grains feel better, live longer, and have more stamina[1] than those patients who do not change their diets or adapt a healthy lifestyle.

______ list
______ comparison/contrast
______ sequence
______ definition
__✔__ cause/effect

5. Before beginning an exercise program, there are several steps you should take. First, consult a doctor. Many people jump into an exercise program without getting confirmation from their physician that what they are about to undertake is safe and will be effective. Then, do research to decide what type of activity you want to engage in. For instance, if you are a homebody, joining a gym or a running group may not be the best thing for you to do, but doing indoor yoga or aerobic exercise may be the right thing for you to do. Next, start slow. People who start exercising at their peak level of heart rate immediately lose stamina[1] quickly and their motivation to exercise. And lastly, look for someone to exercise with. Studies have shown that those who begin an exercise program with a partner stay with the program longer and have greater success in the long run.

______ list
______ comparison/contrast
__✔__ sequence
______ definition
______ cause/effect

6

1. **stamina:** physical strength

* Adapted from Melissa Gotthardt, "Rise and Shine," *O Magazine*, September 2001, 86.

Patterns of Organization

To help readers find and comprehend supporting details more easily, paragraphs are usually organized according to at least one particular **pattern.** So, if you learn the most common patterns found within paragraphs, you'll be able to:

1. Recognize supporting details more quickly and accurately.
2. Better understand the relationships among supporting details.

Both of these skills are essential to good reading comprehension.

This chapter presents five broad patterns of organization: list, sequence, cause/effect, comparison/contrast, and definition. Each pattern type is illustrated by itself first, but it's important to realize that paragraphs often combine two or more of these patterns. The end of this chapter presents some examples of paragraphs that are organized according to two or more patterns.

As you read the example paragraphs and learn to recognize each pattern, note how *the* **topic sentence** *often indicates the paragraph's pattern of organization.* Alert readers know how to watch for clues within topic sentences, clues that indicate how the information is arranged. When you can see these clues, you'll be able to predict the paragraph's framework and see more easily how the details fit into it as you read.

List

Many paragraphs organize supporting details as a list of items. A **list** *is a number of things that come one after the other in succession.* Lists of items all equally support the paragraph's topic sentence; however, the order of the items is usually not important. Sometimes an author will arrange the items in a list from least important to most important, but unlike the *sequence* pattern, the order of items is unimportant.

A paragraph's topic sentence will often indicate that the details will appear as a list of items. For example:

There are ***four types*** of dangerous drivers.

The Google Internet search engine is superior to all other search engines for ***three reasons.***

If you want to screen what your children see on the Internet, you can use ***one of several*** parental screening services such as Net Nanny, Cybersitter, or Cyber Patrol.

As you study the following examples of the list pattern look for clues in the topic sentence that will help you identify the supporting details within the paragraph.

A list paragraph might present a list of examples. This specific pattern is referred to as **illustration**, because it *illustrates the main idea with specific examples*. The following paragraph, for instance, includes a list of examples:

> ***Several conditions*** are known to cause the body to ease its own pain. ***For example,*** endorphins[1] are released by immune cells that arrive at sites of inflammation. ***And*** during the late stages of pregnancy, an endorphin system is activated that will reduce the mother's labor pains. An endorphin system is ***also*** activated when people believe they are receiving a painkiller even when they are not. This may be one reason for the placebo effect.[2] Remarkably, the resulting pain inhibition[3] is experienced in the part of the body where it was expected to occur, but not elsewhere. Physical or psychological stress, ***too,*** can activate natural analgesic[4] systems. Stress-induced release of endorphins may account for cases in which injured soldiers and athletes continue to perform in the heat of battle or competition with no apparent pain.*

This paragraph offers a list of four *equal* examples to explain the topic sentence:

Example #1:	sites of inflammation
Example #2:	labor pains
Example #3:	people who believe they are receiving painkillers
Example #4:	injured soldiers or athletes

6

Another specific kind of list pattern is **classification**, which *sorts things* into a list of *groups, types, or categories*. The following paragraph is an example of a classification:

> Often, unpopular teenagers are placed in one of ***two groups:*** *rejected adolescents* and *neglected adolescents*. *Rejected adolescents* are rarely named as friends by their peers, and they are actively disliked. Many show high levels of aggression, others are extremely withdrawn, and

1. **endorphins:** hormones that reduce the sensation of pain
2. **placebo effect:** beneficial effects that arise from a patient's expectations about treatment rather than the treatment itself
3. **inhibition:** blockage or suppression
4. **analgesic:** related to pain reduction

* Adapted from Bernstein et al., *Psychology,* 6th ed. Boston: Houghton Mifflin, 2003, 135. Copyright © 2003 by Houghton Mifflin Company. Reprinted with permission.

> still others are aggressive and withdrawn. They show poor attitudes toward school (including low attendance and achievement) and discipline problems. *Neglected teenagers* are rarely named by their peers as best friends, but they are not actively disliked. Members of this group show little problem behavior but are not physically attractive, do not seem to have similar interests as other teens, and are not involved in activities socially valued by other adolescents.*

This paragraph classifies all unpopular teenagers into two groups, rejected and neglected. Minor supporting details then provide descriptive information about each group.

Yet another type of list pattern is **division**, which *divides a subject into a series of main parts and describes each part.* For example, read the following paragraph:

> A landfill has ***six basic parts.*** The ***first*** is the bottom liner system. The bottom liner prevents the trash from coming in contact with the outside soil, particularly the groundwater. It is usually some type of durable, puncture-resistant synthetic plastic 30 to 100 millimeters thick. The ***second*** part of a landfill is the cells, the area where trash is stored. Within each cell is one day's worth of compacted garbage. The ***third*** part is the storm water drainage system, which collects rainwater that falls on the landfill. The landfill must be kept as dry as possible to prevent substances from leaking out of it, so plastic drainage pipes and storm liners collect water from areas of the landfill and channel it to drainage ditches surrounding the landfill's base. The ***fourth*** part, the leachate collection system, collects water that does manage to get into the cells. It collects the water that contains *leachates*, or contaminated substances. The methane collection system, the ***fifth*** part, collects the methane gas that is formed during the breakdown of the trash inside the landfill. This gas is then vented, burned, or even used as a fuel source. The ***sixth and last*** part of the landfill is the covering or cap. This covering seals the compacted trash from the air and prevents vermin[1] (birds, rats, mice, flying insects, etc.) from getting into the trash.†

This paragraph divides landfills into six main parts and describes each one.

1. **vermin:** small, destructive animals or insects

* Adapted from Kaplan, *Adolescence*. Boston: Houghton Mifflin, 2004, 194. Copyright © 2004 by Houghton Mifflin Company. Reprinted with permission.

† Adapted from Craig C. Freudenrich, "How Landfills Work," HowStuffWorks.com, http://people.howstuffworks.com/landfill6.htm.

6

In Chapter 3, you learned how to map major and minor supporting details. In a map of a list paragraph, each new reason, example, type, or part is a major detail. For example, read the following list paragraph:

> To ensure the respectful display of the American flag, an emblem of our nation's pride and ideals, certain fundamental rules have been developed. ***First,*** the flag is always hung with the blue union at the top at the observer's left. ***Second,*** when displayed with other flags, the flag of the United States should be in the center and at the highest point. ***Third,*** the flag should never touch anything beneath it, including the ground or the floor. ***Fourth,*** the flag should never be used as wearing apparel, bedding, or drapery. ***Fifth,*** the flag should never be written upon, nor should it be used as a receptacle[1] for holding, carrying, or delivering anything.*

The details in this paragraph are organized into a list of rules. The main idea is, "There are rules that Americans follow to display the national flag," and the paragraph states five rules that support that idea.

Rule #1: Hang with the blue union at top.

Rule #2: Display in middle of and higher than other flags.

Rule #3: Don't let it touch anything beneath it.

Rule #4: Don't use it as clothing, bedding, or drapery.

Rule #5: Don't write on it or carry anything in it.

If you were to map this paragraph, it would look like this:

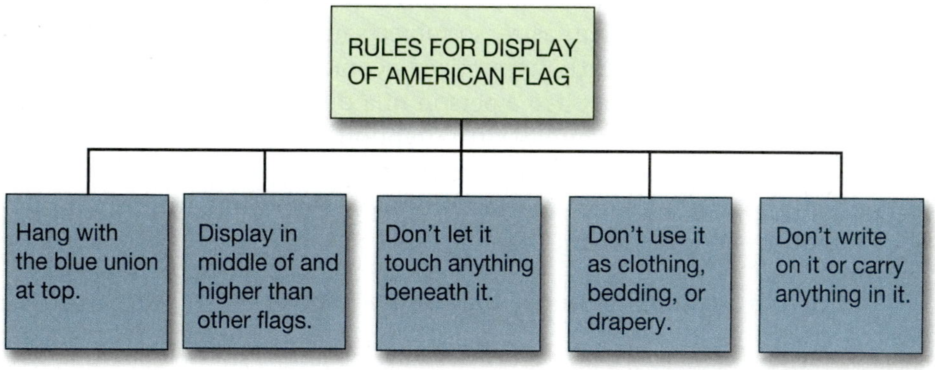

1. **receptacle:** container

* Adapted from *Our Flag* pamphlet. Roseland, NJ: Annin & Co., 1997.

6

As you read, look for transitions that indicate a list to follow.

Words and Phrases That Indicate a List Pattern

Quantity word	*plus*	*List word*	
several		examples	kinds
many		reasons	characteristics
two, three, four, etc.		points	methods
a number of		classes	advantages
numerous		types	ways
		categories	forms
		groups	tips
		goals	

Exercise 6.1

Read each of the paragraphs below and circle the transitions. Then fill in the blank that follows, and insert abbreviated versions of the paragraph's sentences in the outline or map to indicate the list of *major* supporting details. Look for clues in any stated topic sentences.

6

1. Ernest Hilgard described the five main changes people display during hypnosis. First, hypnotized people tend not to initiate actions, waiting instead for the hypnotist's instructions. Second, subjects tend to ignore all but the hypnotist's voice and whatever it points out. Third, hypnosis enhances the ability to fantasize, so subjects more vividly imagine a scene or relive a memory. Fourth, hypnotized people display increased role taking; they more easily act like a person of a different age or a member of the opposite sex, for example. Fifth, hypnotic subjects tend not to question if statements are true and more willingly accept apparent distortions of reality. Thus, a hypnotized person might shiver in a warm room if a hypnotist says it is snowing.*

Word(s) in the topic sentence that indicate a list: five changes

* Adapted from Bernstein et al., *Psychology*, 4th ed. Boston: Houghton Mifflin, 1997, 177–78.

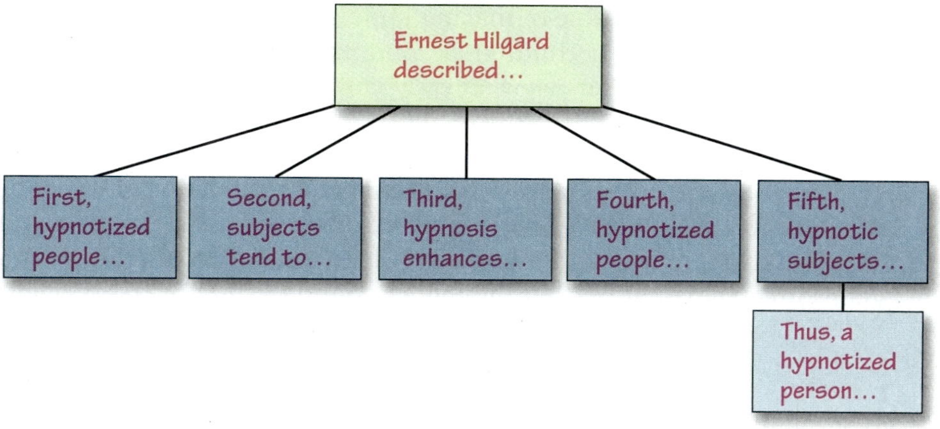

2. Teachers can do several things to turn students' parents into allies. One way is to prepare a short statement to be carried home for the year. Stress that you and they are in a partnership to help their child and have a productive year. Further, let them know how to get in touch with you and that you are looking forward to meeting them. A second suggestion is that once you have established disciplinary and homework policies, a copy should be sent home for parental sign-off. Third, on the first day, get the home and office telephone numbers of each student's parent or parents. Fourth, it is a good idea to call all parents early in the fall. Finally, if problems with a particular student arise or persist throughout the year, insist on a parent visit.*

Word(s) in the topic sentence that indicate a list: several things

I. Things teachers can do to turn students' parents into allies

A. Prepare short statement to be carried home for the year

1. Stress partnership

2. Let them know how to get in touch with you

B. Send home copy of disciplinary and homework policies for parents to sign

C. Get parents' home and office telephone numbers

D. Call all parents early in the fall

E. Insist on parent visit if problems arise

3. Three factors seem to underlie successful early childhood programs, whatever their format and curriculum. First, the staff of successful programs regard themselves as competent observers of children's educational

* Adapted from Ryan and Cooper, *Those Who Can, Teach*, 9th ed. Boston: Houghton Mifflin, 2000, 60–61.

6

needs and as being capable of making important decisions in tailoring a curriculum to particular children. Second, the vast majority of successful programs and teachers view an early childhood curriculum as an integrated whole rather than consisting of independent subject areas of skills. Singing a song, for example, is not just "music"; it also fosters language development, motor skills (if the children dance along), arithmetic (through counting and rhythm), and social studies (if the words are about people and life in the community). Third, successful early childhood programs involve parents, either directly as volunteers in the classroom or indirectly as advisers on governing boards, in certain school activities, or in additional services that support families.*

Word(s) in the topic sentence that indicate a list: three factors

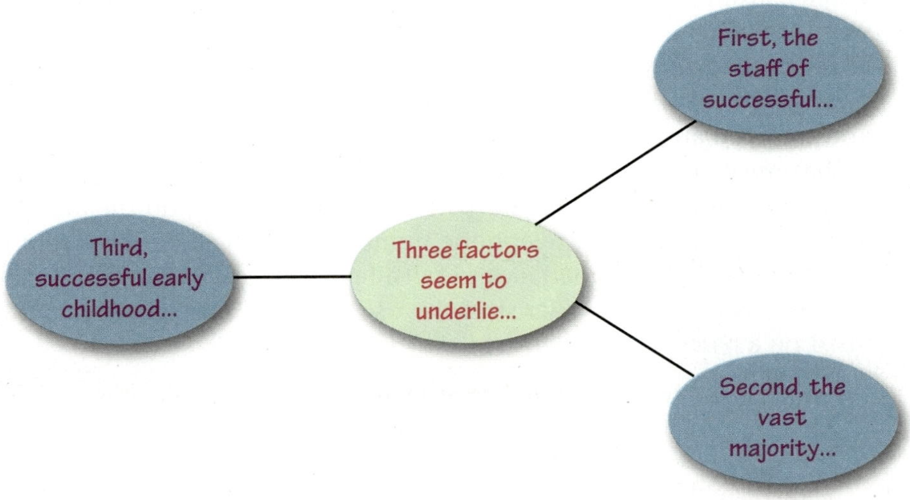

4. Temple University psychologist Frank Farley, a longtime researcher on heroic behavior, says that there are three main types of heroes. The first type, "911[1] heroes," are those who protect people for a living, such as firefighters, police officers, paramedics, and security guards. The second type is the one-time "situational" hero that springs into action when an occasion calls for it. For example, a person who attacks an airplane hijacker or wrestles a gun from a would-be mugger is a situational hero. The last type of hero is the "sustained altruist,"[2] a person who often engages

1. **911:** a reference to the 911 emergency phone number
2. **altruist:** someone who helps others

* Adapted from Seifert and Hoffnung, *Child and Adolescent Development,* 5th ed. Boston: Houghton Mifflin, 2000, 288.

6

in heroic acts over a longer time; this type of hero is more interested in helping people than in making money or doing anything else.*

Word(s) in the topic sentence that indicate a list: three types

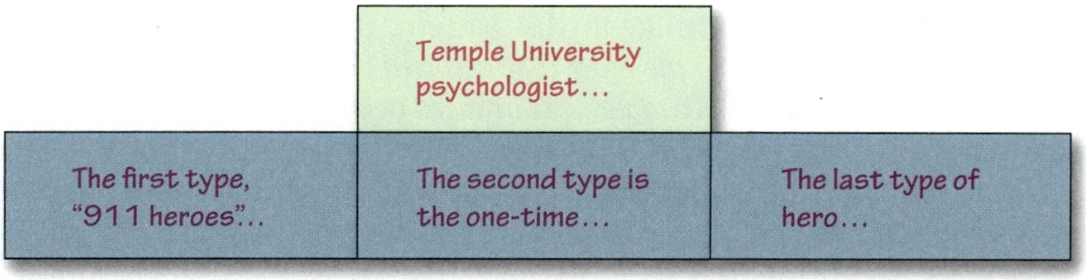

5. I've learned several ways to improve my stamina[1] so I can keep myself going. To begin with, you have to nourish your body and soul. The first thing I do when I get out of bed is meditate for 5 to 10 minutes; that's the grounding work I must do for myself and what makes everything else possible. Second, I'm careful with my diet, and if I'm not, I can feel it. Third, when I get home at night, I don't automatically turn on the television. And fourth, every day I do some sort of exercise. I run four miles every other day—in the winter I do it inside; this morning I ran outside.†

Word(s) in the topic sentence that indicate a list: several ways

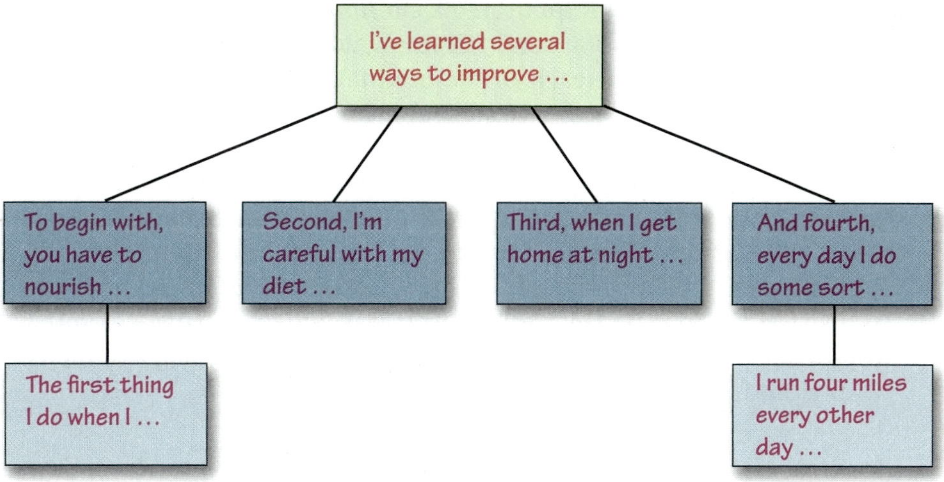

1. **stamina:** physical strength

* Adapted from Marilyn Elias, "Three Kinds of Heroes Emerge," *USA Today*, November 21, 2001, 1D.

† Adapted from Oprah Winfrey, "Secrets of the Staministas," *O* Magazine, September 2001, 196.

Sequence

The next common pattern for organizing details is *sequence. In* **sequence** *paragraphs, the details are arranged according to their chronological relationships.* In other words, sequence paragraphs present details in the order they happened or should happen. Unlike the list pattern, these sequences are events, stages, or steps presented *in the order they occurred or should occur.* Also, unlike list paragraphs, these details *cannot be rearranged* because they would no longer make sense.

Topic sentences in sequence paragraphs will often indicate that a chronology will follow:

A young adult can follow ***three easy steps*** to establish a good credit record.

Construction of the U.S. Capitol Building began in 1793 and continued ***over the next hundred years.***

The history of antibiotics is marked by several key ***events.***

As you read, look for topic sentence words that indicate a sequence pattern.

A sequence paragraph tells a story or recounts a sequence of events. Here is an example of a paragraph that arranges details according to the sequence pattern:

The American flag, also known as Old Glory, was born in 1777 and evolved into its present form by 1960. On ***June 14, 1777,*** Congress adopted the first official Stars and Stripes, which included 13 stars and 13 stripes to symbolize each of the original 13 American Colonies. ***In 1795,*** the flag was given 15 stars and 15 stripes to honor the admission of Vermont and Kentucky to the Union. On ***July 4, 1818,*** Congress restored the original 13 stripes and ordered the addition of a new star for each new state. ***By 1861,*** the flag had 34 stars. During the Civil War (1861–1865), the flag was not changed to reflect the secession[1] of the Southern states. ***From 1867 to 1959,*** fifteen more stars were added. The final fiftieth star was added on ***July 4, 1960,*** following Hawaii's admission into the Union, and the flag assumed its present form.*

1. **secession:** withdrawal

* Adapted from "History of Old Glory," *News Herald*, Morganton, NC, September 23, 2001, 1C, 8C.

In this paragraph, the supporting details are all events presented in the order they occurred:

Evolution of Old Glory

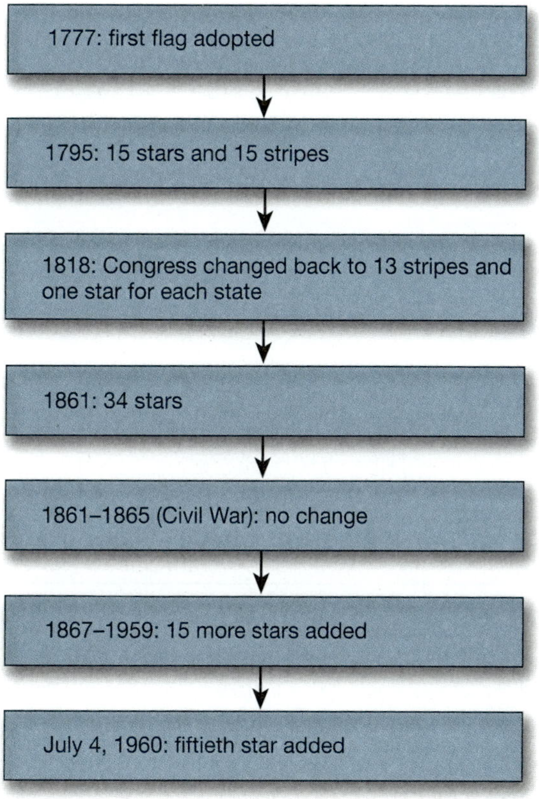

A **process** *paragraph is a type of sequence paragraph that explains how something is done or could be done.* Its details are organized in the steps or stages, in the order they occur. Here is an example:

Kittens require colostrum[1] from the mother ***in the first 24 hours*** after birth. This will protect them from diseases until vaccines begin. They will nurse from the queen ***for 3 weeks. Around 3 to 4 weeks*** of age kittens should be offered canned or moist food. ***Over the next 2 weeks*** they should begin dry food that is moistened with warm water. ***By 6 to 8 weeks*** of age the kittens should be weaned and on solid kitten food. The feedings should be divided into several times a day. It is important when feeding a kitten dry food to feed a size-appropriate diet.*

1. **colostrum:** first milk secreted in the breasts after birth

* Vanhorn, Beth, and Robert W. Clark. *Veterinary Assisting Fundamentals & Applications*. Clifton Park: Delmar, 2011. Print. Ch. 9, p. 125.

Feeding Kittens

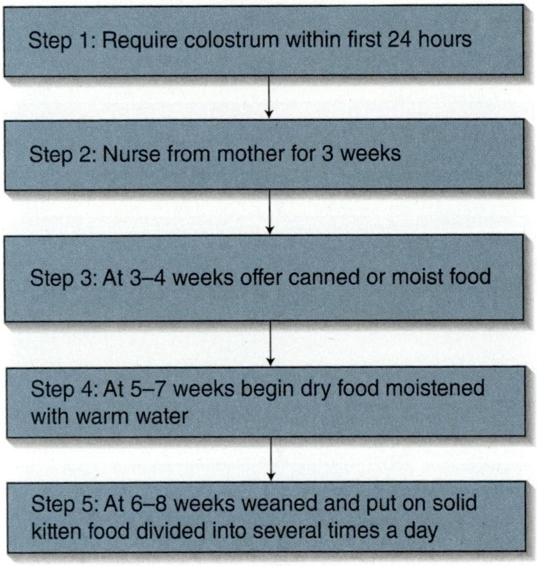

As you read, look for transitions that indicate a sequence pattern.

Words and Phrases That Indicate a Sequence Pattern

Quantity word	*plus*	*Sequence word*
several		events
two, three, four, etc.		steps
a number of		stages
over time		developments
in just one year		procedure
		process

6

Exercise 6.2

Read each of the paragraphs below and circle the transitions. Then fill in the blank that follows. Finally, write abbreviated versions of the paragraph's sentences in the outline or map to indicate the *major* sequence details.

1. Several events take place during jury selection. First, everyone who has been summoned to appear at jury duty must arrive by nine o'clock in the morning and assemble in the jury room. A few minutes later, the court clerk usually shows a movie outlining what is going to happen throughout the day as the jury is chosen for a particular trial. At around ten o'clock,

20 people are chosen from the jurors in attendance and are taken to a courtroom where a judge describes how the process is going to work. About thirty minutes later, 10 people are called to sit in the jury box to be questioned by the lawyers in the case.

Words in topic sentence that indicate sequence: several events

Events of Jury Selection

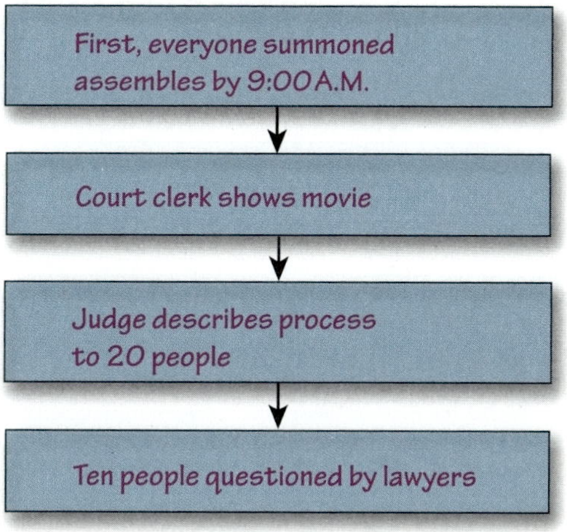

2. Research on memory suggests a certain procedure for taking and using notes effectively. First, realize that in note taking, more is not necessarily better. Taking detailed notes of everything requires that you pay close attention to unimportant as well as important content, leaving little time for thinking about the material. Next, once you have a set of lecture notes, review them as soon as possible so that you can fill in missing details. When the time comes for serious study, use your notes as if they were a chapter in a textbook. Finally, write a detailed outline and think about how various points are related. Once you have organized the material, the details will make more sense and will be much easier to remember.*

Word(s) in topic sentence that indicate sequence: procedure

I. Procedure for taking and using notes effectively

   A. Realize that more is not necessarily better

   B. Review notes as soon as possible to fill in missing details

   C. Write a detailed outline and think about how points are related

* Adapted from Bernstein et al., *Psychology*, 5th ed. Boston: Houghton Mifflin, 2000, 245.

2. Piaget theorized that children progress through four main periods as they attempt to make sense of the world around them and understand their place within it. These four periods, or cognitive schemes, are roughly correlated with age and become increasingly sophisticated with maturity: the sensorimotor period (ages 0–2), the preoperational period (ages 2–7), the concrete operational period (ages 7–11), and the formal operational period (age 11 and up). It is important to be aware of individual differences that may occur and to recognize that development may not always progress in a smooth, continuous manner.*

Periods of Children's Progress

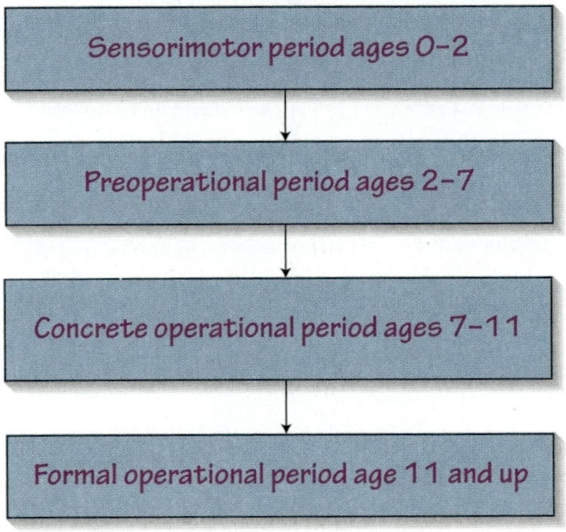

Word(s) in topic sentence that indicate sequence: four main periods

4. A traditional Italian breakfast tends to be light, including coffee with milk (*caffe latte*), tea, or a chocolate drink, accompanied by bread and jam. Lunch is the main meal of the day and may be followed by a nap. It usually starts with an appetizer course of *antipasti,* such as ham, sausages, pickled vegetables, and olives; or *crostini*, crispy slices of bread with various toppings, such as tomatoes or cheese. Next is *minestra* (wet course), usually soup, or *asciutta* (dry course) of pasta, risotto, or gnocchi. The main course is fish, meat, or poultry, roasted, grilled, pan-fried, or stewed. It is served with a starchy or green vegetable, followed by a salad. Bread is served with the meal, often with olive oil and balsamic vinegar for dipping. Dessert often consists of fruit and cheese; pastries or *biscotti* (crunchy twice-baked cookie slices) and ice cream are served on special occasions. Dinner is served at about 7:30 P.M. and is a lighter version of lunch. Wine usually accompanies lunch and dinner. Coffee or *espresso* is enjoyed after

* Hess, Karen M. *Juvenile Justice,* 5th ed. Belmont: Wadsworth, 2010. Print. Ch. 4, pp. 96, 98.

dinner, either at home or in a coffeehouse. Marsala may be served with cheese before the meal for a light appetizer course, or after dinner. It is also often used in the preparation of desserts. One such sweet, now prepared all over Europe, is *zabaglione*, a wine custard.*

Word(s) in paragraph that indicate sequence: starts, next, 7:30, breakfast, lunch, dinner

I. Italian breakfast

A. Coffee with milk, tea, or a chocolate drink

B. Bread and jam

II. Italian lunch

A. Appetizer course

B. Wet or dry course

C. Main course with bread and salad or vegetable

D. Dessert

III. Italian dinner

A. Late version of lunch

B. Wine served with lunch and dinner

C. Coffee or espresso served with dessert

5. During childbirth, labor proceeds in three traditional stages. The first of the three stages begins with brief, mild contractions perhaps 10 to 15 minutes apart. These contractions become increasingly frequent and serve to alter the shape of the cervix,[1] preparing it for the fetus's descent and entry into the narrow birth canal. Near the end of the first stage, which on average lasts about eleven hours for firstborns and about seven hours for later-borns, dilation[2] of the cervix proceeds rapidly to allow passage through the birth canal. The second stage consists of the continued descent and the birth of the baby. This stage usually requires a little less than an hour for firstborns and about twenty minutes for later-borns. It also normally

1. **cervix:** opening to the womb
2. **dilation:** widening

* Kittler, Pamela Goyan, and Kathryn P. Sucher. *Food and Culture,* 5th ed. Belmont: Thomson Higher Education, 2008. Print. Ch. 6, p. 165.

6

includes several reorientations of both the head and shoulders to permit delivery through the tight-fitting passageway. In the third stage, which lasts about fifteen minutes, the placenta[1] is expelled.*

Words in topic sentence that indicate sequence: three stages (or three traditional stages)

I. First stage

A. Begins with brief, mild contractions 10–15 minutes apart

B. Contractions become increasingly frequent to prepare cervix for fetus's descent

C. Near end of first stage, dilation of cervix proceeds rapidly

II. Second stage

A. Continued descent of baby with reorientations of head and shoulders

B. Birth of baby

III. Third stage: placenta is expelled

Cause/Effect

6

When details are arranged *in the* **cause/effect** *pattern, the paragraph intends to show how the details relate to or affect each other.* Like a sequence paragraph, a cause/effect paragraph presents a list of occurrences. However, unlike a sequence, the cause/effect pattern reveals how one occurrence led to another. It might also demonstrate how a list of causes produced one particular effect, or result.

Topic sentences in cause/effect paragraphs will often indicate that an explanation of related occurrences will follow.

Fewer fans are attending football and baseball games ***because*** they are turned off by the commercialism[2] of these sports.

Ethical behavior in business ***results in*** a variety of benefits for an organization.

Parents who cater to their kids' every whim and demand too little of them in return will negatively ***affect*** their children's character development.

1. **placenta:** organ that encloses the fetus during pregnancy
2. **commercialism:** attitude that emphasizes profits

* Adapted from Bukatko and Daehler, *Child Development,* 5th ed. Boston: Houghton Mifflin, 2004, 135. Copyright © 2004 by Houghton Mifflin Company. Reprinted with permission.

The following diagrams will help you visualize some common types of cause/effect patterns. The first diagram shows a *chain reaction* of causes and effect, whereas the second one indicates a *separate series of effects that are not related*. The third diagram shows a pattern in which *several unrelated causes together produce one particular effect*.

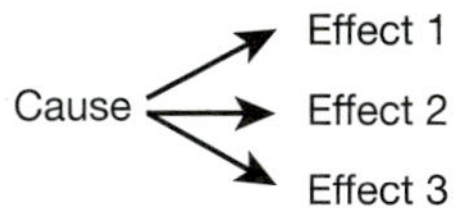

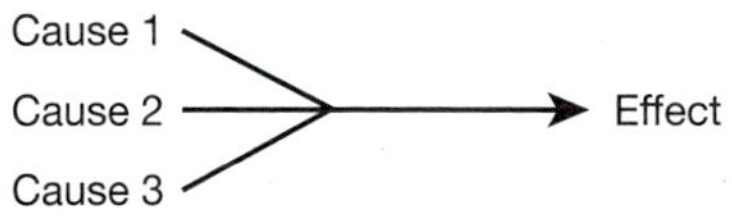

For an example of the cause/effect pattern, read the following paragraph to find the one cause that produces three main effects.

> Obesity is particularly difficult for adolescents who already are struggling to develop a comfortable and realistic view of their changing bodies. It can significantly impair teenagers' sense of themselves as physically attractive people and their overall identity development. In some cases, obesity can severely limit social opportunities ***due to*** both exclusion by peers and self-isolation. ***Because*** overweight adolescents do not conform to the social ideal of thinness, they also suffer from discrimination that limits their access to education, employment, housing, and health care.*

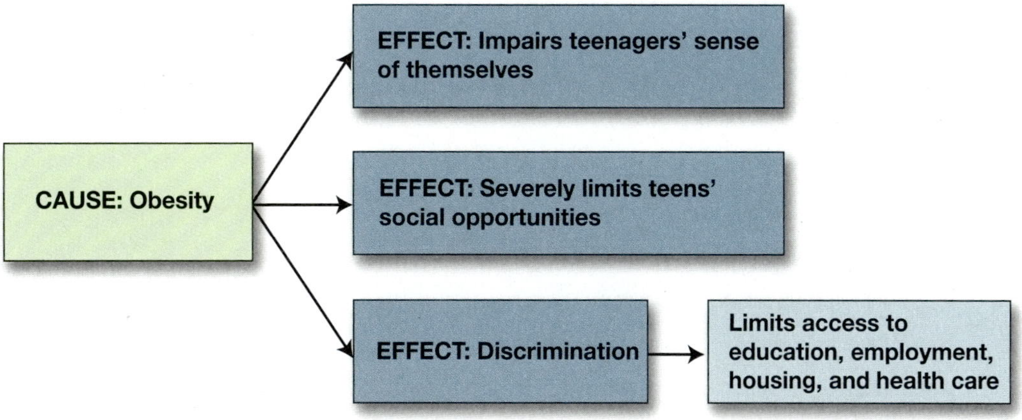

* Adapted from Seifert et al., *Lifespan Development*, 2nd ed. Boston: Houghton Mifflin, 2000, 352. Copyright © 2000 by Houghton Mifflin Company. Reprinted with permission.

Here's a second example that is arranged according to a different cause/effect pattern. In this paragraph read to discover the several causes that produce one effect.

> How could the stunning 1941 attack on Pearl Harbor[1] have happened? After all, American cryptanalysts[2] had broken the Japanese diplomatic code. Although the intercepted[3] Japanese messages told policymakers that war lay ahead, the intercepts never revealed naval or military plans and never specifically mentioned Pearl Harbor. The base at Pearl Harbor was not ready—not on red alert—***because*** a message sent from Washington warning of the imminence[4] of war had been too casually transmitted by a slow method and had arrived too late. Base commanders were too relaxed, believing Hawaii too far from Japan to be a target for all-out attack. Like Roosevelt's[5] advisers, they expected an assault at British Malaya, Thailand, or the Philippines. The Pearl Harbor calamity[6] ***stemmed from*** mistakes and insufficient information, not from conspiracy.*

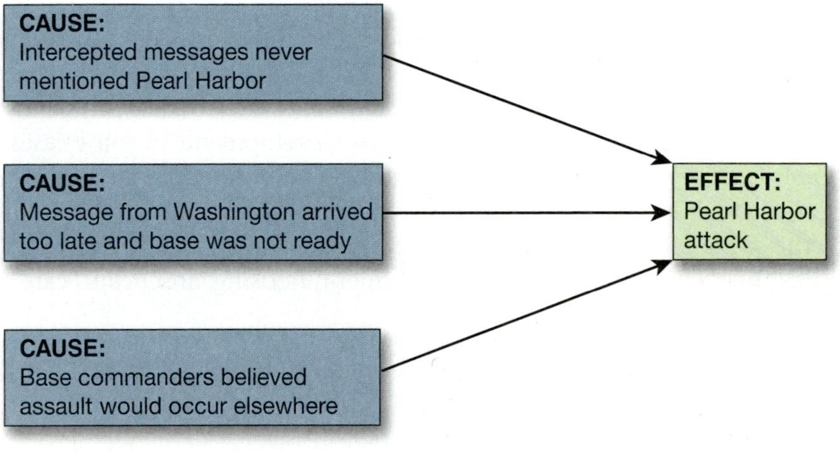

1. **Pearl Harbor:** American military base in Hawaii
2. **cryptanalysts:** people who decipher secret codes
3. **intercepted:** cut off or interrupted
4. **imminence:** state of being able to happen
5. **Roosevelt:** Franklin D. Roosevelt, thirty-second president of the United States
6. **calamity:** disaster

* Adapted from Norton et al., *A People and a Nation,* 5th ed. Vol. II. Boston: Houghton Mifflin, 1998, 774.

As you read, look for the following transitions that signal a cause/effect pattern.

Words and Phrases That Indicate a Cause/Effect Pattern

consequences	was caused by
effects	causes
results	chain reaction
outcomes	leads to
affect	factors
because	

Exercise 6.3

Read each paragraph below and fill in the blank that follows. Then, write abbreviated versions of the paragraph's sentences in the map to indicate the cause/effect relationships between the *major* supporting details.

1. Smoking is responsible for more preventable illnesses and deaths than any other single health-compromising behavior. Smoking is associated with cancer of the lung, larynx, oral cavity, and esophagus; it is also a major risk factor for other cancers throughout the body. Smoking is also related to cardiovascular illness and mortality. Smoking increases the risk of emphysema, chronic bronchitis, peptic ulcers, cirrhosis of the liver, and respiratory disorders and aggravates the symptoms of allergies, diabetes, and hypertension. In women, smoking increases the risk of osteoporosis and lowers the age of menopause.*

   Word(s) in topic sentence that indicate cause/effect order: ________

   is responsible for

6

* Adapted from Seifert et al., *Lifespan Development*, 2nd ed., Boston: Houghton Mifflin, 2000, 428. Copyright © 2000 by Houghton Mifflin Company. Reprinted with permission.

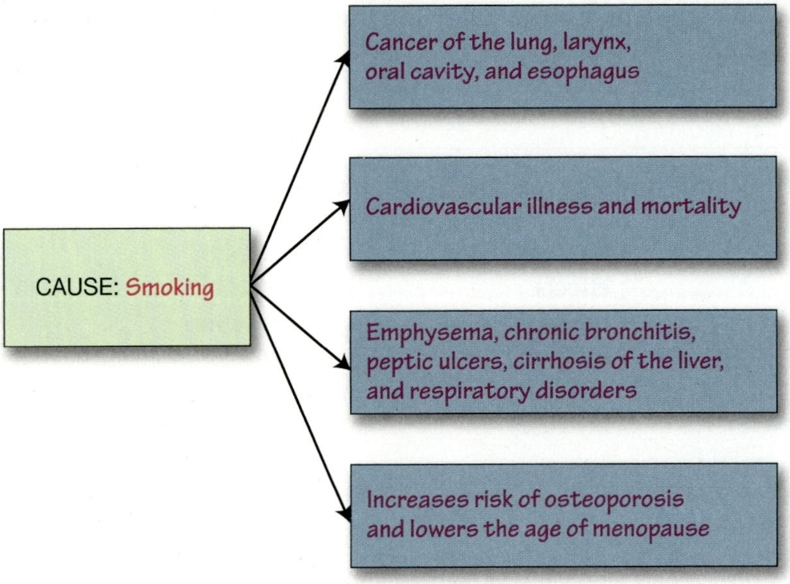

2. Another effect of the AIDS pandemic is the loss of productive young adult workers and trained personnel such as scientists, farmers, engineers, teachers, and government, business, and health-care workers. The essential services they provide are therefore lacking, and there are fewer of them available to support the very young and the elderly. Within a decade, countries such as Zimbabwe and Botswana in sub-Saharan Africa could lose more than a fifth of their adult population. Such death rates drastically alter a country's age structure.*

Word(s) in topic sentence that indicate cause/effect order: effect

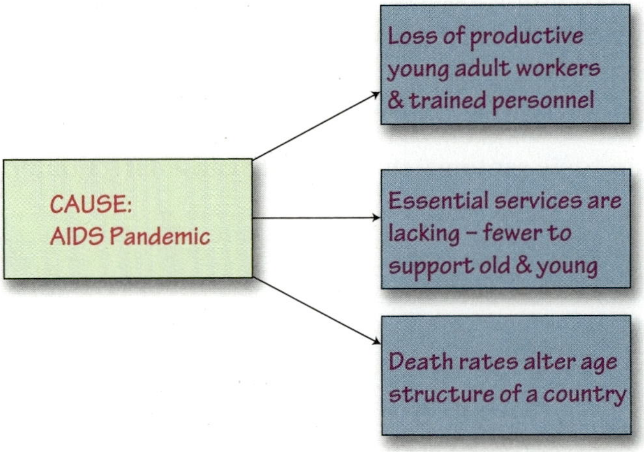

* Miller, G. Tyler, Jr., and Scott E. Spoolman. *Environmental Science,* 13th ed. Belmont: Brooks/Cole, 2010. Print. Ch. 6, p. 103.

3. Experts have identified several factors that lead to a child biting another person, whether it is a parent, caregiver, sibling, or another child. Biting often occurs when children are playing together in close quarters, in a family or preschool setting, and may occur because of conflicts over favorite toys or snacks. It also happens more frequently during unstructured time, such as free playground periods, or when children are tired. Changing dynamics at home or in a childcare setting (brought on by such events as moving to a new room in a childcare center, having a new child come into a room, or the arrival of a new sibling) can cause stress, leading a toddler or preschooler to bite out of frustration or anger.*

Word(s) in topic sentence that indicate cause/effect order: several factors

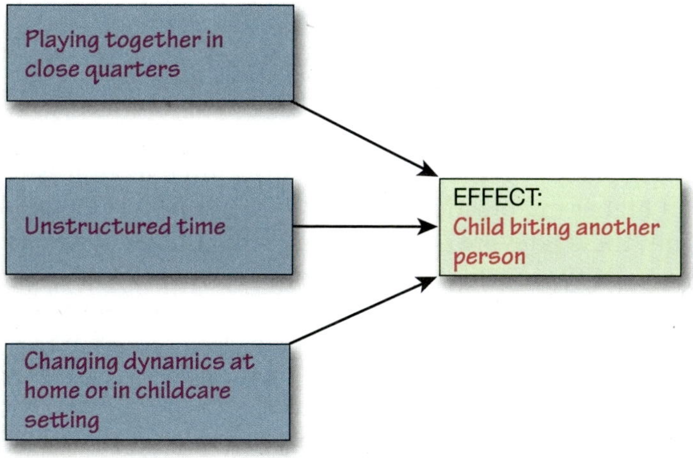

4. World War I had enormous effects on the cinema. The outbreak of hostilities triggered a severe cutback in French production, and the country lost its leading position in world markets. Italy soon encountered similar problems. The growing Hollywood film industry stepped in to fill the gap in supply, expanding its distribution system abroad. By the war's end, American films had an international grip that other countries would struggle, usually with limited success, to loosen.†

Word(s) in topic sentence that indicate cause/effect order: effects

* Adapted from Laurie A. Cavanaugh, "Nipping Biting in the Bud," *Westchester Family*, October 2001, 32.

† Thompson, Kristin. *Film History: An Introduction,* 3rd ed. New York: McGraw-Hill, 2010. Print. Ch. 1, p. 2.

6

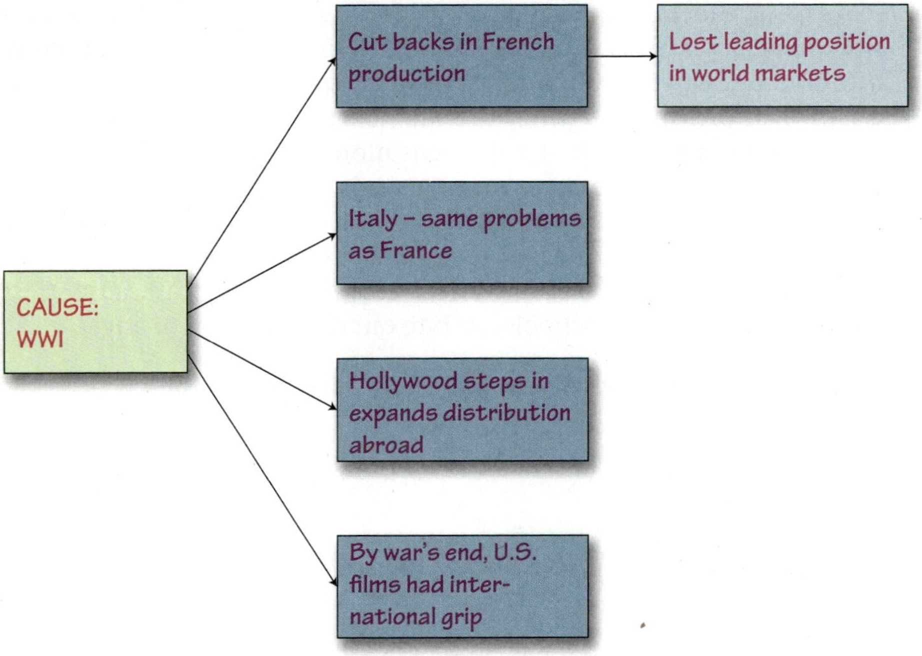

5. Medical malpractice litigation[1] that results in large awards for patients results in higher malpractice insurance premiums for doctors. For many physicians, these rates are soaring so high that they're forced to quit their profession. Of those who continue to practice, many are being forced to raise the cost of their services, which is contributing to skyrocketing medical costs. Thus, the end result of the growing number of malpractice claims is unaffordable health care for all American citizens.

Word(s) in topic sentence that indicate cause/effect order: results in

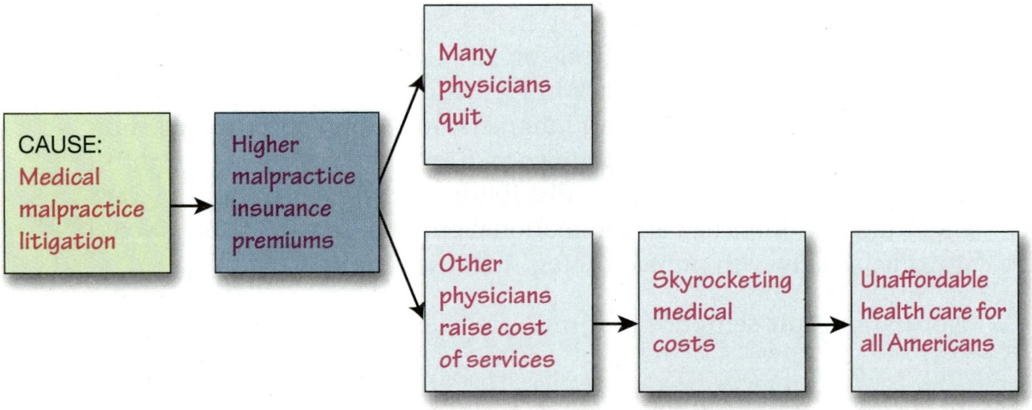

1. **litigation:** legal proceedings

6

Comparison/Contrast

A third common pattern is comparison/contrast. **Comparison** means explaining the *similarities* between two or more things. **Contrast** means examining the *differences* between things. A paragraph can compare or contrast or do both.

In comparison/contrast paragraphs, the supporting details concentrate on certain aspects or features of the subjects and explores their likenesses and/or differences in those areas. For example, a comparison of two different male singing groups might focus on the similarities in their style, the subjects of their songs, and the audiences they attract.

Topic sentences in comparison/contrast paragraphs often indicate that an explanation of similarities and/or differences is to follow:

> There are some fundamental ***differences*** between Greek and Roman mythology.
>
> ***In comparison*** to American women, many women in Middle Eastern countries have fewer rights, freedoms, and opportunities.
>
> Research on identical twins has shown that they tend to demonstrate remarkable ***similarities*** in traits.

Comparison/contrast paragraphs arrange the details in one of two ways. One option is to focus on each subject in turn. The following paragraph, which deals only with similarities, provides an example of this pattern:

> England's Stonehenge and the colossal statues on Rapa Nui, or Easter Island, share quite a few ***similarities.*** The monoliths that compose the circular Stonehenge are huge. Some of them weigh as much as 45 tons and measure seven feet tall. The transport of stones this size was a marvel of preindustrial age engineering. Modern scientists speculate that the stones were moved by laying each one on a sledge[1] and then pulling it with ropes over log rollers. Their purpose is still a mystery, but many believe that Stonehenge was some kind of temple used for sacred rituals. One theory claims that ancient Druids[2] conducted religious ceremonies, including human sacrifices, at the site. Similarly, the carved stones of Rapa Nui are gigantic. On average, each stands over 13 feet high and weighs about 14 tons. Like the stones of Stonehenge, they may have been moved from the quarries[3] where they

1. **sledge:** low vehicle drawn by work animals, used to transport loads
2. **Druids:** an ancient order of priests
3. **quarries:** pits from which stones are cut or dug

originated with sledges, ropes, and logs. They may have had a sacred purpose as well; the people of Rapa Nui might have viewed them as ceremonial conduits[1] for communication with the gods.

This paragraph groups the points of comparison by subject, discussing first Stonehenge and then the statues of Rapa Nui. It would be outlined like this:

I. Similarities between Stonehenge and Rapa Nui

  A. Stonehenge
    1. Size
    2. Transport
    3. Purpose

  B. Statues of Rapa Nui
    1. Size
    2. Transport
    3. Purpose

A comparison/contrast paragraph can also be arranged so that it alternates back and forth between the two subjects.

Debit cards and credit cards may look alike, ***but*** there are important ***differences.*** A debit card, or check card, electronically subtracts the amount of your purchase from your bank account the moment the purchase is made. ***In contrast,*** when you use your credit card, the credit card company extends short-term financing, and you do not make a payment until you receive your next statement. Using a debit card means you do not pay an interest or finance charge for your purchase. If you use a credit card and do not pay off the balance when you receive your statement, you end up paying interest, which results in higher costs for the items you buy. Finally, banks usually do not charge debit card users an annual fee. Many credit cards do.*

This paragraph contrasts three aspects of debit cards and credit cards: when you pay for the purchase, whether or not interest applies, and whether an annual fee applies. It would be outlined as follows:

I. Differences between debit cards and credit cards

  A. When you pay
    1. Debit cards
    2. Credit cards

1. **conduits:** pipes or channels

* Adapted from Pride et al., *Business*, 6th ed. Boston: Houghton Mifflin, 1999, 492–93.

B. Interest
   1. Debit cards
   2. Credit cards

C. Annual fee
   1. Debit cards
   2. Credit cards

As you read, look for the following transitions that indicate a comparison/contrast pattern.

Words That Indicate a Comparison/Contrast Pattern	
similarities	differences
alike	different
likenesses	

Exercise 6.4

Read the following comparison/contrast paragraphs and answer the questions that follow. Circle the letter of the correct answer or write your answer on the blank provided.

Although my husband and I have many common interests, we couldn't be more different. Both of us love to go to the movies, but I love action/adventure movies, and he enjoys romantic comedies. We even eat differently at the movies—I love popcorn, whereas he enjoys chocolate. We also share a love of the outdoors, but whereas I love to go camping, hiking, and rafting, he enjoys just sitting in our backyard, reading the paper. We also enjoy eating good food; I love to cook and he hates it! However, he enjoys cleaning up after I cook a gourmet meal, so I can do the thing we both love to do—relax.

1. This paragraph (circle the letter of one answer)
   a. compares.
   b. contrasts.
   c. compares and contrasts. (circled)

2. Which two subjects are being compared and/or contrasted? wife and husband

3. How are the two subjects compared? List four similarities on the blanks provided.
   1. Both love movies.
   2. Both eat at movies.

6

3. Both love outdoors.

4. Both love good food.

4. How are they contrasted?

1. Type of movies each enjoys

2. Type of food each eats at the movies

3. Specific outdoor activities each enjoys

4. Each spouse's feelings about cooking

Not all reading is alike. Active readers use different strategies for different purposes. Skimming and scanning are two strategies that you will use often. When you skim a chapter, you quickly glance through it to get a general idea of what it covers—the topic, author's purpose, and key ideas. Skimming the introduction, headings, and summary will give you the big picture and may also help you determine how difficult the reading will be and how much time you should plan to spend on it. Skimming is different from reading in depth. Skimming the chapter first will help you anticipate what is to come when you read the chapter in depth and begin to think critically about the author's ideas. Like skimming, scanning is also rapid reading, but for a different purpose. When you scan, you are searching for a specific fact or detail. Let's say you have already read a chapter and are now doing an assigned exercise. You might scan the chapter to find a specific fact or definition of a term that will help you answer a question.*

6

5. This paragraph (circle the letter of one answer)

a. compares.

b. contrasts.

c. compares and contrasts. (circled)

6. Which two subjects are being compared and/or contrasted? skimming and scanning

7. How are the subjects alike? Both are rapid-reading strategies.

The two systems of communication also have differences. First, nonverbal communication is perceived as more honest. If verbal and nonverbal behaviors are inconsistent, most people trust the nonverbal behavior. There is little evidence that nonverbal behavior actually is more trustworthy than verbal communication; after all, we often control it quite deliberately. Nonetheless, it tends to be perceived as more trustworthy.

* Kanar, Carol C., *The Confident Student,* 7th ed. Boston: Wadsworth, 2011. Print. Ch. 7, p. 164.

Second, unlike verbal communication, nonverbal communication is multi- channeled. Verbal communication usually occurs within a single channel; oral verbal communication is received through hearing, and written verbal communication and sign language are received through sight. In contrast, nonverbal communication may be seen, felt, heard, smelled, and tasted. We often receive nonverbal communication simultaneously through two or more channels, as when we feel and see a hug while hearing a whispered "I love you."

Finally, verbal communication is discrete, whereas nonverbal is more continuous. Verbal symbols start and stop; we begin speaking at one moment and stop speaking at another moment. In contrast, nonverbal communication tends to flow continually. Before we speak, our facial expressions and posture express our feelings; as we speak, our body movements and appearance communicate; and after we speak our posture changes, perhaps relaxing.*

8. This paragraph (circle the letter of one answer)

   a. compares. c. compares and contrasts.

   (b.) contrasts.

9. Which two subjects are being compared and/or contrasted?

   verbal communication and nonverbal communication

10. On what three major differences between the two subjects do these paragraphs focus?

    1. Trustworthiness
    2. How communication is received
    3. Flow of communication

Dating norms in other cultures differ, sometimes drastically, from norms among most Americans. A survey of college students from a U.S. midwestern state university and a Chinese university in Shanghai showed dating behaviors and attitudes that varied greatly. American college students held more liberal attitudes toward who initiates a date, dated younger, dated more frequently, and were more likely to develop a sexual relationship. Chinese students dated later, dated less frequently, and were less likely to develop a sexual relationship. American students in this sample had their first date during their 14th year, whereas the average age for Chinese students' first date was 18. Social pressure to date is greater in the United States, and the ability

6

* Wood, Julia T., *Communication in Our Lives,* 6th ed. Boston: Wadsworth, 2012. Print. Ch. 6, p. 124.

to have dates indicates popularity. In China, however, dating in junior high or even high school is considered somewhat unusual, and opportunities for dating are more limited. American society encourages dating, whereas Chinese society frowns on it.*

11. This paragraph (circle the letter of one answer)

    a. compares.

    b. contrasts.

    c. compares and contrasts.

12. Which two subjects are being compared and/or contrasted?

    American dating norms and Chinese dating norms

13. On what six differences between the two subjects does the paragraph focus?

    1. Who initiates dates
    2. Dating ages
    3. Dating frequency
    4. Likelihood of sexual relationship
    5. Average age of first date
    6. Social pressure

6

Group therapy offers features not found in individual therapy treatment. First, group therapy allows the therapist to observe clients interacting with one another, whereas individual therapy relies on the patient and the therapist only. Second, clients often feel less alone as they listen to others and realize that many people struggle with difficulties at least as severe as their own. In contrast, individual therapy patients benefit from one-on-one contact with their therapists, who get to know their patients well during treatment. Third, group members can boost one another's self-confidence and self-acceptance as they come to trust and value one another. In a therapist–patient relationship, the patient must develop trust only with his or her therapist in order for the therapy to work in that setting. Fourth, clients learn from one another, which is something that obviously cannot happen in a one-on-one situation. They share ideas for solving problems and give one another honest feedback about their attitudes and behavior. Fifth, perhaps through mutual modeling, the group experience makes clients more willing to share their feelings and more sensitive to other people's needs, motives, and messages. In a one-on-one therapy situation, the patient shares his or her feelings with the therapist

* From Kaplan, *Adolescence*. Boston: Houghton Mifflin, 2004, 204. Copyright © 2004 by Houghton Mifflin Company. Reprinted with permission.

alone. Finally, group therapy allows clients to try out new skills in a supportive environment, whereas one-on-one patients can take what they've learned out into the world and try it out there.*

14. This paragraph (circle the letter of one answer)

   a. compares.
   b. contrasts.
   c. compares and contrasts.

15. Which two subjects are being compared and/or contrasted?

   Group therapy and individual therapy

16. On what six similarities or differences between the two subjects does the paragraph focus?

   1. People involved
   2. Benefits of each type
   3. Development of trust
   4. Opportunities to learn from others
   5. Willingness to share feelings
   6. Where clients can try new skills

Definition

One last pattern you should learn to recognize is the definition pattern. **Definition** *usually states the meaning of a particular word, term, or concept, and then goes on to illustrate it with one or more examples.* Textbooks often use this pattern to explain a term being introduced for the first time.

Topic sentences will often indicate that a definition will follow:

A triathalon ***is*** a long-distance race that usually includes phases of running, swimming, and bicycling.

Evolution can be ***defined*** as a process of changes that occur over several generations in a particular population.

One ***meaning*** of Zen is the process of identifying and reducing attachments to the beliefs, attitudes, and ideas that cause human suffering.

* Adapted from Bernstein and Nash, *Essentials of Psychology,* 2nd ed. Boston: Houghton Mifflin, 2002, 464.

The following paragraph is organized according to the definition pattern.

> Permanent whirlpools are not just ancient myths; these churning areas of ocean actually exist. A *whirlpool* ***is*** a marine phenomenon created by a combination of tide, current, wind, and seabed features. When fast-moving water flows over rocks, shelves, ridges, and peaks of the ocean floor, the water eddies[1] and swirls, creating extremely dangerous whirling waves that can grind up all ships that pass through incautiously, turning them into matchwood. Only five whirlpools in the world are wild enough and big enough and famous enough to earn the name. The most notorious of them all is the Maelstrom in Norway, which added a word for "violent or turbulent situation" to the English language. It is a huge area of furious water that appeared on maps as early as 1555 and still threatens sailors today.*

The example or examples within a definition paragraph may be arranged according to one of the other patterns. For example, the definition might be followed by a list of examples or other details. Or, one example might be told using the sequence format. This next paragraph is a good example:

> For some people, *anxiety takes the form of* ***panic disorder.*** People suffering from panic disorder experience recurrent terrifying *panic attacks* that often come without warning or obvious cause and are marked by intense heart palpitations,[2] pressure or pain in the chest, dizziness or unsteadiness, sweating, and a feeling of faintness; often, victims believe they are having a heart attack. They may worry constantly about suffering future panic episodes and thus curtail activities to avoid possible embarrassment. ***For example,*** Geri, a 32-year-old nurse, had her first panic attack while driving on a freeway. Afterward, she would not drive on freeways. Her next attack occurred while with a patient and a doctor in a small examining room. A sense of impending[3] doom flooded over her and she burst out of the office and into the parking lot, where she felt immediate relief. From then on, fear of another attack made it impossible for her to tolerate any close quarters, including crowded shopping malls. She eventually quit her job because of terror of the examining rooms.†

6

1. **eddies:** moves in a circular motion, against the main current
2. **palpitations:** rapid, irregular beating
3. **impending:** upcoming, nearby

* Adapted from Simon Winchester, "In the Eye of the Whirlpool," *Smithsonian,* August 2001, 84–94.

† Adapted from Bernstein, *Psychology,* 4th ed. Boston: Houghton Mifflin, 1997, 503.

As you read, look for the following transitions that may indicate a definition pattern.

Words That Indicate a Definition Pattern	
means	definition
meaning	is/are
define	

Exercise 6.5

Read each of the following definition paragraphs and answer the questions that follow. Write your answers on the blanks provided.

(1) The police culture or police subculture is a combination of shared norms, values, goals, career patterns, lifestyles, and occupational structures that is somewhat different from the combination held by the rest of society. (2) The police subculture, like most subcultures, is characterized by clannishness, secrecy, and isolation from those not in the group. (3) Police officers work with other police officers during their tours of duty. (4) Many socialize together after work and on days off, often to the exclusion of others—even old friends and family. (5) When socializing, off-duty officers tend to talk about their jobs.*

1. Which term is defined in this paragraph? police culture
2. Which sentence states the definition? sentence 1
3. How many examples are given as illustrations? two
4. Which pattern organizes the examples? list

(1) The word *crater* (Greek *krater*) means bowl-shaped, and lunar craters are small- and large-diameter depressions believed to be caused by the impact and explosion of small and large meteorites. (2) The craters are rather shallow (their depths are small in comparison with their diameters), and their floors are located below the lunar surface. (3) The moon's South Pole-Aiken impact basin is the largest known in the solar system, with a diameter of 2,500 km (1,550 miles) and a depth that averages

* Dempsey, John S., and Linda Forst, *An Introduction to Policing,* 5th ed. Clifton Park: Delmar, 2010. Print. Ch. 6, p. 168.

6

about 12 km (7.4 miles). (4) The youngest impact basin on the moon is Orientale, which is about 1,000 km across and was formed 3.8 billion years ago.*

5. Which word is/are defined in this paragraph? crater

6. Which sentence(s) states the definition? sentence 1

7. How many examples are given as illustrations? two

8. Which pattern organizes the examples? list

(1) Many public schools in the United States are adopting a "uniform only" policy regarding how their students dress. (2) What is a uniform? (3) A uniform is a standard outfit worn by both girls and boys at their school. (4) Taking their cue from parochial[1] schools around the country, some school administrators are requiring students, who formerly wore whatever they wanted to school, to wear a uniform that is determined by the school and sold only at specific locations. (5) It is the equivalent of a dress code with the "dress" being mandated by the school administration. (6) An example of this would be blue pants, white shirt, and a tie for boys, and for girls, a jumper, white blouse, and knee socks. (7) Some schools have even determined that students should wear a specific type of shoe, but many still allow students and their parents to pick the shoes to go with the uniform.

9. Which word is defined in this paragraph? uniform

10. Which sentence states the definition? sentence 3

11. How many examples are given as illustrations? two

12. Which pattern organizes the examples? list

(1) In a simple sense, e-business, or electronic business, can be defined as the organized effort of individuals to produce and sell, for a profit, the products and services that satisfy society's needs through the facilities available on the Internet. (2) American Online, or AOL, is an example of an e-business that invented itself on the Internet. (3) Another example is Amazon.com, which gives customers anywhere in the world access to the same virtual[2] store of books, videos,

1. **parochial:** relating to a church parish
2. **virtual:** existing in computers

* Adapted from Shipman et al., *An Introduction to Physical Science*, 9th ed. Boston: Houghton Mifflin, 2000, 445.

and CDs. (4) And at e-Bay's global auction site, customers can, for a small fee, buy and sell almost anything.*

13. Which term is defined in this paragraph? e-business
14. Which sentence states the definition? sentence 1
15. How many examples are given as illustrations? three
16. Which pattern organizes the examples? list

(1) Most young people would like to have more influence, status, and popularity. (2) These goals are often achieved through identification with an authority figure or a role model. (3) A role model is a person you most admire or are likely to emulate.[1] (4) Preschoolers are most likely to identify their parents as their role models. (5) At this early stage, parents are seen as almost perfect, as real heroes. (6) During early elementary school, children begin to realize that their parents have flaws, and they search for other heroes—perhaps a popular athlete, a rock star, or an actor. (7) During later stages of development, new role models are adopted.†

17. Which term is defined in this paragraph? role model
18. Which sentence states the definition? sentence 3
19. How many examples are given as illustrations? three
20. Which pattern organizes the examples? sequence

Combination of Patterns

Often, paragraphs include more than one pattern of organization. The major supporting details may be arranged according to one pattern, and minor details are arranged according to another. For example, read the following paragraph:

In 1994, the Women's Bureau of the Department of Labor conducted a landmark survey of how working women in America feel

1. **emulate:** imitate

* Adapted from Pride, Hughes, and Kapoor, *Business*, 7th ed. Boston: Houghton Mifflin, 2002, 104–105. Copyright © 2002 by Houghton Mifflin Company. Reprinted with permission.

† Adapted from Reece and Brandt, *Effective Human Relations in Organizations,* 7th ed. Boston: Houghton Mifflin, 1999, 151.

> about their jobs. More than a quarter of a million women told of their concerns and experiences. ***After*** the results of the survey were studied, the workplace was identified as the greatest single source of stress. The ***causes*** of such stress can range from the anxieties produced by corporate downsizing to factors that ***result*** in physical disorders such as carpal tunnel syndrome.[1] Stress ***also*** can ***result*** from simply a feeling on the part of the individual worker that he or she is not appreciated on the job or is being overwhelmed by family obligations.*

This paragraph is mostly a cause/effect paragraph that explains two major causes of stress in the workplace. However, it begins with some sequence of details regarding a 1994 survey about how workers in America feel about their jobs.

Here is one more example:

> Time-starved Americans now spend as much time eating out as they do eating at home. How often do you pick up a quick lunch at a Burger King or Taco Bell? ***In the 1950s and 1960s,*** this trend was just beginning. Consumers wanted more restaurants and fast-food outlets. ***As a result,*** McDonald's, Wendy's, Big Boy, White Castle, Pizza Hut, Godfather's Pizza, and other fast-food outlets flourished. The trend toward eating away from home reached a fevered pitch in the ***late 1970s,*** when the average number of meals per person eaten out (excluding brown-bag lunches and other meals prepared at home but eaten elsewhere) exceeded one per day. In the ***1980s,*** people wanted the fast food but didn't want to go get it. By emphasizing delivery, Domino's Pizza and a few other fast-food outlets became very successful. ***In the 1990s,*** the "takeout taxi" business—where restaurant food is delivered to homes—grew 10 percent per year.†

Most of the details in this paragraph are arranged in the sequence pattern. The paragraph points out the development of the fast-food trend over five decades. The results of consumer desires are also included, so this paragraph combines the sequence and cause/effect patterns.

6

1. **carpal tunnel syndrome:** pain, numbness, and weakness in the thumb and fingers

* Adapted from Andrews et al., *Public Speaking*. Boston: Houghton Mifflin, 1999, 124.

† Adapted from Boyes and Melvin, *Fundamentals of Economics*. Boston: Houghton Mifflin, 1999, 45. Copyright © 1999 by Houghton Mifflin Company. Reprinted with permission.

Exercise 6.6

In the list following each paragraph, write a check mark beside each pattern used to organize the supporting details. Circle the transitions to help determine which patterns are being used.

1. In denial, impulses and associated ideas reach awareness, but their implications[1] are rejected or denied. For example, an unwillingness to check on medical symptoms could indicate the presence of denial, as does "gallows[2] humor," the tendency of soldiers to engage in banter and jest as they near an engagement with the enemy. Although denial may be functional for soldiers marching off to combat, it can be damaging for the individual. To deny the possible diagnostic implications of a persistent swelling that may be symptomatic of cancer is to risk the possible consequences of failing to take advantage of early treatment. Denial can also result in profound psychological consequences as, for example, when one refuses to acknowledge negative traits in a potential spouse.*

   ______ list ✔ comparison/contrast
   ______ sequence ______ definition
   ✔ cause/effect

2. Soaring eagles have the incredible ability to see a mouse move in the grass from a mile away. Similarly, cats have the amazing ability to see even in very dim light, thanks to special "reflectors" at the back of their eyes. Through natural selection, over time, each species has developed a visual system uniquely adapted to its way of life. The human visual system has also adapted to many things well: it combines great sensitivity and great sharpness, enabling people to see objects near and far, during the day and night. Our night vision is not as acute[3] as that of some animals, but our color vision is excellent. This is not a bad trade-off, because being able to appreciate a sunset's splendor seems worth an occasional stumble in the dark.†

   ______ list ✔ comparison/contrast
   ______ sequence ______ definition
   ✔ cause/effect

6

1. **implications:** significance
2. **gallows:** related to the place where executions by hanging occur
3. **acute:** sharp

* From Feshbach et al., *Personality*, 4th ed. Boston: Houghton Mifflin, 1996, 84. Copyright © 1996 by Houghton Mifflin Company. Reprinted with permission.

† Adapted from Bernstein et al., *Psychology*, 5th ed. Boston: Houghton Mifflin, 2000, 107.

3. Finland and the United States approach education differently. Children in Finland start at age 7, two years later than children in the United States start. Educational spending in Finland is only $5,000 a year per student, there are no gifted programs, as there are in America, and there are often 30 Finnish children in one classroom. In America, class sizes tend to be smaller. Therefore, one would expect America's schools to be better. On the contrary, an international survey showed that Finland is number one in the world in literacy and in the top five in both math and science. Many experts attribute Finland's high academic ranking to the higher quality and social standing of its teachers. Educators must have at least a master's degree, and teaching is a highly respected profession. Universities in Finland have to turn down the majority of applicants for teaching programs. In contrast, American schools often have trouble finding enough teachers for a profession that is not highly regarded.*

_____ list　　　✔_____ comparison/contrast

_____ sequence　　　_____ definition

✔_____ cause/effect

4. The major side effects of anabolic steroid abuse include liver tumors and cancer, jaundice (yellowish pigmentation of skin, tissues, and body fluids), fluid retention, high blood pressure, increases in low-density lipoproteins (LDL, or bad cholesterol), and decreases in high-density lipoproteins (HDL, or good cholesterol). Other side effects may include kidney tumors, severe acne, and trembling. Many gender-specific side effects are associated with these drugs. Many men suffer shrinking testicles, reduced sperm count, infertility, baldness, development of breasts, and increased risk of prostate cancer. Women may suffer growth of facial hair, male-pattern baldness, changes in or cessation of the menstrual cycle, enlargement of the clitoris, and a deepened voice. Adolescents' growth may be halted through premature skeletal maturation and accelerated puberty changes, meaning that they risk remaining of short stature for the rest of their lives if they take anabolic steroids before the typical adolescent growth spurt. In addition, people who inject anabolic steroids run the added risk of contracting or transmitting HIV/AIDS, which is potentially fatal, or hepatitis, which causes serious damage to the liver.†

6

* From Lizette Alvarez, "Educators Flocking to Finland, Land of Literate Children," *New York Times*, April 9, 2004, www.nytimes.com.

† France, Robert C., *Introduction to Sports Medicine and Athletic Training*, 2nd ed. Clifton Park: Delmar, 2011. Print. Ch. 9, p. 160.

✔ list ______ comparison/contrast

______ sequence ______ definition

✔ cause/effect

5. An overwhelming amount of evidence shows that social support has therapeutic[1] effects on both our psychological and physical health. David Spiegel, of Stanford University's School of Medicine, came to appreciate the value of social connections many years ago when he organized support groups for women with advanced breast cancer. Spiegel had fully expected the women to benefit, emotionally, from the experience. But he found something else he did not expect: These women lived an average of 18 months longer than others who did not attend the groups. In another study, Lisa Berkman and Leonard Syme surveyed seven thousand residents of Alameda County, California; conducted a nine-year follow-up of mortality rates; and found that the more social contacts people had, the longer they lived. This was true of men and women, young and old, rich and poor, and people from all racial and ethnic backgrounds. James House and others studied 2,754 adults interviewed during visits to their doctors. He found that the most socially active men were two to three times less likely to die within 9 to 12 years than others of similar age who were more isolated.*

✔ list ______ comparison/contrast

______ sequence ______ definition

✔ cause/effect

Reading Strategy: Taking Notes

Learning how to take notes effectively is a vital skill for college students. You will often be tested on the information in reading selections such as textbook chapters, so you will need to make sure you're using all of the tools at your disposal to understand and retain this information.

One of those tools is an active reading technique known as *note taking*. **Taking notes** *means recording in writing the major information and ideas in a text.* You might choose to take these notes in the margins of the book itself, or in a notebook, or on separate sheets of paper.

1. **therapeutic:** having healing powers

* Adapted from Brehm et al., *Social Psychology*, 5th ed. Boston: Houghton Mifflin, 2002, 528. Copyright © 2002 by Houghton Mifflin Company. Reprinted with permission.

Regardless of where you write them, notes offer two important benefits. First of all, writing down information and ideas helps you to remember them better. For many people, taking the extra time to handwrite the main points helps implant those points in their memory more securely. As a result, retention and test performance tend to improve. Secondly, good notes are often easier to study because they provide the student with a condensed version of the main points.

Good notes always begin with highlighting or underlining main ideas or key terms as you read, just as you learned to do in Chapter 1. When you write notes, they might take one or more of the following forms:

- **A list of the main ideas in all of the paragraphs.** Put them in your own words and condense them whenever possible. Don't try to include all of the details, just the most important points.
- **A summary of the chapter or article** (for an overview of this strategy, see Chapter 5).
- **An outline.** In previous chapters of this book, you've practiced filling out outlines that reveal the relationships between the details. You can use a Roman numeral outline, but the notes are usually for your eyes only, so you could also adopt or create a more informal system. No matter what kind of outline you use, though, make sure it clearly demonstrates the general and specific relationships between the ideas.

No matter what form they take, effective notes always possess three important characteristics. They should be:

1. *Neat.* Skip lines between points and write legibly.
2. *Clearly organized.* Group related points together so they're easier to remember.
3. *Factual and objective.* Like summaries, notes should be free of your own opinions.

Actively read one of the following reading selections. Then, take notes by creating a list of the paragraphs' main ideas, by writing a summary, or by mapping or outlining the selection.

The following websites will help you to learn more about taking better notes in college—both in class and in your textbooks.

WEB LINK

http://www.howtostudy.org/resources_skill.php?id=9
http://www.studygs.net/booknote.htm

Reading Selections

Practicing the Active Reading Strategy

Before and While You Read

You can use active reading strategies before, while, and after you read a selection. The following are some suggestions for active reading strategies that you can employ before you read and as you are reading.

1. Skim the selection for any unfamiliar words. Circle or highlight any words you do not know.
2. As you read, underline, highlight, or circle important words or phrases.
3. Write down any questions about the selection if you are confused by the information presented.
4. Jot notes in the margin to help you understand the material.

BIOGRAPHY:
Clara Barton: Founder of the American Red Cross

Though she never received any formal medical training, Clara Barton's instincts helped her to provide nursing assistance during the Civil War. Her greatest legacy, though, lies in founding the American Red Cross, which serves thousands of Americans every year.

1 Clarissa Harlowe Barton, founder of the American Red Cross, was born in 1821 in Massachusetts. For two years as a young teenager, Barton helped care for one of her seriously ill brothers. This experience helped Barton overcome an acute shyness and became her primary medical training.

2 At the age of eighteen, Barton began teaching school. In 1854, she ended her teaching career when she moved to Washington, DC, to work as a recording clerk at the U.S. Patent Office; she was paid an equal salary to her male peers, $1,400 annually. However, the following year, Secretary of the Interior Robert McClelland, who was opposed to women working in government offices, reduced her position from clerk to copyist with a lower salary. In 1857, the Buchanan administration eliminated her position at the Patent Office, but in 1860 she returned to her position as copyist after the election of President Abraham Lincoln.

6

3 Barton was working in Washington, DC, when the Civil War broke out in 1861. The 6th Massachusetts Infantry was attacked en route to Washington, DC, by southern sympathizers, and were in bad shape when they arrived. Barton heard about their condition and brought supplies from her home to aid them. This act started a lifelong career of aiding people in times of conflict and disaster.

4 Barton continued to aid wounded soldiers in Washington, DC, and established a distribution agency of supplies. In 1862, she received official permission to transport supplies to battlefields. Throughout the Civil War, she was at all of the major battles in Maryland, Virginia, and South Carolina, providing supplies to doctors and surgeons, and tending to the wounded and ill, too, even though she had no official medical training. After the end of the war in 1865, Barton helped locate missing soldiers, find and mark thousands of graves, and testified in Congress regarding her experiences during the war.

5 In 1869, upon the advice of her doctor, Barton traveled to Europe to regain her health. While in Switzerland, she learned about the Red Cross organization that was established in Geneva in 1864.

6 Upon her return home, Barton focused her attention on educating the public and obtaining support for the creation of an American society of the Red Cross. She wrote pamphlets, lectured, and met with President Rutherford B. Hayes. On May 21, 1881, her efforts paid off, and the American Association of the Red Cross was formed; Barton was elected president in June. Over the years, local chapters were formed throughout the country to help people during times of natural disasters. In March 1862, President Chester A. Arthur signed the Treaty of Geneva and, with the unanimous ratification of the U.S. Senate, the United States joined the International Red Cross.

7 Barton spent most of the rest of her life leading the Red Cross, lecturing, attending national and international meetings, aiding with disasters, helping the homeless and poor, writing about her life and the Red Cross, and lecturing on women's rights and suffrage. In 1904 she resigned as president of the American National Red Cross and established the National First Aid Association of America, an organization that emphasized basic first aid and instruction, emergency preparedness, and developed first aid kits.

8 Barton died in 1912, at the age of 90, at her Glen Echo home in Maryland. Glen Echo became the Clara Barton National Historic Site in 1975, the first National Historic Site dedicated to the accomplishments of a woman.*

6

* Source: http://www.nwhm.org/education-resources/biography/biographies/clara-barton/

Vocabulary

Read the following questions about some of the vocabulary words that appear in the previous selection. Before you look up the word, try to use the context of the passage to figure out the meaning. Then circle the letter of the correct answer for each question or write the definition that best fits the context on the line provided.

1. What is *acute* shyness in paragraph 1?

   a. slow c. unnoticed

   b. slight (d.) severe

2. Barton established a *distribution* agency of supplies. What kind of agency is this? (paragraph 4)

   a. crisis c. war

   (b.) source d. medical

3. In paragraph 4, what is *transport*? carry

4. Barton wrote *pamphlets* to help gain support for establishing the AmericanRed Cross. What are *pamphlets*? (paragraph 6)

   a printed work consisting of a few sheets of paper stitched together, but not bound

5. The U.S. Senate gave *ratification* to the Treaty of Geneva. What is *ratification*? (paragraph 6)

   a. decline c. delay

   (b.) approve d. veto

Reading Skills

Respond to each of the following questions by circling the letter of the correct answer or by writing your answer on the blank provided.

1. What is the overall pattern of organization used for the biography?

   a. cause/effect c. comparison

   b. list (d.) sequence

2. Write the contrast transition from paragraph 2. however

3. What is the main idea of paragraph 4? Clara Barton worked throughout the Civil War and for years afterward providing any assistance she could for soldiers and their families.

4. Write the topic sentence of paragraph 6. Barton focused her attention on educating the public and obtaining support for the creation of an American society of the Red Cross.

5. Create a time line of events from this reading selection. Answers will vary.

Practicing the Active Reading Strategy

After You Read

Now that you have read the selection, answer the following questions, using the active reading strategies that you learned in Chapter 1.

1. Identify and write down the point and purpose of this reading selection.
2. Did you circle or highlight any words that are unfamiliar to you? Can you figure out the meaning from the context of the passage? If not, then look up each word in a dictionary and find the definition that best describes the word as it is used in the selection. You may want to write the definition in the margin next to the word in the passage for future reference.
3. Predict any possible questions that may be used on a test about the content of this selection.

Questions for Discussion and Writing

Respond to each of the following questions based on your reading of the selection.

1. What event led Clara Barton to begin a career in helping people during difficult times?

   For two years as a young teenager, Barton helped care for one of her seriously ill. brothers.

2. What has been the main function of the Red Cross over the years?

   to assist people in times of natural disasters

3. What is significant about the Clara Barton national Historic Site?

   It was the first National Historic Site dedicated to the accomplishments of a woman.

Practicing the Active Reading Strategy

■ Before and While You Read

You can use active reading strategies before, while, and after you read a selection. The following are some suggestions for active reading strategies that you can employ before you read and as you are reading.

1. Skim the selection for any unfamiliar words. Circle or highlight any words you do not know.
2. As you read, underline, highlight, or circle important words or phrases.
3. Write down any questions about the selection if you are confused by the information presented.
4. Jot notes in the margin to help you understand the material.

TEXTBOOK READING: FASHION DESIGN

Fashion Emphasis, 2000–Present: You Make the Call!

How much attention do you pay to fashion trends? Are you someone who always has to have the latest trend? What do you think influences the changes in fashion? As you read this selection try to underline the factors that influence fashion change.

1 Identifying the magnitude of fashion trends poses some difficulty if society is currently experiencing the trend. Some trends are visible, but it is much easier to study major fashion trends in retrospect. Styles that are currently in fashion have yet to complete their life cycle, so the degree of popularity or the speed of the cycle cannot be determined. However, because a new fashion usually grows out of a preceding fashion, some generalizations can be made, especially about the earlier years of the twenty-first century.

2 The terrorist attacks on the World Trade Center towers in New York City on September 11, 2001, and the subsequent military involvement shed fashion light on patriotic colors and camouflage prints. Red, white, and blue color combinations in fashions increased in popularity in the seasons following the attacks. The camouflage prints that had been popular during the mid- to late 1990s were waning in popularity by the end of the twentieth century. However, the renewed interest in the military after the terrorist attacks of 2001 also may have renewed the fashion interest in camouflage in the first decade of the twenty-first century.

3 In the early 2000s, fashions became dressier, and the fashion industry heralded the return of the one-piece dress as a new direction in women's wear. Comfort remained an important part of dressing, but

people were dressing up more than previous years. The 1970s disco glam look reappeared in the early 2000s and featured glitter and sequin embellishments on clothing and accessories. By the middle of the decade, the 1960s retro fashions emerged in styles that included A- line and tubular silhouettes. Geometric print and mod styles were mid-decade fashions.

4 The distressed jeans look featuring tears, holes, and threadbare patches diminished in popularity although it remained a part of the male and female teen wardrobe beyond the first half of the decade. Darker denims with higher rises gradually replaced the low-rise destroyed and distressed denims. Layered tops complemented the denim fashions. Women's knit tops lengthened to several inches below the waist, replacing the cropped tops of the late 1990s and early years of the 2000s. By the mid-2000s, the tunic-length top was a pervasive fashion trend.

5 When fashion experts predict the movement of fashion, differences of opinion exist on the emerging trends and the upcoming popular fashions. A perusal of the 2007 fashion editorials identified references to retro fashions from the 1950s, 1960s, 1970s, and 1980s. Although designers may incorporate ideas from all these decades into collections for a particular year, the consumers ultimately decide which styles they adopt. In 2007, the fashion editor predictions and opinions varied on the emerging trends. For example, in February 2007, the New York Fashion Week event showed designer collections for the fall/winter 2007 to 2008 season. The subsequent write-ups by fashion editors represented dichotomous viewpoints. One editor wrote that the designers showed "color, flowing lines and loose cuts." A second editor wrote that the fall/winter 2007 to 2008 season was "all about tighter lines and a closer cut." Could both predictions be correct?

6 For menswear, the term *metrosexual* defined the fashion-forward male who dressed with care in colorful clothing, hinting at a more feminine side. The more conservative male wore comfortable and colorful sport shirts with neutral-colored slacks, jeans, or the wardrobe classic cargo pants or shorts. Popular neckties prints included bold and colorful patterns, such as repeating stripes (reps) and geometric patterns.

7 Manufacturers offered conservatively cut suits, featuring moderate-width lapels, single-breasted coats, and straight-legged trousers. As is usually the case, designers concentrated fashion-forward looks in shirts and accessories that could easily be updated each season, rather than in the wardrobe basics, such as men's suits, that often required a higher initial investment.

8 Variations on the Gothic, hip-hop, gangsta, and skateboarder looks continued well into the first decade of this century, although for the most part they were in the declining stages for mainstream fashions. Until about 2005, retailers featured the distressed or destroyed denim look for adolescent denim fashions, but this look

soon moved into the decline stage. By 2007, the preppy look, retro of the 1980s, gained momentum. It included woven button-up shirts, polo knitted shirts, Lacoste alligator logos, wrinkle-free cotton khaki pants, and darker denim jeans. Denim jeans were the item of the decade.*

Vocabulary

Read the following questions about some of the vocabulary words that appear in the previous selection. Before you look up the word, try to use the context of the passage to figure out the meaning. Then circle the letter of the correct answer for each question or write the answer on the line.

1. What does the phrase "in *retrospect*" mean in paragraph 1?
   a. looking ahead
   b. not clear or visible
   c. looking back
   d. in society

2. In paragraph 3, what do you think *heralded* means?
   a. ushered in
   b. ended
   c. closed
   d. permitted

3. The author writes, "By the mid-2000s, the tunic-length top was a *pervasive* fashion trend" (paragraph 4). Which of the following definitions IS NOT the meaning of *pervasive*?
   a. extensive
   b. universal
   c. limited
   d. prevalent

4. What does *perusal* mean in paragraph 5?
   a. sign
   b. examination
   c. page
   d. skimming

5. "The subsequent write-ups by fashion editors represented *dichotomous* viewpoints" (paragraph 5). What does *dichotomous* mean?
   a. puzzling
   b. incorrect
   c. similar
   d. divided into two parts

6. Using context clues of explanation, briefly describe the "*disco glam*" look(paragraph 3).

   featuring glitter and sequin embellishments on clothing and accessories

* Stall-Meadows, Celia. *Fashion Now: A Global Perspective*. Upper Saddle River: Pearson Education, Inc., 2011. Print. Ch. 4, pp. 77–79.

6

Reading Skills

Respond to each of the following questions by circling the letter of the correct answer or by writing your answer on the blank provided.

1. What is the main idea of paragraph 2? The terrorist attacks of September 11, 2001, and subsequent military involvement had an effect on fashion.
2. In paragraph 6, what word or term is defined? What is the definition? Metrosexual; the fashion-forward male who dresses with care in colorful clothing, hinting at a more feminine side.
3. What is the implied main idea of paragraph 4? The fashion trends of denim and tops changed during the early 2000s.
4. Write the minor detail transition word/s used in paragraph 5. for example
5. What pattern organizes the details of paragraph 2?

   a. sequence
   b. series
   c. cause/effect (circled)
   d. compare/contrast

6

Practicing the Active Reading Strategy

After You Read

Now that you have read the selection, answer the following questions, using the active reading strategies that you learned in Chapter 1.

1. Identify and write down the point and purpose of this reading selection.
2. Did you circle or highlight any words that are unfamiliar to you? Can you figure out the meaning from the context of the passage? If not, then look up each word in a dictionary and find the definition that best describes the word as it is used in the selection. You may want to write the definition in the margin next to the word in the passage for future reference.
3. Predict any possible questions that may be used on a test about the content of this selection.

Questions for Discussion and Writing

Respond to each of the following questions based on your reading of the selection.

1. What effects did the terrorist attacks on September 11, 2001, and the military involvement have on fashion?
   Patriotic colors (red, white, and blue color combinations) in fashion increased; people began to wear more camouflage print.

2. The author writes, "Denim jeans were the item of the decade." Compare and/or contrast the different ways in which denim has been worn over the decade of the early 2000s.
   In the first half of the decade, people wore torn/ worn jeans, but their popularity began to diminish; darker denim became trendier. Higher-rise jeans replaced lower-rise jeans.

3. Why is it difficult to study major fashion trends while society is currently experiencing the trend?
   "Styles that are currently in fashion have yet to complete their life cycle, so the degree of popularity or the speed of the cycle cannot be determined."

4. Write three generalizations about fashion trends of the early 2000s.
   Answers will vary. Suggested answers: 1. Hip-hop looks are diminishing. 2. The distressed denim look is being replaced with darker denim. 3. The preppy, retro look of the '80s has gained momentum.

Practicing the Active Reading Strategy

Before and While You Read

You can use active reading strategies before, while, and after you read a selection. The following are some suggestions for active reading strategies that you can perform before you read and as you read.

1. Skim the selection for any unfamiliar words. Circle or highlight any words you do not know.
2. As you read, underline, highlight, or circle important words or phrases.
3. Write down any questions about the selection if you are confused by the information presented.
4. Jot notes in the margin to help you understand the material.

NEWSPAPER READING: HEALTH

Women React to Pain Differently Than Men

by Rita Rubin

Who is a bigger "baby" when they are sick—men or women? Do you know someone who complains of pains constantly? Man or woman? This article discusses some of the reasons why there are gender differences to feeling pain.

1 Recent studies now show that pain is not gender neutral. From the intensity of their pain to the way they deal with it, men and women are different, suggests a growing body of evidence. One result, many scientists say, is that women's pain is not taken as seriously as men's. "Pain is not simply a physical experience," says Diane Hoffmann, director of the Law & Health Care Program at the University of Maryland School of Law. "Men and women have been shown to give different meaning to their pain."

2 Two common scenarios illustrate some of the differences between the sexes: A man awakens with chest pain and writes it off as indigestion. His wife urges him to go to the emergency room, where he is diagnosed as having a heart attack. In contrast, a woman awakens with chest pain and thinks she might be having a heart attack. She goes immediately to the emergency room, where all tests of her heart function are normal. Doctors throw up their hands and send her on her way.

3 Possible explanations for these differences are complex, ranging from the physiological to the cultural. It's not clear whether women actually feel pain more intensely, as some—but not all—laboratory experiments have found, or whether they simply tend to describe their pain more expansively. "It's complicated, because you have to separate out reporting style," says Arthur Barsky, director of psychiatric research at Brigham and Women's Hospital in Boston. "What's a twinge for you may be an agonizing, crushing pain for me. It's hard to separate the vocabulary from the actual sensual experience."

4 Anita Tarzian, a health law researcher at the University of Maryland and a hospice[1] nurse, notes that women do have thinner skin and a higher density of nerve fibers than men. And estrogen, the so-called *female hormone*, influences women's pain response in many ways, Tarzian says. Fluctuations in hormone levels might contribute to variations in the severity of women's pain symptoms across the menstrual cycle, during pregnancy and immediately after delivery, and during and after menopause.

5 Menstrual cramps and childbirth themselves might help explain

1. **hospice:** related to a program that provides care for terminally ill people

differences in how women and men perceive pain, scientists say. "We have a regular experience of pain that can be somewhat severe," says Anita Unruh, an occupational therapist and social worker at Dalhousie University in Halifax, Nova Scotia. "You have to learn to be attuned to when pain is actually abnormal."

6 When women feel pain, their brains don't respond the same as men's do, says psychologist Karen Berkley of Florida State University. Because women are brought up to be more nurturing than men, Berkley says, they're more likely to regard pain as a call to action. In other words, she says, women tend to think, "OK, it hurts. Now, let's go do something about it." Men, on the other hand, are taught from boyhood that crying and other expressions of distress are for sissies, Barsky says. And, partly because women tend to seek medical help more often than men, their pain complaints are often less likely to be taken seriously, says Tarzian, who with Hoffmann wrote a paper titled "The Girl Who Cried Pain: A Bias Against Women in the Treatment of Pain" in an issue of *The Journal of Law, Medicine & Ethics*.

7 Some doctors might discount a woman's pain because they think it's all in her head. Even if doctors do acknowledge the validity of a woman's pain, they may think she has a higher pain tolerance because she's built to give birth, Tarzian and Hoffmann write. Either way, they say the outcome is the same: less aggressive treatment of women's pain.

8 Further complicating matters are the reasons for women's pain, or the apparent lack thereof. Women are far more likely than men to suffer from painful conditions with no obvious cause, such as migraines or fibromyalgia, characterized by tender, aching muscles. "The whole issue of just treating symptoms isn't dealt with much in medical education," Barsky says. "The real objective is to make a diagnosis and treat the underlying problem." Doctors are at a loss when confronted by patients whose pain has no obvious cause, he says. As a result, says James Campbell, director of the pain treatment center at Johns Hopkins Hospital in Baltimore, "people who have illnesses that are not well understood end up getting rotten care."

9 That shouldn't dissuade women from seeking medical advice when they feel pain, Unruh says. "You have to trust your own knowledge about who you are and what your body is like," she says. Women need to tell their doctor when they are seeking information rather than treatment and ask themselves, "Do I have a pain to worry about or not?" Unruh says. "A good doctor will say when he or she doesn't know."*

6

* Adapted from Rita Rubin, "Women React to Pain Differently Than Men," *USA Today*, October 9, 2001, 10D.

■ Vocabulary

Read the following questions about some of the vocabulary words that appear in the previous selection. Circle the letter of the correct answer.

1. In paragraph 1, what do you think *gender neutral* means?
   a. the same for men and women
   b. different for men and women
   c. more intense for men
   d. less intense for women

2. What is *indigestion*? (paragraph 2) "A man awakens with . . . *indigestion*."
   a. cramps
   b. inability to digest
   c. leg pain
   d. headache

3. "Possible explanations for these differences are complex, ranging from the *physiological* to the cultural" (paragraph 3). What does *physiological* mean?
   a. related to the brain
   b. related to the functions of the body
   c. the study of illnesses
   d. the study of plants

4. What are *fluctuations*? (paragraph 4) "*Fluctuations* in hormone levels might contribute to variations in the severity of women's pain symptoms. . . ."
   a. ideas
   b. moments
   c. changes
   d. definitions

5. "Because women are brought up to be more *nurturing* than men. . . ." (paragraph 6) What does it mean to be *nurturing*?
   a. helping to grow or develop
   b. helping to decide
   c. providing shelter
   d. providing food

6. What does it mean to *dissuade*? (paragraph 9) "That shouldn't *dissuade* women from seeking medical advice when they feel pain. . . ."
   a. encourage
   b. protect
   c. discourage
   d. enhance

6

Reading Skills

Respond to the following questions by circling the letter of the correct answer.

1. What pattern organizes the details in paragraph 4?

   a. sequence
   b. list
   (c.) cause/effect
   d. comparison/contrast

2. In paragraph 4, what word or phrase is defined?

   (a.) estrogen
   b. nerve fibers
   c. hospice
   d. hormone

3. In paragraph 6, what pattern organizes the details?

   a. sequence
   b. list
   c. cause/effect
   (d.) comparison/contrast

4. What is the implied main idea of paragraph 2?

   a. Men often get indigestion.
   b. Men have more heart attacks than women.
   (c.) Men and women react differently to pain, which confuses doctors.
   d. Women don't have heart attacks.

5. Which of the following is a comparison/contrast transition that appears in the reading selection?

   (a.) on the other hand
   b. and
   c. as a result
   d. because

Practicing the Active Reading Strategy

After You Read

Now that you have read the selection, answer the following questions, using the active reading strategies that are discussed in Chapter 1.

1. Identify and write down the point and purpose of this reading selection.
2. Did you circle or highlight any words that are unfamiliar to you? Can you figure out the meaning from the context of the passage? If not, then look up each word in a dictionary and find the definition that best describes the word as it is used in the selection. You may want to write the definition in the margin next to the word in the passage for future reference.
3. Predict any possible questions that may be used on a test about the content of this selection.

Questions for Discussion and Writing

Answer the following questions based on your reading of the selection. Write your answers on the blanks provided.

1. State one interesting fact that you learned from this selection. Why was this fact interesting to you?

   Answers will vary.

2. Do you think that the information in this selection stereotypes men and women? Why or why not? Does the author provide enough evidence to support her assertion that "pain is not gender neutral"? Why or why not?

   Answers will vary.

3. What do you think Diane Hoffmann means in paragraph 1 when she says, "Men and women have been shown to give different meaning to their pain"? Do you agree? If so, provide an example from your own life where this was true.

   Answers will vary.

Vocabulary Strategy: The Example Context Clue

You've learned that a *context clue* is a word, phrase, or sentence that helps you understand the meaning of an unfamiliar word you encounter as you read. In Chapter 4, you practiced recognizing the definition/restatement context clue. In Chapter 5, you learned about the explanation context clue. The **example** is a third type of context clue that can give you a sense of a particular word's definition. In this type, *an example somewhere near a word provides an illustration that allows you to draw a conclusion about the word's meaning.* For example, read the following sentence, which comes from one of the paragraphs in this chapter:

> Singing a song, for example, is not just "music"; it also fosters language development, ***motor skills*** (if the children dance along), arithmetic (through counting and rhythm), and social studies (if the words are about people and life in the community).

What does the term *motor skills* mean in this sentence? You get a clue in the form of the phrase "if the children dance along." If dancing is an example of using motor skills, then they must have something to do with moving the body. Therefore, you can conclude that *motor skills* means "the performance of movements."

Vocabulary Exercise 1

The following sentences all come from paragraphs in this chapter and previous chapters. In each one, underline the example context clue that helps you understand the meaning of the boldfaced, italicized word. Then, on the blank provided, write a definition for the boldfaced, italicized word.

1. They may worry constantly about suffering future panic episodes and thus ***curtail*** activities to avoid possible embarrassment. For example, Geri, a 32-year-old nurse, had her first panic attack while driving on a freeway. Afterward, she would not drive on freeways. limit, cut short

2. It also happens more frequently during ***unstructured*** time, such as free playground periods, or when children are tired. not regulated or organized

3. From the 1880s onward, popular newspapers increasingly nurtured people's fascination with the ***sensational.*** Joseph Pulitzer, a Hungarian immigrant who bought the *New York World* in 1883, pioneered this trend by filling his newspaper with stories of disasters, crimes, and scandals.
intended to arouse strong interest, curiosity, or reaction, especially by
exaggerated or lurid details

4. [Tennis players] Tilden and Johnston played five acts of incredible ***melodrama,*** with a thrill in every scene, with horrible errors leading suddenly to glorious achievements, with skill and courage and good and evil fortune. drama marked by exaggerated emotions

5. Countless monuments, from the pyramids of Egypt to ordinary tombstones, have suffered drastic deterioration from freezing water, hot sunshine, and other ***climatic*** forces. relating to climate or weather

6. The types of fat in these oils can improve the levels of cholesterol and other ***lipids*** in your blood and combat the narrowing of arteries that often occurs with age. fatty substances in the body

7. In addition to good values on down-home classics, New York serves up thrifty East Indian curries, Moroccan couscous, Greek kebabs, West Indian callaloos, Senegalese thiebu djen (fish stews), Mexican chimichangas, and many more ***culinary*** treats from around the globe.
relating to food or eating

6

8. This covering seals the compacted trash from the air and prevents ***vermin*** (birds, cats, mice, flying insects, etc.) from getting into the trash.

small, destructive animals or insects

Vocabulary Exercise 2

In each of the following passages, underline the example context clues that help define the boldfaced, italicized words.

A. Any candle factory worth its wicks will produce 1,000 to 2,000 varieties. Candles are highbrow ***horticulture,*** with creations of Bulgarian Roses and Mexican Orange Blossom. Candles are ***cuisine,*** in flavors of Oatmeal Cookie, Candy Corn, and Toasted Marshmallow. Appealing to Generation X, there are Jumpin' Java candles with whipped wax "served" in Irish coffee mugs. There are hometown candles with ***regional*** flavors: That's not a leafy clump of weeds burning on your coffee table! It's a kudzu candle from Mississippi. And no fewer than 10 varieties are considered ***aphrodisiacs.*** Ylang Ylang, for example, is said to inspire romance.*

B. The scientific study of memory has influenced the design of the electrical and mechanical devices that play an increasingly important role in our lives. Designers of computers, cameras, and even stoves are faced with a choice: Either place the operating instructions on the ***contraptions*** themselves, or assume that the user remembers how to operate them. Understanding the limits of both working memory and long-term memory has helped designers distinguish between information that is likely to be stored in (and easily retrieved from) the user's memory, and information that should be presented in the form of labels, instructions, or other ***cues*** that reduce memory demands. Placing unfamiliar or hard-to-recall information in plain view makes it easier to use the device as intended, and with less chance of errors.

Psychologists have influenced advertisers and designers to create many other "user-friendly" systems. For example, in creating toll-free numbers, they take advantage of ***chunking,*** which provides an efficient way to maintain information in working memory. Which do you think would be easier to remember: 1-800-447-4357 or 1-800-GET-HELP? Similarly, automobile designers ensure that the turn signals on your car emit an audible cue when turned on, a feature that reduces your memory load while driving.†

6

* Adapted from Dennis McCafferty, "Stop and Smell the Candles," *USA Weekend*, July 27–29, 2001, 12.

† Adapted from Bernstein et al., *Psychology*, 5th ed. Boston: Houghton Mifflin, 2000, 245.

Reading Visuals: Line Graphs

A **graph** *is a visual aid composed of lines or bars that correspond to numbers or facts arranged along a vertical axis, or side, and a horizontal axis.* The purpose of a graph is to show changes or differences in amounts, quantities, or characteristics. Two types of graphs are line graphs and bar graphs. Each one presents information differently. The bar graph is covered in Chapter 7 of this text.

A **line graph** *is composed of points plotted within a vertical axis and a horizontal axis and then connected with lines.* Line graphs typically reveal *changes or trends* in numerical data over time. They demonstrate how two factors interact with each other. The vertical axis is labeled with increments of time, such as years or minutes. The vertical axis is labeled with quantities. For each point in time, a dot on the graph indicates the corresponding quantity. Then, these dots are all connected to show upward and downward movement.

Line graphs contain the following parts:

- **Title.** The title points out the type of numbers being examined. It corresponds to the label of the vertical axis.
- **Vertical axis.** This line, which runs up and down, is divided into regular increments of numbers that correspond to the type of data being tracked. This axis is labeled to identify the type of data.
- **Horizontal axis.** This line, which runs from left to right, is divided into segments of time. It, too, is labeled to identify the kind of time factor being used.
- **Points.** Numerical data is plotted at the points where numbers and time factors intersect on the grid. These points may be labeled with specific amounts.
- **Lines.** Points are connected with lines to show trends.
- **Source line.** The source line identifies who collected or compiled the information in the graph.

These parts are labeled on the following line graph.

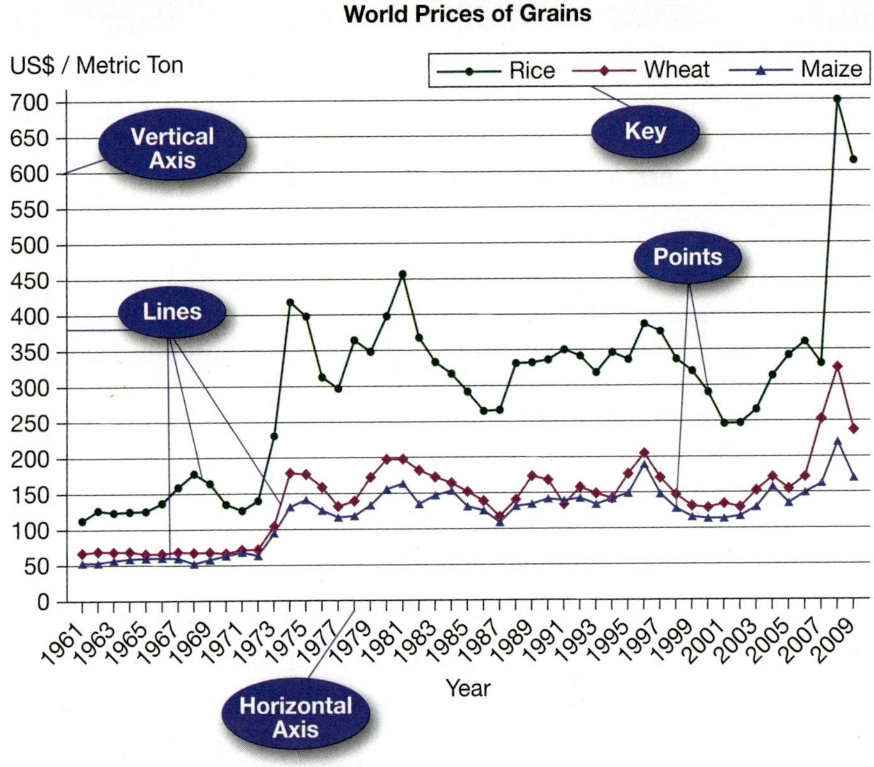

Source: Norton, George W., *Economics of Agricultural Development: World Food Systems and Resource Use*, 2nd ed. New York: Routledge, 2010. Print. Ch. 1, p. 7.

To read a line graph, begin with the title. Read it carefully to understand the numerical value on which the graph focuses. Then, read the labels on the vertical and horizontal axes to understand what two factors are interacting. Finally, examine the line that connects the points and try to state in your own words the trends being revealed by the numbers. Do the numbers increase, decrease, or both? When? How much overall change has occurred during the time span indicated on the horizontal axis?

As the title indicates, the line graph above illustrates the cost trends of grains used around the world. The vertical axis is divided into increments of U.S. dollars for a metric ton. The horizontal axis is divided into years. The points plotted on this grid are connected by three lines, which are labeled in the key. These three lines clearly reveal that between 1961 and 2009 to the cost of various important food grains around the world. Although wheat and maize (corn) costs have grown gradually, the cost of rice has shown dramatic ups and downs, with a very large spike in 2008. Rice is consumed by a large portion of countries in the Far East and their populations have increased dramatically in the last few decades, creating a greater demand for rice.

Now, study the following line graph and then answer the questions that follow.

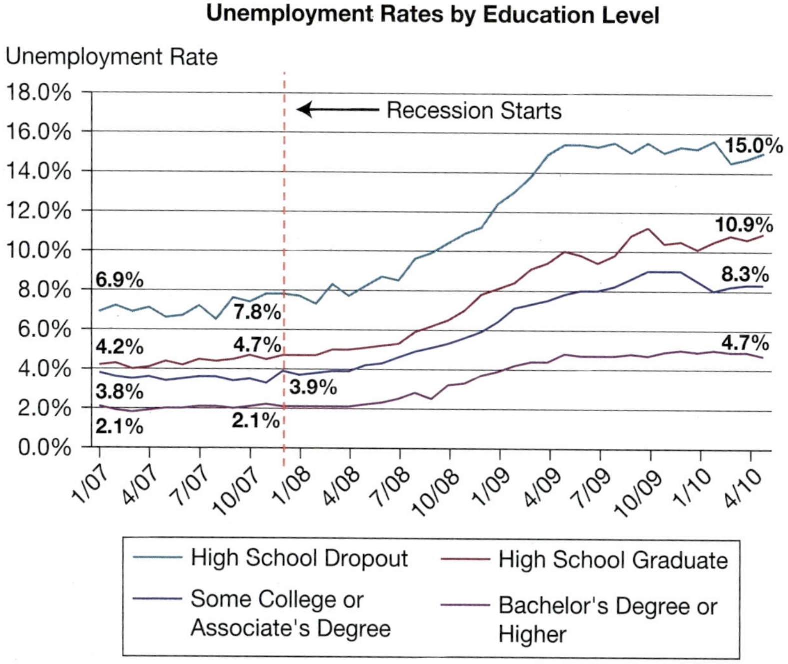

Source: http://www.all4ed.org/publication_material/straight_as/06282010 Web.

1. What was the unemployment rate of high school dropouts in 1/09? 12%
2. In 1/10, what percentage of high school graduates were unemployed? 10%
3. In what month/year was the unemployment rate of people with some college or an associate degree 6%? 1/09
4. What was the unemployment rate of people with a bachelor's degree or higher in 1/09? 4%
5. When the recession started, what percentage of high school graduates were unemployed? 4.7%
6. Based on this graph, which group of people consistently has the highest rate of unemployment? Lowest?

high school dropouts; people with a bachelor's degree or higher

Chapter 6 Review

Fill in the blanks in the following statements.

1. A pattern is a consistent, predictable form or method for putting something together.
2. Patterns help readers find supporting details and understand their relationships.
3. Five broad patterns for organizing details include list, sequence, cause/effect, comparison/contrast, and definition.
4. Topic sentences often include clues to a paragraph's pattern of arrangement.
5. A list is a number of things that follow each other in succession. Lists in paragraphs may be examples, reasons, types, or other points.
6. Sequence paragraphs, which include narratives and processes, arrange details chronologically.
7. Cause/effect paragraphs explain how supporting details are related to each other.
8. Comparison/contrast paragraphs examine two or more subjects' similarities, differences, or both.
9. The definition pattern includes a term's meaning plus one or more examples as illustration.
10. Paragraphs often use a combination of patterns to organize supporting details.
11. List three important characteristics of good notes.

    a. Good notes are neat.

    b. Good notes are clearly organized.

    c. Good notes are factual and objective.
12. An example context clue provides an illustration of a word that is being defined within the context of a paragraph.

Alistair Berg/Digital Vision/Getty Images

Inferences

CHAPTER 7

Goals for Chapter 7

- Define the term *inference.*
- Explain how inferences are made.
- State three reasons for asking readers to make inferences.
- Use guidelines to make accurate inferences from reading selections.
- Write an entry in a reading journal.
- Read and understand information in a bar graph.

Reading selections don't always state everything you should know about a subject. Instead, you're expected to figure out information that's not actually in the text by drawing inferences, or conclusions. To see how well you already do this, take the pretest below.

Pretest

Read the following sentences and answer the questions that follow. Circle the letter of the correct answer.

When I returned home from the store, I took off my wet clothes and dried my hair.

1. What you can infer about the weather?

   a. It was dry and sunny.
   b. It was raining.
   c. It was warm.
   d. It was cold.

Dora spent the day raking leaves.

2. What can you infer about the season?

   a. It was autumn or fall.
   b. It was spring.
   c. It was summer.
   d. It was winter.

Charlie is on a fixed income, so he uses coupons when he shops at the grocery store.

3. What can you infer about coupons?

   a. They are the same as money.
   b. They can only be used at the grocery store.
   c. They can save you money at the grocery store.
   d. They are good to use only with certain items.

Earphones on, eyes on the computer screen, the ninth grader types the word he hears: I-M-I-G-E-S. Wrong, the computer tells him. He tries again: I-M-U-G-E-S. Still wrong. He starts the next word: T-E-C-N-O-L. In a flash of frustration, he leaves the spelling program and clicks into a reading drill, where he correctly answers questions about the Blue Man group, and then, calmer, he returns to the spelling program.*

* From Tamar Lewin, "In Cities, a Battle to Improve Teenage Literacy," *New York Times,* April 14, 2004, www.nytimes.com.

7

4. What can you infer about the ninth grader from this passage?
   a. He is not a good speller.
   b. He is not computer literate.
   c. He is very computer literate.
   d. He is working on a computer in his home.

While wearing either a sweater or swimsuit in front of a mirror, male and female students took a challenging standardized math test. All students' scores on this test were adjusted based on their scores from standardized college entrance math examinations. The men's scores were unaffected by what clothes they were wearing. The women's scores were affected. Women did significantly worse on the test if they were wearing a swimsuit than if they were wearing a sweater.*

5. What can you infer about women from this passage?
   a. They do poorly on math tests.
   b. They feel uncomfortable around men.
   c. They feel uncomfortable in bathing suits.
   d. They like to wear sweaters all year.

Inferences

Writers do not write down everything they want you to understand about a topic, but they expect you to figure out this information anyway. How? They know you make inferences while you read. *An* **inference** *is a conclusion you draw that's based upon the stated information, the implied information, and your own knowledge of the subject.* You made one type of inference when you learned how to determine implied main ideas in Chapter 4. When you consider a group of related supporting details and draw a conclusion about the point they suggest, you're inferring that main idea. But you make many more kinds of smaller inferences, too, as you read. For example, read the following passage.

> A woman's voice in the dark, a voice that meant death. That is what they talk about, the children who survived, even as the decades pass and their hair grays. Not just about the two famous killers with a

7

* Adapted from Brehm et al., *Social Psychology*, 5th ed. Boston: Houghton Mifflin, 2002, 172. Copyright © 2002 by Houghton Mifflin Company. Reprinted with permission.

> flashlight and a gun wresting a boy from his bed, but about those who helped them. Simeon Wright, who was lying next to his cousin Emmett Till[1] that fateful Mississippi night, remembers the intruders well enough. But he also recalls a third man out on the porch. And he repeats his deceased father Mose's recollection that "they took Emmett out to the truck to ask 'Is this the one?' And a female voice said, 'He's the one.'" Mose Wright used to repeat this often.*

After you read this short passage, did you conclude that many years ago, in the middle of the night, Emmett Till was abducted and killed by two men in revenge for something he said or did to a woman? If you did, you made several inferences to reach that conclusion. First of all, the paragraph never says exactly when this crime took place, but decades have passed and the children who survived now have gray hair, so you concluded that it happened quite a long time ago. Next, the passage never says that Emmett Till was abducted, but you figured that out based on the information that the men, one with a gun, "wrest" the boy from his bed. How do you know that Emmett was murdered? You based that conclusion on the information that the other children "survived." Also, the two men who took Emmett from his bed are called "killers," and the woman's voice "meant death." How do you know the murder was an act of revenge? The men have a woman outside identify him to make sure they have the right person.

Therefore, even though the passage does not tell you exactly what happened, you still understand because of your ability to make inferences. You see more than what is actually there because you bring your own knowledge, experiences, and observations to your reading, allowing you to fill in the gaps. For instance, you've seen cars broken down on the side of the highway. Therefore, when you see a parked car on the shoulder of the interstate and people standing next to it, you conclude that the vehicle has malfunctioned and the people are stranded, so they're waiting for a ride and a tow truck. You apply these same experiences and observations as you read.

1. In 1955, the murder of 14-year-old Emmett Till fueled support for the Civil Rights Movement, especially black Americans' boycott of the segregated buses in Montgomery, Alabama, later that same year. Although Roy Bryant and J. W. Milam stood trial for Till's murder and were acquitted, Milam later confessed to the crime.

* Adapted from David Van Biema, "Revisiting a Martyrdom," *Time,* May 24, 2004, 57.

Exercise 7.1

Look at the following photographs and write a check mark next to each accurate inference.

Ariel Skelley/Flirt/CORBIS

1. ______ This family is wealthy.

   ______ The family is having an Easter brunch.

   __✓__ The family is having a Christmas dinner.

   ______ This is a very happy family.

7

Flame/CORBIS

2. ______ The woman is getting ready for work.

 ✔ The woman is a working mother.

 ______ The woman is a top executive at a company.

 ______ The woman is a nanny.

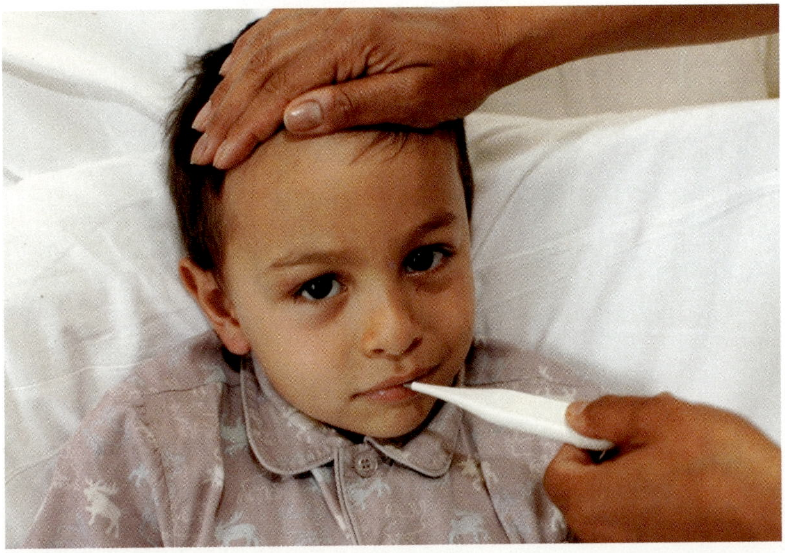

Philippe Lissac/Godong/Terra/CORBIS

3. ✓ The boy is not feeling well.

______ The boy is getting ready for school.

______ The boy is tired.

______ The boy is about 10 years old.

Shen Hong/XinHua/XinHua Press/Corbis News/CORBIS

4. ______ The boys are dressed up like clowns.

✓ The boys are at a St. Patrick's Day parade.

______ The boys are going to the circus.

______ The boys are funny.

Photographer's Choice/Mike Timo/Getty Images

5. ______ This cliff is in Arizona.

✔ The man in the photo is a stunt man.

______ The man bought the chair at Wal-Mart.

______ The man in the photo is crazy.

Exercise 7.2

Read the following paragraphs and respond to the questions that follow by circling the letter of the correct answer.

The 20s are a black box, and there is a lot of churning in there. One-third of people in their 20s move to a new residence every year. Forty percent move back home with their parents at least once. They go through an average of seven jobs in their 20s, more job changes than in any other stretch. Two-thirds spend at least some time living with a romantic partner without being married; marriage occurs later than ever. The median age at first marriage in the early 1970s, when the baby boomers were young, was 21 for women and 23 for men; by 2009 it had climbed to 26 for women and 28 for men, five years in a little more than a generation.*

1. What can you infer about 20-somethings?
   a. They are confused about their educational goals.
   b. They are immature and apathetic.
   c. They are not certain of their career goals.
   d. They are taking longer to reach traditional milestones.

* http://www.nytimes.com/2010/08/22/magazine/22Adulthood-t.html?_r=1 Web.

The period that followed Columbus's landing witnessed a complete overhaul of cuisines all over the world, as ingredients from the Americas reached other parts of the world, and Asian and European ingredients reached the Americas. Out of the Americas came foods like turkey, tomatoes, corn, chiles, potatoes, sweet potatoes, squashes, beans, avocados, pineapples, vanilla, and chocolate. Many of these quickly became common ingredients in both Europe and Asia (chiles and beans), whereas others took longer for acceptance (tomatoes and potatoes were resisted for decades or more). Conversely, citrus, melons, onions, garlic, cilantro, Asian spices, rice, wheat, domesticated pork, chickens, cows (and thus dairy products), and grapes all were introduced to the cuisines of the Americas.*

2. What does the author want you to infer about the effect on cuisine when Columbus arrived in the Americas?

   a. Foods never before seen in Europe were found in the Americas.

   b. Foods never before seen in the Americas were introduced.

   c. No one liked potatoes and tomatoes.

   d. A dramatic change occurred in worldwide cuisines as an exchange of foods took place.

One of the defining moments of my life came in the fourth grade—the year I was Ms. Duncan's student. I really came into myself in her class. For the first time, I wasn't afraid to be smart. She encouraged me to read as much as I could, and she often stayed after school to work with me. For many years after that, I had one goal for myself: I would one day become a fourth-grade teacher who would win the Teacher of the Year Award.

Ron Clark is living my dream. I met him last fall in Los Angeles. He'd not only traveled from East Harlem to Los Angeles to receive his award but he'd raised more than $25,000 to bring his entire class with him. As I watched the video about Ron's life and his decision to relocate from North Carolina to one of the toughest areas of Harlem, I was moved to tears. What I saw in Ron that day left me humbled and inspired—I could literally feel his deep sense of love for and connection with his students.†

3. What can you infer about Ron Clark from this passage?

   a. He had a profound effect on the writer of this passage.

   b. He was one of Ms. Duncan's students.

   c. He never thought he'd win.

   d. He had never been to Los Angeles before.

7

* MacVeigh, Jeremy, *International Cuisine*. Clifton Park: Delmar, 2009. Print. Ch. 12, p. 301.

† Adapted from Oprah Winfrey, "Mr. Clark's Opus," *O* Magazine, November 2001, 110.

Telltale holes, each about the size of a dime, recently started appearing in the soft spring earth beneath big trees on the University of Maryland campus in College Park. Entomologist[1] Mike Raupp can hardly contain his excitement. In a few weeks, the massive community known as Brood X will suddenly emerge from the ground after lurking underfoot for 17 years. Billions of them will fly clumsily around 15 eastern states in a brief mating frenzy, shrieking in a daytime din[2] that can rival a jet engine.*

4. What can you infer about Brood X?

   a. They are fish.

   b. They are insects.

   c. They are rats.

   d. They are tropical birds.

Howard Schultz, CEO of Starbucks Coffee Company, grew up in a lower-middle-class family in federally subsidized[3] housing in Brooklyn. His father was a blue-collar worker who held a variety of jobs. Schultz says, "He was not valued as a worker; the system he was part of beat him down, and he became a bitter person who lost his self-esteem." Schultz is now working hard to make sure every employee feels valued and respected. At Starbucks, the employee, not the customer, comes first. This policy is based on the belief that enthusiastic, happy employees will keep customers coming back. Starbucks offers workers an employee ownership plan, excellent training programs, full medical and dental benefits (available even to part-time employees), and career advancement opportunities.†

5. What does the author want you to infer about Howard Schultz's memories of his father?

   a. They don't mean anything.

   b. They are responsible for shaping his philosophy toward his workers at Starbucks.

   c. They created his determination to become a very wealthy man.

   d. They contributed toward his success at Starbucks.

7

1. **entomologist:** scientist who studies insects
2. **din:** loud noise
3. **subsidized:** supported with financial assistance

* Adapted from Nell Boyce, "Summer of the Cicada," *U.S. News and World Report,* April 19, 2004, 70.

† Adapted from Reece and Brandt, *Effective Human Relations in Organizations,* 7th ed. Boston: Houghton Mifflin, 1999, 4.

Guidelines for Making Accurate Inferences

Writers rely on readers' ability to make inferences for three reasons. First of all, passages that spelled out every detail would be boring and tedious to read. Second, they would be unnecessarily long. And finally, they would deprive readers of the pleasure they experience in figuring out some things for themselves.

So how can you make sure you're drawing the right conclusions from information in a text? Follow these guidelines.

- **Focus only on the details and information provided, and don't "read into it" anything that's not there.**

It's surprisingly easy to take just a little bit of information and jump to unfounded conclusions. For example, think back to the earlier example about the murder of Emmett Till. What do you suppose Emmett Till did to the woman who identified him? The men killed him for his misdeed, so you might conclude that Till assaulted her in some way. However, the passage does not reveal exactly what Till did. (In fact, he is reported to have whistled at the wife of one of the men who killed him.) Now, without looking back at the passage, answer this question: Did a third person escape being charged with Emmett Till's murder? Did you answer yes? Why? You probably inferred that because Till's cousin Simeon Wright recalls a third man out on the porch, there were three killers rather than just two. Actually, though, we don't get enough information to be able to answer that question, so we should not leap to possibly inaccurate conclusions.

Next, read another passage.

> One of two escaped inmates holed up in a North Texas house freed his two captives early today, then shot the second fugitive to end the standoff. While jail escapee John Leroy Weston slept inside the house, his partner, Joe Bob Smith, helped free the two hostages, whose hands had been tied. The hostages then escaped through a bathroom window, law enforcement officers said. Harold Thompson and his wife, Dede, fled to shelter behind hay bales near the house. Before Smith could escape, officers said, Weston awoke and the two suspects began talking. Law officers, who had been negotiating with Smith, then heard gunfire at 3:50 A.M. Smith surrendered and Weston was sent to a hospital for treatment of a wound to the abdomen. A large cache[1] of weapons was found inside the farmhouse. Smith, who was unhurt,

1. **cache:** hiding place

7

surrendered after the shooting and was taken to Wilson County Jail, where arraignment[1] was scheduled for later this morning. The freed hostages were uninjured.*

Would it be accurate to infer from this passage that the house is in a rural area? Yes, that's correct. Why? Because the hostages take shelter behind hay bales near the house and because the house is referred to as a farmhouse. Could you infer that one inmate shot the other one with a gun? Most readers would. However, the passage refers only to "weapons" and a "wound in the abdomen." Although it's unlikely, the weapons could have been crossbows. Why did one of the fugitives free the hostages and shoot his fellow escapee? We're told only that he had been negotiating with law officers. We can infer that they talked him into ending the standoff.

■ Don't ignore any details.

The details provide the important clues. For instance, in the earlier example, was Emmett Till kidnapped during the day? The passage says that the woman's voice was "in the dark," the killers had a flashlight, and the children were in bed. If you conclude that the crime occurred during the day, you have ignored these details.

Here's another paragraph in which you must notice the details to make the right inferences:

> Like other dutiful mothers, Lisa Jillani took her newborn daughter, Samantha, to the doctor for required immunizations. As months passed, she began to notice "a gradual fading away" in her daughter. After the fourth of five sets of shots, Samantha "acted like she was in her own little world," Jillani said. "She acted like she was drunk sometimes."
>
> Samantha, now 9, was 3 when she was diagnosed with sensory integration dysfunction, a milder-than-autism[2] disorder. Doctors couldn't identify a cause. After some research, Lisa and her husband, A. J., agreed that their second daughter, Madison, now 5, would get no vaccinations.
>
> The Jillanis's pediatrician refused to see them anymore. And when Madison was born, the couple felt hospital nurses and doctors tried to intimidate them into accepting shots. "It was just a very hostile experience that I didn't think other people should have to go through,"

1. **arraignment:** calling an accused person into a court of law to answer the charge made against him or her
2. **autism:** abnormal withdrawal and concentration upon oneself

* Adapted from Angela K. Brown, Associated Press, "Escapee Frees Hostages, Shoots Other Fugitive," *News Herald,* Morganton, NC, October 15, 2001, 7A. Reprinted with permission of The Associated Press.

7

Lisa said. A few months later, she started PAVE (People Advocating Vaccine Education), a group that advises parents not to vaccinate their children.*

Now, try to recall the details as you consider whether or not the following inferences are correct:

Lisa and A. J. Jillani believe that vaccinations caused their daughter Samantha to develop sensory integration dysfunction.

Samantha's doctors agreed with the Jillanis's conclusion.

Many doctors and nurses join the PAVE organization.

Think about how the details affect the inferences you make. The first statement is correct because the Jillanis did some research after their first daughter became ill and because they subsequently refused to vaccinate their second daughter. The second statement, however, is incorrect. The passage says Samantha's doctors could not identify the cause of her illness. The third statement is incorrect, too. The Jillanis's pediatrician would no longer treat their children, and hospital doctors and nurses pressured them to vaccinate their second child. Therefore, it would be correct to infer that most doctors and nurses advocate immunizations and incorrect to infer that they would want to join a group that advises against immunizations.

■ Make sure nothing contradicts your conclusion.

Try not to overlook one or more details that may conflict with any preliminary conclusion you make about a passage. For example, read the following:

> The mighty Tyrannosaurus rex deserved its reputation for viciousness, but in some ways, T. rex was a T. wreck, research suggests. The fearsome thunder-lizards lived wretched lives, says Wyoming paleontologist Robert Bakker. "They were beat up, limping, had oozing sores, were dripping pus and disease ridden, and had to worry about their children starving and other T. rexes coming in and kicking them out." Bakker, of the Wyoming Dinosaur Society, bases his characterization on research conducted by Elizabeth Rega, a physical anthropologist[1] at Western University in Pomona, California, and University of Iowa

7

1. **anthropologist:** scientist who studies the origins and development of human beings

* Adapted from Karen Garloch, "Debate Simmers Over Vaccinations," *Charlotte Observer,* Charlotte, NC, October 15, 2001, 1E, 4E. Reprinted with permission from the *Charlotte Observer.* Copyright owned by the *Charlotte Observer.*

paleontologist[1] Chris Brochu. The pair has examined three T. rexes, including Sue, one of the most complete specimens in the world. Sue's lower leg bone had an infection that healed but probably leaked pus at times. "I don't know if this would have debilitated[2] the animal, but it probably would have been really smelly in life," says Rega, who presented her findings at the recent meeting of the Society of Vertebrate Paleontology at Montana State University–Bozeman. Sue also had several broken ribs, and several bones in her spine and tail had stiffened and begun to fuse.*

In this passage, you can infer that the Tyrannosaurus rex dinosaur was often injured. Can you also infer that the three T. rex specimens the paleontologists studied ultimately died of old age? Probably not. Not only is there no information to support that conclusion, most of the details actually contradict it. An animal suffering from multiple wounds, infections, and broken bones probably did not live long enough to be considered "old."

■ **Don't let stereotypes and/or prejudices color your interpretation.**

When you think back to that story about Lisa Jillani and her People Advocating Vaccine Education group, did you infer that she and her husband were wrong to deny their second child immunizations? The only information in the passage that supports this conclusion is the doctors' and nurses' reactions to the parents' refusal to allow their baby to be vaccinated. If you agree with the doctors and nurses, you probably will be prejudiced against the Jillanis and their decision, and you will likely judge their decision as irresponsible. *You should be aware that some of your inferences will be colored by your own personal beliefs and attitudes, and that these can lead us to form generalizations that may be incorrect.*

7

For example, read the following passage.

Scientists claimed bittersweet[3] victory in the experiment that used technology they hope can be used to shore up the numbers of endangered animals. The Asian gaur, a bull calf named Noah, was born Monday at Trans-Ova Genetics in Sioux Center, Iowa, and died Wednesday. It was a project that united the technology of cloning with that of an interspecies birth.

1. **paleontologist:** scientist who studies prehistoric life forms
2. **debilitated:** made weak or feeble
3. **bittersweet:** bitter and sweet at the same time

* Adapted from Michelle Healy, "T. Rex Played Hard, Lived Hard," *USA Today,* October 16, 2001, 7D.

Noah was the first animal to gestate[1] in the womb of another species and survive through the late stages of fetal development. Five other cows that became pregnant with cloned gaur fetuses spontaneously aborted the fetuses. To create Noah, scientists used the single cell of a dead gaur implanted into a cow's egg. They first removed the DNA from the cow's egg, ensuring that the interspecies pregnancy produce a gaur, not a gaur-cow mix.

Gaur, native to India and Burma, are brownish-black animals with white legs, a pronounced shoulder hump, and horns that curve inward. The largest of wild cattle, an adult male gaur can reach a shoulder height of six feet and weigh up to a ton with horns two feet long.

"The data collected clearly indicates that cross-species cloning worked, and as a scientist, I'm pleased," said Philip Damiani, a researcher with Advanced Cell Technology. "Despite this setback, the birth of Noah is grounds for hope," said Robert Lana, vice president of Medical and Scientific Development at ACT. "We still have a long way to go, but as this new technology evolves, it has the potential to save dozens of endangered species."

Bessie, an ordinary black and white Angus cow, gave birth under the watchful gaze of geneticists. The experiment cost Advanced Cell Technology around $200,000, Damiani said.*

Would you say that Noah died and the other cows aborted their fetuses because nature disagrees with human attempts at cloning? If you answered "yes," you're letting your opinions about cloning color your interpretation of the information. Actually, the scientists believed that they were successful in their experiment, and they express optimism about their future attempts. Yet, many people who oppose cloning for moral or religious reasons might conclude that the animals' deaths are proof that scientists should not be tampering with such technology.

7

Exercise **7.3**

Read the following passages and circle the letter of the correct answer for each of the questions that follow or write your answer on the lines provided.

In July 1861, Georgia matron[2] Gertrude Clanton Thomas wrote, "Events transcending in importance anything that has ever happened within

1. **gestate:** develop in the womb
2. **matron:** a married woman or widow

* Adapted from "Rare Ox Clone Dies After Birth," as it appears at http://my.abcnews.go.com, October 19, 2001. Reprinted with permission of The Associated Press. http://abcnews.go.com/Technology/story?id=99174&page=1

the recollection of any living person in our country, have occurred since I have written in my journal. War has been declared." Fort Sumter in South Carolina had surrendered; Lincoln had called for 75,000 troops; four more southern states—Virginia, North Carolina, Arkansas, and Tennessee—had left the Union; the newly formed Confederate government had moved from Montgomery, Alabama, to Richmond, Virginia; and thousands of troops had passed through Augusta, Georgia, on their way to the front. "So much has taken place," Gertrude Thomas declared. "I appear to be endeavoring to recall incidents which have occurred many years instead of months ago."*

1. What can you infer about the war that Gertrude is referring to?
   a. It was the Civil War.
   b. It was World War I.
   c. It was the Revolutionary War.
   d. It was the War of 1812.
2. What can you infer from this passage about how Gertrude feels about the events?
   a. She was angry about what had happened.
   b. She was overwhelmed by all that had happened.
   c. She was frightened.
   d. She was happy and excited.
3. What can you infer about Gertrude?
   a. She probably supported the Confederate government.
   b. She probably supported keeping the Union intact.
   c. She probably opposed the war.
   d. If women had been able to vote, she would have voted for Lincoln.

Working strange shifts of duty, especially 4-to-12s (4:00 P.M. to 12:00 midnight) and midnights (12:00 midnight to 8:00 A.M.), and working weekends and holidays makes it difficult for the police officer to socialize with the average person, who works a 9-to-5 job Monday through Friday. Many police officers find it difficult to sleep after a tense, busy evening tour. If officers want to socialize or relax after work instead of going home to a house whose inhabitants

7

* Adapted from Boyer et al., *The Enduring Vision,* 5th ed. Boston: Houghton Mifflin, 2004, 437. Copyright © 2004 by Houghton Mifflin Company. Reprinted with permission.

have to get up at 6:00 A.M. to go to regular jobs, many tend to socialize with their comrades from the job. When officers work weekends, their days off fall during the average person's workweek, so again, many tend to socialize with other officers. Police spouses tend to socialize with other police spouses, and police families tend to associate with other police families. After a while, the police world is the only world for many officers.*

4. What inference can you make about police officers from this paragraph?
   a. They might have a difficult time relating to anyone who is not a police officer.
   b. They have trouble making friends with anyone other than police officers.
   c. They have difficulty maintaining their marriages.
   d. They are not involved in their children's lives.
5. What can you infer about the effects of a police officer's unusual schedule?
   a. This type of schedule is easy to adapt to.
   b. This type of schedule creates a strong bond among police officers.
   c. Families of police officers like this type of schedule.
   d. Police departments are working to change this type of schedule.

Test anxiety is stress that is related to a testing situation, and it may affect students in different ways. Test anxiety is of two types: situational and chronic. Situational test anxiety is the most common and may occur only when you are unprepared or when the test has a lot riding on it. Final exams, certification or board exams, and other tests of skill that determine whether you move forward or stay behind are anxiety provoking for most students. Some situational test anxiety is both rational and expected. Chronic test anxiety is more severe and less common. Students who have this type of anxiety get nervous at the mere mention of a test. Their fear of testing may be so paralyzing that it affects their performance. Chronic test anxiety that does not respond to relaxation techniques combined with adequate test preparation is best dealt with by professionals who can provide the kind of help needed to overcome the anxiety.†

7

* Dempsey, John S., and Linda S. Forst, *An Introduction to Policing,* 5th ed. Clilfton Park: Delmar, 2010. Print. Ch. 6, p. 168.

† Kanar, Carol C., *The Confident Student,* 7th ed. Boston: Wadsworth, 2011. Print. Ch. 11, p. 279.

6. What can you infer about the difference between situational test anxiety and chronic test anxiety?

   Chronic test anxiety is much more serious and severe. Situational text anxiety is much easier to find solutions for than chronic test anxiety.

7. What can you infer about the treatment for chronic test anxiety?

   Students who suffer from chronic test anxiety will need to seek professional help and this treatment may take both time and money to solve.

My conversation with the insurance agent went as I'd expected. She assumed, correctly, that the house my husband and I were buying (and were to move into with our two children) was protected by deadbolt locks and smoke detectors. She was satisfied the wood stove had been properly installed. She wasn't concerned about the lack of hydrants on our country road; a pond a quarter mile away would provide plenty of water in case of a fire. Only one fact troubled her. "You've got the size of the house listed as 1,200 square feet," she said. "That's just the first floor, right?" No, I said. That's the whole house, first and second floors. She paused. "That can't be," she insisted.*

8. What can you infer about the insurance agent?
   a. She thinks the house is too small for the author and her family.
   b. She loves small houses.
   c. She thinks families with children should buy houses with two stories.
   d. She likes being an insurance agent.

9. What can you infer about the author of this selection?
   a. She doesn't like climbing stairs.
   b. She doesn't like her insurance agent.
   c. She wishes the house were bigger.
   d. She thinks the house is big enough for her family.

10. What can you infer about the house in the selection?
    a. It is the size of a barn.
    b. It is smaller than the average American home.
    c. It is smaller than the house the author used to live in.
    d. It is much bigger than the average American home.

7

* Adapted from Barbara Stith, "When Half as Big is More Than Enough," *Newsweek,* April 30, 2001, 22.

Exercise 7.4

Read the following passages and then write a check mark beside all of the accurate inferences in the list.

1. Any dog can sleep all day. The profoundness of my dog's laziness comes not from his immobility[1] but from his almost predatory[2] pursuit of ease. Example: He long ago learned that he can avoid the inconvenience of walking down the hall for a drink of water before bedtime by standing beside my own bedside cup of water and making a discontented, growly noise that sounds and functions exactly like a fussy old man clearing his throat. I am supposed to hold the cup under his nose for him so he can lap up all the water, then get out of bed to refill it. When I return, he will be sitting on my pillow, having taken my warm place on the bed. This happens every night. It used to be cute.*

   __✓__ 1. The dog sleeps in the bed with the narrator.

   __✓__ 2. The narrator loves the dog.

   ______ 3. The narrator works as a dog trainer.

   ______ 4. The dog is very old.

   ______ 5. The dog is disabled.

2. If there are 1,000 square feet in the two-bedroom flat, then a good 80 percent of that space is devoted to Jim Breidenbach's passion. Yes, there are those commemorative[3] programs that vendors hawk at most sporting events. But much of Breidenbach's collection consists of one-of-a-kind items, like a poster from the 1971 Muhammad Ali/Joe Frazier fight at Madison Square Garden. He has part of a seat from the old Madison Square Garden in one bedroom. He also has the ticket stub from the last hockey game played at the old Garden at 50th Street and Eighth Avenue—right next to a ticket stub from the first hockey game played at the new one. And somebody could just about outfit a whole hockey team in sticks, jerseys, and pucks in Breidenbach's apartment.†

   __✓__ 1. Jim Breidenbach is a fanatical sports fan.

   ______ 2. Jim Breidenbach lives in Brooklyn, New York.

1. **immobility:** lack of movement
2. **predatory:** victimizing others for one's own gain
3. **commemorative:** serving as a reminder or memorial to something

* Adapted from David Dudley, "The Laziest Dog in the World," *Modern Maturity,* January/February 2002, 54.

† Adapted from Clem Richardson, "Stuck on Pucks," *New York Daily News,* March 22, 2004, 15.

______ 3. Jim Breidenbach is not married.

______ 4. Jim Breidenbach has an impressive collection of sports memorabilia.

______ 5. Jim Breidenbach enjoys hockey.

3. Located in the heart of Tokyo's government district, the Kasumigaseki subway station is one of the city's busiest stations. But what strikes a Westerner accustomed to American subways is the almost surreal[1] orderliness of the place. People line up at appointed places. Trains arrive at precisely scheduled times a few minutes apart. Uniformed attendants are posted throughout the gleaming, well-lit station—a dependable oasis of rational order in the hectic urban whirlwind that is modern Tokyo.*

______ 1. Tokyo does not have many subways.

______ 2. People like to decorate Tokyo subway stations with graffiti (spraypainted artwork).

__✔__ 3. Americans do not line up at appointed places in subway stations.

______ 4. Tokyo's subways are the world's most modern and technologically advanced.

__✔__ 5. Trains at American subway stations are often late.

4. Every surface in my bathroom is covered with bottles of face moisturizer, body lotion, volumizer, night cream, and eye serum.[2] On the shelves in my shower, I have 9 shampoos, 5 conditioners, and 10 bath gels. When I leave every morning, I cart 6 mascaras and 12 lip glosses in my makeup bag, just for the day, just for the office. I find myself wandering into beauty boutiques and drugstores every day scanning whether I'd truly tried each beauty potion available in the store.†

__✔__ 1. The author shops a lot.

______ 2. The author is allergic to many cosmetics.

__✔__ 3. The author cares about her appearance.

__✔__ 4. The author enjoys using body lotion, shampoo, bath gels, and other beauty products.

______ 5. The author is in her 20s.

1. **surreal:** having on odd, dreamlike quality
2. **serum:** fluid

* Adapted from Malcolm Jones, "Notes from the Underground," *Newsweek,* April 30, 2001, 78.

† Adapted from Linda Wells, "The High Road, and the Low," *Allure,* October 2001, 70.

7

5. Even now, at 63, when my mother speaks of home, she does not mean the house that she and my father rented before I was born. She does not mean the house they bought soon after I turned five, or even the one after that, a bigger house, perched on the edge of a ravine. What she means by home—what she has always meant—is my grandmother's 100-acre farm in Dacada, Wisconsin: the white clapboard house at the end of a country road, yes, but also the barn and the milk house across the courtyard, the smokehouse and the chicken coop out back. What she means is the gently sloping hill that rolls from the root-cellar door down to the apple orchard, the grape arbor reaching long and low to either side, humming with bees. She means the twin cherry trees my grandfather planted before his death, and the view from the vegetable garden: flat fields stretching in all directions; weathered fence posts crowned with meadowlarks; the clean, dark line where the land meets the sky.*

______ 1. The author's mother is confused and may have Alzheimer's disease.[1]

______ 2. The author's mother is dead.

___✔___ 3. The author's mother has very fond memories of her childhood home.

______ 4. The author did not like her grandparents' home.

___✔___ 5. Dacada, Wisconsin, is a rural town.

Making Inferences in Literature

7

When you read literary selections, such as novels, short stories, poetry, plays, and essays, you'll often be required to make inferences. Creative writers tend to describe situations, people, objects, and ideas with specific details, and then they let the reader draw conclusions based on those details. Therefore, improving your ability to make inferences will help you understand and appreciate literature more. For example, read this passage from the classic novel *Wuthering Heights* by Emily Brontë:

> One fine summer morning—it was the beginning of harvest, I remember—Mr. Earnshaw, the old master, told Joseph what was to be done during the day, he turned to Hindley, and Cathy, and me—for

1. **Alzheimer's disease:** a disease marked by progressive loss of mental capacity

* From A. Manette Ansay, "One Hundred Acres," *Real Simple*, October 2001, 149. Reprinted by permission.

> I sat eating my porridge[1] with them—and he said, speaking to his son, "Now, my bonny man, I'm going to Liverpool to-day, what shall I bring you? You may choose what you like: only let it be little, for I shall walk there and back: sixty miles each way, that is a long spell!"
>
> Hindley named a fiddle, and then he asked Miss Cathy; she was hardly six years old, but she could ride any horse in the stable, and she chose a whip.
>
> He did not forget me, though he was rather severe sometimes. He promised to bring me a pocketful of apples and pears, and then he kissed his children good-bye, and set off.*

The reader can draw several important conclusions from this brief passage. First, we learn about the kind of person Mr. Earnshaw is. He's about to undertake a long journey, but he's thinking about bringing back presents for his children. He obviously loves them and wants to make them happy by giving them gifts. What can you infer about the speaker of this passage? Is the person telling the story male or female? There's nothing in the passage that indicates the speaker's gender. Is the narrator one of Mr. Earnshaw's children? No, the narrator must be a servant or employee. Cathy and Hindley will get expensive gifts—a fiddle and a whip—but the narrator will receive only apples and pears. The narrator also tells us that Mr. Earnshaw "did not forget me," suggesting that he brings gifts for others besides his children. This, too, is a further indication of his kindness.

Next, take a look at a passage from Mark Twain's nonfiction memoir entitled *Life on the Mississippi:*

> My father was a justice of the peace, and I supposed he possessed the power of life and death over all men and could hang anybody that offended him. This was distinction enough for me as a general thing; but the desire to be a steamboatman kept intruding, nevertheless. I first wanted to be a cabin-boy, so that I could come out with a white apron on and shake a tablecloth over the side, where all my comrades could see me; later I thought I would rather be the deckhand who stood on the end of the stage-plank with the coil of rope in his hand, because he was particularly conspicuous.[2] But these were only daydreams,—they were too heavenly to be contemplated as real possibilities. By and by one of our boys went away. He was not heard of for a long time. At last he turned up as apprentice engineer or "striker" on

7

1. **porridge:** soft food made by boiling oatmeal or another meal in water or milk
2. **conspicuous:** obvious, easy to notice

* Adapted from Emily Brontë, *Wuthering Heights*. New York: Bantam, 1947.

a steamboat. This thing shook the bottom out of my Sunday-school teachings. That boy has been notoriously worldly, and I just the reverse; yet he was exalted[1] to this eminence,[2] and I left in obscurity and misery. There was nothing generous about this fellow in his greatness. He would always manage to have a rusty bolt to scrub while his boat tarried[3] at our town, and he would sit on the inside guard and scrub it, where we could all see him and envy him and loathe him. And whenever his boat was laid up he would come home and swell around the town in his blackest and greasiest clothes, so that nobody could help remembering that he was a steamboatman; and he used all sorts of steamboat technicalities in his talk, as if he were so used to them that he forgot common people could not understand them. He would speak of the "labboard" side of a horse in an easy, natural way that would make one wish he was dead. And he was always talking about "St. Looy" like an old citizen; he would refer casually to occasions when he "was coming down Fourth Street," or when he was "passing by the Planter's House," or when there was a fire and he took a turn on the brakes of "the old Big Missouri"; and then he would go on and lie about how many towns the size of ours were burned down there that day. Two or three of the boys had long been persons of consideration among us because they had been to St. Louis once and had a vague general knowledge of its wonders, but the day of their glory was over now. They lapsed into a humble silence, and learned to disappear when the ruthless "cub"-engineer approached. This fellow had money, too, and hair oil. Also, an ignorant silver watch and a showy brass watch chain. He wore a leather belt and used no suspenders. If ever a youth was cordially[4] admired and hated by his comrades, this one was. No girl could withstand his charms. He "cut out" every boy in the village. When his boat blew up at last, it diffused[5] a tranquil contentment among us such as we had not known for months. But when he came home the next week, alive, renowned,[6] and appeared in church all battered up and bandaged, a shining hero, stared at and wondered over by everybody, it seemed to us that the partiality[7] of

1. **exalted:** elevated
2. **eminence:** high rank or standing
3. **tarried:** remained, stayed, lingered
4. **cordially:** warmly; strongly felt
5. **diffused:** spread
6. **renowned:** famous
7. **partiality:** prejudice or favor

7

> Providence[1] for an undeserving reptile had reached a point where it was open to criticism.*

What can you infer from this passage about how the author and his fellow townspeople feel about steamboatmen? Many clues in the passage tell readers that they greatly admire the men who work on the boats. Do the author and his friends really hate the boy who goes off to work on a steamboat? No, they are jealous of him. The author tells us that he dreams of being a steamboatman, so he and his friends envy the boy for his job, his money, his attractiveness to girls, and his heroism when he survives an explosion. Is the boy humble about his job? No, he likes to advertise the fact that he is a steamboatman and uses his position to increase his status in the community.

Poetry is yet another type of literature that requires the reader to make inferences. As a matter of fact, poetry is such a condensed form of expression that it relies heavily on the reader's ability to draw the right conclusions. For example, read the following poem by Theodore Roethke:

My Papa's Waltz†

The whiskey on your breath
Could make a small boy dizzy;
But I hung on like death:
Such waltzing was not easy.

We romped until the pans
Slid from the kitchen shelf;
My mother's countenance[2]
Could not unfrown itself.

The hand that held my wrist
Was battered on one knuckle;
At every step you missed
My right ear scraped a buckle.

You beat time on my head
With a palm caked hard by dirt,
Then waltzed me off to bed
Still clinging to your shirt.

1. **Providence:** God
2. **countenance:** facial expression

* *Source:* Mark Twain, *Life on the Mississippi.*

† *Source:* "My Papa's Waltz," copyright 1942 by Hearst Magazines, Inc., from *The Collected Poems of Theodore Roethke* by Theodore Roethke. Used by permission of Doubleday, a division of Random House, Inc.

The poet expects you to make a number of inferences based on the details he includes. What kind of person is the father? He's got whiskey on his breath and battered and dirty hands. These details suggest that he's a hardworking, rough sort of person. He may even be drunk. What can you conclude about father and son's "dance"? Their movements cause pans to fall from shelves, the child scrapes the father's buckle, and his father "beats time" on his head. The mother disapproves probably because their game is making noise and a mess. All of these details suggest that the game is rough, too. Does the child enjoy this game? He says he "hung on like death" as they "romped," and he clings to his father's shirt. He also calls their game a "waltz," which is a graceful, elegant dance. His actions and his description of their game seem to indicate that he likes it. Also, he's a boy, and experience tells us that boys tend to enjoy rough-and-tumble games. The reader must examine these details carefully, though, to make the right interpretation.

Exercise 7.5

Read the following selection by Mitch Albom from his book, *Tuesdays with Morrie*. Although the selection is only four short paragraphs, you can infer a lot about Morrie, the narrator, and the nature of their relationship. Respond to the questions that follow by circling the letter of the correct answer.

The First Tuesday: We Talk About the World

1 Connie opened the door and let me in. Morrie was in his wheelchair by the kitchen table, wearing a loose cotton shirt and even looser black sweatpants. They were loose because his legs had atrophied[1] beyond normal clothing size—you could get two hands around his thighs and have your fingers touch. Had he been able to stand, he'd have been no more than five feet tall, and he'd probably have fit into a sixth grader's jeans.

2 "I got you something," I announced, holding up a brown paper bag. I had stopped on my way from the airport at a nearby supermarket and purchased some turkey, potato salad, macaroni salad, and bagels. I knew there was plenty of food at the house, but I wanted to contribute something. I was so powerless to help Morrie otherwise. And I remembered his fondness for eating.

3 We sat at the kitchen table, surrounded by wicker chairs. This time, without the need to make up sixteen years of information, we slid quickly into the familiar waters of our old college dialogue, Morrie asking questions, listening to

1. **atrophied:** wasted away

7

my replies, stopping like a chef to sprinkle in something I'd forgotten or hadn't realized. He asked about the newspaper strike, and true to form, he couldn't understand why both sides didn't simply communicate with each other and solve their problems. I told him not everyone was as smart as he was.

4 Occasionally, he had to stop to use the bathroom, a process that took some time. Connie would wheel him to the toilet, then lift him from the chair and support him while he went. Each time he came back, he looked tired.*

1. Which can you infer about Morrie from the selection?

    a. He is a young man.

    b. He is seriously ill.

    c. He has lived his life in a wheelchair.

    d. He is married to Connie.

2. What can you infer about Morrie and the narrator's relationship?

    a. They have just met.

    b. They met two years earlier.

    c. They have known each other a fairly long time.

    d. They often argue.

3. What can you infer about the location of the meeting between Morrie and the narrator?

    a. They are visiting in Morrie's hospital room.

    b. They are at a college campus.

    c. They are in Detroit.

    d. They are in Morrie's home.

4. From the information provided, what do you think the narrator does for a living?

    a. He is a college professor.

    b. He works for a newspaper.

    c. He takes care of Morrie.

    d. He is a wheelchair salesman.

* From *Tuesdays with Morrie,* by Mitch Albom, copyright © 1997 by Mitch Albom. Used by permission of Doubleday, a division of Random House, Inc.

Reading Strategy: Keeping a Reading Journal

In Chapter 1 of this book, you learned that active readers are those who interact with the text by thinking about what they read and by consciously trying to connect the text's information to their own experiences and beliefs. One useful strategy for understanding and absorbing new information you read is to keep a reading journal, a notebook in which you record your thoughts about the things you read. These thoughts could include a brief summary of the selection, a list of new ideas or new information you learned, or your reactions to or opinions about the text.

Keeping a reading journal offers two important benefits. First of all, the act of writing helps your thoughts become clearer. You may have some vague ideas or reactions after finishing a text. When you write them down, however, you'll find that trying to find the right words to express what you think will actually result in a better understanding of those thoughts. Therefore, the act of writing your response becomes a tool for learning about that response. A second benefit comes from creating a written record of your ideas. An entry for each article, chapter, or essay you read for a class, for example, can provide you with a handy reference for study. Later, when you're preparing for a test or completing an assignment, you can simply reread your entries to refresh your memory about the content of each text.

To keep a reading journal, obtain a notebook with blank pages inside. Immediately after you read a text, first write down its title, the author's name, and the date you read it or finished reading it. Then, let your purpose for reading the text determine the type of response you compose. If you'll be expected to discuss the content of the selection in class or write about its topic for an assignment, you may want to record several or all of the following:

- A brief summary of the text.
- Your reaction (your feelings or your own opinions about the subject).
- Your judgment of the selection's merit or accuracy.
- A comparison of this work to other works you've read.
- Your experiences or observations that either support or refute the text's ideas and conclusions.
- Your questions about the text.

If you're reading for your own pleasure or to expand your general knowledge about a particular topic, you might want to focus on just

7

one or two of the items in the list above. No matter what your purpose, though, plan to put forth the little bit of extra effort it takes to better understand what you've read.

Read one of the following selections and then write a reading journal entry that includes at least three of the items in the bulleted list above.

The following web link is an article that discusses why it is important for college students to keep different kinds of reading journals.

WEB LINK **http://www.lifehack.org/articles/productivity/back-to-school-keep-an-academic-reading-journal.html**

Reading Selections

Practicing the Active Reading Strategy

■ Before and While You Read

You can use active reading strategies before, while, and after you read a selection. The following are some suggestions for active reading strategies that you can perform before you read and while you read.

1. Skim the selection for any unfamiliar words. Circle or highlight any words you do not know.
2. As you read, underline, highlight, or circle important words or phrases.
3. Write down any questions about the selection if you are confused by the information presented.
4. Jot notes in the margin to help you understand the material.

BIOGRAPHY: The Diary of a Young Girl

by Anne Frank

How would you cope if you had to go in to hiding with your family for over two years? No one could know you were in a secret room. Anne Frank, whose story is known today to millions of people around the world, told of her early teen age years in hiding from the Nazis during World War II in the form of a diary. Anne's father, Otto, the only survivor in the family, found Anne's diary after the war and had it published so others could understand not only what the family had endured but Anne's hopeful, positive spirit that even the most difficult of circumstances could not dim.

Wednesday, July 8, 1942

Dearest Kitty,

1 It seems like years since Sunday morning. So much has happened it's as if the whole world had suddenly turned upside down. But as you can see, Kitty, I'm still alive, and that's the main thing, Father says. I'm alive all right, but don't ask where or how. You probably don't understand a word I'm saying today, so I'll begin by telling you what happened Sunday afternoon.

2 At three o'clock (Hello had left but was supposed to come back later), the doorbell rang. I didn't hear it, since I was out on the balcony, lazily reading in the sun. A little while later, Margot appeared in the kitchen doorway looking very agitated. "Father has received a call-up notice from the SS,"[1] she whispered. "Mother has gone to see Mr. van Daan." (Mr. van Daan is Father's business partner and a good friend.)

3 I was stunned. A call-up: everyone knows what that means. Visions of concentration camps[2] and lonely cells raced through my head. How could we let Father go to such a fate? "Of course he's not going," declared Margot as we waited for Mother in the living room. "Mother's gone to Mr. van Daan to ask whether we can move to our hiding place tomorrow. The van Daans are going with us. There will be seven of us altogether." Silence. We couldn't speak. The thought of Father off visiting someone in the Jewish Hospital and completely unaware of what was happening, the long wait for Mother, the heat, the suspense—all this reduced us to silence.

4 Suddenly the doorbell rang again. "That's Hello," I said.

5 "Don't open the door!" exclaimed Margot to stop me. But it wasn't necessary, since we heard Mother and Mr. van Daan downstairs talking to Hello, and then the two of them came inside and shut the door behind them. Every time the bell rang, either Margot or I had to tiptoe downstairs to see if it was Father, and we didn't let anyone else in. Margot and I were sent from the room, as Mr. van Daan wanted to talk to Mother alone.

6 When she and I were sitting in our bedroom, Margot told me that the call-up was not for Father, but for her. At this second shock, I began to cry.

1. **the SS:** a unit of Germany's Nazi Party, which served as German dictator Adolph Hitler's personal guard and special security force; a call-up notice from the SS was a command to report for removal to a concentration camp

2. **concentration camps:** camps where prisoners of war, enemies, and political prisoners are locked up, typically under harsh conditions

7

Margot is sixteen—apparently they want to send girls her age away on their own. But thank goodness she won't be going; Mother had said so herself, which must be what Father had meant when he talked to me about our going into hiding. Hiding . . . where we would hide? In the city? In the country? In a house? In a shack? When, where, how . . . ? These were questions I wasn't allowed to ask, but they still kept running through my mind.

7 Margot and I started packing our most important belongings in a schoolbag. The first thing I stuck in was this diary, and then curlers, handkerchiefs, schoolbooks, a comb and some old letters. Preoccupied by the thought of going into hiding, I stuck the craziest things in the bag, but I'm not sorry. Memories mean more to me than dresses.

8 Father finally came home around five o'clock, and we called Mr. Kleiman to ask if he could come by that evening. Mr. van Daan left and went to get Miep. Miep arrived and promised to return later that night, taking with her a bag full of shoes, dresses, jackets, underwear, and stockings. After that it was quiet in our apartment; none of us felt like eating. It was still hot, and everything was very strange.

9 We had rented our big upstairs room to a Mr. Goldschmidt, a divorced man in his thirties, who apparently had nothing to do that evening, since despite all our polite hints he hung around until ten o'clock.

10 Miep and Jan Gies came at eleven. Miep, who's worked for Father's company since 1933, has become a close friend, and so has her husband Jan. Once again, shoes, stockings, books, and underwear disappeared into Miep's bag and Jan's deep pockets. At eleven-thirty they too disappeared.

11 I was exhausted, and even though I knew it'd be my last night in my own bed, I fell asleep right away and didn't wake up until Mother called me at five-thirty the next morning. Fortunately, it wasn't as hot as Sunday; a warm rain fell throughout the day. The four of us were wrapped in so many layers of clothes it looked as if we were going off to spend the night in a refrigerator, and all that just so we could take more clothes with us . . . I was wearing two undershirts, three pairs of underpants, a dress, and over that a skirt, a jacket, a raincoat, two pairs of stockings, heavy shoes, a cap, a scarf and lots more. I was suffocating even before we left the house, but no one bothered to ask me how I felt.

12 Margot stuffed her schoolbag with schoolbooks, went to get her bicycle and, with Miep leading the way, rode off into the great unknown. At any rate, that's how I thought of it, since I still didn't know where our hiding place was.

13 At seven-thirty we too closed the door behind us; Moortje, my cat, was the only living creature I said goodbye to. According to a note we left for Mr. Goldschmidt, she was to be taken to the neighbors, who would give her a good home.

14 The stripped beds, the breakfast things on the table, the pound of meat for the cat in the kitchen—all of these created the impression that we'd left in a hurry. But we weren't interested in impressions. We just wanted to get out of there, to get away and reach our destination in safety. Nothing else mattered.

15 More tomorrow.

*Yours, Anne**

Vocabulary

Read the following questions about some of the vocabulary words that appear in the previous selection. Circle the letter of the correct answer.

1. What does it mean to be *agitated?* "A little while later Margot appeared in the kitchen doorway looking very *agitated*" (paragraph 2).

   a. happy
   b. joyful
   c. depressed
   d. disturbed

2. "Margot and I started packing our most important *belongings* in a school-bag" (paragraph 7). What does *belongings* mean?

   a. possessions
   b. underwear
   c. legal documents
   d. boots

3. "I was *suffocating* even before we left the house, but no one bothered to ask me how I felt" (paragraph 11). What does it mean to be *suffocating* in this context?

   a. overly chilly
   b. overly hot
   c. happy
   d. depressed

Reading Skills

Respond to the following questions by circling the letter of the correct answer.

1. Can you infer who "Kitty" is?

   a. Kitty is Anne's best friend.
   b. Kitty is the name that Anne gave her diary.
   c. Kitty is another cat in the Frank household.
   d. Kitty is the nickname that Anne has given Margot.

* From Anne Frank, *The Diary of a Young Girl*. Copyright © 1991, the Anne Frank-Fonds, Basel, Switzerland. Used by permission of Anne Frank-Fonds.

2. What can you infer about the relationship between Anne and Margot?

   a. They are sisters.
   b. They are best friends.
   c. They are cousins.
   d. They are not blood relatives.

3. Based on the information presented in the selection—the date of the diary entry (July 8, 1942), the fact that Anne lives in Europe, and the fact that Margot was called up by the SS—what can you infer about the Franks?

   a. They are Catholic.
   b. They are Africans.
   c. They are Jewish.
   d. They are Dutch.

4. Based on your reading of this selection, what can you infer about Miep and Jan Gies?

   a. They are committed to helping the Franks.
   b. They are going to take care of the cat when the Franks leave the house.
   c. They will provide Margot with a good home.
   d. They will eventually turn the Franks in to the SS.

5. What can you infer about the mood in the Frank house from this diary entry?

   a. The Franks are happy-go-lucky.
   b. The Franks are extremely tense.
   c. The Franks are depressed.
   d. The Franks are joyful.

6. What pattern of organization arranges the details in paragraph 8?

   a. list
   b. sequence
   c. comparison/contrast
   d. definition

7. What type of transition helps the reader follow the pattern in paragraph 2?

   a. list
   b. sequence
   c. comparison/contrast
   d. cause/effect

8. Which sentence states the main idea of paragraph 7?

   a. "Margot and I started packing our most important belongings in a schoolbag."
   b. "The first thing I stuck in was this diary, and then curlers, handkerchiefs, schoolbooks, a comb, and some old letters."
   c. "Preoccupied by the thought of going into hiding, I stuck the craziest things in the bag, but I'm not sorry."
   d. "Memories mean more to me than dresses."

Practicing the Active Reading Strategy

After You Read

Now that you have read the selection, answer the following questions, using the active reading strategies that are discussed on Chapter 1.

1. Identify and write down the point and purpose of this reading selection.
2. Did you circle or highlight any words that are unfamiliar to you? Can you figure out the meaning from the context of the passage? If not, then look up each word in a dictionary and find the definition that best describes the word as it is used in the selection. You may want to write the definition in the margin next to the word in the passage for future reference.
3. Predict any possible questions that may be used on a test about the content of this selection.

Questions for Discussion and Writing

Answer the following questions based on your reading of the selection. Write your answers on the blanks provided.

1. What hints are you given about Anne as a person from this passage, if any? Based on her diary entry, think about what kind of person Anne was and create a description. Use examples from her diary entry.

   Answers will vary.

2. If you were in a similar situation and had to leave your home suddenly, would memories mean more to you than dresses, as Anne states in paragraph 7? Describe how you would react in a similar situation. What would you bring on such a journey and why?

   Answers will vary.

3. Look up Anne Frank on the Internet and write a brief summary of what happened to her and her family.

   Answers will vary.

Practicing the Active Reading Strategy

■ Before and While You Read

You can use active reading strategies before, while, and after you read a selection. The following are some suggestions for active reading strategies that you can employ before you read and as you are reading.

1. Skim the selection for any unfamiliar words. Circle or highlight any words you do not know.
2. As you read, underline, highlight, or circle important words or phrases.
3. Write down any questions about the selection if you are confused by the information presented.
4. Jot notes in the margin to help you understand the material.

TEXTBOOK READING – WEATHER AND CLIMATE

Aircraft Icing—A Hazard to Flying

Flying in the winter creates special hazards. Although delays can be frustrating, ice on an airplane can be deadly.

1 The formation of ice on an aircraft—called aircraft icing—can be extremely dangerous, sometimes leading to tragic accidents. In fact, aircraft icing may have been responsible for the downing of a commuter plane that plummeted from the sky onto a house near Niagara International Airport at Buffalo, New York, in February, 2009—killing all 49 on board and one person on the ground.

2 How does aircraft icing form? Consider an aircraft flying through an area of freezing rain or through a region of large supercooled[1] droplets in a cumuliform[2] cloud. As the large, supercooled drops strike the leading edge of the wing, they break apart and form a film of water, which quickly freezes into a solid sheet of ice. This smooth, transparent ice—called clear ice—is similar to the freezing rain or glaze that coats trees during ice storms. Clear ice can build up quickly; it is heavy and difficult to remove, even with modern de-icers.

3 When an aircraft flies through a cloud composed of tiny, supercooled liquid droplets, *rime* ice may form. Rime ice forms when some of

1. **supercooled:** cooled below the freezing point without solidification or crystallization
2. **cumuliform:** a dense puffy cloud form having a flat base and rounded outlines often piled up like a mountain

7

the cloud droplets strike the wing and freeze before they have time to spread, thus leaving a rough and brittle coating of ice on the wing. Because the small, frozen droplets trap air between them, rime ice usually appears white. Even though rime ice redistributes the flow of air over the wing more than clear ice does, it is lighter in weight and is more easily removed with de-icers.

4 Because the raindrops and cloud droplets in most clouds vary in size, a mixture of clear and rime ice usually forms on aircraft. Also, because concentrations of liquid water tend to be greatest in warm air, icing is usually heaviest and most severe when the air temperature is between 32°F and 14°F (0°C and 10°C).

5 A major hazard to aviation, icing reduces aircraft efficiency by increasing weight. Icing has other adverse effects, depending on where it forms. On a wing or fuselage, ice can disrupt the airflow and decrease the plane's flying capability. When ice forms in the air intake of the engine, it robs the engine of air, causing a reduction in power. Icing may also affect the operation of brakes, landing gear, and instruments. Because of the hazards of ice on an aircraft, its wings are usually sprayed with a type of antifreeze before taking off during cold, inclement weather.*

■ Vocabulary

Read the following questions about some of the vocabulary words that appear in the previous selection. Before you look up the word, try to use the context of the passage to figure out the meaning. Then circle the letter of the correct answer for each question.

1. ". . . a commuter plane that *plummeted* from the sky . . ." (paragraph 1). What is *plummeted?*

   a. plunged (circled)
   b. soar
   c. leveled off
   d. appeared suddenly

2. Use your knowledge of the definition pattern to define the following terms:

   a. *clear ice* smooth, transparent ice
   b. *rime ice* rough, brittle, appears to be white

3. What does *transparent* mean in paragraph 2?

   a. milky
   b. rough
   c. black
   d. clear (circled)

7

* Ahrens, C. Donald, and Perry Samson, *Extreme Weather and Climate*. Belmont: Brooks/Cole, 2011. Print. Ch. 6, p. 160.

4. ". . . icing reduces aircraft *efficiency* . . ." (paragraph 5) What is *efficiency?*

   a. capacity for luggage
   b. ability to work easily
   c. passenger total
   d. distance limit

■ Reading Skills

Respond to each of the following questions by circling the letter of the correct answer or by writing your answer on the blank provided.

1. What is the major detail transition in paragraph 1? In fact
2. What is the major pattern of organization used in paragraph 2?

   a. list
   b. comparison
   c. contrast
   d. sequence

3. What can you infer about the dangers of ice if the temperature is below zero? Why? There will be little if any icing when temperatures are below zero. Colder air cannot hold as much moisture, limiting the ability of water to freeze on airplanes.
4. What can you infer about the effectiveness of de-icers? They are quite effective with rime ice, but not as effective with clear ice. When conditions are right for clear ice to form there is a greater hazard to airplane flight.
5. What is the implied main idea for paragraph 5? Icing has numerous hazardous effects on an airplane.

7

Practicing the Active Reading Strategy

■ After You Read

Now that you have read the selection, answer the following questions, using the active reading strategies that you learned in Chapter 1.

1. Identify and write down the point and purpose of this reading selection.
2. Did you circle or highlight any words that are unfamiliar to you? Can you figure out the meaning from the context of the passage? If not, then look up each word in a dictionary and find the definition that best describes the word as it is used in the selection. You may want to write the definition in the margin next to the word in the passage for future reference.
3. Predict any possible questions that may be used on a test about the content of this selection.

Questions for Discussion and Writing

Respond to each of the following questions based on your reading of the selection.

1. Which is more hazardous to aircraft, rime ice or clear ice? Why? Clear ice is more hazardous because it is heavier, it builds up quickly, and is difficult to remove even with modern de-icers.

   Clear ice is more hazardous because it is heavier, it builds up more quickly, and it is difficult to remove even with modern de-icers.

2. Identify the specific effects of icing of aircraft that are discussed in paragraph 5. reduces the aircrafts efficiency by increasing weight

3. Can disrupt the airflow and decrease the plane's flying capability

   robs the engine of air, causing a reduction in power

   may also affect the operation of brakes, landing gear, and instruments

3. Should planes be allowed to fly when temperatures and ice conditions may cause hazards? Why or why not?

   Answers may vary.

Practicing the Active Reading Strategy

Before and While You Read

You can use active reading strategies before, while, and after you read a selection. The following are some suggestions for active reading strategies that you can employ before you read and as you are reading.

1. Skim the selection for any unfamiliar words. Circle or highlight any words you do not know.
2. As you read, underline, highlight, or circle important words or phrases.
3. Write down any questions about the selection if you are confused by the information presented.
4. Jot notes in the margin to help you understand the material.

WEBSITE READING – HEALTH

Real Men Do Wear Pink

by Bethany Kandel

Each October, Arnaldo Silva seems to be the lone man in a sea of pink. "I feel a little left out," the two-time breast-cancer survivor says of the products, races, and T-shirts promoting National Breast Cancer Awareness Month. "I want people to know it is not just a woman's disease."

1 Since most men aren't aware of the risk because the incidence is so low, Silva, 60, is making it his mission to tell people about breast cancer in men. Of the estimated 209,060 new cases of invasive breast cancer diagnosed in the United States this year, 1,970 will be in men, according to the American Cancer Society. In September 2006, the New York City native noticed a pimple-size lump near his right nipple while in the shower. "It didn't hurt, so I kept quiet about it," Silva says. "But a few months later, it was bigger, and I knew something wasn't right."

2 His primary-care physician told him it was fatty tissue—nothing to worry about. But his wife, Maria, a nurse, urged him to get a second opinion, and the new doctor sent him for a mammogram, sonogram, and biopsy. That's how the burly, 6-foot-2 Silva, who maintains the boilers in a junior high school, ended up sitting in a hospital waiting room full of women and dressed—you guessed it—in a pink gown. "They were all looking at me, wondering why I was there."

3 He wondered the same thing. "I didn't even know men had breasts," he says. When he complained as his chest was squeezed into the mammogram machine, the female technician said, "Now you know how we feel," Silva recalls. "But I have a mother, daughter, and four sisters. My older sister died of breast cancer at 47. I felt I already understood their pain."

4 Still, nothing prepared him for the news that he had the same disease. Diagnosed at stage 2, he underwent a mastectomy to remove some breast tissue, his nipple, and most of the area's lymph nodes. Silva also tested positive for BRCA2—a breast-cancer gene mutation that carries an increased risk for developing breast, ovarian, and other cancers. Four months later, his daughter Vanessa Silva-Welch, then 32, learned that she too was BRCA2-positive—and had cancer in one of her breasts. With the support of her husband, Mark, she decided to undergo a double mastectomy as a preventive measure, since the chance of recurrence of cancer in her healthy breast was high. (Vanessa's younger brother, Arnaldo III, tested BRCA2-positive as well but has remained cancer-free.)

5 Father and daughter ended up going through chemotherapy together, sometimes hooked up to adjacent IVs. "We were the rock stars of the hospital," Silva says. "The staff

had seen mothers, daughters, and sisters with breast cancer, but they'd never seen a father and daughter before."

6 "I constantly thank him for saving my life," says Silva-Welch, a New York City school administrator. "If it wasn't for his diagnosis, I would have waited until 40 to get a mammogram. It might have been too late." Since her three children are at risk, they will be tested when they reach their 20s.

7 Silva's story didn't end there. During his annual mammogram last spring, doctors found a lump in his left breast, and he had a second mastectomy. "I have matching scars," he jokes. Determined to turn their pain into purpose, father and daughter have started a nonprofit organization, LIFE (Live in Faith Everyday), to spread the word about male breast cancer, especially in minority neighborhoods. (Silva is Latino.) "Those communities are underserved in learning about nutrition, exercise, and staying healthy to prevent cancer," Silva-Welch says. "African-Americans and Latinos often don't get tested even when they feel something."

8 Her father has also been speaking to boys at school health classes. "Girls have their mothers and doctors talk to them about breast cancer. Nobody talks to young men," Silva says. "I tell them, 'This is your body; don't be embarrassed to examine it. If you feel something strange, don't stay silent. It could be deadly.' I want the same awareness for men as there is for women so guys won't feel like freak shows." Someday, Silva says with a grin, "I hope the pink ribbon has a tinge of blue. It doesn't have to be split in the middle—just give us a corner."

9 Even though having the BRCA1 or BRCA2 gene significantly raises one's chances of developing breast, ovarian, and other cancers, routine testing is not recommended, according to Dr. Sharon Rosenbaum Smith, the New York City breast surgeon who treated both Arnaldo Silva and Vanessa Silva-Welch. That's because less than 1% of Americans possess these gene mutations. But if you have a blood relative who has had breast or ovarian cancer, ask your physician if you should get screened. The test requires a blood sample, which is usually combined with genetic counseling to accurately assess your risks.

10 Although breast cancer is rare in men, it is often deadly. Fewer than 2,000 men are expected to be diagnosed with the disease in 2010, but an estimated 390 will die from it, according to the American Cancer Society. "Men often are diagnosed at a later stage than women, because men do not get yearly mammograms," explains Dr. Sharon Rosenbaum Smith, the breast surgeon who treated both Arnaldo Silva and Vanessa Silva-Welch at St. Luke's Roosevelt Hospital in New York City. "Men think that they are immune to breast cancer because it's a 'woman's disease.' When a man detects a lump in the breast, he should never ignore it. By the time a cancer becomes palpable, it is more likely to be invasive and at an advanced stage. Our goal

is to pick up cancer before it gets to that point."

11 Currently, there is no specific treatment for men with breast cancer, Dr. Rosenbaum Smith says. In Silva's case, he received chemotherapy similar to what is used to treat women. He also takes tamoxifen, a hormone therapy prescribed to lower the risk of the cancer's recurrence disease in women, and as a result, he experiences some of the same side effects, including hot flashes and night sweats.*

Vocabulary

Read the following questions about some of the vocabulary words that appear in the previous selection. Before you look up the word, try to use the context of the passage to figure out the meaning. Then circle the letter of the correct answer for each question.

1. In paragraph 1, what does the word *invasive* refer to?
   a. confined
   b. tending to spread
   c. painful
   d. fatal
2. What does *burly* mean in paragraph 2?
   a. frail
   b. sick
   c. thin
   d. large in bodily size
3. In paragraph 3, the author writes about "a breast-cancer gene *mutation*. . . ." What is a *mutation?*
   a. inaction
   b. decrease
   c. stagnation
   d. alteration
4. What does the word *adjacent* mean in paragraph 4?
   a. distant
   b. neighboring
   c. separate
   d. stinging
5. In paragraph 10, the author writes, "By the time a cancer becomes *palpable,* it is more likely to be invasive and at an advanced stage." What is the meaning of *palpable*?
   a. apparent
   b. unclear
   c. obscure
   d. uncomfortable

* http://www.parade.com/health/2010/10/17-real-men-do-wear-pink.html Web.

7

Reading Skills

Respond to each of the following questions by circling the letter of the correct answer or by writing your answer on the blank provided.

1. Silva writes in paragraph 2, "They were all looking at me, wondering why I was there." Can you infer how Arnaldo Silva felt when he had to sit in a hospital waiting room full of women dressed in a pink gown?
He probably felt a bit embarrassed, uncomfortable, and out of place.

2. Can you infer what conclusions a man may come to after reading this piece?
   a. breast cancer is a woman's disease
   b. a lot of men get breast cancer
   c. breast cancer is not just a woman's disease
   d. all men should be screened for breast cancer

3. Can you infer what kind of judgments someone could make about men's attitudes about breast cancer after reading this piece? Men often think that they are immune to breast cancer because it occurs most frequently in women.

4. What is the main idea of paragraph 10? Although breast cancer is rare in men, it is often deadly.

5. What pattern of organization arranges the details in paragraph 2?
   a. sequence
   b. compare/contrast
   c. definition
   d. cause/effect

6. What patterns of organization arranges the details in paragraph 4?
   a. sequence
   b. compare/contrast
   c. definition
   d. cause/effect

Practicing the Active Reading Strategy

After You Read

Now that you have read the selection, answer the following questions, using the active reading strategies that you learned in Chapter 1.

1. Identify and write down the point and purpose of this reading selection.
2. Did you circle or highlight any words that are unfamiliar to you? Can you figure out the meaning from the context of the passage? If not, then look up each word in a dictionary and find the definition that best describes the word as it is used in the selection. You may want to write the definition in the margin next to the word in the passage for future reference.
3. Predict any possible questions that may be used on a test about the content of this selection.

Questions for discussion and Writing

Respond to each of the following questions based on your reading of the selection.

1. How did Arnaldo Silva and his daughter turn their "pain into purpose"?

   They started a nonprofit organization, LIFE (Live in Faith Everyday), to spread the word about male breast cancer, especially in minority neighborhoods.

2. Why do you think some people chose to have a double mastectomy even when they only have cancer in one breast? They want to ensure that the cancer does not affect their remaining breast; as a preventative or cautionary measure.

3. What is BRCA2 and what are its risks? It is a breast-cancer gene mutation that carries an increased risk for developing breast, ovarian, and other cancers.

4. Based on this article, what kind of person do you think Arnaldo Silva is?

   Answers will vary.

5. Do you think that the breast cancer ribbon or color will change in the future if there are an increased number of men who are diagnosed with the disease? Why or why not?

   Answers will vary.

7

Vocabulary Strategy: The Contrast Context Clue

In Chapters 4, 5, and 6, you learned about the three different types of context clues: definition/restatement, example, and explanation. One last type of context clue is **contrast.** *In this type of clue, nearby words, phrases, or sentences may give the opposite meaning of the unfamiliar word, allowing you to conclude what it means by noticing this contrast.* For example, read this next sentence, which comes from one of the paragraphs in this chapter.

> That boy had been notoriously worldly, and I just the reverse; yet he was exalted to this ***eminence,*** and I left in obscurity and misery.

If you're wondering what *eminence* means, you can look to the remainder of the sentence, which includes a contrast clue using the transitions "yet." The word is contrasted with "obscurity and misery"; therefore, it must mean "famous, with high rank or standing."

Vocabulary Exercise **1**

The following examples all come from paragraphs in Chapters 5, 6, and 7. In each one, use the explanation context clue to help you determine the meaning of the boldfaced, italicized word, and write a definition for this word on the blank provided.

1. Second, the vast majority of successful programs and teachers view an early childhood curriculum as an ***integrated*** whole rather than consisting of independent subject areas of skills. united or joined
2. Carrying a ***grudge*** around saps your energy and happiness. For this reason, you should learn to forgive the mistakes or thoughtlessness of other people. deep resentment
3. The numbers suggest that if Hispanics acted together, they would wield considerable ***clout,*** but their diversity has led to fragmentation and powerlessness. power or influence
4. Thus, the otherwise ***staid*** *New York Times* resorted to wild hyperbole to summarize a 1920 tennis match between Bill Tilden, the national champion, and challenger William Johnston. sedate and dignified
5. Again, as in the case of failure rates, the truth about the prospects of starting or working for a small company is different—and brighter—than the traditional ***fallacy*** suggests. false belief

7

Vocabulary Exercise 2

In the following passage, underline the contrast context clues that help define the boldfaced, italicized words.

Twelve Things You Must Know to Survive and Thrive in America

1 Those of us with forebears[1] branded by history hold in our hearts an awful truth: to be born black and male in America is to be put into shackles[2] and then challenged to escape. But that is not our only truth, or even the one most relevant. For in this age of new possibilities, we are learning that the shackles forged in slavery are far from ***indissoluble,*** that they will yield, even break, provided that we attack them shrewdly.

2 Today's America is not our grandfathers' or even our fathers' America. We are no longer forced to hide our ambition while masking our bitterness with a grin. We don't face, as did our forefathers, a society committed to relentlessly humiliating us, to forcing us to play the role of inferiors in every civilized sphere. This doesn't mean that we are on the verge of reaching that lofty state of exalted[3] consciousness that sweeps all inequities away. What it does mean is that we have a certain social and cultural leeway: that, in a way our forefathers could only dream about, we are free to define our place in the world. That freedom is nowhere near absolute. But today's obstacles are not nearly as daunting[4] as those faced by our ancestors. It's the difference between stepping into the ring with both hands ***lashed*** behind your back and stepping in with one hand swinging free. Still, if the one hand is all you have, you must use it twice as well as your opponent uses his. And because you have so much less room for error, you must fight strategically, understanding when to retreat and when to ***advance*** and how to deflect the blows that inevitably will come your way. You must understand, in short, how to compete in this new arena, where the rules are neither what they seem nor quite what they used to be. So what I have set out below is a list of things that may help us in our competition.

3 **Complain all you like about the raw deal you have gotten in life, but don't expect those complaints to get you anywhere.** America likes winners, not whiners. And one of the encouraging developments of this new, more enlightened age is that Americans even, at times, embrace winners who are black.

1. **forebears:** ancestors
2. **shackles:** devices used to restrain someone
3. **exalted:** elevated
4. **daunting:** discouraging

7

4 **Don't let the glitter blind you.** Almost invariably when I have spoken to people who have made their living selling drugs, they talk a lot like "Frank," who said, "I didn't want to be the only dude on the streets with busted-up shoes, old clothes." They talk of the money, the women, the cars, the gold chains—the glamour, the glitter of the dealer's life. Only later do most acknowledge that the money, for most dealers, is not all that good, and that even when it is, it generally doesn't last very long—partly because the lifestyle so often leads to either prison or an early grave. Maybe you don't care about that. Nonetheless, I urge you to realize that you have a better chance (providing you prepare for it) of getting a big job at a major corporation than of making big money for a long time on the streets—and the benefits and security are a hell of a lot better.

5 **Recognize that being true to yourself is not the same as being true to a stupid stereotype.**[5] A few years ago when I visited Xavier University, a historically black college in New Orleans, I was moved by a student who proudly proclaimed the university to be a school full of nerds. At a time when many black men and boys are trying their best to act like mack-daddies and badass muthas, Xavier (which sends more blacks to medical schools than any other university) is saying that it has another image in mind: blackness really has nothing to do with projecting a manufactured, crude street persona. Xavier celebrates accomplishment instead of ***denigrating*** it, and it makes no apologies for doing so. We desperately need to promote archetypes[6] other than rappers, thugs, and ballplayers of what it is possible and desirable for us to be—if for no other reason than that so few of us can find success on such limited terrain.[7]

6 **Expect to do better than the world expects of you; expect to live in a bigger world than the one you see.** One of the most unfortunate realities of growing up as a black male in America is that we are constantly told to lower our sights; we are constantly nudged, unless we are very lucky and privileged, in the direction of ***mediocrity.*** Our dreams, we are told in effect, cannot be as large as other folks' dreams; our universe, we are led to believe, will be smaller than that of our nonblack peers. When Arthur Ashe wrote that his "potential is more than can be expressed within the bounds of my race or ethnic identity," he was speaking for all of us. For those of us who are accustomed to hearing, "You will never amount to much," dreams may be all that give us the strength to go on. And as we dream big dreams, we must also prepare

5. **stereotype:** an oversimplified generalization about a group

6. **archetypes:** original models or ideal examples

7. **terrain:** ground

7

ourselves to pursue them, instead of contenting ourselves with fantasies of a wonderful existence that will be forever beyond our reach.

7 **Don't expect support for your dreams from those who have not accomplished very much in their lives.** The natural reaction of many people (especially those who believe they share your background) is to feel threatened or intimidated or simply to be dismissive if you are trying to do things they have not done themselves. Don't share your dreams with failures; people who have not done much in their own lives will be incapable of seeing the potential in yours. That is certainly not true in all cases, but it is true much too often. You owe it to yourself to tune out the voices around you telling you to lower your sights.

8 **If someone is bringing out your most self-destructive tendencies, acknowledge that that person is not a friend.** No one should toss away friendship. People who will care for you, who will support and watch out for you, are a precious part of a full and blessed life. But people who claim to be friends are not always friends in fact—as Mike Gibson, an ex-prisoner who is now a Morehouse student, ultimately learned. His time behind bars taught Gibson to "surround myself with people who want to see me do good." On the streets he learned that when things got tough, the very buddies who had encouraged him to break the law were nowhere to be found: "When I was in the cell, I was there by myself. . . . I always found myself alone." It's easy to be seduced by those who offer idiotic opinions disguised as guidance.

9 **Don't be too proud to ask for help, particularly from those who are wiser and older.** Mathematician Philip Uri Triesman has had astounding success teaching advanced mathematics to black students who previously had not done very well. Unlike Chinese-American students who typically studied ***en masse,*** blacks, he had discovered, tended to study alone. For blacks, the solitary study ritual seemed to be a matter of pride, reflecting their need to prove that they could get by without help. By getting them, in effect, to emulate[8] some of what the Chinese-Americans were doing, Triesman spurred the black students to unprecedented levels of accomplishment. Whether in schools, in the streets, or in corporate suites, too many of us are trying to cope alone when we would be much better off if we reached out for help.*

8. **emulate:** imitate

* Adapted from Ellis Cose, "12 Things You Must Know to Survive and Thrive in America." Reprinted by permission of Don Congdon Associates, Inc. Originally published by *Newsweek* and published in *The Envy of the World* (Pocket Books, 2002). Copyright © 2002 by Ellis Cose.

7

Reading Visuals: Bar Graphs

In Chapter 6, you learned about line graphs. A second kind of graph is a **bar graph.** *Bar graphs indicate* ***quantities*** *of something with bars, or rectangles.* These bars can run upward from the horizontal axis, or sideways from the vertical axis of the graph. Each bar is labeled to show what is being measured. Although the line graph includes a time factor, the bar graph may not; it focuses on varying quantities of some factor or factors, although it may include several sets of bars that correspond to different time periods.

A bar graph includes the following parts:

- **Title.** The title reveals the entity that's being measured. Depending on how the graph is arranged, this subject may correspond to either the vertical or the horizontal axis.
- **Vertical axis.** This line, which runs up and down, is labeled with either a kind of quantity or the entities being measured.
- **Horizontal axis.** This line, which runs from left to right, is labeled to identify either a kind of quantity or the entities being measured.
- **Bars.** Each bar rises to the line on the grid that matches the quantity it represents. Each bar may be labeled with a specific number.
- **Key.** If entities are broken down into subgroups, the graph may include bars of different colors to represent each group. In that case, a key, or explanation of what each color signifies, may accompany the graph.
- **Source line.** The source line identifies who collected or compiled the information in the bar graph.

These parts are labeled on the bar graph below.

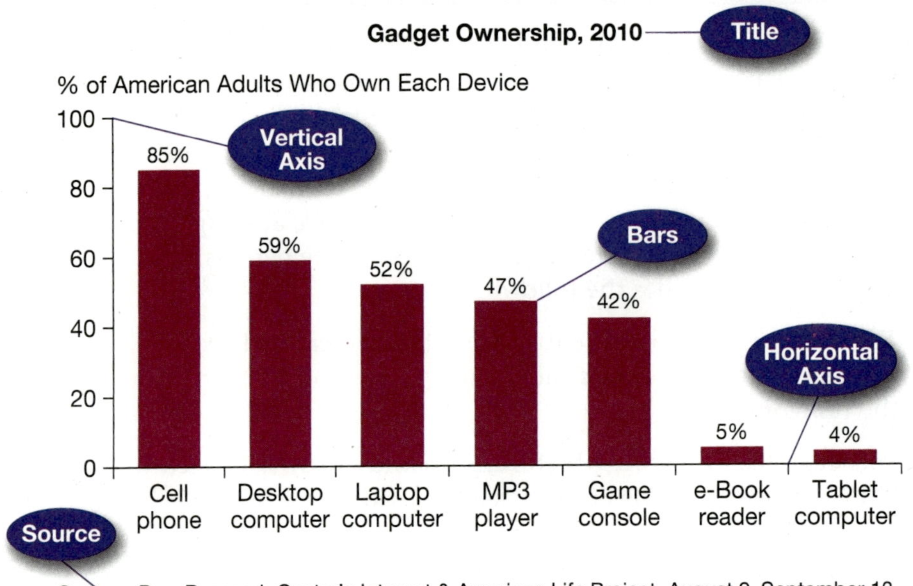

Source: Pew Research Center's Internet & American Life Project, August 9–September 13, 2010 Tracking Survey. N = 3,001 adults 18 and older, including 1,000 reached via cell phone. Interviews were conducted in English (n = 2,804) and Spanish (n = 197).

http://bits.blogs.nytimes.com/2010/10/18/its-a-mobile-nation-as-cellphones-and-tablets-take-hold/?ref=technology

7

To interpret the information in a bar graph, read the title first to find out what is being measured. Next, read the labels of the vertical and horizontal axes to understand how the graph is arranged and what type of quantity is being used. Finally, examine each bar, and try to state, in your own words, the relationship among them. Which entity is largest? Smallest? Are there large discrepancies between two or more of the entities?

The bar graph above shows the percentage of Americans who owned particular electronic gadgets in 2010. Among the notable relationships indicated by the bars are the following:

The cell phone is the most owned gadget by a large percentage.

Newer items, such as e-book readers and tablet computers are owned by a very small percentage of the population.

Game consoles appeal to a smaller group of people than laptop or desktop computers. Also, where people will have their own computers, a game console is often a "shared" gadget therefore accounting for its smaller percentage of ownership.

Now, study the bar graph on the next page and then answer the questions that follow by writing your answers on the blanks provided.

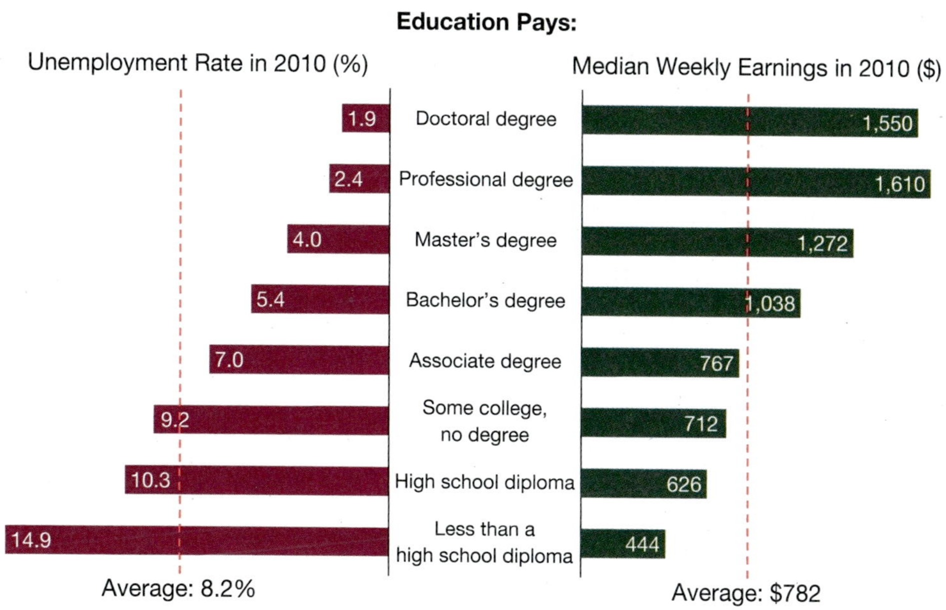

Source: Bureau of Labor Statistics, Current Population Survey

http://www.bls.gov/emp/ep_chart_001.htm. Web. 11/18/2010

1. What does this bar graph show? How education pays – Unemployment and median weekly earnings in 2009

2. What was the median weekly earnings of a worker with a doctoral degree in 2009? How about a worker with less than a high school diploma? $1,532; $454

3. How much education did a worker have who earned $699 a week in 2009? Some college; no degree

4. In 2009, what was the average unemployment rate of all workers? What was the average median weekly earnings? 7.9%; $774

5. What was the unemployment rate of a high school graduate? 9.7%

6. What is the source of this graph? U.S. Bureau of Labor Statistics

7

Chapter 7 Review

Fill in the blanks in the following statements.

1. An inference ________ is a conclusion you draw that's based upon the stated information.

2. Readers ________ use their knowledge, experiences, and observations to help them make inferences.

3. Writers ask readers to make inferences to keep their writing brief ________, interesting ________, and fun for the reader.

4. To make accurate inferences, readers should avoid "reading in" ________ information that's not in a text. Conversely, they should not ignore any details provided.

5. To make accurate inferences, readers should make sure nothing contradicts ________ a conclusion, and they should avoid letting stereotypes or prejudices ________ affect their conclusions.

Scott Stulberg/Comet/Corbis

Critical Reading

Goals for Chapter 8

- Define the term *critical reading.*
- Explain the difference between a fact and an opinion.
- Label statements as either facts or opinions.
- Distinguish informed opinions from uninformed opinions.
- Define the terms *connotative meaning* and *denotative meaning.*
- Recognize connotative meanings of words.
- List the three purposes for writing.
- Recognize the author's purpose for writing.
- Define the term *bias.*
- Explain why readers should learn to detect bias in texts.
- Identify examples of positive and negative bias.

CHAPTER 8

- Define the following terms: *circular reasoning, red herring, hasty generalizations, argument to the person (ad hominem), bandwagon appeal, testimonial.*
- Identify different types of logical fallacies in passages.
- Explain and apply the steps of the REAP strategy.
- Read and understand information in a map.

Complete the pretest below to see how much you already know about critical reading skills.

Pretest

Read the following passages and circle the letter of the correct answer for each of the questions that follow or write your answer on the lines provided.

(1) Never has there been a greater need for athletic trainers than today. (2) In 1972, federal legislation was enacted that prohibited discrimination on the basis of sex as to participation in athletics in schools. (3) *Title IX*, as it was called, also governed overall equity of treatment and opportunity to participate. (4) This legislation accorded female athletes equal treatment under the law. (5) Since the enactment of Title IX, the number of females participating in athletics has grown substantially. (6) Youth sports have also seen a large increase in participation. (7) With the number of individuals participating in athletics at an all-time high, the need for qualified people to support their overall well-being is considerable.*

1. Identify two sentences that contain only facts.

   a. Sentences 2

   b. Sentences 3 or 4

2. Identify two sentences that contain only opinions.

   a. Sentence 1

   b. Sentence 6

8

Some nonrenewable resources, such as copper and aluminum, can be recycled or reused to extend supplies. Reuse is using a resource over and over in the same form. For example, glass bottles can be collected, washed, and refilled many times. Recycling involves collecting waste materials and processing them into new materials. For example, discarded aluminum cans

* France, Robert C. *Introduction to Sport Medicine and Athletic Training,* 2nd ed. Clifton Park: Delmar, 2011. Print. Ch. 2, p. 17.

can be crushed and melted to make new aluminum cans or other aluminum products. But energy resources such as oil and coal cannot be recycled. Once burned, their energy is no longer available to us.*

3. What is the primary purpose of the above passage?

   a. to inform

   b. to entertain

   c. to persuade

Recycling nonrenewable metallic resources takes much less energy, water, and other resources and produces much less pollution and environmental degradation than exploiting virgin metallic resources. Reusing such resources takes even less energy and other resources and produces less pollution and environmental degradation than recycling does.†

4. What is the primary purpose of the above passage?

   a. to inform

   b. to entertain

   c. to persuade

The American Kennel Club (AKC) recognizes 155 breeds of dogs categorized into seven groups. The seven groups are the sporting dogs, hounds, working dogs, terriers, toys, herding dogs, and nonsporting dogs. A miscellaneous group has been established to classify popular breeds that have not been admitted to one of the seven groups. Hybrid or designer breeds are also increasing in popularity. An example of a designer dog breed is the labradoodle, or a mixture of a Labrador retriever and a poodle. These are crosses between two common purebred breeds. A purebred dog is a dog that is from parents that are registered and have known parentage. Some dogs are mixed breeds, or a mixture of two or more breeds of dogs that has no known parentage.‡

5. Does this passage reveal positive bias, negative bias, or is it neutral?

   a. positive bias

   b. negative bias

   c. neutral

We must put a stop to raunchy cheerleading dance routines. Moves like hip thrusts and shaking bottoms are just not appropriate for young girls representing a school.

* Miller, G. Tyler, Jr., and Scott E. Spoolman, *Cengage Advantage Books: Sustaining the Earth,* 9th ed. Belmont: Brooks/Cole, 2009. Print. Ch. 1, p. 12.

† Miller, G. Tyler, Jr., and Scott E. Spoolman, *Cengage Advantage Books: Sustaining the Earth,* 9th ed. Belmont: Brooks/Cole, 2009. Print. Ch. 1, p. 12.

‡ Vanhorn, Beth, and Robert W. Clark, *Veterinary Assisting: Fundamentals & Applications.* Clifton Park: Delmar, 2011. Print. Ch. 8, p. 91.

5. What logical fallacy is contained in the passage above?

   a. red herring
   b. argument to the person
   c. circular reasoning
   d. hasty generalization

Critical Reading

Now that you have mastered the basics of reading presented in the previous chapters of this text, you are ready to begin to probe a text more deeply to understand *what* it says and *how* it says it through critical reading.

Critical reading does not mean reading to criticize or find fault with a text. Instead, **critical reading** *involves noticing certain techniques the writer is using to try to convince you of the validity and worth of his or her ideas or information.* Once you learn to recognize these techniques, you are better able to evaluate a reading selection and decide what it means to you.

The ultimate goal of critical reading is critical thinking, an important skill in all areas of life, not just your academic courses. Critical thinkers don't just believe everything they hear or read. Instead, they approach new ideas and information with a healthy skepticism. They have learned how to analyze texts and ideas to not only understand them better, but also to decide whether they should accept those ideas, reject them, or think about them further.

Distinguishing Fact from Opinion

The most basic critical reading skill is the ability to distinguish between facts and opinions. **Facts** *are information presented in a way that is verifiable.* They are based upon direct experience and observation, so they often include specific data such as numbers, dates, times, or other statistics. They also include information like names of people, places, or events. Therefore, *facts can be proven.* The following statements are all examples of facts:

8

The San Francisco Giants won the 2010 World Series.

So many products are priced $10.99, $15.99, and $199.99 because research has shown that people think prices that end in nine are a bargain.

Women in troubled marriages are three times more likely than women with stressful jobs to be hospitalized for heart problems.

You should be aware as you read that a statement presented as a fact can be incorrect. Writers are not always right, and, sometimes, they include inaccurate information by accident or even on purpose. Also, sometimes research has discovered new data.

Opinions *are statements that express beliefs, feelings, judgments, attitudes, and preferences.* They cannot be verified because they are based on an individual's perceptions of the world. Thus, they are subject to change as a person modifies his or her views. They can also be argued or disputed. Here are some examples of each kind of opinion.

BELIEF: If you want to live an ethical life, you must follow the Ten Commandments.

FEELING: We should be ashamed of our failure to get homeless people the help they need.

JUDGMENT: People who don't keep their lawns neatly trimmed are lazy and inconsiderate toward their neighbors.

ATTITUDE: A mother with a preschooler should not work outside the home full time.

PREFERENCE: Singers should not try to improve upon "The Star-Spangled Banner" because the melody is fine the way it was written.

When you are trying to decide whether a statement is a fact or an opinion, you can look for some *clue words that often appear in statements of opinion.* One kind of clue is words that indicate the **relative nature of something**, words like *bigger, most important, strangest,* and *silliest.* These words relate and compare the subject to something else. For example, notice the boldfaced, italicized words in the following opinions:

The ***best*** time of the year to control wasps is in June after the queen has established her colony and while the colony is still small.

The ***most*** important subject to study in college is philosophy.

For many reasons, multimedia encyclopedias are much ***better*** than traditional printed encyclopedias.

Another kind of clue is words that either qualify or limit statements or turn them into absolutes. **Qualifying words and phrases** include *some, several, many, quite a few, a lot, most, majority, large numbers, usually, often, sometimes, frequently, seldom,* and *rarely.* **Absolute words** include *all, every, never, each, always, none,* and *no.* For example, notice the boldfaced, italicized words in the following opinions:

Everyone should get a flu vaccine every October before flu season hits in November.

Many kids who are taking Ritalin[1] for attention deficit/hyperactivity disorder should not be using the drug.

The ***majority*** of handgun owners in America are Republicans who are out of touch with the violence problem.

1. **Ritalin:** drug that helps calm people with attention deficit/hyperactivity disorder

8

One last type of clue is words or phrases that admit there are **other possibilities.** These terms include *may be, could be, seems, appears, probably, possibly, apparently,* and *seemingly.* This type of clue is boldface italic in the following examples:

> Children of very involved mothers ***may*** not have adequate opportunities to be independent and make mistakes because their mothers are always there to smooth the way.

> Inflammation in the blood stream ***might*** be a reliable predictor of a heart attack.

> Patrick has been very cranky lately; ***possibly*** he's not getting enough sleep or he's overworked.

So, why do you need to recognize the difference between a fact and opinion? The distinction matters because you are going to see both used to explain and support ideas in reading selections. If you need to evaluate whether a text is valid, you'll have to sort out what is definitely true from what the writer *believes* is true. Understanding the difference allows you, the reader, to make more sound interpretations and, thus, more reliable judgments about the worth of information and ideas.

Exercise **8.1**

Read the following statements carefully and then label each of them **F** if it is a fact and **O** if it is an opinion.

__O__ 1. I think Toyotas are the most reliable cars on the road today.

__O__ 2. *Newsweek* is a very informative magazine.

__O__ 3. Summer is my favorite season.

__F__ 4. The weatherman on the news said that last Saturday was the hottest day of the year.

__O__ 5. The Great Wall of China is a magnificent structure.

8

Exercise **8.2**

Read the passages and then label each of the sentences in the list **F** if it offers a fact and **O** if it offers an opinion.

A. **(1)** Most people hold the automotive industry in high esteem. **(2)** Two segments of the industry, sales and service, are the exceptions. **(3)** Much of this distrust stems from the high cost of vehicles and their repairs. **(4)** Further supporting this distrust is the fact that most people do not understand the workings of an automobile, and they have no reference with which to compare the costs of buying and maintaining a car to that of other large purchases. (5) Educating customers is one way to resolve the problem. (6) Very few automobile owners understand that their vehicle's computer is as powerful as the personal computer they have at home or that the technicians are constantly attending training. (7) A business will survive much better in today's highly competitive automotive arena if it can educate its customers to some extent. (8) A customer may pay well over $1,000 for a personal computer (PC) and balk at paying $600 for a vehicle computer.*

___O___ Sentence 1

___O___ Sentence 2

___O___ Sentence 3

___O___ Sentence 4

___O___ Sentence 5

___O___ Sentence 6

___O___ Sentence 7

___O___ Sentence 8

B. (1) To me, presenting an engagement ring is the height of romantic gestures, and I don't believe women should play much of a role in its purchase. (2) Other than announcing a preference on metal or a stone's cut, they shouldn't dictate its precise design. (3) And they certainly should not mandate its expected value. (4) An engagement ring represents a guy's commitment to the woman in his life, not his commitment to make her ring finger stand apart amid her friends and family. (5) The value of the ring is in its sentiment, represented by the effort a man puts into its selection, not the dollars he puts into its acquisition.†

___O___ Sentence 1

___O___ Sentence 2

___O___ Sentence 3

___O___ Sentence 4

___O___ Sentence 5

C. (1) *E Pluribus Unum* means "out of many, one." (2) No other country on earth is as multiracial and multicultural as the United States of America. (3) This diversity is a popular topic and common buzzword in newspaper and magazine articles focusing on the future of American organizations. (4) The strength of many other nations lies in their homogeneity.[1]

1. **homogeneity:** state of being similar

* Owen, Clifton E., *Today's Technician: Basic Automotive Service and Systems,* 4th ed. Clifton Park: Delmar, 2011. Print. Ch. 2, p. CM30.

† Opdyke, Jeff D. "Bridging the Engagement-Ring Divide," *The Sun News,* May 30, 2004, 11D.

8

(5) Japan is mostly made up of persons of Japanese descent, and their economy and business transactions reflect this heritage. (6) The People's Republic of China is populated mostly with persons of Chinese ancestry, whose values and culture are a major part of their global economic strength. (7) But America has always been the "melting pot" of all the world's cultures. (8) This diversity now represents the country's biggest crisis as well as its greatest opportunity.*

F Sentence 1 F Sentence 5

F Sentence 2 O Sentence 6

O Sentence 3 O Sentence 7

O Sentence 4 O Sentence 8

D. (1) A few years later the refrigerated boxcar was invented. (2) This innovation allowed the transportation of meat anywhere in the country anytime during the year. (3) Now not only could animals be slaughtered any time of the year, but also the meat could be stored for a long period of time. (4) This meant that meat could be distributed to everyone in the country. (5) This had the added effect of lowering the price of meat. (6) Americans began to enjoy a healthy diet at a relatively low cost.†

F Sentence 1 O Sentence 4

F Sentence 2 O Sentence 5

O Sentence 3 O Sentence 6

E. (1) Your child may be at risk of being swept up in one of the fastest-growing health epidemics to hit kids in recent years. (2) That's the bad news. (3) The good news is that protecting your kid may be as simple as turning off the tube, hoofing it around the block, or stocking the fridge with fruits and veggies instead of cakes and cookies. (4) One out of every four children in this country is dangerously overweight. (5) And with increasing obesity rates, there has been an explosion in Type 2 diabetes, a disease once so rarely seen in children it was called "adult-onset diabetes." (6) Ten years ago, it accounted for just 4 percent of diabetes cases in children. (7) But today, that figure has jumped to as high as 45 percent in some parts of the country. (8) Of the children diagnosed with Type 2 diabetes, 85 percent are obese. (9) "It's a very serious problem" says Janet H. Silverstein, M.D., the American Academy of Pediatrics' representative on the U.S. Health

* Adapted from Reece and Brandt, *Effective Human Relations in Organizations,* 7th ed. Boston: Houghton Mifflin, 1999, 388–89.

† Herren, Ray V., *Exploring Agriscience,* 4th ed. Clifton Park: Delmar, 2011. Print. Ch. 2, p. 31.

8

Care Financing Administration's Diabetes Quality Improvement Project Leadership Council. (10) "It is really an epidemic."*

F	Sentence 1	F	Sentence 6
O	Sentence 2	F	Sentence 7
O	Sentence 3	O	Sentence 8
F	Sentence 4	F	Sentence 9
F	Sentence 5	O	Sentence 10

Informed vs. Uninformed Opinion

Some opinions are more **informed** *than others; that is, they are supported by a sound body of factual or verifiable information.* **Uninformed** *opinions are those that are based on an insufficient amount of evidence, questionable facts, or on simply more opinions instead of solid proof.* For example, read the following paragraph.

> The population of orca whales off the coast of Washington is in decline, down more than 20 percent in six years. Scientists say that people are to blame. Adoring whale watchers are disrupting the whales' feeding and mating behaviors and polluting their air and water. Because of people's interference, seven whales died during the summer of 2001. The easiest way to find those still alive is to search for the flotilla[1] of slow-moving boats that constantly surrounds them. Researchers estimate that whale watching is now worth tens of millions of dollars, and they're concerned that noise from the boats is contributing to the problem.†

This paragraph offers the opinion that people who like to watch whales are contributing to their deaths. In support of this point, the author mentions that the reasons include disruption of the whales' behaviors, noise, and pollution caused by the whale watchers' boats. However, *no real evidence—no facts or data—is ever offered to support these speculations*. Therefore, *this opinion is relatively uninformed*. Without any concrete evidence, it's difficult to accept the point of this argument.

8

1. **flotilla:** small fleet

* Adapted from Debra Gordon, "The Type 2 Diabetes Epidemic," *Westchester Family*, October 2001, 26. Used by permission of the author.

† Adapted from Carol Kaesuk Yoon, "Struggle to Survive for an 'Urban Whale,'" *New York Times*, October 16, 2001, www.nytimes.com.

Exercise 8.3

Read the paragraphs that follow and decide whether each offers an informed opinion or uninformed opinion. Place a checkmark on the blank beside the correct answer.

1. Once a divorce happens, children frequently are made to go live with one of the parents, either on a full-time or part-time basis. In cases of full custody, the loss of access to the other parent can have devastating consequences for youth. In cases of joint custody, youth commonly face a future of shuffling between residences and may feel like neither place seems like "home." Such transient residential status has also been identified as a risk factor for delinquency.*

   ______ Informed   ✔______ Uninformed

2. All together, Americans are tremendously generous, but many folks of modest means probably give even more than they should (bless their hearts), whereas many of the most fortunate give remarkably little. On average, Americans at almost all income levels give about 3 percent of their income to charity—a lot for those struggling to get by, not much at all for the well off. One very decent millionaire I know felt too stressed to grant an important $10,000 request because, he said, he had just spent $80,000 on wall coverings.

   Contrast that with the late Oseola McCarty, a Mississippi laundress of very modest wants (she never owned a car and walked a mile for groceries) who, at 87, astonished the world by giving $150,000—her life savings—to establish a college scholarship.†

   ✔______ Informed   ______ Uninformed

3. Public schools are better than private schools. In my opinion, public schools are more diverse in their student population. You never see a diverse student population in a private school class, yet public school classes often have students from all over the globe.

   Public schools also offer more programs, and have better teachers. People think private school teachers are better educated than public school teachers, but they're not. Public school teachers are very knowledgeable and caring.

   Public school buildings are more modern because many were built in the 1970s, like the ones in my town. The buildings in my town are clean, fairly new, and updated often. Private school buildings are often from the

* Hess, Karen M., *Juvenile Justice,* 5th ed. Belmont: Wadsworth, 2010. Print. Ch. 4, p. 115.

† Adapted from Velvet Key, "Letters," *USA Today*, October 1, 2001, 14A.

8

early 1900s and look it. For this reason, and the others mentioned above, I think public schools are better.

_____ Informed ✔ Uninformed

4. I must take issue with the conclusion that military schools outscore civilian schools. The data presented simply do not justify the conclusion that military students are attaining higher test scores. The scores reported for the Nation's Report Card exam were only in the area of eighth-grade writing, a trivial and statistically insignificant component of the entire scope of skills for all grades. The only scores that are statistically significant are SAT scores. Military students scored worse on the SAT[1] in math and equal in verbal compared with students overall. One could make the case that SAT scores are the best measure of an overall education, because they measure students after they've completed all grades. If military students in the eighth grade score better than average on a writing test, they must then lose ground later in their education to end up average at the end of high school.*

✔ Informed _____ Uninformed

5. I agree that businesses need to be willing to suffer short-term losses in order to provide stability for their employees and, in the big picture, for the economy as a whole. The president of my company made in excess of $12 million last year in total compensation. Last week, he made an announcement regarding layoffs and terminations totaling more than 12,000 workers. He himself has indicated no plans to cut his own pay, and I am unaware of any other top executives at our organization who plan to take a reduction in their pay. If the business leaders of our country want the state of the economy to improve, then they have to be willing to sacrifice a little, too. If they invest in their employees, then employees won't continue to fear the loss of their positions, and we'll begin to spend again.†

_____ Informed ✔ Uninformed

In addition to evaluating whether the evidence is adequate, you should consider whether the evidence seems *accurate*. Where does the author get the information? If you are provided with any details about the sources of the evidence, you should examine those details to decide

1. **SAT:** Scholastic Aptitude Test, a college entrance exam

* Adapted from Burt Ward, "Letters," *USA Today*, October 15, 2001, 16A.

† Adapted from Andrew Tobias, "Smart Ways to Be Generous," *Parade Magazine*, November 4, 2001, 20.

how trustworthy the information is. Even facts can be misrepresented or misinterpreted, so it's important to know who collected them and what methods they used.

Connotative and Denotative Meanings

When you are evaluating a text and trying to decide whether the author reveals a certain bias, you will want to notice any connotative meanings attached to the words that the author chose. *Although the* **denotative meaning** *of a word refers to its literal, dictionary definition, the* **connotative meaning** *of the word refers to all of the associations and emotions that people tend to attach to that word.* The denotative meaning of the word *father*, for example, is "the male parent of a child." However, the word also carries connotative meanings for many people. For some people, usually those who had positive experiences with their own fathers, the word carries a positive connotation. For others, who had negative experiences, the word may carry a negative connotation.

Connotations of words are attached by people; therefore, they vary from individual to individual. However, many words have absorbed general positive or negative associations. As the chart below shows, connotations are relative. The word *fearless*, for example, may be neutral to some people and have positive connotations for others, but it seems more neutral, or even positive, when compared to a word like *reckless*.

POSITIVE	NEUTRAL	NEGATIVE
diminutive	short	stunted
cuisine	food	grub
eccentric	different	odd
part company	leave	abandon
cottage	cabin	shack
brave	fearless	reckless

8

Exercise 8.4

For each pair of words, write a check mark in the blank beside the one that has the more **positive** connotation.

1. ✔ scent ______ odor
2. ✔ disabled ______ crippled

3.	______ cop	✓	police officer
4.	✓ assertive	______	aggressive
5.	______ housewife	✓	stay-at-home mom
6.	______ abortion	✓	reproductive freedom
7.	______ blind	✓	visually impaired
8.	______ sweat	✓	perspire
9.	✓ downsized	______	fired
10.	______ vomit	✓	spit up
11.	✓ passed away	______	died
12.	______ fat	✓	voluptuous
13.	______ old	✓	mature
14.	✓ fib	______	lie
15.	______ cheap	✓	inexpensive
16.	✓ stroll	______	straggle
17.	______ flawed	✓	irregular
18.	✓ disagreement	______	argument
19.	______ lie around	✓	relax
20.	______ poor	✓	disadvantaged

Purpose

To begin to read more critically, one question you should ask yourself as you read any text is: *What is the author's purpose?* Every book, article, or any other document you read has a purpose behind it. The writer recorded his or her thoughts for one or more of three main purposes:

1. **Entertain:** to entertain or amuse you
2. **Inform:** to give you more information about a topic
3. **Persuade:** to convince you to change an attitude, belief, or behavior

Everything you read has been written for at least one of these purposes. It's important to realize, too, that *a particular reading selection can have more than one purpose*. For example, a persuasive essay can also be informative. An entertaining novel might also teach you something new. Good reading comprehension includes the ability to recognize these different purposes so you'll know what the author wants you to do with the information.

Purpose: To Entertain

Some works are written to either entertain or amuse you. Much creative writing, such as *novels, stories, poems,* and *plays,* is created solely for the reader's enjoyment. For example, read the following newspaper column:

The Pie That Ate My Thanksgiving

By Jacquelyn Mitchard

I married very young—into an Italian family that owned restaurants. For a geeky little biology major raised by a mother who thought that adding a can of Campbell's Cream of Mushroom soup exalted anything into a gourmet tour de force, this made the prospect of preparing my first Thanksgiving dinner like getting up from the audience to sing along with the Three Tenors and the Boston Pops. The fact that I would be judged by someone who now dwelt in the right apron pocket of God was a consideration, too.

I had never met my mother-in-law, who died young five years before I met my husband. She appeared to me only in one of those hand-tinted postwar photos, her neatly nipped waist and thick folds of chestnut hair making her look a little like Donna Reed. She was a legend: Her "gravy" (Italian for spaghetti sauce) seemed to have more ingredients than 1,3-dichlorocyclobutane. Most daunting of all, she made pumpkin pie from actual pumpkins. I didn't even know that this was possible. Yet my love for my husband was so big that I set out to butcher me a head of pumpkin. There was no Internet then. There was no CookaPunkin.com. Perhaps as a tribute to my personality, I hadn't received any cookbooks as wedding gifts, although I would later find *The Baking Book* at a tag sale. (I would have settled for *Baking to Avoid Ridicule*.) I knew this much: Every pumpkin pie contained cinnamon and sugar, but there was probably also nutmeg and cloves. I asked my friend Annette, whose mother cooked from scratch—even lamb cakes for Easter ("What you need for a lamb cake is another mother," my mom had explained to my child self before turning back to her novel). Annette said, "Stuff like that always has canned milk in it. But I think you have to bake the pumpkin first and then puree it." So it really was like 1,3-dichlorocyclobutane.

Now my husband thought that I was delightful and didn't expect me to bake anything at all. He hadn't wanted to marry his mother. Giving me her recipes for "gravy" and for stuff like Chicken Scallapalooza Magnificata and Barcarole Glory Hallelujah was not meant to be the curse of the cat people but a gesture of sweet homemaking hope. But it was not really for him or my brother and sister-in-law or our friends that I was doing this. It was for the beloved icon

8

in the shirtwaist dress. For if there really was a heaven, my mother-in-law was up there with my own beautiful mom, who'd be wearing Capri pants, smoking Salems, reading *Frenchman's Creek*, and pointing out that she hadn't raised her daughter to be the first person in our family to graduate from college—only to have me be brought to grief by a gourd.

I got up at 3 A.M. With a scientist's efficiency, I scored and measured and seasoned. While the pumpkin baked, I crumbled from-scratch bread into stuffing crumbs and chopped onions and celery and tiny bits of apple. Then I scraped that squash into the blender that we used to make margaritas, added some sugar and two cans of condensed milk, hit the button, and sent a prayer to the kitchen gods who had not come to my bridal bower. I put everything into the oven, went upstairs, got a hurricane headache and a sore throat, and slept right through the holiday.

Fifteen years after that first Thanksgiving, I would be a young widow with three little boys, so poor that knowing how to make my own pies (and even pizza dough) turned out to be a blessing. I still do this, in honor of the grandmothers whom my oldest kids never met and will not remember, realizing with no small irony that someday I will be the one in the photograph shown to a bride. It will be given to her along with recipes that will at least be legible because I typed them—though despite my biology background, instead of an exact measurement the word "some" precedes every ingredient.

When I cook, every day, it's with a novel propped open in the stand meant for the cookbook. It turns out that nothing much can daunt a good, plain cook. She really needs no recipe—for food or probably anything else—just hope, strong will, and the guidance of her better angels.*

The sole purpose of this story is to entertain you and make you laugh. How do you know? It's a personal story, for one thing. And, it includes humor such as exaggeration and amusing descriptions. It makes no attempt to teach you anything or convince you of something.*

Purpose: To Inform

Much writing is intended to increase your knowledge or understanding about a subject. A work with an informative purpose is designed to teach you something. *Textbooks, most of the newspaper, and reference works such as encyclopedias are created with an informative purpose in mind.* For example, read this passage from a hospitality textbook.

Bottled Water

Between 1984 and 2003, annual per capita consumption of bottled waters in the United States rose from four gallons to almost twenty-four gallons.

* *Source:* http://www.parade.com/articles/editions/2010/edition_11-21-2010/Views.html

8

The increased consumption of bottled waters is the result of several factors occurring in the marketplace. The first is the growth of the market segment concerned with health, including baby boomers concerned about aging. These consumers believe that drinking six to eight glasses of water each day contributes to general health. Some bottled waters have been marketed as "pure," and therefore seem more healthful than ordinary tap water. Second, the acceptance of bottled waters is part of the broader trend in consumer willingness to purchase specialized or premium products. Bottled water marketers thus have sought to invest their products with a special "cachet" or set of ostensibly unique characteristics. The third factor involves packaging. Spring water bottled in an attractively shaped plastic container with a spiffy label and squirt top is convenient for people to take to an athletic club and drink on the treadmill. Carrying that same container to the office or the mall conveys the impression that the individual lives an active, healthy life.

The challenge faced by the marketers of bottled water is to persuade consumers to pay for a product that they can get for free (or for significantly less) by turning a tap. In the late 1980s, a small number of producers overstated the health- inducing benefits of "pure" bottled waters. Further, in several of these cases, bottled spring water was found to contain significantly more impurities than tap water. Consumers were, in effect, paying a premium for bottled water that was worse for them than what was available from their municipal water supply. In the 1990s, the Food and Drug Administration proposed new labeling standards for bottled waters to prevent misrepresentation. Today, many hotel companies offer "signature" bottled water for sale. Placing it in guest rooms is a suggestive selling technique designed to generate additional incremental profits from room sales.*

The topic of this passage is about factors influencing the sales of bottled water. The authors also discuss the challenges of marketing bottled water. The authors attempt to present neutral and factual information about the subject. They are not attempting to persuade you to think one way or another, so the purpose here is simply informative.

Purpose: To Persuade

Works with a persuasive purpose attempt to convince you to change a belief, an attitude, or a behavior. These readings are said to be arguments, for they argue a point in hopes of getting the reader to agree. *An editorial in a newspaper,* for example, may argue that you should support a particular cause. A *self-help book* may urge you to think and act differently to improve a personal problem. *An essay in a magazine* might attempt to convince you to interpret a current

* Chon, Kaye (Kye-Sung), and Thomas A. Maier, *Welcome to Hospitality,* 3rd ed. Clifton Park: Delmar, 2010. Ch. 8, pp. 272–73.

event in a certain way. For example, look at the following opinion piece that appeared on the AOL News website.

Administrative Bloat Drives College Costs

Between 1993 and 2007, student enrollment at America's leading universities rose by 14.5 percent. Over those same years, the number of full-time administrators employed per 100 students at America's leading universities climbed more than 39 percent. Meantime, the number of employees engaged in teaching, research, or service climbed 17.6 percent. What's more, inflation-adjusted spending on administration per student increased by nearly 66 percent during the same period, while instructional spending per student rose by 39 percent.

In short, universities are suffering from administrative bloat, expanding their bureaucracies significantly faster than their numbers of instructors and researchers, which should be the core missions of any university.

A big reason that university administrators get away with this is that students pay only a fraction of the expense, despite the rapid increases in tuition rates. These leading public and private universities spent an average of $41,337 per student in 2007 and collected an average tuition of $10,929 per student.

The lion's share of university resources come from the federal and state governments, as well as private gifts and fees for non-educational services. The increasing rate of direct and indirect government subsidies for higher education encourages expansion of bureaucracy by shielding students from the full costs of operating a university.

Scaling back government subsidies likely would prompt students and their families to pay much closer attention to how universities spend their money. A good example of this can be found at the University of Michigan. By 2003, that university's funding from the state had dropped to less than 10 percent of its budget. Meanwhile, the University of Michigan reduced its number of administrators between 1993 and 2007, while increasing the number of instructors and researchers by 68 percent.

An old saying holds that when something can't go on forever, it won't. The higher education bubble has been inflating for decades, but college costs cannot outpace family incomes forever.

With dozens of states looking for ways to trim their budgets, now is a good time for policymakers to consider reducing state appropriations to colleges and universities and let students and institutions sort through what they want from a university education and how much it's worth.

This may sound scary, but it's nothing to fear. Michigan has done it, and the quality of their flagship public university hasn't suffered.*

In this excerpt, the author hopes to persuade the reader to agree with the opinion that college costs are rising due to an excess of administrators. He cites a recent study conducted by the Goldwater Institute. He also compares the percentage of administrators hired to the percentage of those directly engaged in student services. Finally, he cites the example of the University of Michigan and the results they have had of cutting administrators to support his point of view.

Determining the Purpose

When you read a passage, how can you determine the author's purpose? The passage itself will usually provide a number of clues that will help you decide on the author's intentions.

The Main Point An entertaining passage may not have a main point at all, or the main point may focus on something that the writer learned from some experience. The main point of an informative passage will usually state a fact or describe some state of affairs without offering any judgment about it. The main point of a persuasive passage, however, will be an opinion. Its persuasive purpose is often indicated with words like *should, must,* and *have to*, because the author wants to convince the reader to change a belief or a behavior.

The Supporting Details In entertaining passages, supporting details are often stories or descriptions, both of which might be humorous. In an informative passage, the details take the form of facts that can be verified, and they do not offer the writer's opinions about those details. A persuasive passage, too, can include facts; however, watch also for more opinions that are used to justify the main point.

The Sources of the Information In an entertaining passage, there are usually no sources provided. An informative passage will often cite sources, and those sources will usually be informative in nature themselves. Persuasive passages may cite sources as well, but those sources may very well be ones that favor the author's point of view.

The Author Pay attention to any information you get about the writer's background, qualifications, experience, and interests, because these characteristics will help you evaluate what he or she intended by writing the passage. Sometimes authors will directly state their purpose by announcing it or by summarizing their credentials. They may offer you some details about their background that led them to write about the topic. However, even if a text reveals little or nothing about the writer, you will still be able to gain a sense of who the writer is and what he or she hopes to achieve. The words authors choose, and even the way

* Source: http://www.aolnews.com/opinion/article/opinion-administrative-bloat-drives-college-costs/19602287?icid=main|main|dl8|sec4_lnk2|166115 Web. 11/22/2010

they put their sentences together, can reveal a great deal about their feelings, their attitudes, and their goals. Specifically, you can learn to recognize bias and to determine the tone of a text, which are discussed in the next section.

You should get in the habit of examining all of these aspects of a reading selection so that you can begin to think more critically about the ideas and information it includes.

Exercise 8.5

Circle the letter of the primary purpose of each of the following passages.

The Plague eliminated as much as one-third of the European population over a five-year period. Smallpox was never that devastating in Europe, becoming endemic[1] and occasionally outbreaking. Widespread resistance reduced the losses to local impacts of about 10 percent. However, introduction of smallpox to America quite rapidly depleted the population. For example, the Spanish attempted to settle Hispanola[2] for sugar cane plantation in 1509. By 1518 all of the 2.5 million aboriginals[3] had perished, and the labor population had to be restored with African slaves.*

1. In this passage, the author's primary purpose is to

   a. entertain. c. persuade.

   b. inform.

In addition to teaching skills and facts, schools help society run more smoothly by socializing young people to conform. They emphasize discipline, obedience, cooperation, and punctuality. At the same time, schools teach students the ideas, customs, and standards of their culture. In American schools, we learn to read and write English, we learn the Pledge of Allegiance, and we learn the version of U.S. history that school boards believe we should learn. By exposing students from different ethnic and social-class backgrounds across the country to more or less the same curriculum, schools help create and maintain a common cultural base.

Schools are like gardeners; they sift, weed, sort, and cultivate their products, determining which students will be allowed to go on and which will not. Grades and test scores channel students into different programs—or out of school altogether—on the basis of their measured abilities. Ideally, the school system ensures the best use of each student's particular abilities.

1. **endemic:** widespread in a particular region or among a certain group of people
2. **Hispanola:** island of the West Indies east of Cuba
3. **aboriginals:** people who have existed in a region from the beginning

* Adapted from "Smallpox: History," October 22, 2001, http://seercom.com/bluto/smallpox/history.html.

8

Schools also act as change agents. Although we do not stop learning after we leave school, new knowledge and technology are usually aimed at schoolchildren rather than at the adult population. In addition, schools can promote change by encouraging critical and analytic skills. Colleges and universities are also expected to produce new knowledge.*

2. In this passage, the author's primary purpose is to

   a. entertain.
   b. inform.
   c. persuade.

I love Halloween because it reminds me of a simpler, more innocent time—a time when I dressed up as a goblin and ran around the neighborhood shouting, "Trick or treat!"

But that was last year. This year I think I'll have a more subdued costume. Maybe I'll dress up as a large piece of lumber and carry around a cardboard box labeled "Interest Rates," and every few steps, I'll drop it. Get it? It's the Federal Reserve "Board!" Dropping interest rates! Ha-ha! I bet *that* will get a big reaction from the neighborhood kids! Probably in the form of eggs.

That's the problem with kids today: They don't know what Halloween is all about. It has been commercialized to the point where our young people think it's just "fun and games." They know nothing about the somber origin of this holiday, which dates back to 1621, when the Pilgrims,[1] having survived a difficult first winter in America, decided to express their thanks by dressing up in comical outfits with knickers and hats shaped like traffic cones (ordinarily, the Pilgrims wore bowling attire) and then went around playing pranks with what—turned out tragically—to be their last remaining roll of toilet paper. And thus as you can imagine their second winter was no picnic, either. THAT is what Halloween is about, but try explaining it to these spoiled kids today, with their inexhaustible supplies of Charmin.[2†]

3. In this passage, the author's primary purpose is to

   a. entertain.
   b. inform.
   c. persuade.

8

Was Elvis' song "That's All Right" the birth cry of rock 'n' roll? Or is that all wrong?

1. **Pilgrims:** English settlers who founded Plymouth Colony in 1620
2. **Charmin:** a brand of toilet paper

* Brinkerhoff, David B., Lynn K. White, Suzanne T. Ortega, and Rose Weitz, *Essentials of Sociology,* 8th ed. Belmont: Wadsworth, 2011. Print. Ch. 12, pp. 284, 285.

† Adapted from Dave Barry, "Hairum-Scarum," *Boston Globe Magazine,* October 28, 2001, 6. Copyright, 2001, Tribune Media Services, Inc. All Rights Reserved. Reprinted with permission.

On July 5, 1954, Elvis Presley stepped into Sun Studio in Memphis to record "That's All Right," his first single. The event has been declared the birth date of rock 'n' roll by a host of commercial celebrators, from BMG, which controls his catalog, and Elvis Presley Enterprises to the Hard Rock Cafe and the Memphis Convention & Visitors' Bureau.

But rock's genesis has long been debated by critics, historians, and pioneers themselves. (Little Richard and Chuck Berry might have a beef with Elvis.) "Obviously, it's a pretty nuanced[1] thing to stick a needle in the timeline and say it's the moment rock 'n' roll was birthed," says Alan Light, editor of music magazine *Tracks*. "There's never a definitive answer, partly because there's no simple, universal definition of rock to begin with."

"It's impossible to pin the birth of rock on one day or even one year," says Pete Howard, publisher of *Ice* magazine. "One could make a strong argument for the late '40s as well as the early '50s. It was a long, gradual process. July 5, 1954, is probably the best single date to settle on, even though it's like trying to pick the date live music began," he says. "We do it just for fun, because people love lists and anniversaries. If Elvis were alive, he'd probably argue for Wynonie Harris' 'Good Rockin' Tonight' or Jackie Brenston's 'Rocket 88.'"*

4. In this passage, the author's primary purpose is to

   a. entertain.
   b. inform.
   c. persuade.

You may not be serving your country in an official status, but you can help those who are. Let the families of military personnel know you recognize their efforts and appreciate what they do. By helping a military family, you are supporting and giving peace of mind to a military member who is risking so much for us.

If you know a family suffering through deployment,[2] consider adopting them. Invite them over for meals, offer to help baby-sit, help fix that leaky faucet. If they are able to correspond with the deployed member, provide a few long-distance phone calls or stationery. Or if you have computer skills, help set up a family website or e-mail account. Use your photography skills so the deployed spouse can have an updated picture of the family. If you're a business owner, post job openings at the Family Support Center on base, hold Military Appreciation Days, and provide military discounts.†

1. **nuanced:** subtle
2. **deployment:** bringing troops into action, ready for combat

* Adapted from Edna Gundersen, "Elvis' First Single Crowns Rock's 50th Anniversary," *USA Today*, July 2, 2004, 4E.

† Adapted from Patty Erickson, "Honor Military Families," *Charlotte Observer*, November 11, 2001, 3D. Copyright, 2001, Knight Ridder/Tribune Media Services. Reprinted with permission.

8

5. In this passage, the author's primary purpose is to

   a. entertain.

   b. inform.

   c. persuade.

Exercise 8.6

Circle the letter that corresponds to the primary purpose of each of the following passages.

Frankly, it seems pretty easy to come up with a new exercise. You just take something people are already doing—like eating—and add "ercise." Or say it's cardio-friendly. So how's about:

R.C. Colaerobics: Soda shopping? Don't just grab a Coke. Stretch waaaaay down to reach the Royal Crown! Your abs will be glad—and so will your wallet!

Karaoke[1] Swim: Tired of singing on that stupid bike? Start singing as you swim across the pool! Pounds peel away as you struggle to clear your lungs and stay afloat. You go, gurgle!

Lego Lifts: Step 1: Invite a child to play with Legos on your rug. Step 2: Have child leave after "cleaning up." Step 3: Remove your socks and run around. Yeow! Ouch. There's another one he missed! You're hopping your way to health!*

1. In this passage, the author's primary purpose is to

   a. entertain.

   b. inform.

   c. persuade.

In his book *The Revolt of the Elites*, the late Christopher Lasch wrote that only in the course of argument do "we come to understand what we know and what we still need to learn. . . . We come to know our own minds only by explaining ourselves to others." If we wish to be engaged in serious argument, Lasch explained, we must enter into another person's mental universe and put our own ideas at risk.

Exactly. When a friend launches an argument and your rebuttal sounds tinny[2] to your own ears, it shouldn't be that hard to figure out that something's wrong—usually, that you don't really agree with the words coming

8

1. **karaoke:** performance in which someone sings the words to a song
2. **tinny:** weak, thin, flimsy

* From Lenore Skenacy, "I'm Rock Hard Thanks to Lie-ercize," *Daily News*, June 13, 2004, 47.

out of your own mouth. Arguing can rescue us from our own half-formed opinions.*

2. In this passage, the author's primary purpose is to
   a. entertain.
   b. inform.
   c. persuade.

Somewhere along the line, *The Times* got out of the news business and into the nation-building business. Its primary intent is no longer to provide objective information and fair-minded analysis to its readers, but to convince them to support a brave new world in the United States. The power of *The Times* is being used to promote the formation of a new America, a bright, shining progressive city on a hill of steep government entitlements.[1]

Why should you care what an individual newspaper does? Even with a circulation of more than a million, most Americans don't read the *Times*. But consider this: Every morning, the powerful barons and anchorpeople who run the network TV news operations read the *Times* first thing. They often take editorial direction from the paper, sometimes duplicating story selection and even point of view. All-news radio does the same thing, and the *Times'* wire goes out to thousands of newspapers across the country and around the world. This is one extremely powerful outfit.†

3. In this passage, the author's primary purpose is to
   a. entertain.
   b. inform.
   c. persuade.

Truck-only toll (TOT) lanes, which are the brainchild of Robert Poole, an engineer who oversees transportation studies at the Reason Foundation, are extra lanes that would be added to our nation's highways to separate cars from trucks in an attempt to expand capacity, improve traffic, and move freight more efficiently. This year, Poole identified 10 stretches of interstate highways in 16 states, including I-80 through Illinois and Iowa, as ideal for testing TOT lanes. But trucking industry leaders are wary. They worry about the financial burden of truckers being forced to pay more tolls, especially on roads they already use for free. "Separating cars and trucks, for the trucking industry, would be an improvement," says Darrin Roth of the American Trucking Associations. "The issue becomes how do you pay for it."

1. **government entitlements:** guaranteed benefits to particular groups

* From John Leo, "Instead of Arguments, We Get Shouts and Insults," *Daily News*, June 15, 2004.

† From Bill O'Reilly, "The Worst of Times," *Daily News*, June 21, 2004. By permission of Bill O'Reilly and Creators Syndicate, Inc.

But TOT lanes are gaining favor in Congress. That's mainly because the Federal Highway Administration has predicted a 31 percent increase in truck freight by 2015. In 2003, 77 million trucks hauled 13.2 billion tons of freight. Combined with the growth of other traffic, the nation's highways are rapidly approaching capacity. TOT lanes would allow highways to be widened without using tax dollars. Construction would be paid for with toll money.*

4. In this passage, the author's primary purpose is to

a. entertain. c. persuade.

(b.) inform.

Does the lie detector, or polygraph, test really work? Many people think it is foolproof, but scientific opinion is still split. Some researchers report accuracy rates of about 90 percent. Others say that such claims are exaggerated and misleading. One well-documented problem is that truthful persons too often fail the test. For example, a study of polygraph records obtained from police files revealed that although 98 percent of suspects later known to be guilty were correctly identified as such, 45 percent of those who were eventually found innocent were judged deceptive. A second problem is that the test can be faked. Studies show that you can beat the polygraph by tensing your muscles, squeezing your toes, or using other countermeasures while answering the control questions, which ask yes/no questions that are not relevant to the crime. By artificially inflating the responses to the "innocent" questions, one can mask the stress that is aroused by lying on the crime-relevant questions.†

5. In this passage, the author's primary purpose is to

a. entertain. c. persuade.

(b.) inform.

Bias

One of the main reasons to determine an author's purpose is so that you can detect any bias the author might have about his or her subject. **Bias** *is an inclination toward a particular opinion or viewpoint.* The term describes our tendency to feel strongly that something is right or wrong, positive or negative. Even authors who try to present information neutrally, without revealing any of their own feelings about the topic, will often allow their own prejudices to creep into their writing. Conversely, authors can also make their bias perfectly clear. They often do so in hopes that they will influence the reader to agree.

* Adapted from Debbie Howlett, "Truckers Leery of Toll-Lanes Idea," *USA Today*, June 28, 2004, 3A.

† Adapted from Brehm et al., *Social Psychology*, 5th ed. Boston: Houghton Mifflin, 2002, 446. Copyright © 2002 by Houghton Mifflin Company. Reprinted with permission.

Recognizing Bias

Authors communicate their bias by using words that urge the reader to feel a certain way about a topic. Many of these words are emotional, and they provoke strong reactions in readers, encouraging them to feel either *positive or negative.* For example, the word *recruiter* is a respectful term, but the word *headhunter* is negative and derogatory. In the following pairs of sentences, the first sentence includes words that are relatively neutral. Notice how the substitution of a few more emotional words injects bias into the statement.

Neutral: Pharmaceutical company representatives influence doctors to write prescriptions for their products by giving them gifts and buying them meals.
Negative Emotional: Pharmaceutical company salesmen seduce doctors into hawking their products by showering them with gifts and wining and dining them.

Neutral: Prisoners serving life sentences should lose all of their freedoms, including their right to procreate[1] with their spouses.
Negative Emotional: Convicted criminals do not deserve any freedoms, including the right to make babies while they're locked up.

Neutral: Drive-in movie theaters are not obsolete; on the contrary, those still in operation are improving their technology to increase their number of customers.
Positive Emotional: Some drive-in movie theaters are still thriving; their cutting-edge, crystal-clear pictures and stereo sound are attracting a new generation of customers who will create a new golden age like the 1950s.

In the second sentence of each pair, you can see that the choice of words makes the author's opinion more emotionally forceful.

8

Exercise **8.7**

In each of the following statements, underline the words or phrases that reveal the author's bias. Then, on the blank, write POSITIVE if the words encourage you to feel positive about the subject and NEGATIVE if they urge you to feel negative.

1. This summer, TV is giving us too much of a bad thing. With Fox and NBC in the forefront, the networks have offered viewers an unusually full schedule

1. **procreate:** conceive and produce children

of flat sitcoms, dull dramas, and cheap, mean-spirited, copycat reality shows. Viewer response has been a resounding "no thanks."* negative

2. That the world has changed in meaningful ways since 1954 is beyond question. Oprah Winfrey and her activities were driving forces in many of those changes. Her enormously influential talk show, her philanthropic work with children in Africa and elsewhere, her popular book club and magazine, her empowering spiritual message, her contribution (by action and example) to improving race relations—all speak to the human family, touching hearts and leaving each one uplifted.† positive

3. When we think of felines, we think of selfish, indulgent, petulant independence. It's a personality that makes us slightly uneasy: Although we believe we have a certain level of control—after all, we do feed and house this beast—we also know that the cat is quite capable of acting against immediate best interests by biting the finger of the hand that feeds it. You can't relax around a cat, which is why cats may be this era's pet. We can't relax anymore, period. Cats mock our pretensions to power, show no gratitude, and hide when we want to display them to company. They are tiny terrorists, reminders of our vulnerability.‡ negative

4. At the broadest level, education is the institution within the social structure that is responsible for the formal transmission of knowledge. It is one of our most enduring and familiar institutions. Nearly 3 of every 10 people in the United States participate in education on a daily basis as either students or staff. As former students, parents, or taxpayers, all of us are involved in education in one way or another.

   The obvious purpose of schools is to transmit knowledge and skills. In schools, we learn how to read, write, and do arithmetic. We also learn the causes of the American War of Independence and the parts of a cell. In this way, schools ensure that each succeeding generation will have the skills needed to keep society running smoothly.§ positive

8

5. From the time they are born, girls are treated in one way and boys in another—wrapped in blue blankets or pink ones, encouraged to take up sports or sewing, described as cute or as strong before they are old enough to truly exhibit individual personalities. In these ways, as symbolic interactionist

* Adapted from Robert Bianco, "Networks Are Sweating Out Their Own Long, Hot Summer," *USA Today*, June 30, 2004, 3D.

† Sidney Poitier, "Heroes and Icons: Oprah Winfrey," *Time*, April 26, 2004, 123.

‡ Adapted from Robert Lipsyte, "Uncertain Times Turn Us into Cat People," *USA Today*, June 30, 2004, 13A.

§ Brinkerhoff, David B., Lynn K. White, Suzanne T. Ortega, and Rose Weitz, *Essentials of Sociology*, 8th ed. Belmont: Wadsworth, 2011. Print. Ch. 12, p. 284.

studies illustrate, children learn their gender and gender roles. By the age of 24 to 30 months, they can correctly identify themselves and others by sex, and they have some ideas about what this means for appropriate behavior.

Young children's ideas about gender tend to be quite rigid. They develop strong stereotypes for two reasons. One is that the world they see is highly divided by sex: In their experience, women usually don't build bridges and men usually don't crochet. The other important determinant of stereotyping is how they themselves are treated. Substantial research shows that parents treat boys and girls differently. They give their children "gender-appropriate" toys, they respond negatively when their children play with cross-gender toys, they allow boys to be active and aggressive, and they encourage their daughters to play quietly and visit with adults. When parents do not encourage gender-stereotypic behavior, their children are less rigid in their gender stereotypes.

As a result of this learning process, boys and girls develop strong ideas about what is appropriate for girls and what is appropriate for boys. However, boys are punished more than girls for exhibiting cross-gender behavior. Thus, little boys are especially rigid in their ideas of what girls and boys ought to do. Girls are freer to engage in cross-gender behavior, and by the time they enter school, many girls are experimenting with boyish behaviors.* negative

Logical Fallacies

When you are evaluating the main point or evidence in a text, you should be aware that authors can try to divert you away from the real issue. They can also oversimplify so that you're more inclined to accept a particular viewpoint. Sometimes authors use these tactics intentionally to manipulate readers. But sometimes, authors—especially inexperienced ones—can also use such tactics without realizing they're doing so. They may unknowingly allow faulty evidence or careless thinking to creep into their writing. Regardless of the writer's intention, however, the reader should learn to recognize the most common **logical fallacies,** *the errors in reasoning that weaken the quality of the evidence presented.* Get in the habit of asking the fourth critical reading question: *Does the text attempt to distract you from the issue or oversimplify the point or the evidence?* By learning to recognize these distractions, you'll never be misled by an author's tricks or mistakes in thinking. Some fallacies you should watch out for are illustrated in the rest of this chapter.

8

* Brinkerhoff, David B., Lynn K. White, Suzanne T. Ortega, and Rose Weitz, *Essentials of Sociology,* 8th ed. Belmont: Wadsworth, 2011. Print. Ch. 9, p. 214.

Fallacies Related to a Lack of Sound Evidence

Some errors in reasoning arise due to a lack of good evidence in defense of an idea. Three specific fallacies of this kind are *circular reasoning,* the *red herring,* and the *hasty generalization.*

Circular reasoning is simply *repeating the main idea in different words without adding any reasons or evidence that actually supports that idea.* In other words, the sentence or paragraph merely circles back to where it began without adding any new development. The following statements, for example, include circular reasoning:

We should prevent teenagers from driving. They're just not old enough to handle driving.

We must not permit scientists to engage in stem-cell[1] research on newly formed embryos. These embryos may not look like babies, but we should not destroy them for scientific experiments.

To end school shootings, we have to remove children's access to guns. If a kid can't get his hands on a gun, then he can't blow away his classmates, right?

The second sentence in each example does not offer any proof for the point. Instead, it merely states the point again in different words.

The **red herring** *is an idea or information that distracts you from the real issue or point.* The term comes from a smelly fish that was used to confuse tracking dogs following a scent trail. Similarly, a red herring in a text leads the reader down an irrelevant path. Authors can inadvertently or intentionally toss these into passages when they run out of valid evidence, or when they want to disguise the fact that their evidence is flimsy. The following statements all include red herrings.

Taxpayers should not have to pay the pensions of ex-presidents. We live in a country where the rich just keep getting richer and the poor keep getting poorer.

Children who commit murder should be tried as adults. Too many parents are not disciplining their children, so it's no surprise that these kinds of crimes are happening.

Sport-utility vehicles should be taken off the American car market. Americans think they're superior to all other nations, and Europeans are tired of their arrogant boasting.

These examples state a point and then, rather than offering some proof or evidence, they quickly change the subject to something related but irrelevant.

1. **stem cell:** related to unspecialized cells that give rise to specific, specialized cells, such as blood cells

One last fallacy related to a lack of good evidence is the **hasty generalization.** This happens when the author *bases a conclusion on very little evidence.* The generalization is hasty because it's made without enough proof to support it. The following examples all demonstrate hasty generalizations:

> A firefighter in our community was killed last week in a burning building. That just goes to show that our fire department is not concerned enough about the safety of its employees.

> One study showed that pet owners experience lower stress levels. People who work in high-stress occupations, therefore, should all go get themselves a cat or a dog.

> Winters in New England are still freezing, so the theory of global warming is obviously inaccurate.

In all three of these examples, one instance or incident is the sole basis for the writer's conclusion. Therefore, all of these generalizations are hasty because they do not arise from enough evidence.

Exercise 8.8

Read each of the following statements and then circle the letter of the type of fallacy it includes.

1. One woman in the news said her cancer went into remission[1] after she began practicing yoga, so yoga must cure cancer.

   a. circular reasoning
   b. red herring
   c. hasty generalization

2. Marcy isn't mature enough to see that movie. She's just too childish to go.

   a. circular reasoning
   b. red herring
   c. hasty generalization

3. People who are unemployed shouldn't get unemployment checks. The lines are too long at all government offices anyway.

   a. circular reasoning
   b. red herring
   c. hasty generalization

1. **remission:** subsiding of disease symptoms

8

4. A tree fell in our backyard last night. All of the trees in our yard must have weak roots.

   a. circular reasoning
   b. red herring
   c. hasty generalization

5. Our town's officials are all corrupt. They are more concerned with lining their own pockets than with bringing improvements to our community.

   a. circular reasoning
   b. red herring
   c. hasty generalization

Fallacies in the Form of a Personal Attack

One particular type of fallacy attacks the person who holds the opposing viewpoint. It diverts the reader's attention from the real evidence by focusing on deficiencies in the opponent's character. Known as an **argument to the person**, or the Latin **ad hominem**, this fallacy resorts to *discrediting an individual rather than dealing with the argument itself*. Here are examples of arguments to the person:

> College football coaches should not be making million-dollar salaries. Most of them are just has-beens with gigantic egos anyway.

> The people who criticize MTV as being childish or immature should look in the mirror. They're all just a bunch of middle-aged ex-hippies who smoked too much pot in the 1960s and 1970s.

> Dr. Paul Wilson, a physical education professor, wants to ban dodgeball from schools. He's obviously just a wimp who got his feelings hurt a few too many times during his childhood PE classes.

All three of these examples do not offer a sound reason in support of the point. Instead, they include personal attacks on the character or background of those who believe the opposing viewpoint.

Fallacies That Appeal to What Other People Believe

One final pair of fallacies involves appeals based on what others think or believe. They attempt to convince the reader that, because a certain person or group accepts an idea, the reader should accept it, too. This type of fallacy includes *bandwagon appeals and testimonials*.

Bandwagon appeals *are suggestions that the reader should accept an idea simply because everyone else accepts it as true*. They encourage the reader to jump on the "bandwagon" and go along with the crowd. This fallacy misleads in two ways. First of all, its claim that "everyone" feels the same way is probably inaccurate. Also, it assumes that "everyone" is right. The following statements include bandwagon appeals:

Millions of Americans have bought the new Wonder Widget. That's why you should buy one, too.

Many people watched the Crazy Aces concert on HBO. You should watch it, too; you'll really like it.

Everyone who lives in New York City roots for the New York Yankees baseball team. If you move here, you should root for them, too.

Another appeal to others' beliefs is known as the **testimonial.** This fallacy suggests that *because a certain individual, usually a celebrity such as a sports hero or movie star, believes an idea to be true, the reader should believe it, too.* Obviously, advertisers use this technique often. Companies are willing to pay famous people huge sums of money to endorse their products because people tend to view a product favorably if they like or admire the person who is offering the testimonial. Yet, the celebrity's opinion really has little to do with the product's quality or worth, so a testimonial is a type of misleading fallacy. These statements all include testimonials:

Michael Jordan wears Nike shoes, so you should, too.

Taylor Swift wears So Young makeup. You should use it, too!

If Oprah Winfrey says we should sing the national anthem at every sporting event, then that's exactly what we should do.

All three of these examples argue that the point must be true because a celebrity says it is.

Exercise 8.9

Read each of the following examples and then circle the letter that corresponds to the specific fallacy it includes.

1. Berkin bags, the trendy new purses from Hermes, are all the rage in New York City this year. Everyone has to have one, even though the cheapest one costs $4,500. You won't be cool without one if you're a woman living in the Big Apple.[1] They are particularly great if you have a lot of stuff to carry around, which most women in New York City do. You'll have plenty of room for all of your makeup, iPhone, brush, and even a small dog, if you have one!

   a. argument to the person c. testimonial

   b. bandwagon appeal

1. **Big Apple:** New York City

2. Our governor says that text.com has the best prices on textbooks and encourages students to buy all of their texts from the website. I bought all of this semester's texts from the site because they must have the best prices. I didn't even check out any of the other textbook sites.

   a. argument to the person
   b. bandwagon appeal
   c. testimonial

3. Most people who host talk shows today make too much money. They are just people who want to spend an hour talking about themselves anyway. They don't really care about the people they are supposed to be interviewing; they just go on and on about themselves, and I think the shows are boring. Also, these talk show hosts all have checkered[1] pasts that include failed marriages, drug abuse, and eating disorders, so their advice just isn't worth all that money they earn.

   a. argument to the person
   b. bandwagon appeal
   c. testimonial

4. Anyone with any sense at all should vote "yes" on the school funding issue. Everyone we know is going to vote for it. It only makes sense to do so. You should vote "yes" on the issue so that the funding passes.

   a. argument to the person
   b. bandwagon appeal
   c. testimonial

5. *Celebrity Chefs* television show only uses Calphalon pots and pans. These must be the best cooking utensils and I should have a set.

   a. argument to the person
   b. bandwagon appeal
   c. testimonial

8

Reading Strategy: REAP

REAP (Read-Encode-Annotate-Ponder) *is a strategy that guides you to respond to a text to improve your reading and thinking skills.* This method provides you with a system of four steps. When you follow these steps, you'll be training yourself to look deeper into the texts you read so you

1. **checkered:** marked by great changes or shifts in fortune

can more fully understand and evaluate them. As a result, your comprehension and critical thinking skills will improve.

- **Step 1: READ.** The first step involves *carefully reading the text* to understand the author's ideas and information.
- **Step 2: ENCODE.** Next, you *translate the text's message into your own words*. This step asks you to paraphrase the ideas or information to put them in language you understand.
- **Step 3: ANNOTATE.** To annotate means to *write notes or comments about a text*. You can record these in the margins of the text, or in a notebook, or on separate sheets of paper. These notes can take the form of objective summaries or more subjective reactions to the ideas and information. For example, you could jot down your own feelings, opinions, or judgments.
- **Step 4: PONDER.** Finally, you *continue reflecting on what you have read and the notes you have written*. In this stage, you also read or discuss other people's responses to the same text in order to more fully explore its content. This sharing can take place formally in classroom settings, or informally, outside of the classroom.

Here is a sample passage annotated according to the REAP method.

Does Watching Violence on Television Make People More Violent?

If observational learning is important, then surely television—and televised violence—must teach children a great deal. For one thing, it is estimated that the average child in the United States spends more time watching television than attending school. Much of what children see is violent; prime-time programs in the United States present an average of 5 violent acts per hour; some Saturday morning cartoons include more than 20 per hour. As a result, the average child will have witnessed at least 8,000 murders and more than 100,000 other acts of televised violence *before graduating from elementary school.*

Children must be affected by all the violence they see on TV.

Psychologists have speculated that watching so much violence might be emotionally arousing, making viewers more likely to react violently

Research suggests that watching TV violence increases violent reactions to frustration, aggressive behavior, and aggressive thoughts and feelings.

Continued

8

to frustration. Televised violence might also provide models that viewers imitate, particularly if the violence is carried out by attractive, powerful models—the "good guys," for example. And recent research suggests that exposure to media violence can trigger or amplify viewers' aggressive thoughts and feelings, thus increasing the likelihood that they will *act* aggressively.

National scientific and psychological organizations believe that watching violent TV increases aggressive behavior.

Many have argued that, through one or more of these mechanisms, watching violence on television causes violent behavior in viewers. Indeed, in 1993 a National Academy of Science report concluded that "overall, the vast majority of studies, whatever their methodology, showed that exposure to television violence resulted in increased aggressive behavior, both contemporaneously[1] and over time." An American Psychological Association commission on Violence and Youth reached the same conclusion.

Anecdotes and case studies show a link between violent TV and violent behavior.

Three types of evidence back up the claim that watching violent television programs increases violent behavior. Some evidence comes from anecdotes and case studies. Children have poked one another in the eye after watching the Three Stooges[2] appear to do so on television. And adults have claimed that watching TV shows prompted them to commit murders or other violent acts matching those seen on the shows.

Long-term studies show a link between violent TV and violent behavior.

Second, many longitudinal[3] studies have found a correlation[4] between watching violent television programs and later acts of aggression and violence. One such study tracked people from the time they were six or seven (in 1977) until they reached their early twenties (in 1992). Those who watched more violent television as children

8

1. **contemporaneously:** happening at the same time
2. **Three Stooges:** three slapstick film comedians of the mid-twentieth century
3. **longitudinal:** long term
4. **correlation:** relationship

were significantly more aggressive as adults and more likely to engage in criminal activity. They were also more likely to use physical punishment on their own children, who themselves tended to be much more aggressive than average. These latter results were also found in the United States, Israel, Australia, Poland, the Netherlands, and even Finland, where the number of violent TV shows is very small.

Finally, the results of numerous laboratory experiments also support the view that TV violence increases aggression among viewers. In one study, groups of boys watched violent or nonviolent programs in a controlled setting and then played floor hockey. Boys who had watched the violent shows were more likely than those who had watched nonviolent programs to behave aggressively on the hockey floor. This effect was greatest for those boys who had the most aggressive tendencies to begin with. More extensive experiments in which children are exposed for long periods to carefully controlled types of television programs also suggest that exposure to large amounts of violent activity on television results in aggressive behavior.*

Lab experiments show the same link.

A lot of evidence suggests that TV violence increases real-life violence, but other factors may be at work, too. I know many people who watch violent programs but don't lash out aggressively.

Now, practice the REAP method yourself by reading and annotating one of the following reading selections. Answers will vary.

WEB LINK

If you are an auditory learner, try this link. This podcast from Australia discusses how to be a better reader.

https://academicskills.anu.edu.au/sites/default/files/skillsoup_tip_13.mp3

If you like to study with a group, you may want to try the KWL strategy that is demonstrated in this link.

http://www.studygs.net/texred3.htm

8

* Adapted from Bernstein et al., *Psychology,* 5th ed. Boston: Houghton Mifflin, 2000, 203–204.

Reading Selections

Practicing the Active Reading Strategy

■ Before and While You Read

You can use active reading strategies before, while, and after you read a selection. The following are some suggestions for active reading strategies that you can employ before you read and as you are reading.

1. Skim the selection for any unfamiliar words. Circle or highlight any words you do not know.
2. As you read, underline, highlight, or circle important words or phrases.
3. Write down any questions about the selection if you are confused by the information presented.
4. Jot notes in the margin to help you understand the material.

BIOGRAPHY

Howlin' Wolf: Booming Voice of the Blues

by John Burnett

His name was Chester Arthur Burnett, but everyone called him Howlin' Wolf. He played harmonica, but some say he was the greatest blues singer of all time. His unique voice mesmerized audiences and hugely influenced rock 'n' roll.

1 Nobody had a voice like Wolf, before or since. Singer and harmonica player Billy Boy Arnold says he remembers playing a bill with Wolf at Silvio's Lounge on a Saturday night in 1957. The lineup was a blues lovers' dream: Arnold's band, Muddy Waters and Howlin' Wolf. Arnold says he heard a lot of great blues singers in those days, but that there was never anyone or anything like Howlin' Wolf.

2 "He had the most unusual voice in the history of blues," Arnold says. "That was his trademark. A lot a people tried to imitate him. But he just had that big, booming voice." Singer Ronnie Hawkins said it was "stronger than 40 acres of crushed garlic." Bonnie Raitt said he was "the scariest . . . bit of male testosterone I've ever experienced." Legendary record producer Sam Phillips heard Wolf on the radio and said, "This is where the soul of man never dies." Maybe his guttural voice was a result of severe tonsillitis he had as a child. Or maybe Chester Burnett's travails[1] had somehow come out in his voice.

1. **travails:** hardships

3 He was born a hundred years ago, black and destitute, in Clay County, Miss.—cast out of his home, raised by an abusive uncle who whipped him with a leather plow line. He was so poor, he once tied burlap sacks around his bare feet, and so hungry he once ate food scraps tossed off a train by railroad workers.

4 While he was a young man sharecropping in Mississippi, Wolf apprenticed[2] with Delta blues legend Charley Patton. As he said on a Chess Records album in 1968, Wolf was deeply influenced by Patton's gritty singing and percussive playing. Wolf started playing on weekends in country juke joints, then moved to Memphis, made a name for himself, and finally settled in Chicago to become—literally—a giant of the blues. "He was a big man, wore size 16 shoe," guitarist Jody Williams says, "and his stage presence—when he talk or sing, people listen to him, you know."

5 Williams played guitar alongside Hubert Sumlin in Wolf's band in 1954. Of all the famous musicians Williams backed up—Bo Diddley, Memphis Slim, Big Joe Turner—Wolf is the one he remembers best. "He even went outside the door of the club," he says. "He had a long, 100-foot cord on his microphone. So Hubert and rest of the band and I were onstage playing, and Wolf just howling and singing. So he went out that door, down the sidewalk to the corner, he [was] just blowing his harmonica and howlin' and carryin' on. But that was the Wolf."

6 Mark Hoffman, co-author of *Moanin' at Midnight: The Life and Times of Howlin' Wolf*, paints a similar picture of the wild-man performer. "Wolf would crawl around on his hands and knees, and he'd howl like a wolf," he says. "He'd pound on the stage. And people would watch him; they couldn't take their eyes off him." With his feral stage presence and growling vocals, Wolf fought his way to the top of the cutthroat Chicago blues scene during the 1950s—neck and neck with his rival, Muddy Waters. In the '60s, young white rockers discovered his music and began to cover his classic renditions of "Little Red Rooster" and "Spoonful."

7 In 1965, The Rolling Stones, fresh from England, appeared on the ABC TV show *Shindig*. They had one condition: Their idol, Howlin' Wolf, had to be there, too. Sure enough, he was. A hulking black eminence, he stood at the microphone in a dark suit, his huge head sweating as he stabbed the air with his finger, shaking his hips salaciously before a bevy of white go-go dancers. It's surely one of the most incongruous[3] moments in American pop music. Music journalist Peter Guralnick, who says he reveres Howlin' Wolf, goes even further. He calls it one of the greatest cultural moments of the 20th century.

2. **apprenticed:** to work as a beginner
3. **incongruous:** not seeming to be fitting or correct

8 "What was so great about seeing Wolf on *Shindig* was it was in a sense reality imposing itself on this totally artificial setting," Guralnick says. "While I was a big fan of the Stones, it was altogether appropriate that they would be sitting at Wolf's feet. And that's what it represented. His music was not simply the foundation or the cornerstone; it was the most vital thing you could ever imagine."

9 Since Chester Burnett died in 1976—in Chicago, the town that made the blues famous—a postage stamp has had his face on it, and there's been a statue in his hometown, a blues festival in his name and numerous Hall of Fame inductions and record reissues. The Wolf keeps howlin'.*

Vocabulary

Read the following questions about some of the vocabulary words that appear in the previous selection. Before you look up the word, try to use the context of the passage to figure out the meaning. Then circle the letter of the correct answer for each question.

1. In paragraph 1, the author describes Howlin' Wolf's voice as "*guttural.*" What kind of sound is *guttural*?

   a. soft, soothing
   b. quiet, mellow
   c. harsh, grating
   d. loud and booming

2. "[B]lack and *destitute*" is used to describe Howlin' Wolf in paragraph 3. What is *destitute*?

   needy or poor

3. What is a *feral* stage presence? (paragraph 6).

   a. savage
   b. tame
   c. upbeat
   d. loud

4. Howlin' Wolf is described in paragraph 7 as a "hulking black *eminence*"? What does *eminence* mean?

   a position of prominence

5. "[S]haking his hips *salaciously*...." How was Howlin' Wolf shaking his hips? (paragraph 7)

   arousing or appealing to sexual desire

*http://www.npr.org/templates/story/story.php?storyId=130276817. Web. 10/4/2010

8

Reading Skills

Respond to each of the following questions by circling the letter of the correct answer or by writing your answer on the blank provided.

1. What is the purpose of this article? to inform or entertain

2. Which sentence in paragraph 1 is a fact?

   a. Sentence 1
   c. Sentence 3
   (b.) Sentence 2
   d. Sentence 4

3. Is the last sentence in paragraph 6 a fact or opinion?

   fact

4. List the words with negative connotation from paragraph 3.

   destitute, cast out, abusive, whipped, poor, hungry, food scraps

5. From the description of Howlin' Wolf's performance in paragraph 5, what can you infer about him as a performer?

   He was a fascinating, charismatic performer who was idolized by many famous musical artists for his unusual voice and performing characteristics.

6. What can you infer from paragraph 6 about the feeling The Rolling Stones had for Howlin' Wolf?

   They thought that he was one of the most important influences to their music and one of the performers they most admired and looked up to.

7. What is the bias illustrated in paragraph 8?

   (a.) Positive
   c. Neutral
   b. Negative

8

Practicing the Active Reading Strategy:

After You Read

Now that you have read the selection, answer the following questions, using the active reading strategies that you learned in Chapter 1.

1. Identify and write down the point and purpose of this reading selection.

2. Did you circle or highlight any words that are unfamiliar to you? Can you figure out the meaning from the context of the passage? If not, then look up each word in a dictionary and find the definition that best describes the word as it is used in the selection. You may want to write the definition in the margin next to the word in the passage for future reference.
3. Predict any possible questions that may be used on a test about the content of this selection.

■ Questions for Discussion and Writing

Respond to each of the following questions based on your reading of the selection.

1. Describe the characteristics that made Howlin' Wolf unique.

   His wild stage presence and growling, raspy voice

2. What evidence does the article provide of Howlin' Wolf's affect on rock and roll singers?

   Young white rockers began to record his songs and The Rolling Stones insisted that he perform on television when they did.

3. What performer today do you think will leave this kind of legacy? Why?

   Answers may vary.

Practicing the Active Reading Strategy

■ Before and While You Read

You can use active reading strategies before, while, and after you read a selection. The following are some suggestions for active reading strategies that you can employ before you read and as you are reading.

1. Skim the selection for any unfamiliar words. Circle or highlight any words you do not know.
2. As you read, underline, highlight, or circle important words or phrases.
3. Write down any questions about the selection if you are confused by the information presented.
4. Jot notes in the margin to help you understand the material.

TEXTBOOK READING – AGRICULTURE

Kefa Village in Eastern Zambia

Anthropologist Else Skjonsberg visited Kefa Village first in 1977 and several times since. Her book Change in an African Village: Kefa Speaks *portrays a traditional agricultural system in Eastern Africa.*

1 Villagers in Kefa depend on land, which is controlled and allocated by the local chief. Some inherit cultivation rights from their parents, others request unused land from the chief, and others borrow land from relatives and neighbors. When land shortages arise, groups of villagers break away and search other areas for unused lands.

2 Households cultivate 1 to 4 hectares, with maize, groundnuts, sweet potatoes, and pumpkins produced for their own consumption, and tobacco and cotton produced for sale. Fortunate farmers have access to wetland dambos, where they grow vegetables year-round. The agricultural year starts before the first rains in October, when the ground is broken by hand hoes. Maize, the most important food crop, is planted first, weeded first, and harvested first. Most villagers plant open-pollinated maize varieties, which have been used for generations. Maize is stored in granaries, and in years of abundance it is used to brew beer or sell. Groundnuts are rotated with maize to maintain soil fertility and provide dietary protein. Hybrid maize varieties, with higher yields and shorter growing seasons, have been introduced, but most Kefa villagers are suspicious of their quality and only produce them for sale. Hybrids require purchased fertilizer, and in dryland farming, exposure to risk invites trouble. Many believe use of fertilizers will breed dependency and bring ruin to adventurous farmers.

3 Family members share work responsibilities. Women prepare meals, carry them to the fields, hand-cultivate all day, then return home with pots and pans, loads of firewood, and water. During December and January, the women take responsibility for weeding. It takes as long as three weeks to weed a hectare of maize, so family time is fully occupied. On rainy days, men make repairs around their huts, while women manage household affairs. When labor is scarce, some mobilize workers by throwing home-brewed beer parties; others trade labor and work together. During April through June, labor is in short supply and entire villages participate in harvests. Women are chiefly responsible for harvest, but men and older children assist. Women headload food crops in 50-kilogram bags from the fields to storage bins. In rare cases where oxen or motorized transport is used, men take responsibility for the task.

4 Although agriculture is the main source of well-being in Kefa, all households are engaged in non-agricultural activities. Some brew and sell beer; others practice crafts such as weaving or woodworking; many

engage in petty trading; and others are healers, scribes, or have specialized skills. Cattle raising and off-farm incomes supplement farm incomes and help families buy farm and household equipment, clothes, and blankets and pay for services such as school fees. Off-farm activities are divided by gender: women brew and sell beer, trade and weave, whereas men more often have specialized skills, work with wood, or do repairs. Incomes earned in these activities are held separately by men and women, and women are eager to engage in such activities because the money they earn provides them a degree of autonomy in decision making.

5 Families in Kefa are structured in different ways. Only about half of the households are nuclear in the sense of two parents and children. About a third of households are headed by women, some divorced or widowed, some whose husband is absent. Children participate actively in household economic life; by age 5 most contribute to household tasks and, past 8 years, farmwork increases. Boys are responsible for tending cattle, whereas girls assist their mothers in the house and care for younger siblings. Most children attend schools, but are excused during periods of peak agricultural labor. The elderly live with their families or are cared for by family members. The poorest of the poor have few relatives and depend on handouts from other villagers.*

■ Vocabulary

Read the following questions about some of the vocabulary words that appear in the previous selection. Before you look up the word, try to use the context of the passage to figure out the meaning. Then write the meaning for each word as it is used in the passage.

1. *allocated* (paragraph 1) to set apart for a special purpose
2. *cultivate* (paragraph 2) to improve and prepare (land), as by plowing or fertilizing, for raising crops
3. *hectares* (paragraph 2) a measure of area, or superficies, containing a hundred acres
4. *dambos* (paragraph 2) a spring-fed marsh
5. *scribes* (paragraph 4) one who writes; a writer
6. *petty* as in "petty trading" (paragraph 4) of small importance
7. *autonomy* (paragraph 4) independence

* Norton, George W., Jeffrey Alwang, and William A. Masters, *Economics of Agricultural Development: World Food Systems and Resource Use,* 2nd ed. New York: Routledge, 2010. Print. Ch. 7, pp. 134–35.

Reading Skills

Respond to each of the following questions by circling the letter of the correct answer or by writing your answer on the blank provided.

1. What is the primary purpose of this reading selection?

   to inform

2. Is the author's bias positive, negative, or neutral?

   neutral

3. What (if any) words reveal the author's bias?

   The words the author uses are neutral and do not express a positive or negative bias.

4. Is the information presented in this article mostly facts or opinions?

   Information is primarily factual.

5. In paragraph 5, the word *elderly* is used. Do you feel this word has a positive, neutral, or negative connotation? Explain your reasoning.

   Answers will vary.

6. What pattern is used to organize paragraph 2?

   a. Sequence
   b. Compare/Contrast
   c. Series
   d. Cause/Effect

7. What pattern is used to organize paragraph 3?

   a. Sequence
   b. Compare/Contrast
   c. Series
   d. Cause/Effect

8. What can you infer about the author's views of this agricultural system in Africa?

   The author is very knowledgeable about this African village, shown by the amount of specific detail that is presented in the selection. The introduction mentions that she has traveled there since 1977 and has written a book about it, too.

9. Based on the information in the paragraph, what can you infer about the history of this agricultural system (i.e., how long has it been in place)?

   The system is very precise and traditional; it has been in place for many generations.

8

10. What inferences can be made about the gender equality or inequality in this culture? Give some examples to support your conclusions.

    Women and men have very separate, yet shared responsibilities that relate to agriculture and other duties in the village. Specific examples from the article will vary.

Practicing the Active Reading Strategy

■ After You Read

Now that you have read the selection, answer the following questions, using the active reading strategies that you learned in Chapter 1.

1. Identify and write down the point and purpose of this reading selection.
2. Did you circle or highlight any words that are unfamiliar to you? Can you figure out the meaning from the context of the passage? If not, then look up each word in a dictionary and find the definition that best describes the word as it is used in the selection. You may want to write the definition in the margin next to the word in the passage for future reference.
3. Predict any possible questions that may be used on a test about the content of this selection.

■ Questions for Discussion and Writing

Respond to each of the following questions based on your reading of the selection.

1. How do you think advances in farm equipment have helped this farming village?

   Answers may vary.

2. Can you relate any aspect of this agricultural system to something similar we may find in the United States? Explain your answer.

   Answers may vary.

3. Using an online source, research more about the Kefa Village and write down three more interesting facts that you learned.

   Answers may vary.

Practicing the Active Reading Strategy

Before and While You Read

You can use active reading strategies before, while, and after you read a selection. The following are some suggestions for active reading strategies that you can perform before you read and while you read.

1. Skim the selection for any unfamiliar words. Circle or highlight any words you do not know.
2. As you read, underline, highlight, or circle important words or phrases.
3. Write down any questions about the selection if you are confused by the information presented.
4. Jot notes in the margin to help you understand the material.

NEWSPAPER READiNG – HEALTH

Pill-Popping Replaces Healthy Habits

by Steven Findlay

How many pills do you take each day? Do you think you take too many? Do you take a pill for any pain or problem you have? According to the following article, Americans are probably overmedicated and the financial cost is enormous. Although this article was written in 2004 during the Bush administration, the problem continues to grow.

1 If you watch enough TV these days, you might get the impression that there's a prescription drug for just about anything that ails you. And that's about right. In recent years, more and better drugs have come along to treat the chronic diseases and conditions afflicting us: arthritis, diabetes, asthma, coronary-artery narrowing, heartburn, allergies, depression, and erectile dysfunction.

2 U.S. pharmacies dispensed more than 3 billion prescriptions in 2003, up from about 2 billion a decade ago. We love our medicines. And why not? They are so easy, and they usually work. We take more and more of them, even as we complain bitterly about their prices and rail against the pharmaceutical industry.

3 But another perspective goes down less easily: Although many Americans don't get the medicines they need, as a nation, we are fast becoming overly reliant on a slew[1] of drugs that essentially substitute for a healthy lifestyle. Most of us don't routinely eat wholesome foods in moderate quantity, stay active, or manage our body weight. One in five of us still smoke. When the inevitable consequences follow, we

1. **slew:** large amount

8

count on pills to counter the ills that our human weaknesses engender and our culture fosters (think ubiquitous fast, fatty foods and physical education's demise in schools).

4 This has every bit as much impact on the steeply rising national tab for prescription drugs as their prices do. Unless Americans, individually and collectively, begin to take more responsibility for their own health, that tab may rise to a point where more serious limits will be imposed on our access to drugs.

5 The predicted costs of medicines compelled Congress to limit the drug benefit it added to Medicare to stay within a self-imposed 10-year budget of $400 billion. Now the Bush administration has raised that projection to $534 billion, even as the AARP[1] and others begin to push to expand the new benefit.

6 The drug industry correctly notes that many medicines can save money by preventing hospitalizations or nursing-home care and reducing disability. But it's just as true that the industry's success builds on our failure. Growth in costs could be reduced sharply if more people took basic steps to maintain their health and so needed fewer drugs or other medical care.

7 Consider the cholesterol-lowering drugs known as statins. They are among the most widely prescribed medicines: Sales topped $13 billion in 2002, up from $1.8 billion a decade earlier. Lipitor alone earned Pfizer more than $6 billion last year in the United States, the most of any drug. Some 15 million Americans take a statin daily.

8 Statins are highly effective, lowering the risk of heart attack and stroke by an average 20 percent to 30 percent among people at risk. But their use has soared largely because more and more people are identified as "at risk" due to obesity, clogged arteries, diabetes, and high blood pressure, which, in turn, are linked to overeating, poor diet, and lack of sufficient physical activity.

9 In 2001, for example, a National Institutes of Health panel changed the at-risk standard for "bad" (LDL) cholesterol and said many more people with other heart-disease risk factors also should lower their cholesterol. This pushed the number of Americans who need to lower their cholesterol from 13 million to 36 million. The panel urged people to eat better and exercise more—but tellingly, its leaders noted that drugs might be an easier solution. "We used to say to try lowering (cholesterol) with diet first, but now we say that if your LDL is above 130 and you have coronary disease, you should be on drug therapy," Scott Grundy, a physician and the panel's chairman, told the *Wall Street Journal*. For people with LDL levels between 100 and 130, he added, "We think the evidence justifies the majority going on drugs."

10 Recent studies add to the momentum. One showed the benefits of lowering LDL to 70 or 80. Two studies last year revealed that children and teens with high LDL levels

8

1. **AARP:** American Association of Retired Persons

show early signs of heart disease. These studies, trumpeted in the media, largely were seen as further evidence that even more Americans, maybe up to 50 million, could benefit from statins.

11 Less noticed was a study out last July that found that a diet rich in fiber and soy protein lowered LDL levels about as much as a statin. OK, OK: Soy protein may be too much to ask. But a large body of research shows that a healthy, balanced diet and regular exercise can keep high cholesterol at bay for most of us—and yields multiple other benefits to boot, including a lower risk of some cancers.

12 The cholesterol story is not unique. This same dynamic plays out for other ills and the drugs that treat them: high blood pressure, Type 2 diabetes, certain kinds of pain, sleep disturbances, heartburn, even mild depression. Yes, millions of Americans with such conditions need medicines. But millions of us are self-afflicted with such ills because we can't or won't get our lifestyle acts together.

13 We devour fad diets, such as Atkins and South Beach. But obesity rates have climbed steadily for 20 years. Two-thirds of us now are overweight. What we really want—admit it—is a trusty, safe anti-fat pill. Indeed, that's the Holy Grail[1] of the pharmaceutical industry.

14 The looming question is whether we can afford in the long run to allow the drug industry to bail us out of our bad habits. Drugs will get better, but not cheaper. It's our choice: Let drug costs spiral upward and drug firms capitalize on our weaknesses. Or take charge of our own health and reduce the overall need for pills.*

Vocabulary

Read the following questions about some of the vocabulary words that appear in the previous selection. Circle the letter of each correct answer.

1. In paragraph 1, the author uses the word *chronic* to describe diseases. In this context, what does *chronic* mean?

   a. final
   b. happening over and over again
   c. minor
   d. disturbing

1. **Holy Grail:** The Holy Grail is generally considered to be the cup from which Christ drank at the Last Supper and the one used by Joseph of Arimathea to catch Christ's blood as he hung on the cross. (From The Holy Grail website, http://www.lib.rochester.edu/camelot/grlmenu.htm, The Camelot Project at the University of Rochester.) In the time of King Arthur and according to that legend, pursuit of the Grail was the highest spiritual pursuit. It is used here to represent something magical and unattainable.

8

* Adapted from Steven Findlay, "Pill-Popping Replaces Healthy Habits," *USA Today,* February 5, 2004, 15A.

2. "We take more and more of them, even as we complain bitterly about their prices and *rail against* the pharmaceutical industry" (paragraph 2). In this context, what does *rail against* mean?

   a. criticize
   b. disagree with
   c. agree with
   d. throw around

3. "When the inevitable consequences follow, we count on pills to counter the ills that our human weaknesses *engender* and our culture fosters" (paragraph 3). What does *engender* mean?

   a. disgust
   b. obey
   c. adjust
   d. produce

4. "[T]hink *ubiquitous* fast, fatty foods and physical education's demise in schools" (paragraph 3). What does *ubiquitous* mean?

   a. disappearing
   b. never-ending
   c. ever-present
   d. inexpensive

5. What does it mean to keep something or someone *at bay?* (paragraph 11)

   a. to keep close
   b. to keep safe
   c. to keep at arm's length
   d. to keep in a box

■ Reading Skills

Are the following sentences from the reading selection facts or opinions? On the blank after each statement, write FACT or OPINION.

1. "In recent years, more and better drugs have come along to treat the chronic diseases and conditions afflicting us: arthritis, diabetes, asthma, coronary-artery narrowing, heartburn, allergies, depression, and erectile dysfunction." fact ______

2. "We love our medicines." opinion ______

3. "One in five of us still smoke." fact ______

4. "When the inevitable consequences follow, we count on pills to counter the ills that our human weaknesses engender and our culture fosters (think ubiquitous fast, fatty foods and physical education's demise in schools)." opinion ______

5. "What we really want—admit it—is a trusty, safe anti-fat pill." opinion ______

8

Circle the letter of the correct answer or write the answer on the line.

6. What is the purpose of this reading selection? To inform

7. Is the evidence presented mostly facts or mostly opinions?
   a. mostly facts
   b. mostly opinions

8. In paragraph 2, identify two words with negative connotation.
   complain, rail

9. In paragraph 10, what is the connotation of the word *trumpeted*? positive

10. What is the author's bias towards taking pills to improve health?
    a. positive
    b. negative
    c. neutral

Practicing the Active Reading Strategy

After You Read

Now that you have read the selection, answer the following questions using the active reading strategies that are discussed in Chapter 1.

1. Identify and write down the point and purpose of this reading selection.
2. Did you circle or highlight any words that are unfamiliar to you? Can you figure out the meaning from the context of the passage? If not, then look up each word in a dictionary and find the definition that best describes the word as it is used in the selection. You may want to write the definition in the margin next to the word in the passage for future reference.
3. Predict any possible questions that may be used on a test about the content of this selection.

Questions for Discussion and Writing

Answer the following questions based on your reading of the selection. Write your answer on the blanks provided.

1. Do you agree or disagree with the following statement from the selection? "Although many Americans don't get the medicines they need, as a nation, we are fast becoming overly reliant on a slew of drugs that essentially substitute for a healthy lifestyle." Why or why not?
   Answers will vary.

8

2. "But a large body of research shows that a healthy, balanced diet and regular exercise can keep high cholesterol at bay for most of us—and yields multiple other benefits to boot, including a lower risk of some cancers." Conduct some additional research to find out what some of the other multiple benefits of a balanced diet and regular exercise might be and summarize your findings in a short essay.

Answers will vary.

3. The author of this selection mentions both the Atkins diet and the South Beach diet. Go online and research both diets. Write a paper in which you summarize the basic rules of each diet, their purported health benefits (beyond weight loss), and their success rates.

Answers will vary.

Vocabulary Strategy: Formal vs. Informal Language

When you read, you should be able to distinguish between formal and informal language. **Formal language** *is usually serious, businesslike, and often sophisticated.* This is the type of language that is most prevalent in *scholarly, academic,* and *professional writing.* Most textbooks, college assignments, and business reports, for example, are written using formal language. **Informal language** *is closer to that of conversation.* It's more casual, often including *colloquial (everyday) words, slang* terms, *idioms* (expressions like "She's trying to butter me up"), and even *humor.*

The level of formality in a reading selection helps the reader know how the author feels about his or her subject. A passage or document written in a formal style communicates the author's belief that the subject is important and significant. A more informal style can suggest that the author is more lighthearted about the topic.

When a text is written in a more formal style, the reader may have to make more of an effort to understand it. One way to increase your comprehension is to use *active reading,* a technique you learned about in Chapter 1 of this text. When you read actively, you look up the definitions of unfamiliar words, underline or highlight main ideas, and jot down notes and questions. All of these tactics will help you better understand the formal language of an academic or professional text. You can also use the *SQ3R technique* you practiced in Chapter 4. Surveying a text; turning its headings into questions; and then reading it, reciting the answers to the questions, and reviewing the information will most likely increase your understanding of a text with a formal style. Or, you might prefer to apply the *REAP reading strategy* presented in this chapter. Experiment with using different strategies to find the ones that help you comprehend the more advanced vocabulary and more complex sentences of a formally written text.

To understand the difference between formal and informal language, first take a look at a formal statement from one of the passages in this chapter:

> Researchers find that many ***affluent*** schools let kids solve real-world math problems and read stories that spark their interest. ***Low-income*** students, ***meanwhile,*** are apt to be seated in rows, kept busy with meaningless worksheets and endless practice tests that focus on vowel sounds or ***arithmetic*** rules to be ***memorized and recited without understanding.***

The sentences in this passage are complex, and the boldfaced, italicized words and phrases are serious and formal. Notice, though, how rewriting the statement and substituting some different words makes the statement more colloquial and casual:

> Researchers find that ***rich kids*** get ***cool*** assignments like real-world math problems and interesting stories. But ***poor kids*** are given ***lame busywork*** assignments they ***don't*** really ***get.***

8

Vocabulary Exercise 1

Use the boldfaced, italicized words in each of the following sentences, which come from Chapters 7 and 8, to decide whether the language is formal or informal. On the blank alongside each sentence, write FORMAL or INFORMAL.

1. Reelection-minded professional ***politicians*** must be ***concerned*** about what their ***constituents*** think and want; ***principled*** amateur legislators ***need not be.*** formal ____________

2. Give a ***kid*** a loving environment over a few extra ***bucks*** any day. informal ____________

3. And thus, as you can imagine, their second winter ***was no picnic,*** either.

   informal

4. The ***profoundness*** of my dog's laziness comes not from his ***immobility*** but from his almost ***predatory pursuit of ease.*** formal

5. Soda shopping? Don't just ***grab*** a Coke. Stretch ***waaaaay*** down to reach the Royal Crown! Your ***abs*** will be glad—and so will your wallet! informal

6. Her elegant, personal autobiography was titled *The Majesty of the Law.* But her own majestic qualities are ***refreshingly devoid of regal pretense.*** They are marked instead by the humility and tolerance and restraint that are the ***true foundations of the constitutional principles*** that she ***endeavors*** both to balance and to obey. formal

7. When his boat blew up at last, it ***diffused a tranquil contentment*** among us such as we had not known for months. But when he came home the new week, alive, ***renowned,*** and appeared in church all battered up and bandaged, a shining hero, stared at and wondered over by everybody, it seemed to us that the ***partiality of Providence*** for an undeserving reptile had reached a point where it was ***open to criticism.***

   formal

Vocabulary Exercise 2

On the blank at the end of each passage, write FORMAL or INFORMAL.

1. We may talk the lean talk. But we are walking—make that waddling—the fat walk. The days of "reduced-fat" snacking aren't dead, but they're in intensive care. Perhaps no one knows that better than Andrea Ratliff. She can't stomach low-fat anything. She recently bought some Yoplait no-fat yogurt—and chucked it before finishing the container. She bought some fat-substitute Wow potato chips—and never finished the bag. She's even got a half gallon of Edy's Vanilla fat-free ice cream stashed in her freezer—with just one spoonful eaten out of it. It's been there for a month. "All you're doing is paying a lot of money for stuff that tastes lousy," says Ratliff. "The more fat they take out of something, the worse it tastes, and the more it costs."* informal

8

* Adapted from Robert N. Pyle, "Letters," USA Today, August 6, 2001, 12A.

2. Consumers report that they are confused by the media's constant barrage of often-conflicting nutritional advice that leads many to eschew nutritional advice altogether. In a time of unprecedented obesity and diet-related disease in the United States, the U.S. Department of Agriculture's food pyramid was designed as a clear, concise guide to healthy eating. It has become an international icon of nutrition and should be supported in its present form.

   Harvard professor Walter Willett's revision of the USDA pyramid, with its base level of "daily exercise and weight control" is at best vaguely worded and confusing and at worse a very dangerous eating plan. That healthy foods such as white rice, white bread, potatoes, and pasta are in the "use sparingly" category is the first clue that Willett's advice is not grounded in sound science.* formal

3. The thermometer read 36 degrees when I walked out the back door at first light to inspect my tomato patch. They're coming along nicely, and if the weather holds, we should be eating summer tomato sandwiches by, oh, mid-December anyway. Shoot, we've had young 'uns faster than this year's 'mater crop has come in.

   We've had several frost warnings, but overall it's been warm, which is why I think we might be lucky enough to have 'mater sandwiches for Christmas dinner.

   The leaves are coming off the trees at a rapid clip now, and even the weakening fall sunlight is doing the Big Boys and the Better Boys a world of good. Right now it's a race against the calendar, and my neighbor is betting Jack Frost will get the tomatoes before I do.

   Me? All I want for Christmas is a good ol' 'mater sammich—the thicker the better. Maybe two, now that I think about it.† informal

Reading Visuals: Maps

A **map** *is a visual depiction of an area and its physical characteristics*. Maps illustrate spatial relationships; for example, they show sizes and borders and distances from one place to another. They can also be used to make comparisons. For instance, a map of the United States may color in the states which apply the death penalty in red, and color those that don't, in blue.

* Adapted from Bruce Horovitz, "Low-fat Industry Loses Out as Consumers Favor Flavor," *USA Today*, October 15, 2001, 2B.

† Adapted from Jack Betts, "Trials of a Shade-tree Farmer," *Charlotte Observer*, November 14, 2001, 18A. Reprinted with permission from the *Charlotte Observer*. Copyright owned by the *Charlotte Observer*.

Here are some parts that might be included in a map.:

- **Title.** The title identifies either the area itself, or the relationship between different areas.
- **A diagram of the area.** A map includes a proportionate drawing that represents the geographical features and spatial relationships.
- **Key.** Many maps incorporate symbols, so the key explains what these symbols mean.
- **Labels.** Maps will usually label parts or features that help the reader understand the overall point stated in the title.
- **Source line.** The source line identifies who collected or compiled the information shown in the map.

The map below labels all of these parts.

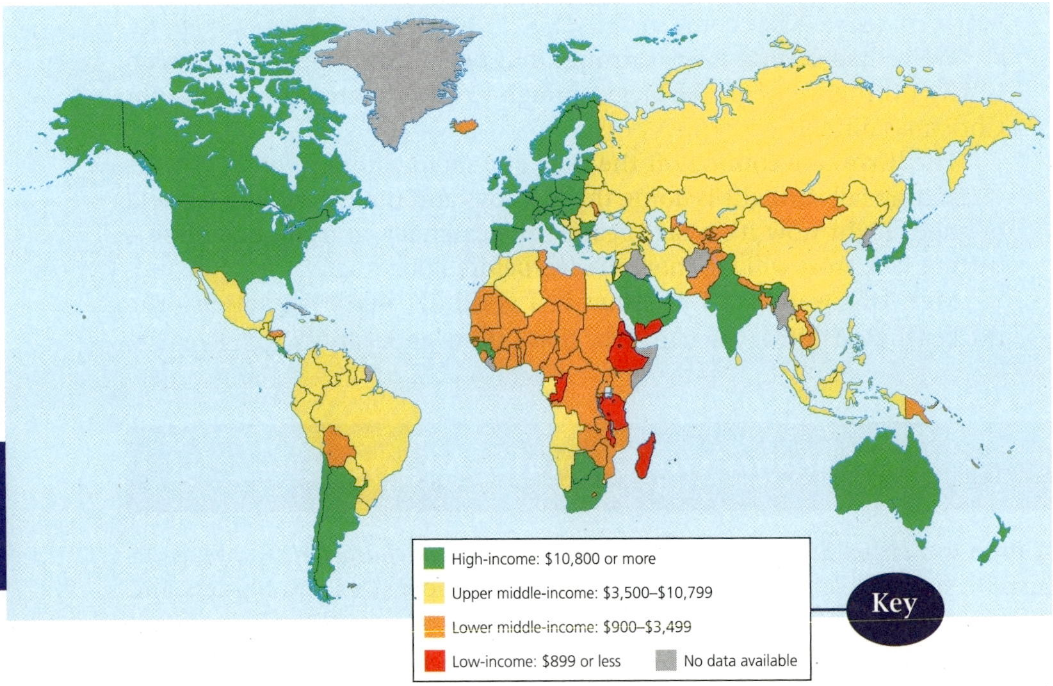

Figure 8.1 **High-income, upper middle–income, lower middle–income, and low-income countries in terms of gross national income (GNI) PPP per capita (U.S. dollars) in 2006**

Source: Data from World Bank and International Monetary Fund — Source

Title

8

The map shown above shows the level of income for countries around the world in 2006 as determined by each country's gross national income per person in U.S. dollars. The key helps the reader locate the countries by income level. The authors chose not to label the countries on this world map.

To interpret a map, read the title first to understand the idea or information on which you should focus. Then, familiarize yourself with symbols in the key (including the scale that indicates distance) and read the labels that name different areas. If the map is illustrating a comparison, try to state in your own words a conclusion based on that comparison.

Now, study the map below and then answer the questions that follow.

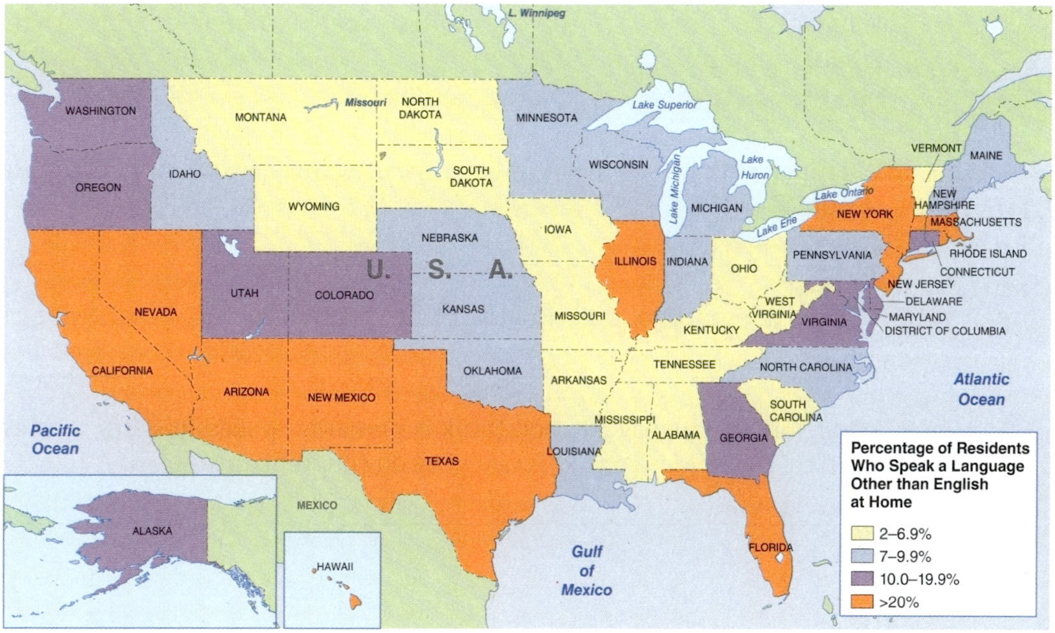

Figure 8.2 **Percent of U.S. Residents 5 Years and Over Who Speak a Language Other than English at Home**

Almost 20 percent of U.S. residents now speak a language other than English at home, leading some Americans to worry that American culture and the English language are at risk. But many of these foreign-language speakers also speak English, and many of their children speak only English.

Source: Map compiled based on data from factfindercensus.gov. Calculated from 2007 American Community Survey data set. Accessed April 2009. In Brinkerhoff, David B., Lynn K. White, Suzanne T. Ortega, and Rose Weitz, *Essentials of Sociology,* 8th ed. Belmont: Wadsworth, 2011. Print. Ch. 2, p. 39.

1. What does this visual represent? the percentage of residents in each state that speak a language other than English at home

2. Name three states in which 20 percent or more of the residents speak a language other than English at home.

   Answers will vary.

3. Name three states in which only 2 to 6.9 percent of the residents speak a language other than English at home.

   Answers will vary.

4. What percent of residents in Colorado speak a language other than English at home?

   10 to 19.9 percent

5. What percent of residents in Indiana speak a language other than English at home?

   7 to 9.9 percent

6. What is the source of this visual? Factfinder.census.gov

7. What "other" language do you think is primarily spoken in states such as California, New Mexico, and Texas? Why do you think this?

   Answers will vary.

Chapter 8 Review

Fill in the blanks in the following statements.

1. Critical reading means noticing certain techniques the writer is using to convince you of the validity and worth of his or her ideas or information.
2. Facts are information that is verifiably true.
3. Opinions are statements that express beliefs, feelings, judgments, attitudes, and preferences.
4. Statements of opinion often contain clue words that indicate the relative nature of something.
5. Informed opinions are supported by a sound body of factual or verifiable information, whereas uninformed opinions are based on an insufficient amount of evidence, questionable facts, or simply more opinions instead of solid proof.
6. The denotative meaning refers to a word's literal dictionary definition. The connotative meaning of a word refers to the emotions or associations that people attach to it.
7. Writers record their thoughts for one or more of three main purposes: to inform, to entertain, or to persuade.
8. A work created solely for the reader's enjoyment or amusement has an entertaining purpose.
9. A work with an informative purpose is designed to teach you something.
10. Works with a persuasive purpose attempt to convince you to change a belief, an attitude, or a behavior.
11. Bias is an inclination toward a particular opinion or viewpoint.
12. Logical fallacies are errors in reasoning.
13. Fallacies related to a lack of sound evidence include circular reasoning, the red herring, and the hasty generalization.
14. The argument to the person is a form of fallacy that includes a personal attack.
15. Two fallacies that appeal to others' beliefs are the bandwagon appeal and the testimonial.

INDEX